PUBLISHED ON THE
LOUIS STERN MEMORIAL FUND

Neutrality
for the
United States

BY

EDWIN BORCHARD

AND

WILLIAM POTTER LAGE

Second Edition
with new material covering 1937–1940

NEW HAVEN

YALE UNIVERSITY PRESS

1940

9406

From

WASHINGTON'S FAREWELL ADDRESS

OBSERVE good faith and justice towards all nations. Cultivate peace and harmony with all. — In the execution of such a plan nothing is more essential than that permanent, inveterate antipathies against particular Nations and passionate attachments for others should be excluded; and that in place of them just and amicable feelings towards all should be cultivated. The Nation, which indulges towards another an habitual hatred, or an habitual fondness, is in some degree a slave. — Antipathy in one nation against another disposes each more readily to offer insult and injury, to lay hold of slight causes of umbrage, and to be haughty and intractable, when accidental or trifling occasions of dispute occur. Hence frequent collisions, obstinate envenomed and bloody contests. The Nation, prompted by ill will and resentment sometimes impels to War the Government, contrary to the best calculations of policy. The Government sometimes participates in the national propensity, and adopts through passion what reason would reject; at other times it makes the animosity of the Nation subservient to projects of hostility instigated by pride, ambition and other sinister and pernicious motives. The peace often, sometimes the Liberty, of Nations has been the victim.

So likewise, a passionate attachment of one Nation for another produces a variety of evils. Sympathy for the favorite nation, facilitating the illusion of an imaginary common interest, in cases where no real common interest exists, and infusing into one the enmities of the other, betrays the former into a participation in the quarrels and Wars of the latter, without adequate inducement of justification: It leads also to concessions to the favorite nation of privileges denied to others, which is apt doubly to injure the Nation making the concessions — by unnecessarily parting with what ought to have been retained — and by exciting jealousy, ill-will, and a disposition to retaliate, in the parties from whom equal privileges are withheld: And it gives to ambitious, corrupted or deluded citizens (who devote themselves to the favorite Nation) facility to betray, or sacrifice the interests of their own country, without odium, sometimes even with popularity; gilding, with the appearances of a virtuous sense of obligation a commendable deference for public opinion, or a laudable zeal for public good, the base or foolish compliances of ambition, corruption, or infatuation.

PREFACE

THE struggle between neutrality and unneutrality is as active as ever. In the minds of many Americans, the intervention of the United States in the recent European war exemplified the operation of " collective security " against an " aggressor." The cult of unneutrality was then born. It received the imprimatur of official approval in the Covenant of the League of Nations. Ever since, the United States has been torn between two conflicting schools of thought — those who desire the nation to continue its interest in collective intervention on behalf of the " righteous " and those who desire it to return to its traditional policy of neutrality and nonintervention in European quarrels. That conflict is implicit in the confused efforts of recent years to frame satisfactory neutrality legislation. The interventionists desire a wide range of presidential discretion; the neutrals an observance of the rules of international law, without Executive discretion. Discretion is urged to enable the United States to " coöperate " with the " peace-loving " nations to " prevent war " or, if it is unpreventable, to " shorten " it by sanctions and thus " enforce peace." These seductive phrases have captured the imagination of many American citizens, although they threaten not only the neutrality, but the independent existence of the United States. The interventionists attack neutrality as a principle; the neutrals defend it. The confusion has been increased by the unavoidable toleration by the interventionists of the word " neutrality," while they read into it, through the proposed flexibility incidental to

Executive discretion, the whole ideology of unneutrality.

Neutrality is an old institution, which finds its source in candor, in the obligation to hold the scales even, to remain a friend of both belligerents, to lend support to neither, to avoid passing judgment on the merits of their war. It assures both belligerents that they are dealing with a friend, not a disguised enemy. The belligerents must know who is in the war and who is not. In return for obligations assumed by a neutral, the belligerents undertake to respect his rights as a neutral, including the right to remain out of other people's wars. There are those who regard this life-preserving role as insufficiently heroic and who recommend mixing in foreign wars as a " world service." But they seem unaware of the humiliations which the " servant of mankind " brings to his own people and the distress which interference in foreign quarrels spreads to the rest of the world.

The case against neutrality and in favor of the " enforcement of peace " through sanctions is supported by arguments never heretofore heard. Not least among them is the contention that since neutrality did not keep the United States out of the War of 1812, or out of the European war of 1917, it should be repealed in favor of a new dispensation by which the United States shall join the " peace-loving " nations either to prevent a foreign war or to starve or otherwise coerce an aggressor to cease and desist from his warlike enterprise. The conclusion is unsound not only because of its impracticability and war-provoking tendencies, but because its major premise is false. Neutrality did not cause the War of 1812, and unhappily, the United States was not neutral

from 1914 to 1917. The failure consistently to apply
the principles and rules of neutrality during the period
1914–17 served largely to drive the United States into
the European war. It was, therefore, not neutrality,
or the laws of neutrality, which were at fault, but
the unwise human administration of laws which, properly administered, would adequately have protected the
United States against intervention.

Neutrality is necessarily incompatible with the new
theory that peace can be produced by coalitions of the
worthy " peace-loving " nations against an " aggressor."
This revolutionary idea has no roots in experience, is
antilegal in its connotations, and has naturally produced, together with the " peace " treaties with which
it was born, a state of international disequilibrium and
distemper unparalleled in modern times. Not least of
its deplorable features is the fact that it has enlisted in
its support the emotional morality of so-called idealists,
particularly in the United States. Far removed from the
turmoil which characterizes Europe, these groups have
cherished and expounded the theory and persuaded governments to support it as the way to peace. Nonintervention has been denounced as immoral. Partiality and intervention have been glorified. No wonder then that
armaments have steadily increased and wars appear
imminent.

The result of these unfortunate contradictions has
been to extol force and war in the name of peace, to
characterize neutrality as an invitation to war, and sanctions and intervention as peaceful devices, to consider
the neutrals as reactionaries and the Noble Interventionists as liberals. A topsy-turvy world of paradoxes has

thus been created in which peace is to be achieved through war.

It is the purpose of this book to expose the fallacies which have so greatly undermined the conception of neutrality, and to indicate the dangerous vistas which unneutrality now opens to the United States. An attempt will be made to present the underlying reasons for neutrality over the centuries, regarded by many down to 1914 as the maximum achievement of international law. The errors in the administration of American neutrality during the period of 1914–17 will then be discussed, and after that the postwar developments, including recent legislative proposals and their effect on neutrality for the United States.

Our debt to Eugene Davidson, the editor of the Yale University Press, is hard to express. He has not only inspired us to proceed with the work, but his constant editorial aid and advice have been invaluable. Professor Samuel F. Bemis has been good enough to examine the chapters dealing with the diplomacy of the war, and we are grateful for a number of useful suggestions. Miss Phoebe Morrison has rendered exceptional service in assisting us in research. Miss Roberta Yerkes has given us important editorial help on the manuscript.

THE wars foreshadowed in the first edition are now upon us. Again the cult of unneutrality persuades the United States to unneutral " methods short of war " — usually the prelude to war. The vicissitudes of the struggle to maintain neutrality during 1937–1940 are considered in the last chapter.

E. B.

W. P. L.

April 7, 1940.

CONTENTS

PART I

INTRODUCTION

PART II

THE PERIOD OF " NEUTRALITY," 1914–1917

NEUTRALITY FOR THE UNITED STATES

PART I

INTRODUCTION

I.

THE CONCEPTION AND THE RULES OF NEUTRALITY

IN the rational days of the nineteenth and early twentieth centuries, the path of progress was deemed to lie in a firm abstention from the wars of other peoples. While every effort was made to conciliate differences, it was not assumed that in a competitive world all conflicts could be avoided, still less that any good purpose could be served by intervening in the affairs of other nations or by judging the merits of their wars and taking sides accordingly. Nor was it thought that foreign countries would view such intervention as other than unfriendly interference, a busybody's concern with matters he did not understand. The belief that nations were each other's keepers or the guardians of each other's consciences would have been regarded as fantastic. It was not assumed that, in a world of sovereign states, nations would or could discard the dictates of political self-interest and adopt the disinterested objective standards ordinarily associated with judicial bodies. Realizing that international law had behind it no sovereign state but only the support of custom and voluntary agreement, nations refrained from subjecting it to excessive strains. Thus, with the intensive cultivation of international trade incidental to the industrial system, voluntary consent was gradually obtained to rules for the greater security of peaceful trade, even in wartime, and the mitigation of the horrors of war for noncombatants.

A system of independent states of varying size and power could not, however, develop a legal system such as prevails within each one of the states. There, a legislature or lawgiver in more or less continuous session relieves social strains by frequent changes in the law, and a balanced division of governmental powers helps to maintain, after a fashion, the social equilibrium. The system of independent states is far too primitive for so organic a legal system. Many of the political errors of recent years have been due to the easy assumption that there is a close analogy between the law within a state, whereby the unruly are hailed before the civil authorities, and the international system, in which no one can hail an unruly nation before the bar of justice without producing conflicts. But this ignores the facts. Law is built on experience with things as they are. The moment even municipal law exacts too much, it proves unenforceable. Witness the experiment with prohibition. International relations are much less susceptible of external control. Any attempt to impose a rule which does not grow out of previous experience is almost sure to fail. Thus, mere hatred of war is not enough to justify extravagant hopes of a fundamental change in international relations. Law follows life; it does not lead it. Granting that the international system consists of a relatively limited number of states, each claiming equality before the law but manifestly unequal in physical power, a legal system must develop among them by slow growth and custom or else by voluntarily contracted treaties bearing a reasonable relation to the current mores. The experience of the ages has shown that such a system was best kept alive and its progress assured by enlarging as far as possible the oases of neutrality and confining to as narrow limits as possible the area of belligerency.

The thirst for speedy solutions of complex problems is, however, unquenchable. After the Great War, it became fashionable in the United States to encourage the promulgation of grandiose schemes for the creation of Permanent Peace. Modest proposals for relieving tensions in a narrow field, such as economic competition, were hardly deemed sufficiently attractive. Not so long ago, a Mr. Charles H. Levermore won a prize of $50,000 in a contest for " the best plan by which the United States may coöperate with other nations to achieve and preserve the peace of the world." Doubtless the $50,000 proved more substantial than the plan, for who can now remember it?

The blithe casualness and optimism with which rules for the conduct of nations are now prescribed, especially in the United States, have damagingly oversimplified a problem whose difficulties have their source in the history and in the weaknesses of man. Far from solving the problem of peace, these easy prescriptions, and the reliance placed in them, have served to weaken respect and support for the gradual and unobtrusive improvement of international relations in practical ways. They have helped to conceal the true state of international affairs; by misdirecting public attention from fact to fancy, they have induced public opinion unwittingly to pursue counsels and policies the opposite of constructive. The present state of the world is the best exemplification of that mistaken ideology. A comparison between the tolerant attitude of peoples in 1899, at the time of the first Hague Conference, and the intolerance of 1937 is eloquent.

The idea that neutrality was necessary to self-preservation, that it was a stabilizing influence in the world, had prevailed for some seven centuries, ever since the Hanseatic and Mediterranean cities of the twelfth, thirteenth and fourteenth centuries had developed an international trade and sought protection for it in a legal system. The maritime codes of those centuries, codifying ancient customs of maritime Europe, became the foundation for the prize law of the modern world. War on enemy shipping and commerce was recognized as an incident of warfare, but the immunity of the goods and ships of a friend — the significant name for a neutral — gave some inducement to neutrality, both in principle and in practice.

During the unity of the Holy Roman Empire, before modern nations had established what is now called sovereignty or independence, neutrality as a political conception had but a limited scope. It has achieved its importance with the growth of the state system, especially after the sixteenth century. The right to stay out of wars and to enjoy the privileges of neutrality was recognized by belligerents only after a struggle lasting over several centuries. Not until the gradual widening of international commercial relations, together with the realization that no single nation was always a belligerent and that excessive impositions on a neutral might turn him into an enemy, was self-interest finally enlisted to support the cause of neutrality as a political and legal status. Then came general acceptance of the idea of a neutral nation, implying by the very name, " two nations at war, and a third in friendship with both." The neutral recognizes the cause of both parties as just; as John Quincy Adams said, " It avoids all consideration of the merits of the contest."

The history of this struggle for the legal right to remain neutral extends over a period of approximately four hundred years.[1] At times the obstacles seemed insuperable. In the seventeenth century especially, the danger of being compelled to fight anyway persuaded Grotius and others to suggest a distinction between just and unjust wars; they advised

---

[1] As late as 1680 Molloy in *De jure maritimo et navali* (Bk. I, ch. ix, Sec. 9), felt able to say: " As a neuter neither purchases friends nor frees himself from enemies, so commonly he proves a prey to the victor; hence it is held more advantage to hazard in a conquest with a companion than to remain in a state wherein he is in all probability of being ruined by the one or the other." In other words, a neutral, to survive, was advised to pick the winning side. That, in effect, is the advice enjoined upon neutrals by the modern proposal to take sides against the " aggressor." Should the " aggressor " win, the result would spell disaster for the small " neutral."

neutrals to help the just, but when a distinction was impossible, to treat both sides alike. The advice was not taken, at least until 1919, because nations found no use for it. It was impractical. The remedy would have been worse than the disease. Consequently, the right of neutrals to stay out of wars and to have their rights respected attained universal recognition and became solidified in the treaties of the sixteenth and seventeenth centuries. Men of good sense perceived that by building up this painfully won right to neutrality they had made a striking contribution to peace, to sanity, to the limitation of the horrors and area of war, and by such limitation, to the framing of workable treaties of peace. An immunity against war had thus been erected.

Following the early maritime codes, these advances in the law were first recorded in treaties for the adjustment of the conflicting interests of belligerents and neutrals, a settlement which could not be worked out on the basis of force alone. The belligerent desire to cripple an enemy's trade clashed with the neutral interest to continue nonmilitary trade and to avoid undue hardships. As a result, a separate system of prize law and prize courts, nationally organized but administering international law, was gradually developed, a system which helped to give some assurance that neutral ships and cargoes at sea had the protection of law against the arbitrary force or reckless caprice of belligerents.

From the fiery crucible of many a war there was evolved a group of principles by which belligerents and neutrals achieved some reasonably definite guides to the conduct of their reciprocal relations on land and sea. This development did not rest on force; that lay with the belligerents. It was not imposed by a superior authority, but grew out of the practice and customs of independent states. It was, therefore, a delicate structure which belligerents were often under temptation to upset. Among independent nations rules of law have behind them no other sanction than the reciprocal recognition that stability and order are necessary to all human activity and that lawlessness will arouse legitimate reprisals, if not war. A nation can less easily conceal its violation of law than can an individual, and the force of public opinion — and in wartime, of neutral opinion — is a potent influence in behalf of legality.

The principles on which neutral rights and belligerent duties were based were these: in return for the neutral's strict abstention from the conflict and observance of genuine impartiality between the belligerents — or the maintenance, as it was called in early treaties, of the position of a friend — the belligerent would not attack the neutral or seek to draw him into the ambit of belligerency. But that abstention and impartiality had to be sensitively preserved. Otherwise, each belligerent was privileged to regard departure from this obligation as unfriendly, as exposing the neutral to legitimate attack.

Another factor in the development of neutrality was, as it is today, the necessity for candor, for open sincerity in international dealings. As Westlake states, " that quality is more important in international than in other relations, because states over which there is no sovereign power must look chiefly to themselves for their security, and if they were harassed by doubts as to the conduct to be expected from powers not openly hostile, their situation would be so confused that they would often feel compelled to extend the area of war in a manner really needless." The belligerent has the right to know who is in the war and who is not, who is an enemy and who is a friend. To depart from the standards of an " honest neutrality," or " fair neutrality " as Jefferson called it, is to take on the character of an enemy while seeking to retain the guise of a friend and the privileges and immunities attaching to friendship. To be neutral and unneutral at one and the same time is a legal monstrosity.

Closely related to this obligation of candor is another consideration now frequently misconceived. That is the necessity for definiteness in the rules of neutrality and certainty as to what action neutrals will take. The current view that neutrality is something adjustable, to be changed from day to day as Executive discretion may dictate, is unsound and dangerous. Without certainty in the rules and their administration, the neutral government is exposed to the fluctuations of sentiment at home and to the suspicions of belligerents abroad, each judging the purpose of the changes by their practical effect on his own fortunes. To substitute for definiteness an Executive license to make daily adjustments is to invite the charge and the consequence of unneutrality.

The growth of trade and the dependence of most seafaring as well as landlocked nations on the exchange of goods, both for their economic life and their prosperity, brought about certain compromises by which private neutral traders were privileged to continue their trade, even with the belligerents and their citizens. This concession was not easily obtained from the dominant Sea Powers. However, since no country was involved in every war, since the Sea Powers had become industrial nations interested in preserving their own privileged trade in nonmilitary goods, and since the law could not be continually shifted from war to war as belligerent interest dictated, a coördinated compromise was brought about between belligerent and neutral rights. That compromise rested on practical rules which were applied by all the agencies that nations possess, such as prize courts, diplomatic negotiations, arbitral decisions, treaties, and domestic legislation. These rules forbade a neutral *government,* under penalty of being considered hostile, to supply arms, ammunition, and implements of war to either belligerent or to lend him money. In addition, it was implicitly understood that governments, as such, would not supply any commodities to a belligerent.

Governments were not then customarily engaged in commerce.

On the other hand, the private citizen or corporation, deemed the natural agent of trade, was restricted by these international rules only to the extent necessary to insure that he would not supply military goods to the belligerents. Moreover, enforcement of even that slight restriction on normal freedom of private trade was so arranged that the neutral government did not assume the responsibility of policing shipments, even though they might consist of arms. Enforcement was left to the visit and search of belligerent cruisers. It might have been preferable to assign responsibility for the nonshipment of arms, ammunition and implements of war to the neutral government, and this might perhaps have helped to limit the category of contraband goods which belligerent countries announce that they will seize when destined for their enemy. But in the eighteenth and nineteenth centuries, when these rules were mainly worked out, the climate of opinion favored freedom for the individual and relieved the neutral government of such responsibility. The solution adopted was for the trader in contraband to assume all the risks of that commerce without protection from his government.

The neutral trader was required not to interfere with the military operations of the belligerents against each other to the extent of not seeking to break through an effective blockade of belligerent coasts or cities. Blockade, like a land siege, was considered a legitimate operation. Again, enforcement of this duty was not imposed on the neutral government, which might have found it difficult, but on the belligerent injured by its nonobservance.

The neutral nation, however, was obliged to make sure that its territory was not used — even by private citizens, national or alien — for the preparation of a military expedition or enterprise against either belligerent. Thus, under the Three

Rules of the Treaty of Washington,[2] Great Britain was held liable to the United States to the extent of $15,500,000 for the depredations on Union shipping committed by the Confederate cruiser *Alabama;* the vessel had been fitted out and allowed to sail from Liverpool, carrying in her hold guns subsequently mounted on deck.

This system has rightly been called a compromise between two otherwise irreconcilable claims — the claim of the belligerent to stop all trade with his enemy, and the claim of the neutral to continue all trade with both belligerents. In return for a concession to permit trade in nonmilitary goods, the neutral government agrees to permit the belligerent to capture — if it can — its citizens' military goods destined for the enemy. That it was a compromise between two claims, either of which if fully exerted would have wiped out the other, does not make it any the less law. It is in this respect no different from many rules in private or constitutional law.

The fact that the responsibility for policing neutral trade, even to the extent of prohibiting the supply of arms and implements of war, was thrown not on the neutral country of shipment but on the belligerent unfavorably affected, indicates that neutral privileges were not merely the generous concessions of a powerful belligerent; they were legal rights wrung from the belligerents and insisted upon through the united force of neutral interest. And they were freely admitted by belligerent prize courts.

These legal rights were confirmed and recorded in multilateral treaties, notably the Declaration of Paris, the conventions of the First and Second Hague Conferences of 1899 and 1907, and the Declaration of London in 1909. The wavering record of some nations in the past, and the advances of commerce and orderly government, had made it seem re-

[2] These rules, requiring a neutral to prevent the use of his territory as a base of naval or military equipment, were adopted for the *Alabama* arbitration. Moore, *Arbitrations*, I, 573 *et seq*. Citizen Genêt's activities were curbed by the Washington administration under these general principles.

ciprocally advantageous to record the growth of law not merely in bilateral treaties — such as characterized the sixteenth, seventeenth and eighteenth centuries — but in multilateral conventions to which all or most maritime states were made parties. The principle of impartiality and abstention having been firmly established, the efforts of progressive statesmen were directed toward uniformity and generalization of supplementary regulations in world-wide conventions.

There were two weaknesses in the earlier rules — one cured in 1856, the other still prevalent. Before 1856, it had been common to seize neutral ships on the ground that they carried enemy goods which, even when noncontraband, were subject to confiscation. This placed on neutral shipowners the enormous responsibility of identifying the owners of their cargoes, a burden increased by certain presumptions as to enemy character arising out of enemy destination. Long before the first Armed Neutrality of 1780 [3] and the second of 1800, traders had brought influence to bear on governments to insist that the neutral flag of a vessel should exempt goods on board from seizure regardless of their ownership, except for legitimate contraband. The United States had, in the first Treaty Plan of 1776 of the Continental Congress, proposed the rule that free ships make free goods, and this doctrine, like the doctrine of immunity from capture of private property at sea, became a traditional American political principle. It has often been asked why the relatively weak United States, through its statesmen of the late eighteenth century, was so successful in its diplomacy. Not least among the reasons is the fact that those statesmen were so eminently practical. Their proposals carried weight because they were well considered and the relative chances of their success were taken into account in advance. The doctrine of free ships,

[3] An association of Russia, Denmark, Sweden, Holland, Austria, Portugal and the two Sicilies, for the protection of neutral rights against violation by Great Britain, Spain and France. Moore, *Digest*, VII, 559. The United States later adopted the principles of the Armed Neutrality.

free goods, backed by European neutrals, was finally adopted
in the Declaration of Paris of 1856 and became thereafter
the universal rule of law, to the great advantage of neutral
shipping and trade. That the rule has at times been violated
by belligerents controlling the sea does not militate against
the magnitude of this victory of law over force.

The other weakness in the rules that still troubles the
world and contributes to the burden of heavy armaments is
the fact that the term " contraband of war " is not defined
in multilateral treaties. During the sixteenth and seventeenth
centuries it was common to define this term in bilateral treaties in order that each country might have a clear guide when
one of the contracting parties became a belligerent and the
other remained neutral. The practice of treaty definition prevailed down to modern times; for example, Article 15 of the
Treaty of 1871 between the United States and Italy defined
the following commodities as constituting contraband of war:

1. Cannons, mortars, howitzers, swivels, blunderbusses, mus-
kets, fusees, rifles, carbines, pistols, pikes, swords, sabers, lances,
spears, halberds, bombs, grenades, powder, matches, balls, and
all other things belonging to, and expressly manufactured for, the
use of these arms.
2. Infantry belts, implements of war and defensive weapons,
clothes cut or made up in a military form and for a military use.
3. Cavalry belts, war saddles and holsters.
4. And generally all kinds of arms and instruments of iron,
steel, brass, and copper, or of any other materials manufactured,
prepared, and formed expressly to make war by sea or land.

Even in the absence of such treaties, however, a long-
continued practice had limited belligerents to the inclusion
within " contraband of war " of commodities exclusively devoted to warlike functions.

Belligerents naturally have an interest in enlarging the
content of the term " contraband " and neutrals in limiting
it, for goods falling within its scope are freely confiscable,

even though they are the property of citizens of friendly countries. On occasions when neutrals have been weak, belligerents have been successful in extending the list to include such items as horses and fuel and similar commodities not primarily of military use but which might be so used. Even so, down to the late European war, there had been a certain sense of restraint in the expansion of these lists by belligerents, so that occasions for dispute were few. They were limited mainly to controversies over the inclusion of particular commodities, such as provisions and coal. During the Spanish-American War, for instance, Spain classed sulphur as contraband, yet Italy, by a well-argued protest on the ground that sulphur also had valuable civil uses, was able to persuade Spain to reconsider and to remove it from her contraband list.

In the late war, the number of belligerents was so large and the unwillingness of neutrals, especially the United States, to adopt a common course was so marked, that belligerents were able to abuse their power and to include in the contraband list hundreds of articles which never had appeared in such a list before. No Italy appeared to contest the inclusion of sulphur. The United States, urged on by Ambassador Page, defaulted badly, although Mr. Lansing had announced that we would be the " champion " of neutrals.

In 1909, the Declaration of London, foreseeing the danger of conflict between belligerent and neutral over the subject of contraband, had endeavored to establish fixed lists. Article 22 of that convention provided:

The following articles and materials are, without notice, regarded as contraband, under the name of absolute contraband:
(1) Arms of all kinds, including arms for sporting purposes, and their unassembled distinctive parts.
(2) Projectiles, charges, and cartridges of all kinds, and their unassembled distinctive parts.
(3) Powder and explosives specially adapted for use in war.

(4) Gun-carriages, caissons, limbers, military wagons, field forges, and their unassembled distinctive parts.

(5) Clothing and equipment of a distinctively military character.

(6) All kinds of harness of a distinctively military character.

(7) Saddle, draught, and pack animals suitable for use in war.

(8) Articles of camp equipment, and their unassembled distinctive parts.

(9) Armor plates.

(10) Warships and boats and their unassembled parts specially distinctive as suitable for use only in a vessel of war.

(11) Implements and apparatus made exclusively for the manufacture of munitions of war, for the manufacture or repair of arms, or of military material for use on land or sea.

There was also promulgated a list of goods which were not contraband,[4] but which might be seized as contraband provided the captor proved out of the ship's papers and in

---

[4] Article 24 of the Declaration of London provided as follows:

The following articles and materials susceptible of use in war as well as for purposes of peace, are, without notice, regarded as contraband of war, under the name of conditional contraband:

(1) Food.

(2) Forage and grain suitable for feeding animals.

(3) Clothing and fabrics for clothing, boots and shoes, suitable for military use.

(4) Gold and silver in coin or bullion; paper money.

(5) Vehicles of all kinds available for use in war, and their unassembled parts.

(6) Vessels, craft, and boats of all kinds, floating docks, parts of docks, as also their unassembled parts.

(7) Fixed railway material and rolling-stock, and material for telegraphs, radio telegraphs, and telephones.

(8) Balloons and flying machines and their unassembled distinctive parts as also their accessories, articles and materials distinctive as intended for use in connection with balloons or flying machines.

(9) Fuel; lubricants.

(10) Powder and explosives which are not specially adapted for use in war.

(11) Barbed wire as also the implements for placing and cutting the same.

(12) Horseshoes and horseshoeing materials.

(13) Harness and saddlery material.

(14) Binocular glasses, telescopes, chronometers, and all kinds of nautical instruments.

a speedy proceeding in the prize court that the goods in question were destined to the enemy government for military use.[5] If the captor could not make this proof in the limited way allowed, ship and cargo had to be released.

The Declaration of London was unratified, so that in 1914 international law was controlling. When then the Allied governments decided arbitrarily to keep all commodities out of Germany, without undertaking to establish a legal blockade, as the law required, they proceeded to expand the list of goods absolutely contraband, so as to include most of the commodities used by human beings. The purported explanation of this abuse was the argument that modern science could now work up raw materials into all kinds of lethal weapons; for example, cotton could be used for explosives and lard to make nitro-glycerin.

In order to insure the continued economic life of noncombatants and to enable neutrals to continue to trade with noncombatants, it had been established ever since the seventeenth century that goods which were capable of both military and nonmilitary use should not be confiscable unless the captor could definitely prove that they were destined for army or navy service. Such goods came to be known as goods conditionally contraband, the principal item of which consisted of foodstuffs. A classic statement of Lord Salisbury in 1900 epitomizes the law on this point: " Food stuffs, with a hostile destination, can be considered contraband of war only if they are supplies for the enemy's forces. It is not sufficient that they are capable of being so used; it must be shown that this was in fact their destination at the time of the seizure." [6]

With various arguments, such as the one that the enemy governments had taken over the distribution of food,[7] the British prize courts in the late war broke down this distinc-

---

[5] Story, *Prize Courts* (London, 1854), pp. 19, 35–36.

[6] Moore, *op. cit.*, VII, Sec. 1253, p. 685.

[7] British note of Feb. 10, 1915, *For. Rel.*, 1915, Suppl., p. 324.

tion between goods absolutely and goods conditionally contraband on the unsustainable ground that the division itself
was ill-founded. In April, 1916, the British Government officially abolished the distinction between the two classifica-
tions. In addition, a change in the rules of evidence, throwing
on the cargo-owner the burden of proving that the goods would
never reach Germany, in place of requiring the captor to prove
that they were destined for the enemy's military forces, deprived neutrals of all remaining protection against belligerent
caprice.

Neutrals like the United States had, in 1915, protested
against these Allied abuses, but since the United States was
unwilling to make the protest effective, the abuses continued.
As a result, the expansion of contraband lists served the same
military purpose as would an actual blockade. It also had the
effect of making postwar prospects of a limitation of naval
armaments illusory.

In this connection another abuse of the law must be mentioned. Prior to 1756 neutrals had attempted to avoid the
prohibition of trading between a belligerent country and its
colony, a trade at that time closed to them even in time of
peace, by breaking the voyage into two parts — from the
colonies to a neutral port and then from the neutral port
to the parent country. The result was a slightly roundabout
but nonetheless effective commerce. This effort to evade
legitimate belligerent prohibitions was expanded in 1793 in
the French Revolutionary Wars. To meet it, belligerents developed a body of rules, known as the doctrine of continuous
voyage. During the American Civil War, the Union invoked
this doctrine so as to bring about the seizure of British ships
bound for Nassau but purposing, either by themselves or
through transshipping, to import Confederate supplies into
Charleston in violation of the Northern blockade. Condemnations, however, were applied only to military goods.[8] This

[8] During the late war, Secretary Lansing failed to make this fundamental
distinction between military and nonmilitary goods, and tried to justify the

American action was not unreasonable, for Nassau had no local or general trade; [9] it was merely a springboard for Charleston, the real destination.

In the Declaration of London the applicability of this doctrine which, if abused, would act to cripple neutral trade, was confined to goods absolutely contraband — that is to say, arms, ammunition, and implements of war. During the late war, however, the doctrine was abused beyond all reasonable limits, first by considering large categories of peaceful goods as absolutely contraband, and then by indulging the presumption, practically impossible of rebuttal, that all goods shipped to neutral countries from which they could reach the Central Powers were in fact destined for them. Furthermore, by rationing schemes and other devices, the economic life of neutral peoples was made dependent upon Allied concession; they were obliged to restrict their own exportation to the Central Powers in accordance with Allied command.

That these were abuses of the rights of neutrals is indicated by the rules of international law which, in 1914, would have been deemed fundamental by nearly every international lawyer. Professor Jessup has adequately summarized these rules:

1. "Paper" blockades are illegal. A blockade to be binding must be effectively maintained by an "adequate" naval force.
2. Even enemy goods are safe on a neutral ship, *if* they are not contraband and *if* they are not destined for a blockaded port: "Free ships make free goods."
3. Neutral goods are safe even on an enemy ship, *if* they are not contraband and *if* they are not destined for a blockaded port.
4. *A fortiori*, neutral goods are safe on a neutral ship *but* only if they are not contraband and if they are not destined for a blockaded port.

British abuses on the ground that the United States had done about the same thing in the Civil War.

[9] As the Scandinavian countries and Holland did have in 1914–17.

5. Contraband goods are divided into two categories: absolute and conditional.

6. Absolute contraband consists of goods exclusively used for war and destined for an enemy country, even if passing through a neutral country en route; the rule of " continuous voyage " applies.

7. Conditional contraband consists of goods which may have a peaceful use but which are also susceptible of use in war and which are destined for the armed forces or a government department of a belligerent state; the rule of " continuous voyage " does not apply.

These were the rules of international law in 1914, and their violation by belligerents in the late war has not changed them. New law is not to be found in the violations of the old. This by no means suggests that modifications may not be agreed upon in a new international conference. In return for an abandonment of visit and search, certification of cargoes at the port of departure might well be justified. Even in the rare case of a general European war, permits or convoys for passenger vessels or special cargoes could be arranged. Organization among neutrals can by skill and candor obtain an enforceable recognition of their rights. But the suggestion that neutrals should surrender those rights merely turns the sea and its trade over to belligerents, thus stimulating belligerent excesses and neutral degradation.

In philosophy and in law the establishment of neutrality and its privileges has until recently been considered a victory for civilization over brute force, for law over anarchy. In 1911, Sir Thomas Barclay, the eminent international lawyer, was able to say: " Neutrality is the most progressive branch of modern International Law. It is also that branch of International Law in which the practice of self-restraint takes the place of the direct sanctions of domestic law most effectively. . . . While the right of war was simply the right of the stronger, there was no room for neutral rights. . . . It is the growth of a law of neutrality, through the modern possibility of concerted action among neutral states, which is bringing about improvement." [10]

While it takes a long time to build up such a legal structure, it takes much less time to destroy it. Nor is war the greatest enemy of law; the maxim *inter arma leges silent* means only that law gives way temporarily to a different forum of arbitrament in which force may occasionally be carried beyond legal bounds. But the law does not cease to exist. The real danger to law and order lies in a different direction. The attempts, of recent years, to create a new system for the collective coercion of unruly or disfavored nations have served largely to distort and enfeeble the long historical evolution of the rules of law, presumably in the belief that the lessons of history had, through the process of science and invention, become obsolete. Unfortunately for this view, man himself is the product of history and his psychology is conditioned by the same factors that animated his ancestors. He is as emotional, and, when hungry and distressed, as unreasoning as those ancestors. Admittedly the process of invention and rapidity of communication have made the world more interdependent and easily subject to general disturbance. All the more reason, therefore, for not predicating an international system on ideas of coercion which in practice repudiate experience, promote exaggerated nationalism, and further division among peoples. Unhappily most of the ideas purveyed since 1919 for the regeneration of the world have ignored all this. The result was foreordained. In the interest of a professed internationalism, there has now been produced an emotional nationalism unprecedented in history.

John Jay, United States Envoy in London in 1794, wrote to President Washington as follows: " As the situation of

---

[10] *Encyclopedia Britannica* (11 ed.), *s. v.* " Neutrality."

the United States is neutral, so also should be their language to the belligerent powers . . . Neither can it be proper to adopt any mode of pleasing one party that would naturally be offensive to the other." [1]

Walter Hines Page, John Jay's successor in London, took a somewhat different view of these questions in 1914.

At the outbreak of the Russo-Japanese War, President Theodore Roosevelt issued an Executive Order directing the officials of the United States to observe an exact neutrality between the belligerents. His order read:

All officials of the Government, civil, military, and naval, are hereby directed not only to observe the President's proclamation of neutrality in the pending war between Russia and Japan, but also to abstain from either action or speech which can legitimately cause irritation to either of the combatants. The Government of the United States represents the people of the United States . . . in the sincerity with which it is endeavoring to keep the scales of neutrality exact and even. . . . It is always unfortunate to bring old-world antipathies and jealousies into our life, or by speech or conduct to excite anger and resentment toward our nation in friendly foreign lands; but in a government employee, whose official position makes him in some sense the representative of the people, the mischief of such actions is greatly increased. . .[2]

During the first week of the European war, President Wilson addressed the Secretaries of War and Navy, terming " highly unwise and improper " public utterances by our military establishment " to which any color of political or military criticism can be given where other nations are involved." [3] On August 18, 1914, supplementing the Neutrality Proclamation, President Wilson addressed the nation as follows:

[1] Jay's correspondence, Sept. 13, 1794, *Works*, IV, 58–59. Note also the attitude of Washington's Cabinet in Hyneman, *The First American Neutrality* (Urbana, 1934), ch. ii.

[2] Executive Order, March 10, 1904, *For. Rel.*, 1904, p. 185.

[3] Taylor, C. C., *Life of Admiral Mahan* (London, 1920), p. 275; Baker, *Life and Letters of Woodrow Wilson*, V, 18, note 2.

. . . It is entirely within our own choice what its effects upon us will be and to urge very earnestly upon you the sort of speech and conduct which will best safeguard the Nation against distress and disaster.

The effect of the war upon the United States will depend upon what American citizens say and do. Every man who really loves America will act and speak in the true spirit of neutrality, which is the spirit of impartiality and fairness and friendliness to all concerned. . . .

. . . It will be easy to excite passion and difficult to allay it. Those responsible for exciting it will assume a heavy responsibility. . .

I venture, therefore, my fellow countrymen, to speak a solemn word of warning to you against that deepest, most subtle, most essential breach of neutrality which may spring out of partisanship, out of passionately taking sides. The United States must be neutral in fact as well as in name during these days that are to try men's souls. We must be impartial in thought as well as in action, must put a curb upon our sentiments as well as upon every transaction that might be construed as a preference of one party to the struggle before another.[4]

[4] Scott, ed., *President Wilson's Foreign Policy*, pp. 66–68.

II.

THE UNITED STATES AND NEUTRALITY

THE American policy of nonintervention in European affairs is sometimes believed to have first received formal expression in Washington's Farewell Address, a profoundly wise legacy of constitutional proportions for the guidance of the American people. But as a matter of fact, in September, 1776, soon after the Declaration of Independence and, curiously, at the very time the proposed and greatly needed treaty of alliance with France was under discussion, John Adams said:

Our negotiations with France ought to be conducted with great caution, and with all the foresight we could possibly obtain; . . . we ought not to enter into any alliance with her which should entangle us in any future wars in Europe; we ought to lay it down as a first principle and a maxim never to be forgotten, to maintain an entire neutrality in all future European wars.

The very obligations that France considered to be imposed on the United States by the treaty of alliance led, in 1793, to a reiteration, in an epoch-making proclamation of neutrality, of our principle of aloofness from European wars, furnished the motives for Washington's Farewell Address, and finally caused that limited conflict with France from 1798 to 1800 which gave rise to the French Spoliation Claims.

A proffered treaty of alliance in 1778 with Spain, by which we undertook to attack Portugal and offered various concessions in return for political aid, only indicates, by countenancing so serious a departure from principle, how great was the need of the struggling colonists. The flexibility of the policy was again demonstrated by the readiness with which the United States undertook to adhere to the Armed Neutrality of 1780, proposed by Catherine of Russia.

Each of these defections from principle had special motives; but nothing better demonstrates the fundamental nature of our policy than the prompt return to it after the momentary need had passed. Thus, on June 12, 1783, Congress passed a resolution which reads in part: " The true interest of the States requires that they should be as little as possible entangled in the politics and controversies of European nations."

In 1780, John Adams had expressed a common sentiment when he wrote from Paris to the President of Congress: " Let us remember what is due to ourselves and to our posterity, as well as to them [European nations]. . . . Our business with them, and theirs with us, is commerce, not politics, much less war; America has been the sport of European wars and politics long enough." [5]

The circumstances which dictated the principles espoused by the colonies that had just become a nation have often been enumerated — the distance from Europe, the insistence upon freedom from the European political system and its perpetual quarrels and upon emancipation from Europe's monarchical and ecclesiastical theories of government, the demand for freedom from the systems of colonial, commercial and navigation monopolies. These facts and aspirations, taken together with the fact that independence found us with a weak government, an immense territory, a small population, a growing maritime commerce, hostile nations in Europe and on the American continent who were less interested in the permanence of American existence or institutions than they were in the use which they could make of America in their political conflicts, presented at once problems which tested to the limit the mettle of our early statesmen. The factors and conditions with which they therefore had to deal gave birth not only to the major principles of

[5] Wharton, *The Revolutionary Diplomatic Correspondence of the United States* (Washington, 1889), III, 623.

America's life as a nation, but also served to shape those collateral policies and politico-legal doctrines which mark the history of our international relations.

It is probably correct to say that the discovery and occupation of the new continent of America is the most important fact in modern history. It vitally disturbed the conventional groupings of Europe. In the two hundred years before the American Revolution, Spain, Holland, France and England — rivals for domination of the Americas — had experienced all the vicissitudes of success and defeat in a series of wars which from time to time changed the boundary lines of the unexplored continent and impressed England with the great lesson that the possession of sea power is the primary source of international strength and influence.

This rivalry of the European nations aided greatly in securing admission for the United States into the family of nations, for France, Holland, and Spain found in American independence an opportunity to gratify historic grudges against England. Whether the governments that welcomed us into the community of nations had no occasion for regret may be doubted; for the independence of a colony in America could not leave Spain unaffected, and the French monarchy always believed, doubtless correctly, that the inspiration of the French Revolution was found in America. The United States, therefore, grew to nationhood, not merely by virtue of its inherent strength, but by reason of the mutual distrust and conflicts among the principal Powers in Europe.

The birth of a new nation in Europe has, as a rule, little effect on international law or relations; the rules of its conduct are prescribed for it either by usage or by the particular group that sponsors its birth. In the case of the United States it was different. The child of a new philosophy of government, at a distance of thousands of miles from the established countries of the world, with a determination to remain free from that European system which had made the colonists sometimes the cause and always the victims of the European struggles for political and commercial supremacy, the new nation had both necessities and opportunities for developing new theories and practices in international relations. It is for these reasons, primarily, that the entrance of the United States into the family of nations has been called epoch-making.

This originality of policy is not only evidenced in the major principle of nonintervention, which gave rise to its corollary, the Monroe Doctrine, and to its natural derivatives, the system of neutrality and the doctrine of recognition of governments *de facto*, but it is reflected in the provisions of our earliest treaties with foreign powers. There, are found stipulations for liberty of conscience; the removal of important disabilities from aliens; mitigation of the rigors and evils of war through humane treatment for prisoners of war; the privileged withdrawal and departure of alien enemies and the immunity of their private property from seizure; restrictions on the belligerent privilege of visit and search; prohibition, under pain of treatment as a pirate, of the acceptance of privateering commissions by citizens of either country from an enemy of the other; and various limitations on belligerent captures at sea, including, in the treaty with Prussia, the reciprocal immunity of merchant ships in case of war between the signatories. Practically all these innovations were proposed by the American negotiators; they reflect a freedom from tradition and an initiative dictated in part by necessity, in part by opportunity. Their substantial merit, not only in promoting our own interest but also in promoting the interests of the world at large, is indicated by the fact that many of these provisions have long since been accepted as among the most settled of the rules of international law.

Not long after the Constitution of the United States had

made it a nation capable of assuming and carrying out international obligations, the French Revolution broke out. The event, as the Revolution grew in intensity and violence, presented to the new American Government its first great problem in foreign affairs, and the solution adopted charted the future course of national policy. As the Revolution could not be promptly suppressed, some of the European governments felt it necessary to intervene. When England's entrance into the conflict in 1793 expanded it into a maritime war, the American Government had to make its great decision.

The French Revolution had aroused mingled feelings in the United States. Americans generally saw in it the counterpart and response to their own recent achievement and enthusiastically approved it. The government realized better the responsibilities attached to association in the French enterprise. It required statesmanship of a high order, in the face of the popular clamor for aid to France, to decline to yield the ultimate good to the immediate popular demand; but then, the leaders of that day were not sounding boards who took their position on public questions and their views of public policy from the morning newspapers.

The country was still weak. Yet American ships of trade were to be found in all the seas. A false step, inviting another war, might have terminated the life of the young nation. Prudence and patriotism therefore dictated a passive attitude toward the French Revolution. Circumstances, however, soon made more positive action necessary. In 1792 Citizen Genêt was sent to the United States by France and made a triumphal tour from Charleston to Philadelphia, enlisting popular support for his cause, and actually commissioning individuals and privateers for service against England. He also adopted a measure, since often imitated, of talking to a people over the heads of their government, with results as disastrous to his cause as the effort was impolitic. To prevent popular excitement which might precipitate unhappy commitments, and to put a stop to the fomentation of hostile enterprises on American soil, which Genêt, claiming authority from the treaty with France and the friendly sentiments of the people, was then sedulously engaged in promoting, Washington and his Cabinet determined to issue a proclamation of neutrality. They hastened in this course for fear that hesitation might result in their being exploited by either France or England, the principal belligerents. Washington's personal policy became the national policy. In March, 1793, he wrote to Jefferson, then Secretary of State: " War having actually commenced between France and Great Britain, it behooves the Government of this country to use every means in its power to prevent the citizens thereof from embroiling us with either of those powers, by endeavoring to maintain a strict neutrality." The colloquy of Oswald, British negotiator of the Treaty of 1783, with John Adams, had not been lost on the Cabinet: " You are afraid," said Mr. Oswald, " of being made the tools of the powers of Europe." " Indeed I am," said Adams. " What powers? " queried Oswald. " All of them," answered Adams.

The disputes arising out of Genêt's exertions to move the government from the course it had adopted, his efforts to violate the principles of neutrality by fitting out privateers and by capturing and condemning British vessels within American jurisdiction, merely confirmed the wisdom of the American policy. His attempt to employ American soil for hostile acts in favor of France against its enemies gave shape to the principles of neutrality enunciated by Jefferson. Neutrality consisted of certain rights and duties, founded primarily on the sovereignty of every nation within its own territory and its obligation of impartiality between the belligerents. Jefferson's principles have been summarized as follows:

As it was " the *right* of every nation to prohibit acts of sovereignty from being exercised by any other within its limits," so it was, he declared, " the *duty* of a neutral nation to prohibit such as would injure one of the warring powers." Hence, " no succor should be given to either, unless stipulated by treaty, in men, arms, or anything else, directly serving for war." [6]

The neutrality proclamation of April 22, 1793, was momentous, for it fixed what seemed until recent times the immutable policy of the United States toward European wars. It did not use the word " neutrality," since Jefferson believed that an avowal of permanent neutrality should not be bartered away without concessions from the belligerents. The proclamation was actually drafted by Randolph, Attorney General, and announced that " the duty and interest of the United States require that they should with sincerity and good faith adopt and pursue a conduct friendly and impartial toward the belligerent powers." Citizens were warned against joining in the hostilities; they were told that they carried contraband at their risk alone, and that violations of the law of nations within American jurisdiction would be punished.

The proclamation created a profound impression in Europe; for it was at least novel that a people which had theretofore been involved in practically every European war to which England, France or Spain had been parties should now assert their complete independence of European quarrels. Yet it was a logical step in the policy of nonintervention in European affairs, a principle to which utterance had already been given by some of the leaders of the government, and it foreshadowed Washington's Farewell Address which definitely made nonintervention a cornerstone of American foreign policy.

Between the open violation of our neutrality by Genêt and his adherents in the United States and the like disregard of our neutral rights at sea by both France and England, the course of the government was difficult. Nor was the United States fortunate in some of its diplomatic appointments to

---

[6] Moore, *Principles of American Diplomacy* (New York, 1918), p. 45.

France. Gouverneur Morris, first sent by Washington, was too cold toward the Revolution for French taste, and his successor, James Monroe, too warm for American.

In view of the vagueness as to what were at that time neutral rights and privileges, it is not surprising that the budding commerce of America paid a heavy price for the prevailing uncertainty and the unwillingness of each of the belligerents to permit American vessels to trade with the other except under severe restrictions. There was no agreement as to what constituted contraband or blockade. Paper blockades and the unlimited extension of contraband lists rendered the fate of neutral trade extremely precarious. The rule that enemy goods, not contraband, on a neutral ship, were exempt from seizure, stated under the formula of " free ships, free goods " and embodied in the Armed Neutrality of 1780 and in the treaty concluded by Benjamin Franklin with Prussia in 1785, was still far from receiving general acceptance; its ultimate survival and inclusion in the rules of international law are in no small degree due to American effort.

The insistence at that time upon neutral rights furnished a critical test for American diplomacy. The subsequent acquisition of concessions for neutrals in the Jay Treaty of 1794 with England [7] was facilitated by the recognition of the corresponding obligations of neutrals which had been embodied in the American proclamation of 1793 and the statute of 1794 carrying those obligations into effect.

In substance, the Act of 1794 forbade within the United States the acceptance of commissions, the enlistment of men, the fitting out and arming of vessels and the setting on foot of military expeditions in the service of any government or people against a government with which the United States was at peace. Provision was therefore made in the Jay Treaty for the compensation of those British subjects who had suf-

[7] From the arbitrations for which the treaty provided, the United States received awards of $11,650,000 — an immense sum for those days — for British violations of American neutral rights.

fered damages from our failure to prevent French privateers from violating our neutrality, a precedent from which we reaped great advantage some eighty years later in the settlement of the *Alabama* claims of American citizens against Great Britain. Hall, the well-known English authority on international law, says of the attitude of Washington's administration:

The policy of the United States in 1793 constitutes an epoch in the development of the usages of neutrality. There can be no doubt that it was intended and believed to give effect to the obligations then incumbent upon neutrals. But it represented by far the most advanced existing opinions as to what those obligations were, and in some points it even went further than authoritative international custom has up to the present time advanced. In the main, however, it is identical with the standard of conduct which is now adopted by the community of nations.[8]

Not long after the proclamation of neutrality of 1793, began that series of mutually retaliatory Orders in Council and decrees by the English and French Governments which made neutral commerce subservient to belligerent expediency. The difficulty of determining which belligerent was doing American commerce the most injury, American military weakness, and the realization that participation in the war would be more disastrous than helpful to our commerce, persuaded the statesmen of that day to overlook the many provocations to war and to negotiate instead. Each belligerent acted, with little qualification, upon the principle reasserted by Great Britain during the recent World War, namely, that if one belligerent is allowed to make an attack upon the other regardless of neutral rights, his opponent must be allowed similar latitude in prosecuting the struggle " and is not limited to the adoption of measures precisely identical with those of his opponent." On this point, complete harmony seems to prevail among belligerents.

[8] Hall, *International Law* (7 ed., 1917), p. 632.

Notwithstanding all their efforts to obtain by negotiation more favorable treatment for American commerce, the United States was, nevertheless, drawn in 1798 into the limited war with France which lasted until 1800. The Peace of Amiens brought a brief respite to American traders and to a much harassed Department of State.

In 1803, the great struggle between France and England was renewed. The reciprocal issuing of retaliatory Orders in Council and Napoleonic decrees again threatened the trade of neutral American merchants and tested the diplomatic resources of our young Department of State, which this time had less success than in the preceding decade. Neutral rights were all but blotted out by the contending belligerents. Paper blockades were the order of the day.

Desperate efforts were made after 1807 to follow the advice of Washington's Farewell Address not to " inter-tangle our peace and prosperity in the toils of European ambition, rivalship, interest, humor or caprice." Not only was American commerce seriously crippled, but in 1807 the British warship *Leopard* had attacked the American frigate *Chesapeake*.[9] Jefferson determined to embargo all our trade with both belligerents which, while painful to the United States, was considered less dangerous than a war with either or both.[10] But it did not work. The first effects of the embargo were to stimulate smuggling, the European consumer paying for the enhanced risk, and to bring about distress at home. After thirteen months, the embargo had to be repealed. Madison's Nonintercourse Act of 1809, while even less strictly enforced, was used mainly as a bargaining lever with England and France.

The issue which ultimately brought on the War of 1812 was not the Orders in Council interfering with American

[9] See the description of this incident in Jefferson's proclamation, *Works*, X, 441–444. Jefferson declined to regard this as a *casus belli*, exhibiting a commendable sense of self-restraint.

[10] Sears, L. M., *Jefferson and the Embargo* (1927), pp. 55, 73 *et seq.*

commerce, which, although reduced, had been going on right along, but the impressment issue which was not so much as mentioned in Madison's message to Congress of 1811. Even that was not the proximate cause but rather the excuse for the war. By that time the " War Hawk " party of Henry Clay and others had determined that it was morally right for the United States to expand to Canada, to Florida, and the Southwest, and that the immersion of Europe in a fratricidal war presented the inspired opportunity. The Embargo and Nonintercourse Acts of Jefferson and Madison had enraged New England to the point of a contemplated secession. The distempers of several groups, therefore, could be allayed, it was assumed, by entrance into the war. With this decision restrictions on American commercial rights had only an indirect connection. Even a declaration of war against England required for its consummation a wily deception by the French ministry, which wrongly informed Mr. Gallatin that the Berlin and Milan decrees had been repealed,[1] thus ostensibly leaving only the British Orders in Council in force. In fact, the British Orders in Council were repealed on June 18, 1812, the very day war was declared. Had the telegraph existed there might have been no war. As it was, a combination of blunders and misstatements caused American intervention. The recent discovery, therefore, that neutrality is impossible for the United States to maintain during a European war and that the War of 1812 proves it, is refuted by the fact that for twenty years, from 1792 to 1812, barring the French reprisals of 1798, peace was maintained in spite of the greatest provocation and war was then entered upon, not because of the difficulty of remaining neutral, but because the War Hawk party forced the issue in what they thought was the national interest.

[1] Moore, *Arb.*, pp. 4454–4455; see also Pratt, *The Expansionists of 1812* (New York, 1932) ; D. R. Anderson, " The Insurgents of 1811," *American Historical Review*, I (1911), 167; J. T. Adams, *The March of Democracy* (1932), pp. 240, 243.

Throughout the many foreign wars in the nineteenth and early twentieth centuries, including the Crimean, the Franco-Prussian, the Chinese-Japanese, the Boer, the Russo-Japanese and the First and Second Balkan Wars, no responsible American statesman suggested that neutrality was not a valuable asset or a satisfactory basis for American nonintervention.

There was always a special reason for American neutrality — the necessity for internal peace. As in the case of Switzerland, the fact that the American population is recruited from various national origins makes neutrality a condition of domestic tranquillity. The fathers of the country seem to have realized this better than their modern successors. Yet Woodrow Wilson had a flash of Jeffersonian inspiration when he remarked on April 20, 1915: " I am interested in neutrality because there is something so much greater to do than fight; there is a distinction waiting for this Nation that no nation has ever yet got. That is the distinction of absolute self-control and self-mastery." [2] We should have a safer and saner world today had Woodrow Wilson not changed his mind.

[2] Baker and Dodd, *Public Papers of Woodrow Wilson* (New York, 1926), III, 305.

III.

"NEUTRALITY," 1914–1917

IT is not a grateful task to record the diplomacy of the
United States during the period 1914–17. Although President Wilson had enjoined on the nation the necessity for
remaining neutral "in thought as well as in action,"
unfortunately he soon found himself entangled in an emotional drift toward intervention in the war. It is possible that
he did not realize the extent to which he was committing
himself. With little if any useful aid from Secretary Lansing,
who seems to have fumbled nearly every legal issue, with an
Ambassador in London who was less interested in his own
country than in the success of what he supposed to be a crusade for civilization,[3] and with a most adroit and effective
propaganda operating to persuade the United States into
seeing only one side of the issue,[4] it required a strong, sophisticated, and detached mind, with a philosophical view of history, to resist the pressure and allurements to which President Wilson was subjected. Volumes have already been written, and more are likely to be written, analyzing the various
factors which served to propel the United States into the
European war. In this book no detailed examination of the
diplomatic history of the time can be attempted; but it is possible to say that the conduct of the American Government
during that period was a negation of nearly all the requirements of neutrality both in thought and in action. The difficulty was not decreased by the profession that we were acting
as neutrals, for neutrality and unneutrality became inextricably confused. There is no doubt that the administration

[3] Page to House, Sept. 15, 1914, Seymour, *Intimate Papers of Colonel House*, I, 333–334.
[4] See Squiers, *British Propaganda at Home and in the United States from 1914 to 1917* (Harvard University Press, 1935), ch. iii.

desired to see the Allies win and declined to take any action even in defense of American neutral rights which would seriously interfere with that objective. Perhaps the objective is understandable — this is not the place to discuss that question — but to suggest that the objective was consistent with the maintenance of American neutrality is a travesty of the truth. We were unneutral and we paid the price.

Our unneutrality began as early as August, 1914. If neutrality was to be the national policy, the struggle to attain it, if such it was, did not last long. As we shall observe, the effort to obtain British adherence to the Declaration of London disclosed an obsequiousness on the part of Ambassador Page, Colonel House and Mr. Lansing which must have forfeited British respect for the American case and for the capacity of America's representatives to defend it. As Ray Stannard Baker says, " By October [1914], perhaps earlier, our case was lost." [5]

Again, in the protest against the British " measures of blockade " which gradually exposed all American trade with the neutrals of Europe to British and Allied control, the United States as early as December, 1914, practically gave away the American case against Allied impositions with the pathetic admission that such trade could not be interfered with " unless such interference is manifestly an imperative necessity to protect their [Allied] national safety, and then only to the extent that it is a necessity." [6] The note appealed to " the deep sense of justice of the British nation " in requesting it to " refrain from all unnecessary interference with the freedom of trade " and to " conform more closely " to the rules of international law. But as long as the belligerents were to be the judges of " imperative necessity," this friendly admonition had the effect of acquiescing in their illegal measures. The British seem so to have construed it. Baker remarks:

[5] Baker, *op. cit.*, V, 181.
[6] *For. Rel.*, 1914, Suppl., pp. 372–375.

". . . One cannot avoid the impression, after a careful study of this document, that the Administration's defense of American policy was in reality a defense of the British blockade, and furnished the British government with a whole arsenal of arguments against our own criticism of that blockade." [7]

Although on August 18, 1914, President Wilson had solemnly urged " every man who really loves America " to " act and speak in the true spirit of neutrality, which is the spirit of impartiality . . . and friendliness to all concerned," and had warned against " partisanship " and " taking sides," on August 30, 1914, only twelve days later, he is recorded as telling Colonel House " that if Germany won, it would change the course of our civilization and make the United States a military nation." [8]

The submarine campaign initiated by Germany in February, 1915, seems to have deeply offended President Wilson and to have fixed his attachment to the Allied cause. This influenced both the tone and contents of his notes to Germany and he began to talk about " strict accountability." Even before the *Lusitania* sinking in May, 1915, Attorney General Gregory attended a Cabinet meeting which he described as follows:

While these conditions existed [i.e., the sinking of ships before the *Lusitania*] a cabinet meeting was held, at which several of Mr. Wilson's advisers expressed great indignation at what they considered violation [by Britain] of our international rights, and urged a more vigorous policy on our part.

After patiently listening, Mr. Wilson said, in that quiet way of his, that the ordinary rules of conduct had no application to the situation; that the Allies were standing with their backs to the wall, fighting wild beasts; that he would permit nothing to be done by our country to hinder or embarrass them in the prosecution of the war unless admitted rights were grossly violated, and that this policy must be understood as settled.

[7] Baker, *op. cit.*, V, 237.   [8] Seymour, *op. cit.*, I, 293.

Like all true-hearted Americans, he hoped that the United States would not be drawn into the war; but he was of Scotch and English blood, and by inheritance, tradition and rearing at all times the friend of the Allies.[9]

On September 22, 1915, Colonel House records Wilson's views as follows: " Much to my surprise, he [Wilson] said he had never been sure that we ought not to take part in the conflict, and, if it seemed evident that Germany and her militaristic ideas were to win, the obligation upon us was greater than ever." [10]

Mr. Tumulty, the President's Secretary, reports the President as believing that the public demand that he keep England within legal bounds was actuated by a " sinister political purpose." The President is reported to have approved Sir Edward Grey's statement that " of course many of the restrictions that we have laid down and which seriously interfere with your trade are unreasonable, but America must remember that we are fighting her fight as well as our own to save the civilization of the world." The President thereupon adopted this idea as his own, stating, according to Mr. Tumulty: " England is fighting our fight and you may well understand that I shall not, in the present state of affairs, place obstacles in her way." He declined to take any action to embarrass England when she " is fighting for her life and the life of the world." [1]

Secretary Lansing admits in his *Memoirs* that as early as July, 1915, he had concluded that " the German Government is utterly hostile to all nations with democratic institutions " and that " Germany must not be permitted to win this war or to break even, though to prevent it this country is forced to

[9] *New York Times*, Jan. 29, 1925.

[10] Seymour, *op. cit.*, II, 84. Yet in a speech before the Associated Press on April 20, 1915, Wilson had said: " If I permitted myself to be a partisan in this present struggle, I would be unworthy to represent you." Scott, *op. cit.*, p. 91.

[1] Tumulty, *Woodrow Wilson as I Know Him* (New York, 1921), pp. 230–231.

take an active part. This ultimate necessity must be constantly in our minds in all our controversies with the belligerents. American public opinion must be prepared for the time, which may come, when we will have to cast aside our neutrality and become one of the champions of democracy." [2]

We shall have occasion to see that the legal positions of the United States in its controversies with the belligerents were highly colored by this view, to which Mr. Lansing gave repeated expression.[3] Describing his notes to England, Mr. Lansing says:

The notes that were sent were long and exhaustive treatises which opened up new subjects of discussion rather than closing those in controversy. Short and emphatic notes were dangerous. Everything was submerged in verbosity. It was done with deliberate purpose. It insured continuance of the controversies and left the questions unsettled, which was necessary in order to leave this country free to act and even to act illegally when it entered the war.[4]

On October 6, 1915, Colonel House wrote to Mr. Page: " We have given the Allies our sympathy and we have given them, too, the more substantial help that we could not offer Germany even were we so disposed — and that is an unrestricted amount of munitions of war and money. In addition to that, we have forced Germany to discontinue her submarine warfare . . ." [5] In 1915, Mr. Lansing wrote to Colonel House: " In no event should we take a course that would seriously endanger our friendly relations with Great Britain, France, or Russia, for, as you say, our friendship with Germany is a thing of the past." [6]

On January 11, 1916, Colonel House records a conference he held with British leaders in which they had asked " what the United States wished Great Britain to do." To this the neutral Colonel replied: " The United States would like Great

[2] Lansing, *Memoirs*, pp. 19, 21.
[3] *Idem*, p. 128.
[4] *Ibid*.

[5] Seymour, *op. cit.*, II, 72.
[6] *Op. cit.*, p. 70.

Britain to do those things which would enable the United States to help Great Britain win the war." [6a] Page admired this " cleverness."

And Mr. Lansing discloses at least one reason for his insincere defense of American neutrality, by stating: " in dealing with the British Government there was always in my mind the conviction that we would ultimately become an ally of Great Britain." [7] His point of view being that of a prospective ally, his conduct was in reasonable accord.

No wonder that Sir Cecil Spring-Rice's biographer could say of him: " As to his value in negotiation, it cannot be overlooked that during the period while America was neutral, all the issues in dispute between England and America were decided as England wished." And Lord Reading adds: " I believe it to be the case that the Allied governments were never forced to recede from their position in any important question owing to American opposition." [8]

The American surrender was, unfortunately, not merely a betrayal of neutrality, of which Lansing declared we were to be the " champions "; it was a surrender of the independence of the United States and of American self-respect. Furthermore, it must have forfeited the respect of Great Britain and her Allies. The surrender was not made through malevolence but through shortsighted emotionalism, a confusion of ideas as to where America's interest lay. It set the mood for that partiality and that incapacity to take and stand upon correct legal positions which ultimately made of the United States an instrument of the foreign policy of certain European belligerents.

We need only refer to the agreement between Colonel House and Sir Edward Grey on February 22, 1916 (of all days!), for the contingent intervention of the United States

[6a] Seymour, op. cit., II, 124.

[7] Lansing, op. cit., p. 128.

[8] Gwynn, The Letters and Friendships of Sir Cecil Spring-Rice (New York, 1929), II, 430–431.

on behalf of the Allies if the Central Powers failed to accept terms of peace suitable to the Allies. Such an agreement is unique in the history of " neutrality."

Nor need more than passing reference be made to the " Sunrise Breakfast Conference " in April, 1916, in which President Wilson sought to find out from Speaker Clark, Floor Leader Kitchin, and Chairman Flood of the Foreign Affairs Committee of the House whether Congress could be persuaded to approve war against Germany.[9]

It is now established that the British Ambassador was often notified in advance that important notes of protest against British violations of American rights were merely formal and not to be taken too seriously. In connection with the American note of October 21, 1915, Ambassador Spring-Rice was requested to send Sir Edward Grey a cable preparing him for a protest. Spring-Rice assured his government that the note was due to the fact that " the United States must defend their rights and they must make a good showing before Congress meets, but that the correspondence should not take a hostile character but should be in the nature of a juridical discussion." [10]

An entirely different attitude distinguishes the correspondence of the United States with Great Britain from that with Germany. Had there been no fundamental prejudice in favor of one group of belligerents, the legal questions might have been approached with greater felicity and understanding.

On the armed merchantmen question, the unsustainable position was taken that, notwithstanding the ability of a single shot to sink a submarine and notwithstanding the British Admiralty orders to ram or fire on submarines at sight, nevertheless the submarine had no right to fire on and sink an armed belligerent merchantman which had American citizens on board. Thus, the neutral United States under-

---

[9] Professor Arnett in *The Nation*, CXLIII (Sept. 26, 1936), 363.
[10] Gwynn, *op. cit.*, II, 282.

took to defend British merchantmen from attack by their enemy, a practice new in history. The real legal issues involved in the *Lusitania* case — her naval status, her cargo, her course in the war zone, the risks the passengers assumed — were not carefully examined, but ultimata were sent to Germany which were not and have not since been justified. The administration declined to inform American citizens, notwithstanding Secretary Bryan's importunities, that they took passage on belligerent vessels at their own risk. It fought the Gore-McLemore Resolutions of 1916 which merely sought to declare this elementary rule of law.

No more than casual reference needs to be made to one of the more egregious lurches into unneutrality, whereby the United States and its people were led into financing the munitions supply of one set of the belligerents, the Allies. In August, 1914, the administration had announced that the flotation of loans for the belligerents was " inconsistent with the spirit of neutrality." In October, 1914, as the munitions traffic developed, a plausible argument was advanced by Mr. Lansing that bank credits for the purchase of supplies were not public loans and hence should not be banned. The President agreed, but was not willing to let the public know that he had approved this qualification of his original position. By August, 1915, this trade had developed to such proportions that the credits needed to be funded and, it was argued, the Allied governments had to have new money to buy their enormous supplies. The 1914 prohibition and its reasons stood in the way. The Secretary of the Treasury made an eloquent plea to the President for authority to permit the Federal Reserve banks to discount bills and acceptances, a flagrantly unneutral act of the United States Government, and to permit the Allied governments to float loans in the United States. Again the President yielded, but again not publicly. He thus committed himself to a policy which could have but one end, for as the need for Allied credit continued — the argument was that American prosperity could not be permitted to decline — and private lenders became reluctant, only public lending could meet the need, and that meant war. Like the impressment issue to the " War Hawks " of 1812, the German submarine note of January 31, 1917, must have been a godsend to the interventionists. The way to the public Treasury was now open. The subsequent record is current history.[1]

The strange thing is that President Wilson apparently failed to perceive that he was inveigled from one misstep to the next and that the end of the trail was intervention. Perhaps his mental attitude in August, 1915, was already such that he conceived it legitimate to reverse Secretary Bryan's and his own sensible position of August, 1914. Those members of the Federal Reserve Board who in August, 1915, were reluctant to permit the Federal Reserve banks' participation in this violation of neutrality were denounced by Secretary McAdoo as " pro-German," then as later a form of psychological terrorism to discourage the well-balanced, the thoughtful, the really neutral devotees of America, its traditions and its independence. The remarkable fact is that under the impact of the mighty forces making for American involvement, including the consistently unneutral attitude of mind and action of the leaders of the administration, American intervention was nevertheless delayed for more than two years. That fact alone attests the fundamental detachment of the American people and their aversion to participation in European wars.

No wonder that the belated effort of President Wilson in December, 1916, to end the war fell in England on unresponsive ears. The British Government had no reason to believe that the United States would exert pressure on England or

---

[1] Nye Report, S. Rep. 944, Part V, 74th Cong., 2d Sess., pp. 59–77; C. A. Beard, *The Devil Theory of War*, 1936, *passim*.

that it would even act impartially. The mediatory or constructive influence of the United States had been frittered away; only its physical power as a belligerent was now sought. That ultimate seduction was not difficult.

Great Britain, well aware of the situation in Washington, timed its replies so as to conceal the downright refusal of practically every American protest; they were almost invariably delivered when the administration was engrossed in the clouds of controversy incidental to American protests against the German submarine. Thus, the American note of October 21, 1915, was answered on April 19, 1916, when the *Sussex* controversy was at its height. This was excellent strategy, like the release of the Bryce reports on German atrocities in Belgium at the time of the *Lusitania* controversy. In like manner, Great Britain made cotton absolute contraband on August 20, 1915,[2] the day following the sinking of the British steamer *Arabic*.

It is not necessary to extend the demonstration of American unneutrality by a discussion of the feeble protest at the seizure of American mails and the diversion of all northern transatlantic shipping into British ports for examination. Nor is it necessary to discuss the forcible removal of passengers from American ships on the high seas if they were thought to be German reservists.

President Wilson thought the " national honor " required him to fight for the right of American citizens to take passage unmolested on British merchant ships. As John Bassett Moore stated to the Senate Foreign Relations Committee in 1936: " We became involved in war directly as the result of our undertaking to guarantee the safety of belligerent merchantmen and our taking the position that armed belligerent merchantmen were to be considered as peaceful vessels." [3]

[2] *For. Rel.*, 1915, Suppl., p. 174.
[3] Hearings on S. 3474, Committee on Foreign Relations, U. S. Senate, 74th Cong., 2d Sess. (Jan. 10–Feb. 5, 1936), p. 185.

It is not necessary to emphasize the fact that scarcely a ton of cargo left an American port from 1915 to 1917 without the control of a British agent. And we need merely call attention to the submission of the United States to the impositions of the British black list which prevented an American citizen from trading with Germans or even Chileans in Chile if their names had been placed on the British black lists — this at a time when Canada refused to submit to such a black list and freely sent shipments to those very firms! [4]

This brief record justifies a few comments. Those who wish to confer on the Executive a wide discretion to embargo commodities during the course of a foreign war may well observe how Executive discretion was employed in 1914–17. Another striking fact to observe is that all the policies for which Mr. Bryan stood — the embargo on arms and munitions, a prohibition on loans, a prohibition to travel on belligerent ships except at the traveler's risk — policies which the rest of the administration firmly opposed, have now received the practically unanimous support of Congress and of the present administration. Mr. Bryan looms larger as a statesman and a prophet. It must also be evident that mere lip service to the yearning to keep out of war, which was as evident during the period 1914–17 as it is now, is no guaranty against partisan policies that have as a natural effect precipitating American entanglement. It may fairly be said that our foreign policy in 1914–17 was, in major matters, consistently unneutral and in some respects, as on the armed merchantmen question, legally unsustainable.

No one can blame the British Government for adroitly safeguarding its own interests and by a most astute propaganda playing on American naïveté, using the United States as an instrument of its national policy. Its intelligence and

---

[4] Cf. Bailey, " The United States and the Black List during the World War," *Journal of Modern History*, VI (1934), 14–35.

skill are to be envied. Great Britain's activities are not to be resented because the leaders and people of the United States permitted themselves to be persuaded by British statesmen to enter suicidal paths in the interests of the Higher Morality or " Civilization " or the " Life of the World." But the record of American statesmanship speaks for itself, as do the results.

IV.

THE WAR AND AFTER

IT is ordinary human frailty for nations at war to idealize their participation. While the submarine provided the juridical ground that ultimately precipitated the entrance of the United States into the European war in 1917, the road had been prepared by a long series of partisan actions. Though the country in general undoubtedly wanted to keep out of war, as was evidenced by the platforms of both parties in the presidential campaign of 1916, a large section of the community, particularly in the East, had manifested a desire for intervention, as the stalemate in Europe became insuperable and shipping losses mounted. Especially after the breaking off of diplomatic relations on February 3, 1917, the yearning for an " overt act " was manifested in large sections of the Eastern press. The propaganda had done its work.[5] The sinkings of the American steamers *Aztec, Healdton,* and *Vigilancia* were regarded less as matters for regret than as manna from heaven. Even though it is probable that at times President Wilson did not wish to enter the war and possibly hoped for some way out, the forces that had been set in motion by earlier administration activities were then too great to stop.

In spite of the fact that Secretary Lansing claims to have written a memorandum to himself in July, 1915, to the effect that the conflict presented an issue between autocracy and democracy and that it was his belief and desire that the country should be prepared for enlistment in the ranks of democracy [6] — a suggestion which might have surprised the Czar of Russia and the Mikado of Japan — it was not until

[5] Parker, " The United States and the War," *Harpers,* CXXXVI (March, 1918), 521–531.

[6] Lansing, *op. cit.,* p. 18.

after the Kerensky Revolution in Russia in March, 1917, that President Wilson saw the issue in this light. In the exaltation of this sacrifice of the United States for the promotion of virtue and the suppression of evil, the President closed his stirring War Address to Congress on April 2 as follows:

It is a fearful thing to lead this great peaceful people into war, into the most terrible and disastrous of all wars, civilization itself seeming to be in the balance. But the right is more precious than peace, and we shall fight for the things which we have always carried nearest our hearts — for democracy, for the right of those who submit to authority to have a voice in their own governments, for the rights and liberties of small nations, for a universal dominion of right by such a concert of free peoples as shall bring peace and safety to all nations and make the world itself at last free. To such a task we can dedicate our lives and our fortunes, everything that we are and everything that we have, with the pride of those who know that the day has come when America is privileged to spend her blood and her might for the principles that gave her birth and happiness and the peace which she has treasured. God helping her, she can do no other.[7]

Not every American citizen was convinced of the practicality of that method of strengthening democracy and enthroning virtue. Fifty members of the House and six members of the Senate voted against the War Resolution.[8] Senator Stone of Missouri, Chairman of the Committee on Foreign Relations, in his address opposing the resolution, said feelingly: " I shall vote against this mistake, to prevent which, God helping me, I would gladly lay down my life." [9] These words are engraved on the Senator's tombstone.

With the entrance of the United States and the speeches of President Wilson, the war took on the attributes of a crusade for righteousness. This was readily accepted by our asso-

[7] Address of President Wilson to Congress, April 2, 1917.

[8] Eight senators and nine members of the House did not vote.

[9] The Senator added, " Even now I lift my voice in solemn warning against this blunder." *Cong. Rec.*, Apr. 4, 1917, p. 154.

ciates, who prudently, however, did not abandon the secret treaties which incorporated the terms on which they expected to make peace. It does not seem important which of the various versions of President Wilson's acquaintance with those treaties is the correct one — whether he knew their contents, as did other citizens who bought the ten-cent pamphlet giving their text in full,[10] and considered them irrelevant; whether he did not know them and therefore proceeded in ignorance; or whether he was aware of their existence but brushed them aside without comprehending their significance. The unfortunate fact remains that the secret treaties became the basis of the 1919 peace treaties which the United States was instrumental in enabling the Allies to write, treaties deeply infected with the germs of future wars.

President Wilson was a conscientious man. It must have troubled him sorely in Paris to realize that peace terms had been written which hardly squared with the idealistic conceptions with which he had entered the war.[1] Unable, however, materially to modify the treaty terms, he embraced the more eagerly the concession which was given him in the form of the League of Nations. In his Fourteen Points he had indicated the necessity for such a league, which he thought of as an association of nations dedicated to mutual coöperation for the prevention of new wars and to the punishment of an " aggressor." This he regarded as a prelude to disarmament.[2]

[10] *New York Evening Post*, Jan. 25, 26 and 28, 1918, reprinted.
Manchester Guardian, Dec. 12, 1917, Jan. 18, 19, 1918, Feb. 8, 1918.
London Herald, May 11, 1918.
Nation (New York), Aug. 3, 1918.
Baker, *Woodrow Wilson and World Settlement* (New York, 1922), I, 41, 42.

[1] Yet he was willing to say: " The object of the war is attained. . . . Armed imperialism . . . is at an end. . . . The arbitrary power of the military caste of Germany . . . is discredited and destroyed." (Message to Congress, Nov. 11, 1918.) Yet soon thereafter a new struggle had to be organized against what had just been destroyed. " It [the world] knows that not only France must organize against [the German peril] but that the world must organize against it." (Speech to French Senate, Jan. 20, 1919.)

[2] " The nations of the world are about to consummate a brotherhood

President Wilson, however, was well aware of the fact that international life is not static but dynamic and that the attempt to solidify the status quo of 1919 would have to be tempered by provisions for its change when circumstances made that seem desirable or even imperative. In his own draft for the guaranty of the independence of existing states, the provision for change was included; what eventually appeared as Articles 10 [3] and 19 [4] of the Covenant were in his draft tied together.[5] The final draft separated the two, and whereas Article 10 has on several occasions given rise to collective efforts at enforcement, Article 19, by the very fact that it requires the consent of the interested states to any change, has remained a dead letter.

But Wilson had hoped that, with the nations committed to a more enlightened management of the world's affairs, the Carthaginian peace embodied in the territorial and economic provisions of the peace treaties would be redeemed. In the period after 1917 he had completely identified America's participation in the war as its contribution to the collective punishment of an evil-doing aggressor and as an enforcement of peace.[6]

---

which will make it unnecessary in the future to maintain those crushing armaments which make the people suffer almost as much in peace as they suffered in war." (Speech to French Chamber of Deputies, Feb. 3, 1919.)

Only a few weeks earlier he had prudently recommended an increase in the American Navy. (Message to Congress, Dec. 2, 1918.)

[3] For the guaranty of the territorial integrity and political independence of all members of the League.

[4] "The Assembly *may* from time to time *advise* the reconsideration by members of the League of Nations of treaties which have become inapplicable and the *consideration* of international conditions whose continuance might endanger the peace of the world." (Italics supplied.)

[5] See Art. 3 of President Wilson's first draft of the Covenant. Miller, *Drafting of the Covenant*, II, 12.

[6] " It [the treaty] seeks to punish one of the greatest wrongs ever done in history, the wrong which Germany sought to do to the world and to civilization, and there ought to be no weak purpose with regard to the application of the punishment. She attempted an intolerable thing, and she must be made to pay for the attempt." (Speech at Columbus, Ohio, Sept. 4, 1919.)

The theory of a collective enforcement of peace provided for in Article 16 of the Covenant also helped to persuade President Wilson that neutrality was " a thing of the past." The second of his Fourteen Points, providing for the freedom of the seas except as they might be closed " by international collective action for the enforcement of international covenants," [7] although announced in January, 1918, had neither been accepted nor rejected by the Allied governments. The President had assumed without any substantial justification that they had committed themselves to these terms. When, in October, 1918, Germany indicated its desire for an armistice and President Wilson obtained German acceptance of the conditions of the Fourteen Points, he then, for the first time, formally requested the Allies to adopt them. When Great Britain replied, Mr. Wilson discovered that in practical effect she refused to accept the freedom of the seas. If then, it is suggested that the maintenance of the " freedom of the seas " was the basis of American intervention, it must also be conceded that the United States lost the war, defeated by its principal ally before the Peace Conference opened. Yet this defeat was seemingly assuaged when President Wilson became impressed with the belief that the Covenant of the League of Nations insured the world against further war by reason of the fact that any recalcitrant nation would find itself opposed by the united front of all the others.

It is not necessary to insist that the Wilson doctrine that

" There is no way, which we ought to be willing to adopt, which separates us in dealing with Germany from those with whom we were associated in the war . . . because I think it is a moral union which we are not at liberty to break." (Conference, Senate Foreign Relations Committee, Aug. 19, 1919.)

" Force, force to the utmost, force without stint or limit, the righteous and triumphant force that shall make right the law of the world." (Speech, April 6, 1918.) And yet, " he [Napoleon] had to record the judgment that force had never accomplished anything that was permanent. Force will not accomplish anything that is permanent." (Speech, New York Press Club, June 30, 1916.)

[7] *For. Rel.*, 1918, Suppl. I, 15.

neutrality is " a thing of the past " became the keystone of the plan for the promotion and idealization of the enforcement of peace through sanctions, but it may be said that supporters of that program of world policy have necessarily had to attack neutrality as a philosophical, legal, and practical conception. The new scheme making any revolter against the status quo both a moral and legal pariah would bring upon the " outlaw " the united force of the rest of the world, and so was to be an assurance against disturbance. This theory was naturally acceptable to the nations that had just written the Treaty of Versailles and appropriated to themselves what they thought helpful. They would thereby receive a world-wide guaranty that their possessions could not be successfully assailed. President Wilson would undoubtedly not have agreed with this analysis, for to him the Covenant presented a method for peaceful change and not for insuring rigidity, but as peaceful change was in practice made impossible under the Covenant, the result has been a guaranty of rigidity. Thus, we witness the strange phenomenon of the " idealists " supporting a plan which inevitably had to employ starvation and force in behalf of a status quo that might prove disastrous, whereas any attempt to change that status quo, however desirable, was in principle condemned as immoral and illegal. This is a discouragement to conciliation, negotiation, and pacification. It is unfortunate that so much moral fervor was aroused on behalf of a system that not only could not produce peace but in effect, when associated with the treaties of 1919, was one of the greatest incentives to war.

But it must not be supposed that the idealism was altogether abstract. For many, the alliances of the war constituted the " collective security " which was to be perpetuated. Hence the armed alignments of the war became the symbol of the ideal of " enforcing peace." The association of the United States with this plan, which was unorganized in 1914, was now to be definitely established in advance under the new phrase, " collective security." This is frankly avowed by Mr. Allen Dulles, an American leader in the movement, in a speech made at a 1935 conference in London:

In the period between 1914 and 1917 there was no real machinery for collective action but circumstances created one. Here collective action took the profit out of war for those who took the last inevitable step to provoke it. If collective action was then possible when there was no provision for it, is there not a better chance that we can achieve it now after the progress, even though admittedly incomplete, of the past fifteen years? [8]

The League was endowed with functions which only a superstate could perform, functions beyond those of the Federal Government in the United States. Its policies, military and economic, were left in the hands of the constituent members, while the economic and military enforcement of those policies was intrusted to the hands of its few principal members, the Great Powers.[9] The conference at Geneva therefore had no power beyond that which the directing nations were willing to supply. It was given responsibility but no initiative and no power.

Yet even if it had been given military power, the result might not have been greatly different. To threaten hostility invites fear and counterhostility. A conference of sovereign states should never have been permitted to symbolize hostility, collective or individual. Such an implication is in direct contrast with the delicate nature and susceptibility of state sovereignty which, far from being weakened, as it might well be, has been infinitely strengthened by the errors of the past twenty years. Appeasement and reconciliation were not made the keynotes of the Covenant — although it speaks of " the good understanding between nations upon which peace depends."

[8] Maurice Bourquin, ed., *Collective Security*, International Studies Conference, 1934–35, League of Nations, p. 462.

[9] Cf. Lord Lothian, " New League or No League," *International Conciliation*, No. 325 (Dec., 1936), 589.

Lord Lothian in his article " New League or No League " [10] analyzes with clarity the fatal defects of the principles of Articles 10 and 16, in both theory and practice. The suggestion that sovereign states, especially populous states, could be successfully coerced, and that the measures of coercion could be called peaceful or could produce peace, was always a " pathetic fallacy." [1] The alluring words " collective security " have by their very association with Articles 10 and 16 produced a degree of collective insecurity hitherto unknown.

One should not hold the Covenant primarily responsible for all the unfortunate results now manifested by these warmaking functions of the League. Its essential defects, associated with " collective security," are the very features which have been exalted as a way to progress by phrase-intoxicated moralists. Judge Moore remarks that " the current delusion that international law ' legalizes ' war, and therefore must yield to the war-tending and warlike processes prescribed by the Covenant comprising ' sanctions,' boycotts, and war itself is merely the legitimate offspring of the new and consoling theory that peoples may with force and arms peacefully exterminate one another, provided they do not call it war." [2]

The disparagement of neutrality, which accompanies the devotion to League theories of collective sanctions, has weakened the only rules the world has ever known for limiting the area of war. For neutrality there are substituted aspirations for " preventing war " and " punishing aggressors " which have converted the world into colossal armed camps where millions of people live with their fears and gas masks and

---

[10] *Supra,* p. 51.

[1] Bernard Shaw remarked, on the occasion of the proposed " sanctions " against Italy in Oct., 1935:

> " Old as I am, I am not yet so pitiably imbecile as to believe that the modern habit of calling torpedoes, mines, blockades, sieges, battles, and bombs ' sanctions' alters their nature so completely that a vote for sanctions is a vote for peace."

Letter to the *London Times,* Oct. 22, 1935, p. 2; also *Time,* Nov. 11, 1935, p. 16.

[2] " An Appeal to Reason," *Foreign Affairs,* July, 1933, p. 560.

spend their substance for armaments to be used in new wars to end war.

And so we have the demand that the United States abandon its neutrality and trust its fate to pacts contemplating peremptory action to " enforce peace." This, not isolation, is the policy that has inflated American armaments and produced a military budget of a billion a year. Intervention is the enemy of neutrality, and its good motive ought not to conceal the fact that it means war. Yet intervention has been urged on the country steadily since 1919, as we shall see, through the League, Kellogg Pacts, consultative pacts, discretionary embargoes. Neutrality, which like many devices of experience and common sense is not nourished by resounding phrases, has had a difficult time surviving the beguilements of this seductive propaganda.

PART II

THE PERIOD OF "NEUTRALITY,"
1914–1917

NO attempt will be made here to deal with the general diplomatic history leading up to American entrance into the war. The discussion will be confined to those outstanding manifestations of unneutrality which helped to steer the United States into the conflict.

The opening negotiations with Great Britain to obtain recognition for the Declaration of London as the criterion of the rights of belligerents and neutrals under international law are important in the main because they disclose a passionate effort on Mr. Page's part both to nullify the attempt of the Department of State to secure recognition for the rights of American citizens under international law, and to back Great Britain in its diplomatic maneuvers to avoid recognition of those rights. The lawyers in the Department of State, believing themselves to be charged with the defense of American rights, did not appreciate the force of Mr. Page's discovery that Great Britain was engaged in a crusade for civilization, in which neutrals should yield their rights to the nobler objective of enabling St. George to dispose of the dragon of militarism for the good of mankind. They were interested in the United States and in obtaining respect for those rules of law which over the years had been developed as the basis for stable relations between neutrals and belligerents.

As early as August, 1914, the question of armed merchantmen was badly confused by the willingness of Secretary Lansing to tolerate guns on British, but not on German ships leaving American harbors; the former were alleged to be defensive, the latter offensive. This discrimination was neither defensible nor neutral. It was only on January 18, 1916, when the impossibility of making the supposed distinction between offensive and defensive armament was realized, that Mr. Lansing proposed to Great Britain that merchant ships disarm. It had then become clear that merchantmen could either arm and expose themselves, their passengers and crew, to all the risks of submarine attack or else would have to disarm as a condition of immunity from attack. Lansing declared it to be " reasonable and reciprocally just " that, while submarines should be required to keep strictly to the rules of international law relating to visit and search, " merchant vessels of belligerent nationality should be prohibited and prevented from carrying any armament whatever." [3]

But so sure were the British of their control of American policy and so great now the partisan pressure on President Wilson, that under impetus of the protestations of Spring-Rice, House, Lodge, and others, the Lansing proposal of January 18, 1916, was withdrawn, and the unsustainable position was reëstablished on March 25, 1916, maintaining the Allies' right to arm belligerent merchantmen and yet denying submarines' right to attack them without warning. Apart from the unheard-of undertaking of a neutral to defend the ships of a belligerent against attack by his enemy, the suggestion that the United States could seek for a British carrier of American passengers or crew an immunity which Great Britain could not claim indicates a confusion of ideas and legal conceptions which makes it surprising that the United States escaped war until April, 1917. If the Congress or public sentiment in general had been as ready for war as were some of the administration leaders, we should probably have become embroiled in 1915.

Had the administration been neutral, it is hardly possible that it would have permitted itself to be pushed out on that limb from which it was later unwilling to retreat. When, then,

[3] *For. Rel.,* 1916, Suppl., pp. 146, 147–148.

President Wilson asserted in his War Message that we would not submit to the German submarine, he overlooked the fact that he had already submitted so completely to the British impositions and to British armaments on merchantmen that, as the administration had remarked in its note of January 18, 1916, the German submarine attacks were invited. To be sure, in 1916, the submarine attack had been directed against belligerent vessels, armed and unarmed. After January 31, 1917, the attacks were directed against all vessels in a war zone around the British Isles. But it was obvious that unless the United States adhered to its position of January 18, 1916, either denying the right of merchantmen to arm, or conceding the right of submarines to attack them, a crisis would shortly develop; the illegal " blockade " of Germany would be followed by an illegal " blockade " of Great Britain.

The distinction between loss of lives and loss of property — there were only three lives lost by torpedo on American vessels before the severance of diplomatic relations with Germany on February 3, 1917 — does not serve to explain the partisanship of the administration. Nor did the bankers, munition makers or traders do anything more than take advantage of the position the administration created and tolerated. And if propaganda helped to undermine the balance and objectivity of our people, it received a powerful stimulus from the partisan attitudes assumed by the government. Propaganda operated in all neutral countries, but those with neutral governments managed to stay out of the war.

President Wilson's position in the matter of intervention was neither clear nor consistent. He had conflicting emotions, the desire to play the part of mediator, the spasmodic desire to keep out of the war, and the desire to see the Allies win. It would have been difficult to maintain a balance between these various motives even under the best of circumstances. Baffled and entrapped by erroneous and unneutral stands on the problems that needed settlement, his position became so confused in 1916 that anything might have happened. He no longer had any definite policy and had made himself the victim of an incident. The situation had gotten beyond his control, and he was unprotected from his own ultimata, which never should have been issued had peace been his policy. But when finally the dilemmas and confusion led him into the war, no suggestion appeared that the mishandling of the American case might have had something to do with our misfortunes. On the contrary, the American position was pictured as un-challengeable — a malevolent aggressor had dragged the American people into war. The debacle was then rationalized not as a defense of the freedom of the seas, even against sub-marine attack, but as a great crusade to end war, a cham-pionship of democracy against autocracy, a kind of religious war which laid the foundation for that current conflict of ideologies which threatens new wars.

It is thus that credulity and misinformation can set in motion hysterical forces incalculable in their capacity for destruction.

I.

EARLY SURRENDERS — THE DECLARATION OF LONDON

AT the outbreak of the war it was at once perceived in Washington that the maritime rights of neutrals would require detailed restatement as a *modus vivendi*. And so an effort was made to obtain the consent of both belligerent groups to a code. But instead of standing on the rules of international law, which were adequate to the purpose, the administration sought to obtain recognition by both sides of the code of rules adopted by the London Conference in 1909. Although these rules, known as the Declaration of London, had not been officially ratified by any Great Powers, they had been incorporated by Germany and by France in their prize codes. Ratification had been advised by the United States Senate, but had not been completed by 1914. The Declaration had also passed the House of Commons in 1910, only to be defeated in the House of Lords on the ground that it was too favorable to neutrals. This might have indicated the trend of British opinion concerning coming events.

The Department of State doubtless suggested the maintenance of the Declaration of London as the rule of law which should govern the relations between the belligerents and the United States because, according to the preamble, " the rules . . . correspond in substance with the generally recognized principles of international law." This was largely true. The rules of international law codified at the Hague Conference had not covered all questions and had left in abeyance certain differences between continental and Anglo-American conceptions as to contraband of war, continuous voyage, transfer of flag from belligerent to neutral vessel during a war, and other topics. The London Conference was designed to reconcile the differences and promote harmony, in preparation for a projected international prize court.

Germany in August, 1914, like Austria, had consented, on request of the Department of State, to adopt the Declaration of London as the rule of law. Great Britain refused to accept the Declaration, however, except with " certain modifications and additions " which effectively impaired neutral rights. It was unwise for the Department to insist on Britain's acceptance of the Declaration of London after the first refusal.[3a] The Department should have fallen back at once on the rules of international law as governing the legal relations between the United States and the belligerents, because there was but little misunderstanding between the United States and Great Britain on these rules and it would have avoided the futile effort to obtain British approval for a document they had not ratified.

The debate, however, from which the United States retreated in defeat on October 22, 1914, served the important purpose of enabling Great Britain to establish that the United States would not insist on a limitation of the exorbitant contraband lists, would not deny clearance to vessels carrying munitions of war, would not establish a competing, government-owned merchant marine, would admit British ships to American ports although armed, and would continue to remain an open market for a unilateral munitions supply, notwithstanding the abuse of American rights through cutting off neutral trade to Holland and the Scandinavian countries. These decisive victories for Allied diplomacy, some of which were vital in the process of sliding America into war, were not merely evidence of superior diplomatic skill. Their more important result was to indicate to Great Britain at once that it had strong friends in the administration who sympathized with the British point of view and would not

[3a] France and Russia made their acceptance of the Declaration contingent on acceptance by Great Britain. Note Aug. 22, 1914, *For. Rel.*, 1914, Suppl., p. 219.

insist on American rights, if such insistence conflicted with British policy.

Among the rules of the Declaration which merely reconfirmed established law was the requirement that " a blockade must not extend beyond the port and coasts belonging to or occupied by the enemy " (Art. 1), and that " whatever may be the ulterior destination of a vessel or of her cargo she cannot be captured for breach of blockade if at the moment she is on her way to an unblockaded port " (Art. 19). It was specifically provided that the " blockading forces must not bar access to neutral ports or coasts " (Art. 18). These rules naturally prevented any blockade of the Dutch or Scandinavian ports or any effort to control traffic for those ports except in munitions of war or goods absolutely contraband, demonstrably destined for Germany or Austria. To this traffic alone could the doctrine of continuous voyage legally apply.

The first British contraband list of August 5 had " corresponded closely with the provisions of the Declaration of London on contraband of war." [4] The only exception related to aircraft, transferred from the list of goods conditionally to the list of goods absolutely contraband. But on August 20, 1914, the British Government issued an Order in Council which materially modified the Declaration of London to the disadvantage of neutrals.[5] Article 33, which prohibited the capture of goods conditionally contraband except on proof of *direct* enemy military destination, was modified so as to permit capture if the goods were destined to a neutral country, under presumptions of ultimate enemy destination which gave Great Britain a practically complete control over all neutral trade. This constituted a flat violation of international law and a flouting of the rule reaffirmed by Lord Salisbury in 1900.[6]

These presumptions devitalized the Declaration of London, for they authorized the capture of any goods bound to neu-

---

[4] *Idem*, p. 215.   [5] *Idem*, p. 219.   [6] *Supra*, p. 14.

tral ports if the shipper or consignee was unable, as an Order in Council of October 29 provided,[7] to prove that the goods would not reach Germany, a burden practically impossible to sustain. The British would thus be able to prevent Holland and the Scandinavian countries, to speak of them only, from dealing with the United States in any goods the British Government saw fit to characterize as contraband, a list which was extended by successive Orders in Council so as to include an unprecedented range of commodities.[8] In April, 1916, Great Britain, without serious protest from the United States, abolished the distinction between goods conditionally and goods absolutely contraband, a distinction which the British prize courts had already in effect wiped out.[9]

It was between August and October, 1914, that the British Government discovered just how far it could press the United States and to what extent American official aid in this process could be expected. On September 26, the Solicitor's Office of the Department of State, headed by Cone Johnson of Texas, prepared a reasoned presentation,[10] probably revised by President Wilson, of the legal rights of neutrals, especially of the United States, and of the violations of those rights embodied in the modifications of the Declaration of London which the British Government had announced on August 20.

---

[7] *For. Rel.,* 1914, Suppl., p. 262.

[8] First list of contraband, Aug. 5, 1914, *For. Rel.,* 1914, Suppl., pp. 215–216. It was amended Sept. 30, 1914, to list copper, lead, iron ore, rubber, and raw hides as conditional contraband, *idem,* p. 236. The list was revised Oct. 29, 1914, and certain raw materials were listed as absolute contraband, *idem,* pp. 261–262. The definition of absolute contraband was expanded by lists of Dec. 23, 1914, *idem,* pp. 269–270; March 13, 1915, *For. Rel.,* 1915, Suppl., p. 138; May 29, 1915, *idem,* p. 165, and Oct. 15, 1915, *idem,* pp. 175–177. "Lubricants" were defined by the list of March 10, 1915, *idem,* p. 137 as amended April 10, 1915, *idem,* p. 160. "Foodstuffs" were defined March 13, 1915, *op. cit.*

[9] Announcement of April 13, 1916, with list. *For. Rel.,* 1916, Suppl., pp. 385–387. The matter was closed by the Order in Council of July 7, 1916, which revoked orders based on the Declaration of London, *idem,* pp. 413–415.

[10] *For. Rel.,* 1914, Suppl., pp. 225–232.

The protest was sent to Ambassador Page by mail, but it never reached the British Government.

Colonel House arrived in Washington September 27. The President showed him the document. Although it seems a little doubtful whether Colonel House fully understood the legal contentions and the reasoning, he immediately objected to the note as " exceedingly undiplomatic." The President apparently yielded at once, and instructed Mr. Lansing to draft a briefer cablegram.[1] Even this Colonel House considered " objectionable." [2] On the following day, House at his own suggestion conferred with Spring-Rice with a view to toning down the protest. House says that Spring-Rice was

thoroughly alarmed over some of the diplomatic expressions. One paragraph in particular he thought amounted almost to a declaration of war. He said if that paper should get into the hands of the press, the headlines would indicate that war with Great Britain was inevitable, and he believed one of the greatest panics the country ever saw would ensue.[3]

Possibly Spring-Rice was shocked at the idea that the United States had the temerity to stand up for its rights under international law, but it is regrettable that Colonel House was so readily impressed by Spring-Rice's show of emotion. However, he was in a sympathetic mood. So, to avoid offending British " amour-propre," as Colonel House terms it, the two gentlemen outlined " the despatch which we thought [Spring-Rice] should send Sir Edward Grey." That despatch doubtless contained the outline of the substituted instruction that on September 28 was to be cabled to Page, withdrawing the note of September 26. Spring-Rice reports to Grey that he and House " had a talk and drew up a scheme, which seemed to offer some good hope of a solution." [4] Thus

[1] Baker, op. cit., V, 205.
[2] Hendrick, Life and Letters of Walter Hines Page, I, 378, House to Page, Oct. 3, 1914.
[3] Seymour, The Intimate Papers of Colonel House, I, 307.
[4] Gwynn, op. cit., II, 234.

did an American diplomat confer with the British Ambassador and help to debilitate the valid legal positions of his own government, so as to conform to the views of the offending government.

The telegram that was actually sent on September 28 bore little resemblance to the original protest.[5] Indeed, it stated " that the President desires to avoid a formal protest." While it mentioned the fact that " this Government is greatly disturbed " by the proposed violations of international law — called " the intention to change the provisions of the Declaration of London," already changed since August 20 — while it spoke of America's " grave concern " and " the President's conviction of the extreme gravity of the situation," it did not speak of the legal rights of the United States and of all neutrals. Instead, it referred to the effect that the British violations would have on American public opinion, the " spirit of resentment . . . which this Government would extremely regret," and to the fact that the changes " would furnish to those inimical to Great Britain an opportunity . . . they would not be slow to seize, and which they are already using in the press." The President, said Lansing, " hopes that the British Government will be willing to consider the advisability of modifying these features of the Order in Council," and expresses " his earnest wish to avoid every cause of irritation and controversy." Furthermore, Mr. Page was to assure Sir Edward Grey " of the earnest spirit of friendship in which [the note] is sent." [6]

This seems like a record low for American diplomacy, far removed from the high levels that Franklin and his colleagues had established. The " champion " of neutrals had become a strange figure of feebleness and subserviency. This impression is strengthened by the bold words with which the telegram closed: " The President is anxious that he [Grey]

[5] *For. Rel.*, 1914, Suppl., p. 232.
[6] *Idem,* pp. 232–233.

should realize that the terms of the Declaration of London represent the limit to which this Government could go with the approbation and support of its people," for the earlier passages in the telegram had vitiated any demonstration of firmness. As we know, on October 22, the United States withdrew its suggestion for the adoption of the Declaration of London, so that even this show of determination collapsed. It is hard to escape the feeling, knowing how little Colonel House and Mr. Page respected the legal position of the United States, that the ostensible resistance was intended less to impress Great Britain than the people of the United States.

No wonder Spring-Rice could advise the President, September 30,[7] that Sir Edward Grey " appreciates the way in which you have raised the question of the Order in Council." He added that Sir Edward Grey had " had a long talk with Mr. Page with whom, as you know, he has very pleasant and cordial relations and whom, if I may say so, he trusts entirely." Well he might. In the interview with Page, Grey yielded not an inch, but explained — to Page's altogether unjustified satisfaction — that "the main point " turned on the doctrine of continuous voyage, which " had been upheld in the United States Courts, and it must remain a part of the accepted doctrine of international law." [8] He blandly added that " the doctrine enunciated in the Order in Council of August 20 had been applied in previous wars," which was as ambiguous as it was false in its implication that similar practices had previously been followed. He stated, without foundation, that " the objects aimed at had been to restrict the supplies for the German Army, and also to restrict the supply to Germany of such materials as could be used in manufacturing war munitions." [9] The real policy, however, was to prevent the entire population, civilian as well as military, from receiving food, raw materials and manufactured goods from any outside

[7] Gwynn, *op. cit.*, II, 234.
[8] Gwynn, *idem*, II, 235. *Infra*, p. 69.
[9] *Ibid.*

source.[10] And that, in the absence of a genuine legal blockade, Britain was unable to accomplish without a fundamental violation of the rights of neutrals.

Even at that early date, Britain felt free to misinform the United States; it had no special reason to respect a government that did not respect itself. In view of Mr. Page's continuous protests to Washington against the vain effort of the law officers of the Department to maintain American rights, Ray Stannard Baker is mild when he suggests that Mr. Page seems often to have blunted the edges of the American case. He had no interest in the American case, and President Wilson rebuked him for his bias.[1] Page probably went further in London than House did in Washington to weaken the American protests. In fact, Page acted as Grey's adviser in contesting the positions of the United States, diluted as they were.[2]

Page thus supported the British " blockade " of Germany before it was fully enforced by Britain, and without any authority from the Department of State. According to Grey,

---

[10] Baker, V, 207, 216.

[1] For. Rel., 1914, Suppl., p. 252.

[2] Viscount Grey remarks in his Memoirs (*Twenty-five Years*, II, 110) that " Page's advice and suggestions were of the greatest value in warning us when to be careful or encouraging us when we could safely be firm. . . ."

Apropos of a Washington instruction to protest against British interference with neutral trade, Grey says:

" 'I am instructed,' Page said, 'to read this despatch to you.' He read, and I listened. He then said: 'I have now read the despatch, but I do not agree with it; let us consider how it should be answered!' " Even the *New York Times,* which was hardly critical of Page's general objective of American support for Great Britain, remarked, on the occasion of the publication of Grey's Memoirs in serial form: " For a parallel to this action [of Page] the records of diplomacy would probably be searched in vain . . . to act as Ambassador Page did was to follow a course . . . which could not be made common in diplomatic practice without demoralizing and disastrous consequences." *New York Times,* Aug. 9, 1935. Grattan, *Why We Fought,* p. 222. Even if uncommon, Page's course had these precise consequences. When Page connived with Grey to have the French seize the American steamer *Dacia,* transferred *bona fide* from a German to an American citizen, and free from condemnation under the rules of international law, he made another unique contribution to American diplomacy. *For. Rel.,* 1915, Suppl., pp. 685–686; Hendrick, *op. cit.,* I, 394; III, 226.

Page informed him that the United States had " no desire to press the case of people who traded deliberately and directly with Germany " — although no such abandonment had been suggested by this government — " but there was great feeling against stopping legitimate American trade with Holland which had always been large, and it was difficult to disentangle the two questions." [3] Page's generosity in handing away the right of American citizens to trade with Germany went unrebuked.

Spring-Rice could say with reasonable justification as early as August 25, 1914, that " all the State Department are on our side except Bryan who is incapable of forming a settled judgment on anything outside party politics. The President will be with us by birth and upbringing." [4] Bryan's objectivity in these matters and his genuine neutrality doubtless irked the good Ambassador, but as we have already observed [5] and will again have occasion to notice, Bryan's judgment on the effect of administration policies was accurate and prophetic. His is the judgment that has been vindicated.

Mr. Lansing was hardly less helpful than Page in whittling down American rights. On the evening of September 28 he was requested by the President to confer with Spring-Rice for the purpose of harmonizing the views of the two governments. The result of the conference is reported in a memorandum of September 29, 1914, filed in the Department by Mr. Lansing.[6] Lansing reports the Ambassador as agreeing with him that the Order in Council " practically made foodstuffs absolute contraband, which was contrary both to British and American traditional policy." He might have added that it was also contrary to international law. Spring-Rice then made an inspired suggestion to the effect that the

[3] Grey to Spring-Rice, Sept. 28, 1914, handed to Acting Secretary of State, Oct. 1, 1914. *For. Rel.*, 1914, Suppl., pp. 236–237; Baker, *op. cit.*, V, 209.

[4] Letter to Sir Edward Grey, Gwynn, *op. cit.*, II, 220.

[5] *Supra*, p. 40.

[6] *For. Rel.*, 1914, Suppl., pp. 233–235.

large quantities of food supplies that had been shipped to Rotterdam were going to the German Army in Belgium, although actually foodstuffs bound for all neutral ports, even Scandinavian, were seized. Lansing yielded the American case further by replying that he " appreciated that such reasons must weigh very heavily with those responsible for the successful conduct of the war," a concession which should have called for reciprocity in appreciation. Then Lansing himself suggested that the British might accomplish " the desired purpose " by getting the Netherlands " to place an embargo on foodstuffs and other conditional contraband or by agreeing not to reëxport such articles." This suggestion must have been welcomed by the Ambassador, for it indicated that other neutrals also might be cajoled into becoming instruments of British policy.

Since the doctrine of continuous voyage could not legitimately be applied to goods conditionally contraband, Spring-Rice suggested the possibility of removing the difficulty by making copper and petroleum and other products having both peaceful and warlike uses, absolute contraband. Lansing thought this " worthy of consideration " and thus supplied another link for the chain by which neutral rights were strangled. Lansing was ostensibly seeking to get rid of the impositions of the August 20 Order in Council, but actually he was proposing or concurring in restrictions which went far beyond that order in violating international law. Possibly Lansing's advice was not especially needed by the British. But the fact remains that the two methods of shutting off neutral trade with the civilian population of Germany were (a) to add items gradually to the list of goods absolutely contraband,[7] and finally, in 1916, to abolish altogether the category of goods conditionally contraband,[8] and (b) to

<hr>

[7] See the contraband lists of Oct. 9, 1914 (*For. Rel.*, 1914, Suppl., p. 244) and Oct. 29, 1914 (*idem*, p. 260).

[8] *Supra*, p. 62.

make the receipt of goods by the neutrals conditional upon their agreeing to embargo exports to Germany.[9]

Spring-Rice immediately cabled Sir Edward the results of the conference with Lansing. On September 30, Page, to whom Grey showed the telegram, cabled his understanding that the suggestion for the new conditions emanated from Mr. Lansing,[1] and that Sir Edward " agrees to two points: (1) To make a new list of absolute contraband, and (2) to prepare a new Order in Council." The latter, Page failed to observe, was to be harsher in its restrictions than previous orders; he felt it would " endeavor to meet our wishes so far as that is possible." [2] Evidently very little was " possible "; but Page was modest in his requirements.

The Civil War Precedents. The British Government also undertook to defend the control of American trade with Holland and the Scandinavian countries on the ground that precedents of the American Civil War had established the doctrine of " ultimate destination " and " continuous voyage." His Majesty's Government pointed out that at that time British ships had been seized en route to neutral ports " as if carrying goods directly to an enemy port." [3] The British Ambassador failed to observe, however, that the " enemy port " was under a lawful blockade, and that the goods seized were intended for the Confederate Army, and hence were absolutely contraband. He was not fortunate in citing Matamoras, Mexico,[4] as such a neutral port of transshipment, for in the *Peterhoff* [5] case the United States Supreme Court refused to consider

---

[9] Consett, *Triumph of the Unarmed Forces*, pp. 72–73; Turlington, *Neutrality*, III, 69 *et seq.*

[1] This must have been the impression that Spring-Rice conveyed to Grey. The State Department considers it a misunderstanding. *For. Rel.*, 1914, Suppl., p. 235, note.

[2] *Idem*, p. 235.

[3] The British Ambassador to the Counselor, Mr. Lansing, Oct. 25, 1914, *idem*, p. 328; Dec. 2, 1914, *idem*, p. 352. On Oct. 29, 1914, shipments to neutral countries had to be consigned to a named consignee, not " to order."

[4] *Idem*, p. 352.

[5] 5 Wallace 28 (1863).

that Matamoras, on the Rio Grande, could be legally blockaded; it condemned only the goods which were absolutely
contraband, i.e., artillery harness, " men's army bluchers,"
" artillery boots," and " government gray blankets." The
Chief Justice stated, " They make part of the necessary equipment of an army." He added: " It is true that even these
goods, if really intended for sale in the market of Matamoras,
would be free of liability; for contraband may be transported
by neutrals to a neutral port, if intended to make part of its
general stock in trade."

In another case arising during the Civil War, the northern
prize courts had condemned a cargo destined for Nassau because there was proof both from the ship's papers and through
the known practice of the owner, a notorious blockade run-
ner, that the particular cargo was intended for the Confederate forces.[6] The ground of condemnation was that the
goods were intended to be transshipped, after stopping at
Nassau, to the blockaded ports of Savannah or Charleston.
In addition, however, the goods captured were goods either
absolutely contraband or belonging to the owner of the contraband. The combination of facts, therefore, that Charleston
was under blockade, that Nassau was merely a springboard
for Charleston, with no local trade or stock in trade, that the
original voyage was made for the purpose of eluding the
blockade, and that the only goods captured were contraband
goods, differentiates the case fundamentally from the British
seizures during the late war of goods of every character, not
destined for a blockaded port but for the unblockaded ports
of Holland and Scandinavia, countries having a large population and a definite stock in trade. When, then, Mr. Lansing in
his letter to the President of December 9, 1914,[7] a document
apparently sent to Senator Stone on January 20, 1915, undertook to suggest that the United States had, with British acqui-

[6] The *Springbok*, 5 Wallace 1 (1866).
[7] Baker, *op. cit.*, V, 225.

escence, established the precedent for the British violations, he was distorting history and law and undermining the rights of the United States. He failed to call attention to the limitations placed on the doctrine of continuous voyage by the Supreme Court in the Civil War. He failed to note that international law had admitted the doctrine only as to goods absolutely contraband.[8]

When Mr. Lansing added,

It is thus seen that some of the doctrines which appear to bear harshly upon neutrals at the present time are analogous to or outgrowths from policies adopted by the United States when it was a belligerent. The Government therefore can not consistently protest against the application of rules which it has followed in the past, unless they have not been practiced as heretofore,[9]

he either was oblivious of the facts or else was misleadingly ambiguous. His last qualifying phrase might have justified the protest he desired to avoid, even if the rest of the quotation were sound. But his frame of mind was such as to minimize points operating in America's favor. Great Britain was seeking to win a war and, as belligerents often do, made exorbitant claims of belligerent privilege in the hope of outmaneuvering the neutrals. With her command of the sea, with her large commercial tonnage, with her coaling stations, she was able to force many neutrals into surrender of their rights. But she used more subtle methods with the United States. Had the United States been seriously interested in maintaining neutral rights, the means of coercion lay mainly in American hands and hardly in the British. As Sir Edward Grey says:

To return to the question of contraband, blockade of Germany was essential to the victory of the Allies, but the ill will of the United States meant their certain defeat . . . The Allies soon became dependent for an adequate supply on the United States.

[8] Cf. F. K. Nielsen in *A. B. A. J.*, Jan., 1937, p. 23.
[9] *For. Rel.*, 1914, Suppl., p. ix.

If we quarrelled with the United States we could not get that supply. It was better therefore to carry on the war without blockade, if need be, than to incur a break with the United States about contraband and thereby deprive the Allies of the resources necessary to carry on the war at all or with any chance of success. The object of diplomacy, therefore, was to secure the maximum of blockade that could be enforced without rupture with the United States.[10]

Sir Edward Grey remarks that " Germany and the neutrals were . . . at the same point of view in this matter." Both the neutrals and Germany had an interest in not permitting their trade to be extinguished. Great Britain was, therefore, fortunate in persuading the United States to act against its own interests in foregoing the freedom of the seas and of trade and in supporting the illegal measures by which Great Britain was able to quash the trade with Germany, except to the extent that she was willing through neutral countries to continue that trade herself.[1] The British policy required a regimentation of the trade of all the neutral countries of northern Europe. These she rationed. And by the black list she prohibited hundreds of traders in foreign countries from engaging in foreign trade. The control effected was more efficient than that of the Napoleonic and French Revolutionary era, and equally contemptuous of neutral rights. Nor was it commercially disinterested, as in Napoleon's day. This would hardly have been possible, however, without the active tolerance, if not support, of the United States Government.

It is needless to detail all the unneutral efforts of Mr. Page in London to hamstring such feeble efforts as the Department of State made to assure some measure of respect for

[10] Grey, *Twenty-five Years*, II, 107. See also Hendrick, *op. cit.*, I, 364 *et seq.*

[1] Consett, *The Triumph of the Unarmed Forces*, ch. xiii. It should be noted that England exerted pressure on the United States by threatening to withhold wool, manganese, rubber and hides, unless certain British conditions were granted. *For. Rel.*, 1914, Suppl., p. 418 *et seq.*

American rights. Great Britain naturally enough took advantage of his coöperation to press still further her belligerent excesses. The fact that Page annoyed President Wilson with his insistence on the waiver of American rights has been adequately commented upon.[2] It is amusing, however, to find Mr. Page harshly criticizing Mr. Lansing for his supposedly legalistic attempts to secure adherence to the Declaration of London as the basis of neutral rights. While Mr. Lansing was not so flagrantly unneutral in 1914 as Mr. Page, he can hardly be said to have helped the lawyers of the State Department to maintain the legal views they endeavored to present. The language of the Department's undelivered note of September 26, 1914, which Colonel House and Spring-Rice had softened into innocuousness, asserts well-established rules of law, but conveys no serious intention to stand upon them. It would be interesting to discover wherein Spring-Rice, apparently with House's concurrence, found it to be practically " a declaration of war " against Britain. But the note does indicate an appreciation of the fact that American submission to British violations might enable the opponents of Great Britain to charge the United States with a lack of neutrality and " evidence of unfriendliness." It observed that the United States could " not permit itself to be placed in a position where its neutrality and impartiality are doubtful or open to question." [3] It seems unfortunate that the Department so soon permitted itself to be placed in that very position.

Sir Edward Grey hardly discussed the Declaration of London at any length. He seemed to feel that its rules would have been broken anyway.[4] He was more concerned with the question of contraband and was encouraged by Page in the unprecedented extensions of the contraband list. Page was greatly irritated at what he seemed to consider the stubborn insistence of the State Department on the Declaration of

[2] Seymour, *op. cit.*, I, 306.   [4] Grey, *op. cit.*, II, 105–106.
[3] *For. Rel.*, 1914, Suppl., pp. 225, 231.

London. On October 6 he wrote the President a long letter urging immediate intervention of the United States on the Allied side.[5]

On October 22, Page threatened to resign if Lansing again brought up the Declaration of London.[6] On that same day, Lansing had announced the United States' withdrawal from that demand and its decision to stand on the rules of international law, rules which by that time had been just as seriously violated as had been the codified terms of the unratified Declaration of London. Lansing admits in his *Memoirs* that the Declaration of London might have operated to tie the hands of the British Government and prevented it " from accomplishing certain things which seemed desirable from the British point of view." [7] Rules of law for the protection of neutrals often do hinder a belligerent's excesses. Restraint is a function of law. That is what the Germans were told by President Wilson in the matter of submarine sinkings of armed merchantmen. It is unfortunate, however, that Mr. Wilson, when he was talking about submarines sinking belligerent merchantmen, was not more accurate in his presentation of the law.

Mr. Lansing adds that under the rules of the Declaration of London " submarine warfare against commercial vessels would have been practically impossible." This may be true because submarine warfare had not then been contemplated. It was justified by Germany as a reprisal against the British attempt to close the North Sea by mines and to starve the German population by illegal measures. Yet Mr. Lansing is again ambiguous when he states " there was no definite code, no fixed standard which could be applied to the relations between neutral and belligerent." If this were true, he was inviting trouble by suggesting that the United States would stand on the rules of international law. But it was not true.

[5] Hendrick, *op. cit.*, III, 172–174. [7] Lansing, *Memoirs*, p. 119.
[6] *Idem*, I, 383, letter to House.

Those rules had in fact served neutrals and belligerents in many a war, and were as certain as most rules of law.[8] Neutrals, however, must be prepared to be neutral and to maintain neutral rights. Mr. Lansing was not prepared for either. His suggestion that " everything seemed to be vague and uncertain by reason of the new conditions " may have been the popular impression; there were plenty of partisans who justified the departures from law as they now justify departure from neutrality on the excuse that the law is " vague and uncertain by reason of the new conditions." But on October 21, 1915, the Department of State had no difficulty in asserting what both then and now were sound rules of law, rules which could and should have been insisted upon had there been any intention on Britain's part to observe the law or any willingness on the part of the United States to use its immense power to see to it that the law was observed. And ironically, Mr. Lansing himself concedes at one point that in spite of what he alleges to be " new conditions," " the long recognized principles were in fact unaffected."

Lansing was apparently more anxious to avoid the irritation of American public opinion against Great Britain than to maintain American legal rights.[8a] On October 16, 1914, he had prepared a memorandum as to how the British ends might be achieved without giving offense. This is another unique contribution to the diplomacy of neutrality. It reads:

. . . In the admirable frankness with which Sir Edward Grey has stated the reasons for the action which Great Britain has deemed it necessary to take in regard to the declaration, this Government feels that it fully understands and appreciates the British position, and is not disposed to place obstacles in the way of the accomplishment of the purposes which the British representatives have so frankly stated.

The confidence thus reported in this Government makes it ap-

[8] Cf. F. K. Nielsen on the certainty of the rules, in *Proceedings of Amer. Soc. Int. L.*, 1935, p. 12.
[8a] Baker, *op. cit.*, V, 211.

preciate more than ever the staunch friendship of Great Britain for the United States, which it hopes always to deserve.

This Government would not feel warranted in offering any suggestion to the British Government as to a course which would meet the wishes of this Government and at the same time accomplish the ends which Great Britain seeks, but you might in the strictest confidence intimate to Sir Edward Grey the following plan, at the same time stating very explicitly that it is your personal suggestion and not one for which your Government is responsible.

Let the British Government issue an order in council accepting the Declaration of London without change or addition, and repealing all previous conflicting orders in council.

Let this order in council be followed by a proclamation adding articles to the lists of absolute and conditional contraband by virtue of the authority conferred by Articles 23 and 25 of the declaration.

Let the proclamation be followed by another order in council, of which the United States need not be previously advised, declaring that, when one of His Majesty's Principal Secretaries of State is convinced that a port or the territory of a neutral country is being used as a base for the transit of supplies for an enemy government a proclamation shall issue declaring that such port or territory has acquired enemy character in so far as trade in contraband is concerned and that vessels trading therewith shall be thereafter subject to the rules of the declaration governing trade to enemy's territory.

It is true that the latter order in council would be based on a new principle. The excuse would be that the Declaration of London failing to provide for such an exceptional condition as exists, a belligerent has a right to give a reasonable interpretation to the rules of the declaration so that they will not leave him helpless to prevent an enemy from obtaining supplies for his military forces although the belligerent may possess the power and would have the right to do so if the port or territory was occupied by the enemy.

When the last-mentioned order in council is issued, I am convinced that a full explanation of its nature and necessity would meet with liberal consideration by this Government and not be the subject of serious objection.

I repeat that any suggestion, which you may make to Sir

Edward Grey, must be done in an entirely personal way and with the distinct understanding that this Government is in no way responsible for what you may say.[9]

This document speaks for itself. Perhaps it is a prototype of the " new neutrality " which would substitute partiality for impartiality, intervention for abstention. Nor, it may be noted, has it been customary for the United States to disavow its own proposals.

President Wilson, in mildly reproving Page for his failure to appreciate the American point of view — due, he felt, to Page's lack of contact with American opinion — wrote: " Lansing has pointed out to you . . . how completely all the British Government seeks can be accomplished without the least friction with this Government and without touching opinion on this side of the water on an exceedingly tender spot." [10]

Although it was clearly realized by both Lansing and the President that what Great Britain sought could not be accomplished without violating American rights and international law, neither gentleman was prepared to exert himself excessively to maintain American rights.

The more the Americans yielded, especially while expressing sympathy for the objectives the British sought to accomplish, the less conciliatory became the British Government. On October 16, the United States threw away an important card by indicating that there would be no interference with the munitions trade between this country and the Allies. On October 22, Lansing withdrew his demand for British acceptance of the Declaration of London and fell back on the rules of international law, a policy that should have been pursued in the first place, or certainly after Britain's first rejection of the Declaration. The interchange demonstrated that the American officials were not competent negotiators, even when they had the law on their side, and that their

[9] *For. Rel.*, 1914, Suppl., pp. 249–250.   [10] *Idem*, pp. 252–253.

sympathy for the British cause, not to mention Page's open partisanship, weakened their willingness to uphold American rights in the face of British opposition.

The Order in Council of October 29, 1914, sealed the British victory by authorizing further departures from the rules of international law, changing the rules of evidence so as to make most cargoes to the Northern neutrals confiscable in the absence of shipper's proof that they would not reach Germany. Presumptions based on statistics, not permitted by prize law, were indulged to accomplish this result. The British were not remiss in building up the propaganda front so as to capture American public opinion, a campaign in which they were naturally aided after February, 1915, by the American attitude toward submarine sinkings. The result was a growing public support for official tolerance of British violations of American rights. The withdrawal of the American proposal for observance of the Declaration of London climaxed a succession of major defeats and charted the course of future developments.

Mr. Ray Stannard Baker,[1] while fully appreciating the nature and effect of the American abdication and noting the fact that Mr. Lansing's arguments were not directed against the British measures on the ground that they were illegal, " the real strength of our position," but because they " would furnish grounds of criticism to [Britain's] enemies in the United States," [2] nevertheless explains the President's acquiescence in this extraordinary diplomacy on the theory that Wilson was dominated by three considerations: (a) the desire to keep America out of the war, (b) a desire to be the instrument for making peace in the conflict and " beyond that . . . a vision of a ' new world order ' " wherein war would be abolished, and (c) a desire to avoid a conflict with the British, a blunder into which Madison had stumbled.

[1] Baker, *op. cit.*, V, 211 *et seq.*   [2] *Idem*, p. 210.

Much allowance must necessarily be made for decisions reached under the stress of an emergency. But making every allowance, it does seem that a better appreciation of the effect of these surrenders might have been asked of American leaders. The Solicitor's Office had suggested the effect in the undelivered note of September 26. To permit one side to violate American neutral rights and hold the other to " strict accountability " was of itself so great a departure from the duty of impartiality urged by Wilson himself that a debacle could scarcely be avoided. This would be true even if the " strict accountability " position had legal validity, which unfortunately it lacked.[3]

The desire " to keep out of war " is certainly commendable. But it is not enough to justify or gloss over reckless measures which can hardly have, in practice, any other effect than that of intervention on one side. Right now we hear much of this desire to keep out of war as a justification for discretionary Executive embargoes which could hardly fail again to evoke the charge of unneutrality and to have all the effects of intervention.[4]

So far as concerns President Wilson's laudable desire to become an instrument of mediation in the European conflict, that also was much weakened by the fact that his deference to Great Britain took from the British all fear of his intent to exercise the power to resist their own impositions, thus depriving him of all genuine influence except as an ally. Although the Germans must have regarded his partiality with distrust, so great was their desire for peace in 1914, 1915, and especially in the fall of 1916, that they still, albeit blunderingly, urged him to proceed with mediation. The possibilities of successful mediation were scarcely promoted by the naïve partisanship of Colonel House. On October 3, 1914, he informed Page with the President's consent, that both the German and Austrian Ambassadors had stated the readiness

[3] *Infra*, p. 129.   [4] *Infra*, p. 327.

80 NEUTRALITY FOR THE UNITED STATES

of their countries for peace talks. Said House: " The attitude, I think, for England to maintain is the one which she so ably put forth to the world. That is, peace must come only upon condition of disarmament and must be permanent." [5] Possibly Lloyd George found herein the inspiration for his proposal of a pacifying " knock-out." [6] Perhaps the greatest tragedy of all, of fatal consequence to the United States and the rest of the world, is the concatenation of circumstances which prevented Wilson from assuming the role of mediator.[6a]

As to his vision of a " new world order," [7] that was always just a dream, tending on the one hand to becloud the objectivity of his view of practical European politics and his perception of the abyss into which he was moving, and on the other, to be a kind of justification and consolation for the many humiliations to which he was exposed by his European colleagues in the making of the peace, a peace which made any realization of a " new world order " worse than hopeless.

But so far as concerned the United States, Wilson exhibited little awareness that in making his various surrenders he was abandoning the fundamental rights of the United States, and indeed its independence. Such action no " vision of a new world order " could justify. Like Tennyson's unfortunate young man in " Locksley Hall," " The individual withers, and the world is more and more." A desire to save the world was to prove costly to the United States and to the world itself. A better realization of the history of past wars, of the place of neutrality in immunizing large areas against disasters and permanent disorder, of the fact that other neutrals and the very principle of neutrality were being abandoned and the world turned over to belligerent excesses — which in turn endangered not only the neutrality but the peace of the United States and of every other neutral —

[5] Hendrick, *op. cit.*, I, 413.
[6] Willis, *England's Holy War*, pp. 225, 234.
[6a] Millis, *The Road to War* (1935), p. 339 *et seq.*
[7] *Infra*, p. 236.

should have led the President to exercise caution, and to call on competent and trusty counselors whose advice was not prompted and controlled by their sympathies. His close advisers exhibited no broad or penetrating perspective and their overwhelming commitment to the crusade theory of the war distorted their view not only of the interests of the United States, present and future, but of the fundamentals of international relations.

The view that war with Germany was inevitable, which House expressed in May, 1915,[8] and Lansing in July, 1915,[9] must have impaired their capacity to deal with any issues from the standpoint of a convinced neutral. It must have materially influenced their judgment, not only on political but on legal issues. It made them incapable of realizing the strength of the American position, which not only had the backing of law and precedent but was fortified by the power to control the Allied munitions supply. Had they been neutrally minded they would have realized what Grey appreciated when he said, " If we quarrelled with the United States we could not get that supply of munitions." [10] Wilson's desire to avoid war with England is praiseworthy enough. But the alleged fear of war with England had no reasonable foundation. At no time was such an issue under serious consideration, and the flurry after the black list order of July, 1916, is not impressive. Colonel House correctly remarked in 1916 to the German Ambassador that there never was a chance of war with England, but there was more than a chance of war with Germany. There was certainly no effective body of public opinion in the United States that demanded war with England or that considered such an idea anything but fanciful. Submission to Great Britain could hardly have been induced by such a fear. What the sugges-

[8] Seymour, *op. cit.*, I, 453.
[9] Lansing, *op. cit.*, p. 19.
[10] Grey, *op. cit.*, II, 107. Cf. *supra*, p. 72.

tion that Wilson yielded because of his fear of war with England does prove, however, is that when a country or an administration does not want to go to war it is difficult to make it do so. In spite of the extraordinary character of the British provocations, which excited public opinion for a while, no responsible group and certainly no responsible official suggested that the remedy was war. The administration even declined to use its many opportunities for reprisal to bring about compliance with American rights and international law.

The recent suggestion that to avoid war we must become a hermit nation, tie ourselves down with mandatory embargoes, or, even worse, confer on the President a discretionary power to lay or lift embargoes as he sees fit, finds no reasonable support or justification in the record of events leading up to American intervention in the European war in 1917. A serious effort to hold Britain to the observance of the rules of law, for which opportunities were plentiful, might have avoided intervention. But unneutrality and sheer errors of law prevented such an effort.

Both Germany and the Allies invoked the argument of necessity to accomplish their military objectives. To the violations of law by one side the United States submitted, not always with regret. To the violations of the other it did not submit, although illegalities in the shape of submarine attack on belligerent, and especially armed belligerent vessels, can hardly be pronounced a violation of *American* rights. Our yielding to the British policy of starving the Central Powers by violating the rights of neutrals necessarily encouraged the Germans to retaliate and to decline to abandon their submarine method of reducing England. And in the German failure to abandon submarine warfare, the United States found a cause for war.

II.

AMERICANS ON ARMED BELLIGERENT MERCHANTMEN

IT may truthfully be said that American intervention in the European war was largely induced by the attempt of the Wilson administration to maintain not only the privilege of British merchantmen to arm but to use their arms against submarines, while yet enjoying immunity from submarine attack because the merchantman had American citizens among her passengers or crew. It was his belief in the soundness of this position that persuaded President Wilson to reiterate from the middle of 1915 to the declaration of war in 1917, " I cannot consent to any abridgment of the rights of American citizens in any respect. The honor and self-respect of the Nation is involved." [1] In taking this position the President was wrongly advised, as we shall endeavor to show. To do this it is necessary to trace the development of the problems connected with the armed merchantman as they presented themselves to the administration for determination.

The subject of armed merchantmen was opened by the British Government. On August 4, 1914, it notified the Secretary of State that German ships carrying arms under deck for mounting on the high seas would be deemed cruisers and that Great Britain would hold the United States responsible " for any damages to British trade or shipping, or injury to British interests generally, which may be caused by such vessels having been equipped at, or departing from, United States ports." [2] This claim of responsibility was based on British objection to the conversion of merchant vessels on the high seas, which was not illegal under international law, and

[1] Cf. letter to Senator Stone, Feb. 24, 1916. Scott, ed., *President Wilson's Foreign Policy*, p. 177. Also in *For. Rel.*, 1916, Suppl., p. 177.
[2] *For. Rel.*, 1914, Suppl., pp. 593, 594.

on the Three Rules of Washington of May 8, 1871, requiring a neutral government to use due diligence to prevent the fitting out, arming or equipping within its jurisdiction and the departure of any vessel which it has reasonable ground to believe will carry on war against a belligerent.[3] Violation of these rules during the American Civil War in the case of the Confederate cruiser *Alabama,* which had carried her arms below deck from Liverpool or Birkenhead but mounted them in the Azores and then raided the shipping of the Union, had cost Great Britain a heavy award in the Geneva arbitration.[4] German vessels suspected of carrying guns were accordingly detained in American ports.

On August 9, 1914, the British Embassy drew the Department's attention to the fact that there would soon be entering the United States a number of British merchant vessels that were armed, but that this was " a precautionary measure adopted solely for the purpose of defense, which under existing rules of international law, is the right of all merchant vessels when attacked." [5] This was followed by a further notification, August 25, 1914, of the " fullest assurances that British merchant vessels will never be used for purposes of attack, that they are merely peaceful traders armed only for defense, that they will never fire unless first fired upon, and that they will never under any circumstances attack any vessel." [6]

On August 31 the German Ambassador telegraphed the Department of State from New York that the White Star Liner *Adriatic* had entered that port " armed with cannons and had not left within twenty-four hours," [7] a requirement imposed on belligerent vessels of war. The following day, he

---

[3] The British filed a direct protest in the case of the *Kronprinz Wilhelm* on Aug. 4, 1914, *idem,* pp. 594–595.

[4] Moore, *Arb.,* I, 496 *et seq.*

[5] *For. Rel.,* 1914, Suppl., p. 598.

[6] *Idem,* p. 604.

[7] *Idem,* p. 605.

called similar attention to the British steamer *Merion*, of 13,000 tons, which had arrived at Philadelphia, armed with six cannons to take freight for Liverpool.[8] On September 3 the *Adriatic* sailed from New York " with four guns mounted and 200 rounds of ammunition . . . 28 first-class passengers, 43 second, and 89 third . . . she had no war material on board and no army reservists." [9] The same day Secretary Bryan telegraphed the German Ambassador that the Department, being satisfied that the *Adriatic* was a " merchantman," had allowed clearance accordingly. In the case of the *Merion* assurance was given the Secretary that the ammunition " will be taken off and guns dismounted and placed in the hold." [10]

At that early date, therefore, the Department conceded in favor of Britain and against Germany the unsustainable distinction between armaments on German and on British vessels, based on the supposedly offensive or defensive intention with which the arms were to be used. The invalidity of this distinction the Department had subsequently (January 18, 1916) to admit; but the admission was retracted on March 25, 1916, when, under circumstances presently to be related, the Secretary of State readopted the erroneous view that British armed merchantmen were legally immune from unwarned submarine attack. This was a fateful mistake into which the administration was led by poor advice, which it went out of its way to demand.[1] Human experience would indicate that when arms are carried, as Bryan observed, they are carried for use, and the very fact of armament would necessarily preclude visit and search and invite attack from enemy warships. And inasmuch as the law does not require a person who believes himself in danger to refrain from shooting until he is fired on — and this was true even before the Admiralty orders

---

[8] *Idem*, p. 605.
[9] Memorandum of British Ambassador, Sept. 7, 1914, *idem*, p. 607.
[10] *Idem*, p. 606.
[1] Lansing, as will be seen, requested an expert opinion which could be used to prevent Congress' warning Americans off belligerent ships.

commanded armed merchantmen to fire on or ram submarines — the supposed distinction between offensive and defensive armament becomes not merely metaphysical but unintelligent. Yet that was the basis on which the issue was debated. Not unnaturally it led to disaster.

The British Government supplied the Department of State with a memorandum on September 9 setting forth the justification for arming merchantmen.[2] This action was due to the fact, it was stated, that Germany was arming merchant vessels as commerce destroyers, claiming the right to arm such vessels in neutral harbors and on the high seas. Arming merchant vessels, it was said, was an ancient English custom; the right to arm and resist capture had been sustained by the British and American prize courts, notably by Chief Justice Marshall in the case of the *Nereide;* [3] and writers and the Institute of International Law supported it. Reference was also made to the United States Naval War Code of 1900, Art. 10 of which provides: " The personnel of merchant vessels of an enemy, who, in self-defense, and in protection of the vessels placed in their charge, resist an attack, are entitled, *if captured,* to the status of prisoners of war." [4] (Italics supplied.)

In its unsuccessful endeavor, presently to be discussed, to obtain from the Dutch Government a recognition of the peaceful status of armed merchantmen, the British Government in quoting this article omitted, doubtless inadvertently, the two italicized words,[5] thus failing to bring out the fact that the personnel was liable to be killed, but nevertheless revealing the vessel's warlike character.

[2] *For. Rel.,* 1914, Suppl., pp. 608–609.

[3] 9 Cranch 388 (1815).

[4] Naval War College, *International Law Discussions,* 1903, pp. 101, 105 (Government Printing Office, 1904). Cf. the Draft Code adopted at the 1913 meeting of the Institute of International Law, Art. 61; *idem,* 1914, pp. 141, 152.

[5] Memorandum prepared by the late Professor A. Pearce Higgins, *A. J. I. L.,* XII, Suppl. (1918), p. 200. The words are not omitted from Professor Higgins' article in *A. J. I. L.,* VIII (1914), 705, 713–714, reprinted in S. Doc. 332, 64th Cong., 1st Sess. (1916), p. 31.

With the United States, however, the British Government was more successful. On the basis of the authorities cited, and without reference to the real issue — the legal consequences and liabilities attached to arming — the British Government concluded with this *non sequitur:*

. . . a merchant vessel armed purely for self-defense is *therefore* entitled under international law to enjoy the status of a peaceful trading ship in neutral ports. . . . They consider that only those merchant ships which are intended for use as cruisers should be treated as ships of war and that the question whether a particular ship carrying armament is intended for offensive or defensive action must be decided by the simple criterion whether she is engaged in ordinary commerce and embarking cargo and passengers in the ordinary way. If so, there is no rule in international law that would justify such vessel, even if armed, being treated otherwise than as a peaceful trader.[6] (Italics supplied.)

There was no connection between premise and conclusion. Merchantmen certainly had been privileged to arm — contrary to a view Germany expressed [7] — but they thereupon lost their immunities as merchant vessels. They could be legitimately treated as war vessels, both on the high seas and in port. As Marshall said of the *Nereide:* " She is an open and declared belligerent; claiming all the rights, and subject to all the dangers of the belligerent character." [8]

But these considerations the British note did not cite. Naturally that government had British interests at heart, not American. But it is distressing to observe that American officials seemed unable or unwilling to answer the weak and unsound contentions of the British and instead garbled the opinion of Marshall in the *Nereide* case by omitting from it the vital sentence quoted above. Thus the President, and the House and Senate also, were misled into taking a position

[6] *For. Rel.,* 1914, Suppl., p. 608.
[7] The practice of arming merchantmen had fallen into disuse in the nineteenth century; its renewal in 1914 made it the more significant.
[8] 9 Cranch 388, 430. " Open and declared belligerent " meant warlike, not merely " British."

which had no foundation either in law or in common sense. Yet on that hollow platform Wilson stood in defending the immunity from attack of British armed merchantmen and of American citizens on board.

Professor Hyde summarizes the law on this subject, after full consideration of the war experience, as follows:

The merchantman when equipped with a gun of great destructive force and long range becomes itself a valuable weapon of offense. The master is encouraged to engage any public vessel of the enemy, of inferior defensive strength and of whatsoever type, which comes within range, and that irrespective of whether the latter initiates hostilities. As the merchantman by reason of its armament may be deemed by the enemy to be justly subjected to attack without warning, the master may fairly regard himself as on the defensive, whenever his ship is pursued by an enemy vessel of war, or even sighted by one. Thus the armed merchantman, although its chief mission be the transportation of passengers and freight, becomes necessarily a participant in the conflict.

* * *

. . . the equipment of a belligerent merchant marine for hostile service, even though defensive rather than offensive, serves, on principle, to deprive the armed vessels of the right to claim immunity from attack without warning.[9]

On September 19, 1914, however, Mr. Lansing adopted a ruling supporting the British contentions. He issued a circular letter setting forth the view of the United States on the status of armed merchantmen, a view which left out of account the practical considerations involved and hence came to legal conclusions which had to be abandoned — but which, however, served to drag the United States into positions so inflexible and acrimonious that they became identified with " National Honor." From these there was no retreat except war. Lansing's circular of 1914 provided:

[9] Hyde, *International Law* (1922), II, 405, 471.

A. A merchant vessel of belligerent nationality may carry an armament and ammunition for the sole purpose of defense without acquiring the character of a ship of war.

B. The presence of an armament and ammunition on board a merchant vessel creates a presumption that the armament is for offensive purposes, but the owners or agents may overcome this presumption by evidence showing that the vessel carries armament solely for defense.

C. Indications that the armament will not be used offensively are:

1. That the caliber of the guns carried does not exceed six inches.

2. That the guns and small arms carried are few in number.

3. That no guns are mounted on the forward part of the vessel.

4. That the quantity of ammunition carried is small.

5. That the vessel is manned by its usual crew, and the officers are the same as those on board before war was declared.

6. That the vessel intends to and actually does clear for a port lying in its usual trade route, or a port indicating its purpose to continue in the same trade in which it was engaged before war was declared.

7. That the vessel takes on board fuel and supplies sufficient only to carry it to its port of destination, or the same quantity substantially which it has been accustomed to take for a voyage before war was declared.

8. That the cargo of the vessel consists of articles of commerce unsuited for the use of a ship of war in operations against an enemy.

9. That the vessel carries passengers who are as a whole unfitted to enter the military or naval service of the belligerent whose flag the vessel flies, or of any of its allies, and particularly if the passenger list includes women and children.

10. That the speed of the ship is slow.[1]

Here the Acting Secretary let himself in for a series of tests designed to establish the *motive* with which the armament was carried. He disregarded the important facts that the armament would necessarily invite attack, that the mere

[1] *For. Rel.*, 1914, Suppl., pp. 611–612.

danger of attack would result in a use of the armament, and that such use determines its character. The truth of these elemental legal considerations was only strengthened by the subsequent instructions issued to merchantmen by the British Admiralty and other Allied governments.

The British had armed their merchantmen primarily as a defensive measure against depredations by individual and isolated surface raiders of the auxiliary-cruiser type, i.e., fast merchantmen converted into cruisers in enemy or neutral ports or on the high seas. The disappearance, for all practical purposes, of this German annoyance to British trade was followed in 1915 by the emergence of the submarine. While the raider, however, had labored under the same limitations as an ordinary surface vessel, it possessed only a fraction of the vulnerability of the submarine. Yet the September, 1914, ruling of the Department was not changed. The impropriety of extending it to cover submarines was not discovered until January, 1916, when Lansing undertook to change it to conform to the new conditions. But by that time a vested political interest in the American error had accrued, and Lansing was forced to retreat to his original untenable position, the impossibility of which he had personally drawn to the President's attention.[2]

British Prewar Measures to Arm Merchantmen

It was to meet the armed cruiser menace that the British had been preparing since 1912 by arming their merchantmen.[3] There was little secrecy about it. On March 26, 1913, Winston Churchill, then First Lord of the Admiralty, included in his annual statement of Navy estimates a few pertinent remarks on foreign converted cruisers as a menace to British trade:

[2] Lansing to Wilson, Jan. 2, 1916, Savage, Doc. No. 149, II, 430, 431. See also *infra*, p. 99.
[3] Hurd, *The Merchant Navy*, I, 120.

. . . substantial progress has been made in the direction of meeting it by preparing as a defensive measure to equip a number of first-class British liners to repel the attack of armed foreign merchant cruisers. Although these vessels have, of course, a wholly different status from that of the regularly commissioned merchant cruisers such as those we obtain under the Cunard agreement, the Admiralty have felt that a great part of the cost of the necessary equipment should not fall upon the owners, and we have decided, therefore, to lend the necessary guns, to supply ammunition, and to provide for the training of members of the ship's company to form the guns' crews. The owners on their part are paying the cost of the necessary structural conversion, which is not great.[4]

Some brief mention might be made of this " Cunard Agreement." Entered into in 1903 as a means of subsidizing the construction and operation of the high-speed liners *Lusitania* and *Mauretania,* the agreement was also designed to provide the British Government " with fast ships available at all times for war service." [5] The government was to advance the cost of the two vessels, not exceeding £2,000,000, at 2¾ per cent, interest to accrue on one half of the loan from the date of the first voyage of the *Lusitania,* and on the other half from a similar point of time in the career of her sister ship. In addition, the line was to receive an annual subsidy of £75,000 for each vessel.[6]

In return, the company entered into an elaborate series of covenants covering not only the two prospective liners but every other unit in its fleet. Some of these merit repetition. The specifications for the two new vessels were to be submitted for Admiralty approval, and any alterations desired by the government were to be carried out.[7] Furthermore, the Company was " to afford to the Admiralty . . . every facility

---

[4] *Parliamentary Debates,* 5th ser., L, 1777.

[5] The Cunard Atlantic Liner *Lusitania; Engineering,* LXXXIV (London, Aug. 2, 1907), 129, 133.

[6] Agreement between the Admiralty, etc., and the Cunard Steamship Company, dated July 30, 1903; [Cd. 1703] 1903, *Accounts and Papers,* XXXVI, 157, Arts. 6, 10, 34.

[7] *Idem,* Art. 3 (2).

for fitting on board all or any of the vessels forming the
Fleet . . . of the Company such fittings and arrangements
for their armament in the event of their being taken for use as
armed cruisers as the Admiralty may think fit. . . ." [8]

The agreement specified that, on the two new vessels,

all certified officers other than engineers and not less than one
half of the crew . . . shall belong to the Royal Naval Reserve
or the Royal Naval Fleet Reserve . . . For the average deficiency
(if any) in each year . . . below the proportion of men [so en-
rolled] . . . liquidated damages at the rate of 12 l. a head shall
be payable by the Company to his Majesty's Government.[9]

The construction contract under which the *Lusitania* was
built at the establishment of Messrs. John Brown and Co.,
Ltd., contained specifications somewhat more exact in detail
than those alluded to in the foregoing summary — and these
specifications appeared in public print even before the great
liner had been placed in actual operation.

One important feature dealt with in fixing the designs had
reference to the use of the ships as cruisers or scouts in time of
war, and the plans which we reproduce on Plate XXV show
that the machinery — which is almost entirely under the waterline — has been so disposed in separate compartments, and with
coal protection along each side, as to counteract, as far as possible, the effect of the enemy's fire at the waterline. For purposes
of attack the Lusitania will be provided with an armament as
satisfactory as the armoured cruisers of the County class, because
on one of the topmost decks there will be carried, within the
shelter of the heavy shell-plating, four 6 in. quick-firing guns attaining a muzzle energy of over 5000 foot-tons, while on the
promenade-deck on each side there will be four more guns on central pivot mountings, also able to penetrate 4–¾ in. armour at
5000 yards range, and 6 in. armour at 3000 yards range. With the
great speed, which can be maintained for three or four times the
period that any modern cruiser can steam even at only 21 knots,
and with the careful subdivision for protection and their satisfactory offensive power, the Lusitania and her consort may be regarded as most effective additions to any fighting squadron. Their

[8] Art. 5 (7).　　　　　　　　　　　[9] Art. 5 (9).

advent is therefore a great advantage from the point of view of British sea power.[10]

It is little wonder, in view of these provisions, that the wartime capabilities of the two vessels should be eulogized:

> They have thus an armament equal to some of the modern first-class cruisers costing a million sterling.[1]

In 1913, some members of the House of Commons questioned the First Lord of the Admiralty about the status of armed merchant vessels in time of war; they were informed that such craft would automatically fall into one of two classes: armed merchant cruisers, or defensively armed merchant ships — rather a subtle distinction. One remark, however, is particularly noteworthy: " The first class is that of armed merchant cruisers, which on the outbreak of war would be commissioned under the White Ensign, and would then be indistinguishable in status and control from men of war. In this class belong the *Mauretania* and the *Lusitania*." [2] There was no secrecy here, and there certainly was none in March, 1914, when Winston Churchill, again addressing Parliament, declared:

> The House will expect me to say a word on the arming of merchant ships . . . Forty ships have been armed so far with two 4.7 guns apiece, and by the end of 1914–1915 seventy ships will have been so armed . . . Vessels so armed have nothing in common with merchant vessels taken over by the Admiralty and converted into commissioned auxiliary cruisers, nor are these vessels privateers or commerce destroyers in any sense. They are exclusively ships which carry food to this country . . . They are, however, thoroughly capable of self-defense against an enemy's armed merchantmen.[3]

---

[10] *Engineering*, LXXXIV (London, Aug. 2, 1907), 135. Diagrams of the deck plan indicate that the side guns were mounted on the shelter deck.

[1] *Idem*, p. 611, Nov. 8, 1907.

[2] *Parliamentary Deb.*, 5th ser., LIII (June 10, 1913), 1431; Hurd, *op. cit.*, I, 123–124.

[3] *Parliamentary Deb.*, 5th ser., LIX (March 17, 1914), 1914. The British fiscal year ends March 31.

These words were uttered five months before the outbreak of war! Just one month after this statement, a list of some forty armed merchantmen appeared in the daily press; [4] as previously intimated by Mr. Churchill, no Cunarders appear in the list.[5] By the start of the war this number had been increased to fifty at the very least,[6] and " by the middle of May [1915] . . . 149 British merchant ships had been fitted with defensive armament." [7] By February 15 of the following year, such vessels numbered 991; on April 12, 1109; and on September 18, 1916, the " defensively armed " merchant squadron counted 1,749 vessels.[8]

Orders to British Armed Merchantmen, 1915

ON February 10, 1915, when submarine warfare began in earnest, the British Admiralty issued orders to its merchant vessels to ram submarines if escape should prove impossible. On February 25, these instructions were amplified by ordering merchantmen to fire on submarines at sight. It is interesting to observe that in spite of the assurances given to the United States that defensively armed merchantmen would not use their arms to attack, the change of instructions was apparently not communicated to the officials in Washington; it reached the State Department in December, 1915, via the American Ambassador in Berlin to whom the amended orders were handed by the German Foreign Office.[9]

The Admiralty instructions of February 10, 1915, read in part as follows:

A. No British merchant vessel should ever tamely surrender to a submarine but should do her utmost to escape.

*   *   *

[4] *London Morning Post*, April 16, 1914, p. 8, col. 2.
[5] They were evidently regarded as armed merchant cruisers.
[6] *London Times*, Feb. 3, 1915, p. 6, col. 5.
[7] Hurd, *op. cit.*, II, 237.
[8] *Idem*, II, 240.
[9] *For. Rel.*, 1915, Suppl., p. 653.

C. If a submarine comes up suddenly close ahead of you with obvious hostile intention, steer straight for her at your utmost speed, altering course as necessary to keep her ahead." [10]

An addendum was more explicit:

It is considered that every ship on sighting a submarine should first endeavor to escape . . . Should it become apparent to the master of the ship pursued that the submarine is rapidly gaining on him, then, unless help is at hand, it will generally be best to turn bow to the enemy before he gets too close, and make straight at him. This will compel him to risk being rammed or dive. If he dives he at once loses speed and drops astern so that the man-oeuvre can be repeated. If he does not dive then there is a fair chance of ramming him, . . .[1]

A fortnight later the Admiralty issued " confidential " orders to all "vessels carrying a defensive armament." These instructions, with a series of other instructions as to how to meet the submarine menace successfully, were found by the Germans on the English steamer *Woodfield*.[2] In the instructions dated February 25, 1915, merchantmen were instructed as follows:

1. Defensively armed vessels should follow generally the instructions for ordinary merchantmen.

2. In submarine waters guns should be kept in instant readiness.

3. If a submarine is obviously pursuing a ship, by day, and it is evident to the master that she has hostile intentions, *the ship pursued should open fire in self-defense, notwithstanding the submarine may not have committed a definite hostile act such as firing a gun or torpedo.* (Italics supplied.)

4. Before opening fire, the British colours should be hoisted.[3]

---

[10] *Idem,* p. 653.

[1] *Idem,* p. 654.

[2] *For. Rel.,* 1916, Suppl., pp. 191–198.

[3] Instruction of Feb. 25, 1915, *For. Rel.,* 1916, Suppl., p. 196. See also instructions found on the *Appam,* dated May 28, 1915, *idem,* p. 173; instructions dated Oct. 20, 1915, in Department of State diplomatic correspondence (*European War, No. 4,* pp. 64–65). Unofficial instructions were published in the *London Times,* Feb. 3, 1915, p. 6, col. 5.

With these instructions the ostensible distinction between offensive and defensive armaments could no longer be seriously maintained.[4] Mr. Winston Churchill, first Lord of the Admiralty, testifies: " Armed small craft were multiplied to an enormous extent, both by building and conversion, the arming of merchantmen was pressed forward, the manoeuvres of decoy ships . . . were perfected, and every scientific device, offensive and defensive against the submarine was made the object of ceaseless experiment and production." [5]

As reports of engagements between armed merchantmen and submarines continued to come in, Lansing became doubtful of the validity of his ruling of September, 1914, with respect to the admission of armed merchantmen into American ports and with respect to the immunity from submarine attack of British merchantmen carrying American citizens. While the United States had not been notified of the arrival of armed British merchantmen after the *Adriatic* and *Merion* cases of 1914,[6] Mr. Lansing advised the British Ambassador on August 25, 1915, that the *Waimana* had arrived at Newport News carrying a 4.7 inch gun for defensive purposes and hoped that the Ambassador would find it possible to " instruct

[4] The British General, Sir Henry F. Thuillier, in speaking before the Royal United Service Institution, Feb. 5, 1936, remarked: " I find a difficulty, being a soldier, in knowing how to distinguish between weapons used in aggression and those used in defence." *Journal* (of the Institute), May, 1936, p. 265. A British Admiral is of like opinion: Richmond, *Sea Power in the Modern World* (New York, 1934), pp. 71–72.

[5] Churchill, *The World Crisis*, III, 217.

On Feb. 15, 1915, the German Ambassador notified the Secretary of State that these hostile methods of armed merchantmen, plus the misuse of neutral flags, made visit and search impractical and dangerous. *For. Rel.*, 1915, Suppl., pp. 104–105.

[6] Mr. Hurd states (*op. cit.*, II, 232) that the British Government had " decided on Sept. 3, 1914, to abandon running defensively armed merchant ships to the United States." But after the Lansing ruling of Sept. 19, " the main purpose of which was to assimilate them to ordinary merchant vessels " (*idem*, II, 243), armed merchantmen again began to arrive. Mr. Hurd says, " a considerable number of vessels under these regulations cleared from New York with their guns mounted aft," *idem*, II, 243.

the captain to remove the gun." [7] The British Ambassador replied September 10 that removal of the gun might be regarded as a precedent and an abandonment of the right which the British Government claimed " to protect the lives and property of British subjects in non-combatant vessels." On September 11, however, the Secretary answered that " it has come to the knowledge of the Department that British merchant vessels which carry arms have used them for offensive purposes in attacks upon submarines "; somewhat more firmly, he again requested the removal of the armament from the *Waimana*, a request which was complied with ten days later.[8]

Finally, on December 31, 1915, Mr. Lansing informed the Italian Ambassador that since September, 1914,

the situation has been changed by the use of submarines as commerce destroyers, and for that reason this Government feels that these [September, 1914] rules should be modified, as a small calibre gun on a merchant ship is just as effective for purposes of attack against the submarine as the large calibre gun. Therefore, the presence of any gun on a merchant ship of a belligerent nationality could well create presumption that the armament was for offensive purposes, thereby causing this Government to treat the ship as a ship of war.[9]

The Secretary was now in accord with the view of British naval authorities prior to the war; as expressed by Mr. Hurd, orders to naval officers

. . . were based upon the well-established principle that the surest way of striking an effective blow at the enemy, and at the same time safeguarding tonnage and territory, was in prompt attack upon the enemy's fighting ships. That principle had guided British policy for centuries.[10]

By this proposed change of ruling the Secretary also concurred with the German view expressed in the note of October 15, 1914, that " as far as determining the warlike char-

[7] *For. Rel.*, 1915, Suppl., p. 848.   [9] *For. Rel.*, 1916, Suppl., p. 749.
[8] *Idem*, pp. 849–850.   [10] Hurd, *op. cit.*, I, 240.

acter of a ship is concerned, the distinction between offensive and defensive arms is irrelevant; the destination of the ship for use of any kind in war is conclusive. Furthermore, restrictions of the extent of armament afford no guarantee that ships armed for defensive will not, in certain circumstances, be used for offensive purposes." [1] Mr. Lansing thereby also repudiated quite properly the position he had assumed in his note to Germany of November 7, 1914, that

the purpose of an armament of a merchant vessel is to be determined by various circumstances, among which are the number and positions of the guns on the vessel, the quantity of ammunition and fuel, the number and sex of the passengers, the nature of the cargo, etc. Tested by evidence of this character the question as to whether an armament on a merchant vessel is intended solely for defensive purposes may be readily answered and the neutral government should regulate its treatment of the vessel in accordance with the intended use of the armament. [2]

He had safeguarded himself somewhat in that, while admitting the right to carry defensive armament, he nevertheless expressed this government's " disapprobation of a practice which compelled it to pass upon a vessel's intended use, which opinion if proven subsequently to be erroneous might constitute a ground for a charge of unneutral conduct." [3]

Evidence of Mr. Lansing's earlier conversion to the view that his original position was wrong, and that the British argument of September, 1914 (maintaining that because merchant ships may arm for defensive purpose they " therefore remain ordinary merchantmen "), was specious, is provided by the fact that early in May, 1915, he had proposed the use of the word " unresisting " in the first *Lusitania* note in preference to the " unarmed " actually used by Bryan in that note. [4] He had preferred the word " unresisting " be-

---

[1] *For. Rel.*, 1914, Suppl., p. 613.
[2] *Idem*, pp. 613, 614.
[3] *Idem*, p. 614.
[4] Savage, *Policy of the United States towards Maritime Commerce in War* (Government Printing Office, 1936), Doc. No. 95, II, 331. Cf. also

cause it avoided the necessary implication that by arming a vessel changed its status.

Writing to the President on January 2, 1916, Lansing pointed out the necessity for a revision of the 1914 ruling because of

the impossibility of a submarine's communicating with an armed merchant ship without exposing itself to the gravest danger of being sunk by gunfire because of its weakness defensively, [and] the unreasonableness of requiring a submarine to run the danger of being almost certainly destroyed by giving warning to a vessel carrying an armament . . .[5]

He suggested, therefore, that merchant vessels discontinue carrying guns. Should they nevertheless continue to arm, they were to be classed as " vessels of war and liable to treatment as such by both belligerents and neutrals." [6] Here, in truth, was the core of the matter, as the Netherlands had realized at the time she issued her declaration of neutrality upon the outbreak of hostilities in 1914. Lansing discovered it over a year later.

The arming of some vessels exposed all of them to the same danger and liability to attack, as Lansing clearly perceived. He said:

The chief difficulty with the situation seems to me to lie in this: If some merchant vessels carry arms and others do not, how can a submarine determine this fact without exposing itself to great risk of being sunk? Unless the Entente Allies positively agree not to arm any of their merchant vessels and notify the Central Powers to that effect, is there not strong reason why a submarine should not warn a vessel before launching an attack?

You will recall the case of the *Baralong* where a German submarine was bombarding a vessel from which the crew had escaped

---

Thomas A. Bailey, " The Sinking of the Lusitania," *American Historical Review*, XLI (Oct., 1935), 54–73; *For. Rel.*, 1915, Suppl., p. 394; *idem*, pp. 436, 438.

[5] Lansing to Wilson, Jan. 2, 1916; Savage, *op. cit.*, Doc. No. 149, II, 430, 431.

[6] *Ibid.*

in boats, when a tramp steamer approached flying the American flag. The submarine remained on the surface and awaited the steamer, which on nearing the submarine lowered the American flag, hoisted the British colors, and with a gun mounted on the stern (a defensive armament according to our early definition) opened fire and sank the German vessel killing all the crew. The British Government would urge that this was merely a *ruse de guerre* and entirely allowable, and so it would have been under old conditions, but under the new conditions it presents a strong argument in favor of submarine attack without warning.

Not only, therefore, should we, in my judgment, rewrite our statement as to the status of armed merchant vessels but show that if any vessels of that class are armed, all merchant vessels are in danger of sudden attack without warning.[7]

By that time, however, it was too late to effect a change. Too many interests, legitimately acquired under the protection of the September, 1914, ruling, had by then solidified into a claim of vested rights.

Attitude of the Netherlands

FROM the very beginning of the war, in August, 1914, the Government of the Netherlands firmly maintained the position that they would regard an armed merchantman, even though armed in alleged self-defense, as assimilated to a warship and, therefore, to be excluded — under Dutch interpretation of its neutral obligations — from Dutch ports. The explanation was that by the armament these vessels were " consequently . . . capable of committing acts of war." [8]

The British Government used an imposing array of arguments to break down this Dutch position, e.g., that only Holland and Mexico thus interpreted their neutral duties; that during the Hague Conference only auxiliary cruisers, and

---

[7] *Idem*, pp. 431–432.

[8] Mr. Chilton, British Minister, to Sir Edward Grey, Aug. 10, 1914, *A. J. I. L.*, XII, Suppl., p. 197.

J. Loudon, Netherlands Minister for Foreign Affairs, to Sir A. Johnstone, April 7, 1915, *idem*, p. 199.

not merchant carriers, were considered to be assimilated to warships; that neutrality did not require such a strict interpretation of neutral duties; that the Hague rules, which prevented a change in the laws of neutrality during the war except to strengthen them in support of neutral duties, presupposed belligerents' conducting themselves according to the laws of war, whereas Germany was carrying on a " campaign of maritime atrocity "; [9] and that self-defense included " the elementary right of a human being to disable his intending murderer." [10]

The Dutch replied that international law gave them the privilege of treating armed merchant vessels as warships and of excluding, or admitting them conditionally; that Holland's special position between the two belligerents required a strict interpretation of neutral duties; that the admission of an armed merchantman might invite danger of belligerent operations in Dutch waters.[1] Dr. Loudon stated:

A belligerent merchant vessel which fights to escape capture or destruction by an enemy warship commits an act the legitimacy of which is indeed unquestionable, but which is none the less an act of war.

The Queen's Government are of the opinion that it would be contrary to the strict neutrality which they have determined to observe from the beginning of the war not to assimilate to a belligerent warship, . . . any belligerent merchant vessel armed with the object of committing, in case of need, an act of war.[2]

During the resumption of the correspondence in 1917, the Dutch derived satisfaction from the view of the United States Government, expressed in its proposal to the Allied governments of January 18, 1916, that

[9] Lord Robert Cecil, *idem*, p. 214.
[10] Sir Edward Grey, *idem*, p. 199.
[1] The Dutch compelled the British armed merchantman, *Princess Melita*, to dump its guns and ammunition overboard before admission to Dutch waters. *Idem*, p. 204.
[2] *Idem*, pp. 202–203.

. . . my [the United States] government is impressed with the reasonableness of the argument that a merchant vessel carrying an armament of any sort, in view of the character of submarine warfare and the defensive weakness of undersea craft, should be held to be an auxiliary cruiser and so treated by a neutral as well as by a belligerent government.[3]

The British sought to weaken the force of this contention by suggesting that it was a proposed compromise based on humanitarian grounds — a half truth only — and that the United States Government had been persuaded to withdraw from its position on March 25, 1916, and had thereafter continued to treat armed merchantmen as ordinary merchant vessels. This was all too true, and how it happened will be noted presently. The British Government added, " His Majesty's Government desire nothing better than the adoption by the Netherlands of the doctrine and practice of the United States as neutrals in this matter." [4]

The British Government in asking for a change in the Dutch rule contended that inasmuch as the few German ships at sea did not need to be armed, the Dutch rule operated to the disadvantage of Great Britain and that " the rules imposed for the purposes of neutrality must be impartial, for impartiality is of the essence of neutrality." [5] It is a satisfaction to observe that at least Great Britain, even in the midst of war, did not forget this cardinal precept.[5a]

The American Proposal of January 18, 1916

THE complexities born of the inconsistent claim that an armed merchantman was a peaceful trader, yet privileged and under orders to attack submarines, and the growing evidence of

---

[3] *Idem*, p. 227; *For. Rel.*, 1916, Suppl., pp. 146, 148.

[4] Mr. Balfour to Sir W. Townley, Nov. 14, 1917, *A. J. I. L.*, XII, Suppl., p. 231.

[5] Lord Robert Cecil to Sir W. Townley, May 18, 1917, *idem*, p. 211.

[5a] Lansing also remembered it when he advised Switzerland that the United States would respect Swiss neutrality if Switzerland maintained it herself and Germany respected it. *For. Rel.*, 1917, Suppl. II, 758.

such encounters [6] finally led the Department of State, possibly at the initiative of the Navy Department, to propose to the Allied governments on January 18, 1916, a so-called *modus vivendi* [7] for the suspension of the practice of arming merchantmen as a foundation for further protests against the sinking of such merchantmen by submarines. Mr. Lansing's note, dropping the propagandistic premise that the submarine was inherently an unlawful instrument of warfare — an argument always advanced when new weapons have been invented [8] — contended that the submarine could not be outlawed since these instruments of war had proved their effectiveness, but that in order to bring them within what he called the general rules of international law and principles of humanity, a formula must be found to modify the practice prevailing " prior to the employment of submarines." He therefore proposed that an enemy merchant vessel should not be attacked without being ordered to stop. The vessel must then stop, and should not be attacked unless it attempted to flee or resist. If it is impossible to place a prize crew on board or take it into port, it may be sunk, provided crew and passengers have been removed to a place of safety. He added:

Prior to the year 1915 belligerent operations against enemy commerce on the high seas had been conducted with cruisers carrying heavy armaments. Under these conditions international law appeared to permit a merchant vessel to carry an armament for defensive purposes without losing its character as a private com-

[6] *For. Rel.*, 1916, Suppl., pp. 198–201.

[7] *Idem*, p. 146. Lansing, *Memoirs*, pp. 99, 104. Lansing conceived the move as a sop to antiwar opinion. He says (p. 101) that it was necessary " to determine upon a general course of action which would not abruptly challenge that opinion but would guide it in the right direction. We had to be able to show that everything had been done to avoid war in order to arouse a public demand for war." He was still seeking to lead the American people into war against Germany: " The American people will have to be educated to a true vision of the menace that Germany is to liberty and democracy in *America* as well as in Europe " (p. 103). (Italics supplied.)

[8] See General Sir Henry F. Thuillier, " Can Methods of Warfare Be Restricted? " *Journal of the Royal United Service Institute*, May, 1936, p. 273.

mercial vessel. This right seems to have been predicated on the superior defensive strength of ships of war, and the limitation of armament to have been dependent on the fact that it could not be used effectively in offense against enemy naval vessels, while it could defend the merchantman against the generally inferior armament of piratical ships and privateers.

The use of the submarine, however, has changed these relations. Comparison of the defensive strength of a cruiser and a submarine shows that the latter, relying for protection on its power to submerge is almost defenseless in point of construction. Even a merchant ship carrying a small caliber gun would be able to use it effectively for offense against a submarine. Moreover, pirates and sea rovers have been swept from the main trade channels of the seas, and privateering has been abolished. Consequently, the placing of guns on merchantmen at the present day of submarine warfare can be explained only on the ground of a purpose to render merchantmen superior in force to submarines and to prevent warning and visit and search by them. Any armament, therefore, on a merchant vessel would seem to have the character of an offensive armament.[9]

He therefore proposed " that merchant vessels of belligerent nationality should be prohibited and prevented from carrying any armament whatsoever," and expressed the conviction that the Allied governments to whom the note was addressed would consider the humane purpose of saving the lives of innocent people rather than insist upon " a doubtful legal right which may be denied on account of new conditions." [10]

The suggestion that international law " appeared to permit a merchant vessel to carry an armament for defensive purposes without losing its character as a private commercial vessel " is ambiguous. If it were captured, it would probably be put through a prize court as a private vessel, but its armament exposed it to every belligerent risk that a warship incurs. It is true that the old rule approving armed merchantmen had been predicated on the assumption that they might

---

[9] *For. Rel.,* 1916, Suppl., p. 147.　　　　　[10] *Idem,* p. 148.

encounter pirates or privateers, whereas against heavy warships they could offer no effective resistance. With the practical disappearance of pirates and privateers, the reason for armament on merchantmen had disappeared. The practice of arming merchantmen was revived by Great Britain, however, because of the unwillingness of the Second Hague Conference to prohibit the conversion of merchantmen into auxiliary cruisers, or even to prohibit such conversion on the high seas. This privilege had been demanded by nations possessing few overseas ports or naval stations where such conversion might take place.

The vulnerable submarine had made the armed merchantman a much more effective instrument of warfare than it had ever been, and the incongruity of attributing to such an effective weapon a peaceful character with immunity from the risks of its belligerent operations, appeared all the more striking by the record of its achievements against the submarine. Professor Hyde must, therefore, be considered correct when he says:

It is believed that the Secretary of State sought to formulate no new principle of law, but rather to gain recognition of the inapplicability of an old rule to existing conditions of maritime warfare, which were at variance with the theory on which the rule was based, and that he endeavored to encourage a practice both in harmony with that theory and responsive to the requirements of justice. Nor did his proposal indicate the abandonment of any neutral right.[1]

Mr. Hyde might have gone further by pointing out that when the Hague Conference adopted the rule that prizes may not be sunk without providing for the safety of passengers and crew, they necessarily contemplated the continuance of merchantmen *un*armed. Had it been suggested that the rule was applicable to *armed* merchantmen, the proposal would

[1] Hyde, *op. cit.*, II, 467.

have been regarded as eccentric. Secretary Lansing's proposal, therefore, was merely a return to common sense as well as elementary legal considerations.

Reception of the Proposal. Mr. Lansing's proposal was the high point of the American effort at neutrality. It was sound and unassailable, but short lived. Had the position been maintained, it might have been more difficult to find a good ground on which to lure the country into war, which by that time an influential minority seemed to desire. Mr. Page, and Colonel House in somewhat lesser degree, appeared to have already committed themselves to American intervention. Mr. Lansing, although contemplating such intervention, vacillated. But the very appearance of the sane proposal of January 18, 1916, seems to have precipitated a rapid deterioration of neutrality and an insistence upon the earlier position that an American citizen could travel on an armed belligerent merchantman unmolested. If he sank with the ship, it would be considered an affront to the National Honor of the United States and would require vindication by war.

Premonitions of the note of January 18 had appeared in the press. On January 6, 1916, a *New York Times* editorial on the sinking of the armed British Steamer *Persia* mentioned the September, 1914, ruling.[2] The next day the Italian liner *Giuseppe Verdi* arrived with guns mounted.[3] On January 9 it was reported that Baron Zwiedinek, the Austrian Chargé, had called on Lansing to protest this armament and that Lansing had promised that the ship would not depart without settlement of the problem.[4] On January 11, Lansing informed the Italian Ambassador, Count di Cellere, that the ship would be held until the guns were dismounted.[5] On January 14, the *Giuseppe Verdi* sailed with guns, because

[2] *New York Times,* Jan. 6, 1916, p. 12, col. 1.
[3] *Idem,* Jan. 7, p. 1, col. 6.
[4] *Idem,* Jan. 9, p. 1, col. 6.
[5] *Idem,* Jan. 11, p. 1, col. 4.

Lansing had been assured that they were " defensive " only [6]
A few days later Baron Zwiedinek intimated to Lansing that
Austria would sink such ships without warning.[7]

It was only on January 28 that the *New York Times*
reported [1] that Lansing had delivered a note to the Ambassadors of the Allied countries on the subject of armed merchantmen. The full text of the note was not published until
February 12.[2] On February 18 Senator Lodge had it spread
on the records of the Senate.[3]

The reception of the note in Allied countries was hardly
favorable.[4] They seemed to believe that the proposal to disarm merchantmen was a handicap to them in that it would
not be followed by restricted submarine warfare. Sir Edward
Grey spoke of it " as one speaks of a great calamity." [5] Page
says: " His surprise and dismay are overwhelming." Page
pictures it " as a complete German victory over us in the submarine controversy. [The] engendered bitterness against us
will be intense in the Allied countries and such influence as
we might have had with the Allied governments will be lost.
If this proposal be persisted in, the administration will forfeit the confidence [and] the good will of England and
France." [6] Page intimates that the British Government might
construct extra munition plants in England and Canada so
as to curtail their dependence on the American supply. It was
a favorite device of Page's to suggest, whenever the United
States had the temerity to think of American neutrality, that
dire consequences would befall us in loss of trade or financial
panic. In effect, the whole weight of the British Empire was
brought to bear on Washington to cause retraction of the

[6] *Idem*, Jan. 14, p. 3, col. 5; *For. Rel.*, 1916, Suppl., pp. 752–754.

[7] *Idem*, Jan. 18, p. 3, col. 1.

[1] *New York Times*, Jan. 28, 1916, p. 1, col. 7.

[2] *Idem*, Feb. 12, 1916, pp. 3, 4, col. 1.

[3] *Cong. Rec.*, LIII, 2762–2763.

[4] *For. Rel.*, 1916, Suppl., p. 149 *et seq.*

[5] Page to Secretary of State, Jan. 25, 1916, *idem*, p. 151.

[6] *Idem*, p. 152.

Lansing note. Every form of persuasion was employed. As one distinguished American commentator puts it:

I recall, as if it were yesterday, what happened when it was suggested here that armed merchantmen should be put under belligerent restrictions. The British Government, or some of its spokesmen, suggested that, if we did this, British ships would cease to come to our ports, and that we should have to send everything to Halifax. Immediately we ran to cover, and submitted. I could not help wondering whether there was any limit to our credulity and subserviency. Of course, I do not blame the British Government. They were not charged with the maintenance of the independence and the honor of the United States. Their hands were full in taking care of themselves. But I cannot forget the fact that the little Kingdom of the Netherlands, small in territory and population, but governed by a loyal Queen, under the advice of patriotic and capable men, put armed merchantmen on the same footing and under the same restrictions as men-of-war, as declared by our own Supreme Court, through John Marshall, the great Chief Justice, in the case of the Nereide (9 Cranch, 388).[7]

Colonel House seems to have convinced President Wilson in the fall of 1915 that war against Germany was necessary.[8] Sir Edward Grey had tempted the President, through Colonel House, with the suggestion that a League of Nations " to get security for the future against aggressive war " would be a splendid plan for ending the present war.[9] Colonel House then, on October 17, informed Sir Edward of the possibilities of American intervention " upon the broad basis of the elimination of militarism and navalism." He was beset with the idea of the Allies, " with the aid of the United States," bringing about a peace along the lines that they had discussed. He pro-

[7] Statement by John Bassett Moore, Hearings on S. 3474, Committee on Foreign Relations, U. S. Senate, 74th Cong., 2d Sess. (Jan. 10–Feb. 5, 1936), pp. 172, 185.

[8] Seymour, *Intimate Papers of Colonel House,* II, 84. On May 30, 1915, House had confided to his diary that war with Germany was " inevitable." *Idem,* I, 453.

[9] *Idem,* p. 89.

posed a trip to Berlin to announce the President's intention of intervening to stop the war by joining the Allies if the Germans refused to accept the joint proposals of the Allies and the United States.[10]

On December 28 House had sailed for Europe to effectuate his plan of intervention.[1] A fortnight later, Wilson cabled him that the *Lusitania* case appeared close to settlement and that a popular demand for an embargo or retaliatory measures against the British for interfering with American trade with neutral countries was insistent.[2] House countered with the plea that Wilson maintain conditions unchanged as long as possible. In a postscript the Colonel stated, " Of course I do not mean to advise that diplomatic relations should not be immediately broken if the Central Powers sink another passenger ship without warning. If this were not done, it would discredit us everywhere and greatly minimize your influence." [3] Apparently Wilson's influence with the Allies was proportioned to his commitment to join them in the war. Any measure to stay out would, in House's and Page's view, forfeit his influence with the Allied governments. It seems not to have occurred to anyone that his position as a trusted mediator, the role Wilson spasmodically yearned for, might be made impossible, even with his friends, by manifest partiality.

Colonel House left England for Germany on January 20.[4] He left Germany with a feeling that his mission had failed and a belief that Germany would insist on the submarine blockade of Great Britain.[5] While in Paris in the early days of February, he conferred with high French officials and apparently promised American intervention if Allied fortunes ebbed.[6]

---

[10] *Idem*, pp. 90–91.
[1] *Idem*, p. 114.
[2] *Idem*, p. 131.

[3] *Idem*, p. 134.
[4] *Idem*, p. 135.
[5] *Idem*, pp. 145–146.

[6] *Idem*, p. 163; to Briand and Cambon. On Feb. 10 Colonel House had recognized the possibility of two alternatives to end the war: (a) " The United States might wait until the Germans withdrew their submarine promise, and enter the war upon the submarine issue," or (b) " The President might de-

On his return to London he devoted his efforts to the realization of his plan and the appropriate timing of American intervention. Success crowned House's efforts on February 22, when he evolved with Sir Edward Grey his remarkable plan for American intervention in the European war if Germany failed to accept terms pleasing to the Allies, a scheme as novel as it was unneutral.[7]

Into this fraternal atmosphere burst Lansing's proposal on armed merchantmen. Although engrossed in other matters, House nevertheless found opportunity to gather British opinions against disarming merchantmen.[8] He was much annoyed at the Lansing proposal, and on his way back to America on March 4 he complained " that the President and Lansing " had largely interfered with his efforts for American intervention in Europe. He says that " if they had held the situation quiescent, as I urged them to do, I am sure the plan for intervention by the United States to end the war would have gone through without trouble. I am deeply disappointed but I hope matters can be ironed out in a way to yet make the plan possible." [9] The prospect of settling an issue with Germany so as to avert American intervention seemed to the

---

mand a peace conference and, if Germany refused the ' reasonable ' terms which would be offered, the United States would enter the War to enforce them." *Idem*, p. 170. Thus " America could say, '. . . we have come to help in a war to end war. But when the victory is won, we shall insist that you join with us to make a peace of justice and security and not of revenge or selfish profit.' " *Idem*, pp. 170–171.

[7] *Idem*, p. 164, report to Wilson.

[8] Seymour, *op. cit.*, II, 190–192..He asked Lord Bryce for a letter giving his argument against disarming merchantmen so that it might be presented to the President with other arguments. Colonel House suggested to Lord Loreburn, " that it was a war, as far as Great Britain was concerned, to prevent a few selfish individuals from plunging the world into war for their own purposes. I thought if he would strike this high note, it would hurt militarism in Germany and would make clear the purposes of the Allies." *Idem*, p. 193.

Bryce supplied the conclusive argument against disarming merchantmen by saying that German promises as to submarine action could not be trusted. *Idem*, p. 211.

[9] *Idem*, pp. 218–219.

good Colonel an improper interference with his splendid efforts.[10]

On February 16, Mr. Lansing sent another circular to American diplomatic officers in Europe,[1] in which he reiterated his impression that an armed merchant vessel is presumptively armed for offensive purposes if it carries an armament making it superior offensively to the submarine, now a recognized naval weapon, and expressed the hope that the Allies would accept the *modus vivendi* proposed in January. He added, however,

there was no present intention to warn Americans from travelling on belligerent merchantmen armed with guns solely for the purpose of defense; that, if Americans should lose their lives in attack by submarines without warning, upon merchantmen so armed, it will be necessary to record the offense as a breach of international law.[2]

Mr. Lansing seemed unaware of the inconsistency of this position, possibly due to his belief that international law granted an immunity to an armed merchantman from hostile attack, although he conceded the impropriety under present conditions of any such rule. Furthermore, he was in error in believing that there ever had been such a rule, though this government had founded its entire case on the assumption that such a rule existed.

After Colonel House returned from England he had his first conference with Wilson and Lansing on March 6.[3] At this conference he explained the Allied position on the disarmament of their merchant ships. The President apologized

[10] Mr. Balfour had appropriately conditioned Colonel House as to the unfortunate results of disarming merchantmen. *Idem*, pp. 211–214. On Sept. 12, 1915, Balfour evidently had received intimations of the prospective change in the State Department's rules as to armed merchantmen and informed Colonel House of the unwisdom of making such a change. Colonel House was duly impressed. *Idem*, pp. 211–214.

[1] *For. Rel.*, 1916, Suppl., p. 170.

[2] *Idem*, p. 170.

[3] Seymour, *op. cit.*, II, 199.

by blaming himself and Lansing for allowing the issue to have been raised. Lansing then had to find a way out. Availing himself of the Austro-German declaration of February 10 that they would consider armed merchantmen after March 1 as no longer " peaceable vessels of commerce " [4] — precisely what he had himself suggested — and of the allegation that German officials had misunderstood him, he announced America's withdrawal from the policy of January 18, 1916.[5] It was an awkward dilemma. He had admitted he was wrong, and then was obliged by political exigencies doggedly to persist in the error. Mr. Lansing is doubtless correct in saying that the Allied governments lost a great opportunity in rejecting his *modus vivendi*.[6] Not only would many lives have been saved, but had Germany failed to observe the agreement not to sink unarmed ships before making provision for the safety of passengers and crew, she might have aroused neutral opinion to take arms against her. Possibly Lansing does not intend to imply that the *modus vivendi* would have been a more effective agent for intervention than the then current confusion. But he is wrong in believing that " the strict letter of the law " supported either the British or the American position, for, as already observed, the suggestion that armed merchantmen had an immunity from sinking at sight defies both common sense and law. It was a delusion which the Allied propaganda sedulously purveyed in the name of humanity and to which the current emotion in the East for intervention under righteous pretenses made the general public susceptible.[7] Hysteria took the place of law.

[4] *For. Rel.*, 1916, Suppl., pp. 166–167.
[5] *Idem*, pp. 223–224; Lansing, *Memoirs*, p. 110.
[6] *Idem*, p. 110.
[7] The British general, Sir Henry F. Thuillier, K.C.B., addressing the Royal United Service Institution in London, Feb. 5, 1936, remarked, in speaking of the false sentimentality attached to certain projects for limiting the use of submarines against surface ships: " Take the case of submarines: does any one really think it more humane to be killed by a shell from a battleship than by a torpedo from a submarine? Or that if a ship is sunk and yourself drowned you will suffer more if the cause is a torpedo from

The Gore-McLemore Resolutions

THE momentary effort to restore American neutrality by retracting an error, the consternation this aroused in interventionist circles, and the successful campaign to induce the return to error, had produced a confusion of counsels not altogether without its amusing features. In spite of the arguments employed by Lansing to prove the inconsistency between the American position of 1914, on armed merchantmen, and the further insistence on their immunity from submarine attack, President Wilson nevertheless declined to draw the natural inference that if armed merchantmen were subject to submarine attack, American citizens on such vessels were obviously exposed to the same danger. At Topeka on February 2, 1916, in the Preparedness Campaign, the President had urged the need to protect and safeguard " the rights of Americans no matter where they might be in the world." [8] In a letter of February 24, 1916,[1] to Senator Stone, Wilson pictured the right of American citizens to travel unmolested on armed belligerent merchantmen as a matter of national " honor," fundamental " principle," and " of the very essence of the things that have made America a sovereign nation." To yield on that point he regarded as a confession of " impotency as a Nation " and a " surrender " of American independence.[2]

The introduction of the Gore-McLemore Resolutions in

---

a submarine than if it is shell fire from a battleship? Obviously not. The objection to submarines is that they can effect surprise and are difficult to guard against. This is very unpleasant for the bigger ship surprised. The submarine is the weapon of the weaker naval Power and tends to equalize the power of navies. Obviously the stronger Power with superiority in battleships would like to abolish them. But this has nothing to do with inhumanity — We are apt to look at such things as inhumane when others use them against us, but not when we use them against others." *Journal* (of the Institute), May, 1936, p. 266.

[8] Dodd and Baker, *Public Papers of Woodrow Wilson*, II, 89.

[1] *For. Rel.,* 1916, Suppl., p. 177.

[2] Dodd and Baker, *op. cit.,* II, 89.

February, 1916,[3] warning American citizens against taking passage on armed belligerent merchantmen, although approved, according to Speaker Clark's statement to the President, by a majority in Congress, was firmly opposed by the administration. The President summoned the Congressional leaders on February 21 and made the defeat of the resolutions a matter of personal prestige. Many members became convinced that the President would insist on the right of American citizens to travel unmolested on armed belligerent merchantmen, even at the risk of war. To clarify the issue Senator Stone wrote the President on February 24, giving his version of the conference of the twenty-first:

I have stated my understanding of your attitude to be substantially as follows:

That while you would deeply regret the rejection by Great Britain of Mr. Lansing's proposal . . . you were of the opinion that if Great Britain and her allies rejected the proposal and insisted upon arming her merchant ships she would be within her right under international law.

Also that you would feel disposed to allow armed vessels to be cleared from our ports; also that you are not favorably disposed to the idea of this Government taking any definite steps toward preventing American citizens from embarking upon armed merchant vessels.

Furthermore that you would consider it your duty, if a German warship should fire upon an armed merchant vessel of the enemy upon which American citizens were passengers, to hold Germany to strict account.

*   *   *

I find it difficult for my sense of duty and responsibility to consent to plunge this Nation into the vortex of this world war because of the unreasonable obstinacy of any one of the powers upon the one hand, or, on the other hand, of foolhardiness, amount-

---

[3] The two resolutions differed somewhat. The Gore Resolution prohibited the issuance of passports to American citizens taking passage on belligerent vessels, and denied protection to those taking such passage without a passport. The McLemore Resolution provided for the issuance of a warning to Americans not to travel on armed commercial vessels of belligerent nationality.

ing to a sort of moral treason against the Republic, of our people recklessly risking their lives on armed belligerent ships. I can not escape the convictions that such would be so monstrous as to be indefensible.[4]

To this letter, the President immediately replied, in part, as follows:

. . . . But in any event our duty is clear. No nation, no group of nations, has the right, while war is in progress, to alter or disregard the principles which all nations have agreed upon in mitigation of the horrors and sufferings of war; and if the clear rights of American citizens should very unhappily be abridged or denied by any such action, we should, it seems to me, have in honor no choice as to what our own course should be.

For my own part, I cannot consent to any abridgment of the rights of American citizens in any respect. The honor and self-respect of the Nation is involved. We covet peace, and shall preserve it at any cost but the loss of honor. To forbid our people to exercise their rights for fear we might be called upon to vindicate them would be a deep humiliation indeed. It would be an implicit, all but an explicit, acquiescence in the violation of the rights of mankind everywhere and of whatever nation or allegiance. It would be a deliberate abdication of our hitherto proud position as spokesman, even amid the turmoil of war, for the law and the right. It would make everything this Government has attempted and everything that it has accomplished during this terrible struggle of nations meaningless and futile.

It is important to reflect that if in this instance we allowed expediency to take the place of principle the door would inevitably be opened to still further concessions. Once accept a single abatement of right, and many other humiliations would certainly follow, and the whole fine fabric of international law might crumble under our hands piece by piece. What we are contending for in this matter is of the very essence of the things that have made America a sovereign nation. She cannot yield them without conceding her own impotency as a Nation and making virtual surrender of her independent position among the nations of the world.[5]

---

[4] *Cong. Rec.*, LIII (Feb. 29, 1916), 3318; Turner, *Shall It Be Again?*, p. 106.

[5] *For. Rel.*, 1916, Suppl., pp. 177–178. Scott, ed.; *President Wilson's Foreign Policy*, pp. 177–178.

The Gore-McLemore Resolutions were duly defeated, a result which was hailed in Washington and London as a vindication of the President's position.[6] But it meant war. There is something tragic in making a moral issue out of a fundamental mistake. Wilson, of course, thought he was legally right and standing on solid ground. It exemplifies the tricks that emotionalism can play on intelligence. The solemnity of the avowal was inappropriate. Solemnity may well be evoked, however, by the painful consciousness that the President of the United States had by very poor advice been led into a blunder as preposterous as it was fatal.[7]

Had the President been really interested in the law and sought competent advice, he would have been told that Congress needed no legislation to accomplish its object; it was elementary law, as we shall see, that a person sailing under a foreign flag takes his legal position and protection from that flag and cannot look to his own country to protect him from the risks of his location on belligerent " territory." Contrary to Mr. Lansing's view that there was no legal authority in the President to issue such a warning,[8] the President merely had to announce the elementary rule of law, which requires no legislation to confirm it. Indeed, the only objection there is to legislation prohibiting or warning American citizens against taking passage on belligerent merchantmen or treating armed merchantmen as warships in our ports is that such legislation implies that this is not already established law.

The public as represented in Congress was for the most part really desirous of avoiding opportunities to enlist in a foreign war, and the Gore-McLemore Resolutions were a response to this demand. The objections, however, to the

[6] *For. Rel.*, 1916, Suppl., p. 202; Grattan, *op. cit.*, p. 336; Seymour, *op. cit.*, II, 217.
[7] See the comment of Representative Mondell in *Cong. Rec.*, LIII (Feb. 29, 1916), 3319.
[8] *Memoirs*, p. 115.

Lansing proposal of January 18, 1916, and President Wilson's determination to repudiate that proposal, caused the administration to concentrate all its pressure to bring about the defeat of the Gore-McLemore Resolutions which its own policy of January, 1918, had invited. The Congress tried to be neutral. The administration would not permit it.[1]

The Memorandum of March 4, 1916

THE method adopted to justify the withdrawal from the Lansing note of January 18, 1916, was to procure an opinion from special advisers to the effect that merchantmen were privileged to arm, that Marshall had so stated in the case of the *Nereide,* that merchantmen were privileged to resist capture, that since neutral goods on the enemy ship *Nereide* were not condemned, therefore passengers were equally exempt, that inasmuch as submarines could apparently not comply with the alleged rule of international law for bringing passengers and crew to safety before sinking a prize, the submarine would have to abandon its practice as a commerce destroyer; that if the United States admits that its citizens have not the right to travel on armed belligerent merchantmen to the extent of a public warning by Congress against such travel,

it will in the face of its own precedents, in effect consent to a change of international law which will result to the advantage of one belligerent and to the disadvantage of his adversaries. This would be unneutral. Furthermore it would be consenting to a change in international law during a war, a thing against which the United States has earnestly and steadily protested in other international questions that have arisen during the War.[2]

---

[1] *For. Rel.,* 1916, Suppl., p. 186; Millis, *The Road to War,* p. 267 *et seq.*
[2] *President Wilson's Foreign Policy,* Appendix, p. 411, Memorandum on the right of American citizens to travel upon armed merchant ships, transmitted to the Committee on Foreign Affairs of the House of Representatives, March 4, 1916.

The opinion denied the right to destroy any vessel without first providing for the safety of all persons on board, enemy as well as neutral; it held that the submarine warfare was illegal because entered on as a measure of reprisal; that the United States had an obligation not only to protect the lives but also the property of its citizens for, as Marshall said, the rights to travel and to transport goods are legally identical. Anything else, it was said, would be a voluntary surrender of the right of American citizens to trade with belligerents. The opinion ended with the statement that inasmuch as submarines cannot comply with the rules governing surface vessels, neutral governments cannot admit their right to destroy merchant vessels without warning,

in disregard of the requirements of international law, and especially of the one grounded on decency and humanity — the safety of innocent human life — without surrendering national self-respect and national sovereignty, which would be a betrayal of the national honor.

The United States Government cannot without such betrayal publicly warn its citizens to renounce their rights in the face of a belligerent threat to do an illegal act, for such warning would be in effect an admission of the right of submarines to destroy merchant vessels illegally.

This opinion is so vulnerable as hardly to warrant serious discussion. In the language of Justice Holmes, it is a " farrago of irrational irregularities throughout." [3] Some of its errors have already been noticed. In relying so heavily on Marshall's opinion in the *Nereide* case,[4] the opinion failed to observe that Marshall was dealing with a totally different situation from the one which was under consideration. The *Nereide* was an armed British merchant ship, which was chartered in 1812 by a Mr. Pinto, a neutral citizen of Buenos

[3] *Gast Realty and Investment Co.* v. *Schneider Granite Co.*, 240 U. S. 55, 59 (1916).
[4] 9 Cranch 388.

Aires, to carry him and his cargo from London to Buenos Aires. She had sailed under convoy but had become separated from her convoy. After an armed struggle, she was captured by an American privateer, as it was obviously not in the interest of a profit-sharing privateer to sink his prize. When the ship was brought into New York for adjudication the question was whether the neutral property of the charterer was to be condemned, because it had been carried on an armed belligerent ship.

What Justice Marshall had to say about the immunity from condemnation of the neutral cargo was conditioned on the facts of the case, namely, that the ship had been *captured* and not sunk. The mere placing of the neutral cargo on the armed belligerent ship did not expose it to condemnation after it came before the prize court, but he was extremely clear in pointing out what the special advisers had completely overlooked, namely, that if the ship had been sunk the neutral Mr. Pinto's cargo would have been legitimately sunk with it. He was exposed to all the risks that the ship incurred. The classic paragraph, the only one relevant to the liabilities of the *Nereide* and its cargo and passengers, had she been sunk, was omitted by the Department's advisers, by Senators Sutherland and Lodge, by Mr. Lansing and by others vitally concerned. That paragraph reads:

The Nereide has not that Centaur-like appearance which has been ascribed to her. She does not rove the ocean hurling the thunders of war while sheltered by the olive branch of peace. She is not composed in part of the neutral character of Mr. Pinto, and in part of the hostile character of her owner. She is an open and declared belligerent; claiming all the rights, and subject to all the dangers of the belligerent character.[5]

Justice Story considered that by placing himself under belligerent armed protection the neutral had resisted search

[5] *Idem,* p. 430.

of his cargo and for that reason should be deemed an enemy and condemned.[6] He also considered that in availing himself of the protection of armament the neutral took " all the chances and hazards of war." [7] Sailing under convoy constituted resistance to capture and exposed the cargo to condemnation even when brought in,[8] a view with which the British courts agreed.[9] Said Story, " He who puts his property on the issue of battle, must stand or fall by the event of the contest." [10]

Just how the experts happened to omit the only relevant paragraph from Chief Justice Marshall's opinion, relating to the risks that the ship and cargo ran of being sunk by the captor, may never be known. The extracts they did quote at length from Marshall's opinion had no relevance to the issue before them. Even Professor A. Pearce Higgins,[1] the British legal adviser, had pointed out that the rule of the Eleventh Hague Convention, to the effect that the crew of unarmed, captured enemy ships may be released on parole, did not apply to ships taking part in hostilities. Higgins said: " Crews who forcibly resist visit and capture cannot then claim to be released. They remain prisoners of war." [2] In case the crew

---

[6] This was the view of Lord Stowell in the *Fanny* (1814), Dobson, pp. 443, 448–449; cf. Moore, *Digest*, VII, 491. He expressed it as follows: " But if he, the neutral, puts his goods on board a ship of force, which he has every reason to presume will be defended against the enemy by that force, the case then becomes very different. He betrays an intention to resist visitation and search, which he could not do by putting them on board a mere merchant vessel, and so far as he does this he adheres to the belligerent; . . . If a party acts in association with a hostile force, and relies upon that force for protection, he is, *pro hac vice*, to be considered as an enemy. . . . If they choose to take the protection of a hostile force instead of their own neutral character, they must take the inconvenience with the convenience; they must abide by the consequences resulting from the course of conduct which . . . they have thought proper to pursue."

[7] *Idem*, p. 444.

[8] *Idem*, p. 448.

[9] The *Maria;* 1 C. Rob. 340 (1799).

[10] *Idem*, p. 453.

[1] S. Doc. 332, *supra*, p. 86.

[2] *Ibid.*

resist, " their potential membership turns into actual membership in the armed forces of their state and if overpowered they become prisoners of war." Obviously in the course of hostilities they and their ship may legally be sunk. They have " combatant privileges when resisting capture by an enemy warship." [3] Although the special advisers had evidently used the Higgins' opinion in preparing their report of March 4, they neglected to include these observations. They failed, too, to point out that the armed ship was " a ship of force," to use Lord Stowell's expression.[4] They also failed to point out Marshall's statement in the *Nereide* case, that it is impossible for a prize court to distinguish between different degrees of armament.

In the Senate, Messrs. Lodge, Sterling, and Sutherland relied on this opinion of Mr. Lansing's experts to break down Lansing's note of January 18 as well as the Gore-McLemore Resolutions. They relied largely on the same irrelevancy that attracted the special advisers, namely, that a merchant vessel had a privilege to arm. On this they firmly insisted. Inasmuch as no one disputed that, except possibly the Germans, the debate was peculiarly inappropriate and irrelevant. The real question as to the consequences incurred by such armament seems to have escaped the learned debaters. Senator Sterling and Senator Lodge were vigorous in defense of Great Britain and appealed touchingly to the dictates of humanity.[5]

In speaking of the omissions from the *Nereide* opinion, John Bassett Moore has recently said:

[3] *Idem*, p. 34. Even in Higgins' opinion, which was not an objective essay but was written to serve an official purpose, it had to be admitted that as to passengers on an armed ship which resists, " they will, naturally, have to take their chance of injury or death." Enclosure 6 in Instruction of Sir Edward Grey to Sir A. Johnstone, Minister to Holland, June 9, 1915, *A. J. I. L.,* XII, Suppl., p. 201.

[4] *Supra*, p. 120.

[5] *Cong. Rec.*, LIII (Feb. 18, 1916), 2760–2763. Senator Sutherland's quotation of the *Nereide* opinion on March 7, 1916, also omitted the famous paragraph. *Idem*, pp. 3660, 3662. See also Lodge, *The Senate and the League of Nations* (New York, 1925), p. 70 *et seq.*

Of Marshall's opinion in this famous case a garbled version was got out here, a version so false as to constitute practically a forgery; but it was widely disseminated, and was used in speeches even in Congress. I repeat that this version practically involved forgery, because it omitted from Marshall's opinion the passage in which it was declared that the ship, by reason of the fact that she was armed, was to be regarded as " an open and declared belligerent, claiming all the rights, and subject to all the dangers of the belligerent character."[6]

The State Department's Retreat

MARCH 25, 1916, the State Department completely withdrew from its unassailable position of January 18. Doubtless the Allied pressure could no longer be resisted. The new announcement,[7] prepared " by direction of the President," [8] required a belligerent's warship to determine the status, warlike or peaceful, of an armed enemy merchant vessel encountered at sea. Warlike character must rest not on presumption but upon conclusive evidence, arms apparently no longer constituting evidence of warlike character. Again the belligerent must, in the absence of " conclusive evidence of aggressive purpose " act on the presumption that an armed merchantman is of " private and peaceful " character, entitled to all the amenities of an unarmed vessel; an armed merchantman cannot be attacked without regard to the lives of persons on board, and conclusive evidence of a purpose to use the armament for aggression is essential; a warship on the high seas can test by experience the purpose of an armament and so determine by direct evidence the status of a vessel. The distinction between " offensive " and " defensive " armament, which Lansing had exposed as an illusion, was now revived in the fabulous contrast between merchantmen armed " for

[6] Memorandum to Senate Committee on Foreign Relations, Hearings on S. 3474, Committee on Foreign Relations, U. S. Senate, 74th Cong., 2d Sess., Jan. 10–Feb. 5, 1936, p. 185.

[7] For. Rel., 1916, Suppl., pp. 244–248.

[8] Hyde, op. cit., II, 468.

aggressive purposes " and " peaceable armed merchantmen." [9]

It seems hard to believe that such rules were intended to be taken seriously. Their invalidity had been demonstrated by the Department of State itself two months earlier. They must, therefore, be regarded as political rules, and they undoubtedly facilitated a *casus belli*. After Colonel House reached his agreement for intervention with Sir Edward Grey on February 22, 1916, he was scarcely interested in finding ways to escape war. Quite the contrary. The rules of March 25, 1916, were admirably designed to accomplish intervention if that was the aim, and, unhappily for the United States, the ground taken could hardly have been less sustainable.

Professor Hyde, commenting upon the errors of the memorandum of March 25, 1916, calls attention to the following oversights:

(a) It fails to heed the fact that the immunity of merchant vessels from attack at sight grew out of their impotency to endanger the safety of public armed vessels of an enemy, and that maritime States have never acquiesced in a principle that a merchant vessel so armed as to be capable of destroying a vessel of war of any kind should enjoy immunity from attack at sight, at least when encountering an enemy cruiser of inferior defensive strength.

(b) That an armed merchantman may retain its status as a private ship is not decisive of the treatment to which it may be subjected. The potentiality and special adaptability of the vessel to engage in hostile operations fraught with danger to the safety of an enemy vessel of war, rather than the designs or purposes of those in control of the former, however indicative of its character, have been and should be deemed the test of the right of the opposing belligerent to attack it at sight. In view of this fact the lawful presence on board the armed merchantman of neutral persons or property cannot give rise to a duty towards the ship not otherwise apparent. Every occupant thereof must be held to assume that the enemy will use every lawful but no unlawful means to subject the vessel to control or destroy it.

[9] *For. Rel.*, 1916, Suppl., pp. 246–247.

(c) To test the propriety of an attack at sight by the existence of conclusive proof of the aggressive purpose of the merchantman places an unreasonable burden on a vessel of war of an unprotected type, whether a surface or undersea craft, for no evidence of the requisite purposes of the merchantman may be in fact obtainable until the vessel of war encountering the former becomes itself the object of attack. The mere pursuit of the merchantman, prior to any signal made to it, may cause the vessel to attack the pursuer as soon as it gets within range.

What constitutes, moreover, an act by way of defense must always remain a matter of uncertainty. The possession of substantial armament encourages the possessor to assert or claim that it acts defensively whenever it opens fire. Thus in practice the distinction between the offensive and defensive use of armament disappears, for the armed merchantman is disposed to exercise its power whenever it can safely do so. To presume, therefore, that such a vessel has a "peaceable character," on the supposition that it will not when occasion offers open fire on vulnerable vessels of war of the enemy, is to ignore an inference fairly deducible from the conduct of vessels equipped with effective means of committing hostile acts.

It is believed, therefore, that the equipment of a belligerent merchant marine for hostile service, even though designed to be defensive rather than offensive, serves, on principle, to deprive the armed vessels of the right to claim immunity from attack without warning.[10]

[10] Hyde, *op. cit.*, II, 469–472.

III.

AMERICANS ON UNARMED BELLIGERENT MERCHANTMEN

EARLY in the war, pressure exerted by Great Britain to prevent the importation of any goods whatever into Germany, whether contraband or noncontraband, by rationing the neighboring neutrals and obliging them to impose export embargoes on their own citizens indicated that the war was to be fought in disregard of neutral rights. In retaliation, the German Government announced on February 4, 1915, its so-called " submarine blockade " around Great Britain and Ireland, and stated that " all enemy merchant vessels found in those waters after the eighteenth instant [Feb. 18, 1915] will be destroyed although it may not always be possible to save crews and passengers." The German Admiralty added that " neutral vessels expose themselves to danger within this zone of war " because " of the misuse of the neutral flag ordered by the British Government on January thirty-first," and that because " of the contingencies of maritime warfare . . . neutral vessels [might] suffer from attacks intended to strike enemy ships." [1]

An explanatory memorandum of February 7th stated that the British Government had carried on mercantile warfare against Germany " in a way that defies all the principles of international law." It pointed out that the rules of the Declaration of London had been effectively repudiated by British Orders in Council, and that by extending the contraband lists beyond all precedent Great Britain had undertaken to abolish the distinction between absolute and conditional contraband and to seize goods conditionally contraband when destined to neutral ports. Furthermore, the Declaration of

[1] *For. Rel.*, 1915, Suppl., p. 94.

Paris had been violated by the seizure of German noncontraband property on neutral vessels, and German nationals had been taken off neutral vessels and made prisoners of war. In sum, the North Sea had been declared a British war zone and neutral coasts and ports had been blockaded. These measures, it was stated, were designed not merely to strike at German military strength, but to paralyze legitimate neutral commerce, to strangle the economic life of Germany, and to accomplish the starvation of the German people.

Germany charged the neutral governments with acquiescing in these illegal steps by failing to induce their retraction. Moreover, they had aided the British measures in other respects by placing " export and transit embargoes " on peaceful goods. Consequently, the German Government stated that it could not be expected any longer to observe strictly the Declaration of London if Great Britain was to continue to violate it and " neutral powers were to continue to acquiesce in these violations of neutrality to the detriment of Germany." The German Government also pointed out that Great Britain was pleading her " vital interests " as an excuse for these violations, whereas neutral powers contented themselves with mere gestures of protest. The neutrals, it was said, seemed thus to accept the vital interests of belligerents as sufficient excuse for belligerent excesses. Therefore, to its regret, Germany felt impelled to appeal to those same vital interests to justify retaliatory war measures aimed at England; and in reprisal for the war zone between Scotland and Norway,[2] declared the waters around Great Britain and Ire-

[2] The British Government maintained that the laying of contact mines by German vessels around British ports, Aug. 7, 1914, was a violation of international law. Germany and France at The Hague in 1907 had reserved their liberty of action. If the mines did not become harmless when adrift, illegality was probably assertable. The British adopted mine-laying in October, 1914, as a countermeasure. In view of the continuance of German mine-laying on the trade routes, Britain then, on Nov. 5, 1914, declared the whole North Sea a " military area " in which all vessels were exposed to danger from mines and warships. Cf. K. Mori, *Submarines in War* (Tokyo, 1931), pp. 12–15.

land a war zone, " and thus will proceed against the shipping of the enemy."

It was announced that commencing February 18 Germany would endeavor " to destroy every enemy merchant ship that is found in this area of war without its always being possible to avert the peril that thus threatens persons and cargoes. Neutrals are therefore warned against further entrusting crews, passengers and wares to such ships." The German Government announced that it gave early notice of these measures so that shipping might accommodate itself accordingly by landing at ports, and it hoped that neutral powers " will show no less consideration for the vital interests of Germany than for those of England and will aid in keeping their citizens and the property of the latter from this area. This is the more to be expected, as it must be to the interest of the neutral powers to see this destructive war end as soon as possible."

The Norwegian and Swedish Governments had, on November 5, protested against the closing of the North Sea by Great Britain as a " military area," [3] because all neutral shipping would thus be forced through the English Channel. In this protest the Norwegian Government had asked the United States to join with other neutrals. On November 10, however, the State Department declined.[4]

When Germany announced the retaliatory war zone around Great Britain, however, the United States was adamant. It flatly refused to acquiesce in the German declaration or to concede to a warship any departures from the restrictions incidental to the right of visit and search. Had the United States confined itself to protesting the possible destruction

---

[3] The Dutch Government also protested, but tacitly recognized the belligerent right to lay mines on the high seas, merely disputing the area. Mori, *op. cit.*, pp. 14–15. The German war zone proclamation of Feb. 4 was also contested only as " much too extensive." *For. Rel.*, 1915, Suppl., p. 97.

[4] *For. Rel.* 1914, Suppl., p. 466.

of American vessels and of human beings on American vessels, its position would have been legally privileged and probably unexceptionable. The only questions then would have been whether acquiescence in the British illegalities required an acquiescence in the German retaliatory measures and whether the mere protests to Great Britain without effective enforcement constituted a defense to the charge of acquiescence. It is in precisely such circumstances that the correct conduct of the neutral is put to its greatest test and it was the skilful handling of situations like these that enabled Holland and the Scandinavian countries to avoid giving either party a ground for asserting that the attitude of those governments was unneutral.

The United States' note [5] categorically denied Germany the right to attack and destroy any belligerent vessel within a prescribed war zone without first ascertaining its belligerent nationality and the contraband character of its cargo. To do otherwise, it was said, would be an act so unprecedented that in effect the United States would not tolerate it. Even the suspicion that enemy ships were using neutral flags improperly would not create a presumption that all ships traversing the war zone were subject to the same suspicion. By demanding that under all circumstances the right of visit and search must be exercised, the United States proposed to cripple the effective use of the submarine as a commerce destroyer.

Furthermore the note denied that the United States was guilty of the unneutral action with which the German Government charged " certain other neutral nations "; the United States had not acquiesced in measures taken by the Allied governments in restraint of neutral trade but, on the contrary, had taken a position which " warrants it in holding those governments responsible in the proper way for any untoward effects upon American shipping which the accepted principles of international law do not justify." Its uncompromising po-

[5] *For. Rel.*, 1915, Suppl., p. 98.

sition toward Germany was therefore considered entirely proper. A solemn warning was issued against the destruction of any American vessel or of American lives, and the Germans were warned that the United States would hold them to a " strict accountability " for such acts of their naval authorities. Finally assurance was demanded that " American citizens and their vessels will not be molested . . . otherwise than by visit and search."

On the same day the Department protested to Great Britain the use of the American flag by British merchant vessels and called special attention to the fact that it had received reports that the captain of the *Lusitania*, acting under British Government orders, had raised the American flag as his vessel approached the Irish coast.[6] The note conceded the validity, however, of the occasional use of a neutral flag as a *ruse de guerre*, and thereby it defeated its whole purpose. The ruse de guerre doctrine cannot be regarded as according a privilege to use neutral flags promiscuously in dangerous waters. Such general misuse of a neutral flag would jeopardize all neutral vessels. Thus the American concession of an exception amounted to a waiver of the rule and an acquiescence in a continuing British offense against the United States.[7]

The British were not remiss in taking advantage of this loophole; in fact, with their usual foresight, they had anticipated, if indeed they had not suggested, the American concession. Even before dispatch of the American request that they " restrain vessels of British nationality from the deceptive use of the flag of the United States," the British Foreign Office had defended the use of neutral flags in a press communication.[8] It was not surprising, therefore, that on Feb-

---

[6] Colonel House was on the *Lusitania* on Feb. 5 when she hoisted the American flag, and realized that " many possible complications " might thus arise. Seymour, *op. cit.*, I, 361.

[7] *For. Rel.*, 1915, Suppl., p. 100. See proposed Code of Naval Warfare, Art. 17 (b), Int. Law Assn., p. 1920; Mori, *op. cit.*, pp. 19–20.

[8] *Idem*, p. 97. The Dutch Government also protested against such " an abuse."

ruary 20 the British Government categorically refused to abandon the practice.[1]

Meanwhile, on February 17, the German Government sent a long answer to the American note of February 10. It disclaimed any intention " ever to destroy neutral lives and neutral property," and reiterated its purpose to sink only " enemy merchant vessels " in the war zone — not all merchant vessels, as the Germans said the United States appeared to have erroneously assumed. The alleged reason for the measure was self-defense against the British impositions which threatened the German people with starvation because of the failure of neutral governments to obtain any relinquishment of British illegal measures. The United States was again urged to bring Great Britain back to the observance of international law so as " to render possible for Germany the legitimate supply of foodstuffs and industrial raw materials," whereupon the German Government would " draw the necessary conclusions from the new situation thus created." [2] The Germans protested particularly against the unrestricted trade in absolute contraband directly between neutrals and England while trade even in noncontraband goods with the continental neutrals was cut off. Although they did not charge a resulting " formal breach of neutrality," they called attention nevertheless to the desirability of the neutrals stopping the trade in contraband, " especially the trade in arms, with Germany's enemies." [3] Claiming to have hitherto observed strictly the rules of international law, the German Government now saw itself " compelled after six months of patience and watchful waiting to meet England's murderous method of conducting maritime war with drastic counter measures." The neutrals that had submitted to the detrimental consequences of England's war of famine were again asked to display no less tolerance toward German measures, even

[1] *Idem*, p. 117.
[2] *For. Rel.*, 1915, Suppl., pp. 112–114.
[3] *Idem*, p. 113.

if those constituted " new forms of maritime war, as has hitherto been the case with the English measures." Voicing its determination to suppress as far as possible " the supply of war material to England and her allies," Germany assumed that neutral governments which had taken no action to suppress such traffic " do not intend to oppose the forcible suppression of this trade by Germany." With respect to the contemplated " blockade " of the British Isles, the Germans offered to " accord in conjunction with the American Government, the most earnest consideration to any measure that might be calculated to insure the safety of legitimate shipping of neutrals within the seat of war." In the light of American protests against the misuse of the neutral flag, German submarines had been instructed to " abstain from violence to American merchant vessels when they are recognizable as such." It was suggested however that the United States convoy American ships carrying peaceable cargoes in order to assure their being recognizable. Furthermore only ships carrying noncontraband should be convoyed, a matter which they hoped to negotiate. The Germans reaffirmed the " scrupulous consideration for neutrals hitherto practised by them " and stated that the present measures were taken " only under the strongest compulsion of national self-preservation." [4]

The fact that the German Government on January 26, 1915, had placed all foodstuffs under German Government control [5] had been advanced by Great Britain as a justification for regarding all foodstuffs as destined for military use. " All food, in effect, belongs to the Army." Thus the jaws of the " starvation blockade " were closed further, despite the fact that government control of food supplies during a shortage, as in the French Revolutionary Wars, is a well-recognized means of assuring an equitable distribution to all the population. But again Britain had made a plausible argument, and

[4] *Idem,* p. 115.   [5] *For. Rel.,* 1915, Suppl., p. 317.

America accepted it as gospel.[6] The seizure of food cargoes, even when destined to neutral countries, soon became an established British practice and was officially confirmed by the retaliatory Order in Council of March 11, 1915.

On February 20, the United States proposed a compromise by which both Germany and Great Britain would agree to refrain from sowing floating mines and from attacking by submarine any merchant vessels except to enforce the right of visit and search; neither belligerent was to misuse neutral flags as a ruse de guerre; foodstuffs from the United States would, through the coöperation of an American agency in Germany, be controlled for civilian use, and Great Britain would agree not to make foodstuffs absolute contraband and not to interfere with them if consigned to the designated agencies in Germany.[7]

Page dragged his feet in presenting this proposal to the British and settled its fate. Mr. Gerard in Berlin on the other hand actively endeavored to obtain its adoption.[8] Germany suggested modification of the proposal to include raw materials as well as food — materials which Mr. Gerard had stated were needed for industry only, and not for war purposes. The British, however, refused to adopt the American proposal or even to negotiate. Thereupon Colonel House endeavored to evolve another compromise which he entitled " Freedom of the Seas." He suggested:

. . . The contraband list should be restricted so as to include only actual implements of warfare; everything else should be placed upon the free list. The trade of merchant vessels, whether belligerent or neutral, should be allowed to proceed freely outside territorial waters so long as they carried no contraband. They might even enter any belligerent port without hindrance, unless that port were actually and effectively blockaded by the enemy's fleet.[9]

---

[6] Jefferson refused to concede this British argument when applied to France in 1793. *Infra*, p. 201.

[7] *For. Rel.*, 1915, Suppl., p. 120.

[8] Compare Grattan, *op. cit.*, pp. 235–241.

[9] Seymour, *op. cit.*, I, 406.

The Colonel was certainly optimistic in believing that the early American proposal for the immunity from capture of enemy private property at sea, including belligerent vessels carrying noncontraband outside territorial waters, might be adopted by Great Britain. But his first suggestion to restrict the contraband list to lethal weapons was historically sound. The privilege of neutral vessels to trade in noncontraband with nonblockaded ports of the enemy was equally unassailable. Great Britain, however, was not interested in any modification of its plan to stop trade which could reach Germany directly or by way of neighboring neutral countries. Whether the submarine and the airplane will eventually persuade Great Britain to perceive a greater self-interest in the freedom of the seas remains to be seen.

The collapse of the proposed American compromise, the intransigent attitude of Great Britain, combined with the refusal of the United States to accept any of the German suggestions and its insistence on the other hand on holding Germany to " strict accountability " for the safety of American life and property, even on belligerent merchantmen, created an impasse which was bound to lead to trouble.

On March 28 the British steamship *Falaba,* carrying passengers and munitions, was torpedoed in the Irish Sea while en route to West Africa. A considerable number of lives were lost, including that of one American, Leon Thrasher. There had been a warning given; the vessel started to escape, sent out a wireless message that " German submarine was following flying British colors " [10] — an allegation expressly denied by Germany [1] — and finally decided to stop and abandon ship as ordered, after receiving a second warning that otherwise it would be fired upon. It is uncertain just how soon thereafter the torpedo was launched — the testimony variously places the time as between 7 and 23 minutes.[2] There

---

[10] *For. Rel.,* 1915, Suppl., p. 363.
[1] *Idem,* p. 370.
[2] *Idem,* p. 419. Cf. 251 Fed. 715 (1918).

was also evidence to show that the approach of other vessels prompted the submarine commander to hasten the destruction of the ship. No American protest was made at once.

For the sake of chronology, mention should be made here of attacks on two American vessels. On April 29, the steamship *Cushing* was attacked by a German airplane, but no lives were lost and little damage was done. It subsequently developed that the vessel was improperly marked. On May 1, the tanker *Gulflight* was torpedoed off the Scilly Islands but remained afloat. The captain died of heart failure and two of the crew were reported to have jumped overboard. She was apparently following two British patrol boats and had been in communication with one of them. The Germans stated that they assumed she was an enemy vessel under convoy. In the course of the resulting diplomatic correspondence the Germans offered compensation for the attack.[3] It should be observed that the *Gulflight* was the only American vessel torpedoed with loss of life from the beginning of the submarine war down to February 3, 1917, when diplomatic relations with Germany were severed.

Secretary Bryan foresaw the coming of a crisis even before the *Lusitania* was sunk on May 7, 1915. In April the Department had under consideration the sending of a sharp note to Germany protesting the *Falaba* sinking. Mr. Bryan feared that this note might " inflame the already hostile feeling against us in Germany." He realized that the attitude of the United States toward the two belligerents had been quite different — not to speak of the difference in attitude of the two belligerents toward the United States. He feared that the denunciation of the practice of the one and what he called " silence "[4] as to the other " will be construed by some as partiality."

---

[3] *For. Rel.*, 1915, Suppl., pp. 378, 381, 397, 419 *et seq.*
[4] This was not quite accurate, for formal but weak protests had been filed.

Mr. Bryan's letter to Mr. Wilson is so full of common sense that it deserves to be reproduced at length:

As I have not been able to reach the same conclusion to which you have arrived in this case, I feel it my duty to set forth the situation as I see it. The note which you propose will, I fear, very much inflame the already hostile feeling against us in Germany, not entirely because of our protest against Germany's action in this case, but in part because of its contrast with our attitude toward the Allies. If we oppose the use of the submarine against merchantmen we will lay down a law for ourselves as well as Germany. If we admit the right of the submarine to attack merchantmen but condemn their particular act or class of acts as inhuman we will be embarrassed by the fact that we have not protested against Great Britain's defense of the right to prevent foods reaching non-combatant enemies.

We suggested the admission of food and the abandonment of torpedo attacks upon merchant vessels. Germany seemed willing to negotiate, but Great Britain refused to consider the proposition. I fear that denunciation of one and silence as to the other will be construed by some as partiality. You do not make allowance for the fact that we were notified of the intended use of the submarine, or for the fact that the deceased knowingly took the risk of traveling on an enemy ship. I cannot see that he is differently situated from those who by remaining in a belligerent country assume risk of injury. Our people will, I believe, be slow to admit the right of a citizen to involve his country in war when by exercising ordinary care he could have avoided danger.

The fact that we have not contested Great Britain's assertion of the right to use our flag has still further aggravated Germany and we cannot overlook the fact that the sale of arms and ammunition, while it could not be forbidden under neutrality, has worked so entirely for the benefit of one side as to give to Germany — not justification but an excuse for charging that we are favoring the Allies. I have mentioned these things to show the atmosphere through which the Thrasher note will be received by Germany.

Believing that such a note as you propose is, under the conditions that now exist, likely to bring on a crisis, I venture to suggest an alternative, namely, an appeal to the nations at war to consider terms of peace. We cannot justify waiting until both sides, or even one side, asks for mediation. As a neutral we cannot have in mind the wishes of one side more than the wishes of the other side. . . .[5]

Bryan had continually urged, after receipt of the German submarine note of February 4, 1915, that American citizens be warned against traveling on belligerent ships. That they incurred the risks of their location is a self-evident rule of law. It was unfortunate when Mr. Wilson refused to accept Mr. Bryan's suggestion in the *Falaba* case; it was disastrous when he failed to realize that there was no precedent or legal warrant for a neutral to protect a *belligerent* ship from attack by its enemy because it happened to have on board American citizens. The exclusive jurisdiction of the country of the vessel's flag, to which all on board are subject, is an unchallengeable rule of law. By failing to observe it the United States went out of its way to court trouble.

The repeated protestations of Secretary Bryan against permitting Americans to travel on belligerent ships were not without some effect. Mr. Lansing practically admitted the correctness of that view. And yet because of the implied admission that the United States had waited too long in warning its citizens and by its silence had allowed them to believe that they had a legal right to be on belligerent vessels and to be protected by the United States in the enjoyment of that right, Lansing preferred to refrain from issuing any warning. Rather than admit the error tardily and raise the inference that he had failed in his duty months before, he preferred to suppress the admission. And this mistake was fatal. On May 9, 1915, in opposing Mr. Bryan's desire to warn American citizens against traveling on belligerent ships, Mr. Lansing stated:

[5] *Memoirs of William Jennings Bryan*, pp. 396–397. This wise injunction might be read in the light of the agreement concluded Feb. 22, 1916, by Colonel House with Sir Edward Grey providing for " probable " American intervention. *Supra*, p. 38.

After carefully considering the suggestion I am convinced that this Government is in no position to adopt the view. To accept it would be to admit that the Government of the United States failed in its duty to its own citizens and permitted them to run risks without attempting to prevent them from doing so.

. . . this Government has permitted in silence hundreds of American citizens to travel by British steamships crossing the " war zone." It has by its silence allowed them to believe that their Government approved and would stand behind them in case their legal rights were invaded.

I do not see how this Government can avoid responsibility now by asserting that an American in traveling by a British vessel took a risk, which he should not have taken. If it held that point of view it should have declared it at the time it protested against the " war zone." [6]

Again, five days later he argued:

Do you not think that, if this notice is given, it will be said " Why did the Government not give this notice before? Why did it wait after the sinking of the *Falaba, Cushing* [*sic.*] and *Gulflight* until a hundred Americans lost their lives on the *Lusitania?* " Even admitting that the effect on the German Government might be beneficial in influencing their reply, I think that the criticism in this country must be considered. It is a matter of policy which must be viewed from every standpoint.[7]

To Mr. Wilson, the final arbiter in the matter, Lansing's arguments seemed " unanswerable." [8]

In July, 1915, Mr. Lansing became much concerned by receipt of a printed circular indicating that the British consul in Shanghai in 1904 had warned British subjects at the outbreak of the Russo-Japanese War that " the British Government will not undertake to be responsible for the safety of

[6] Lansing to Bryan, May 9, 1915, Savage, *op. cit.*, II, Doc. No. 77, pp. 309, 310.

[7] *Idem*, Doc. No. 85, pp. 318–319.

[8] *Idem*, Doc. No. 83, pp. 314–315.

any British subject leaving this port on a ship of either of the belligerent nations." [9] The British Government, asked by Ambassador Page to establish the authenticity of this warning, claimed that it could not be verified and that it was "extremely unlikely" that any warning was issued.[1] The disclaimer is not as satisfactory as might be desired.

The suggestion of warning American citizens off belligerent ships seems to have become repulsive to Mr. Lansing, and one cannot but wonder whether his oversight in not warning them in the beginning that they were on belligerent vessels at their own risk did not contribute to his aversion. In his *Memoirs* he says that such a warning

would have been contrary to the dignity of the United States and would have been justly condemned by Americans in general, who were, as they always have been, jealous of their rights on the high seas, and who believed that it would be pusillanimous for our government not to insist that those rights should be respected whatever might be the consequences of such insistence.[2]

But, in truth, it was only after American citizens had been misinformed on the law that they became subject to such illusions. Yet Secretary Lansing assures us that President Wilson was of the same mind and "took the position that he could not assume so humiliating an attitude." [3] Mr. Lansing admits that the argument for keeping American citizens off belligerent vessels appealed to the average man as "reasonable." When he adds that "the trouble was that the adoption of the policy would not have solved the difficulty because the submarine controversy would have gone on just the same, the subject being loss of property instead of loss of life," [4] he overlooks the fact that both he and President Wilson had

[9] *For. Rel.*, 1915, Suppl., p. 480.
[1] *Idem*, p. 491.
[2] Lansing, *Memoirs*, p. 115.
[3] *Idem*, p. 116. See also Wilson's letter of Feb. 24, 1916, to Senator Stone. *For. Rel.*, 1916, Suppl., p. 177.
[4] Lansing, *op. cit.*, p. 115.

made the loss of life, as distinguished from the loss of property, the one ostensibly irrefutable reason why the United States had to enter the war. The President was to state, in his War Message of April 2, 1917: " Property can be paid for; the lives of peaceful and innocent people can not be." [5]

If, then, Bryan's sensible and thoroughly legal suggestion had been followed, instead of rejected, the one great justification alleged for entering the war, the loss of American life, would have been wanting. The rejection of Bryan's plea for common sense was therefore crucial to the ultimate dénouement.

Mr. Lansing's further statement that " there was no authority in law for the President to issue such a prohibition or warning to American citizens," [6] overlooks the fact already pointed out that legislation to confirm an elementary rule of law is not needed. And even if Lansing had been correct as to the necessity for legislative authority, it is extremely difficult to reconcile that argument with the administration's refusal to let Congress pass such a law in 1916, although it was manifestly desired by those who wished to remain out of the war.

This attitude of Mr. Lansing and the President, coupled with the ultimata to Germany in the *Lusitania* notes,[7] brought about Mr. Bryan's resignation. In 1935, Congress found nothing humiliating in passing a statute to the effect that American citizens travel on belligerent merchantmen at their own risk,[8] nor was Senator Pittman conscious of any abdication of American pride or honor in proposing in his recent bill an absolute prohibition against such travel.[9] On January 5, 1916, similar resolutions had been introduced in Congress

[5] *For. Rel.*, 1917, Suppl. I, 195, 196.
[6] Lansing, *op. cit.*, p. 115.
[7] *Infra*, pp. 145, 150.
[8] Neutrality Resolution, Aug. 31, 1935, Pub. Res. 67, 74th Cong., 1st Sess.
[9] Pittman Resolution, Jan. 22, 1937, S. J. Res. 51, Sec. 6-A, 75th Cong., 1st Sess.

looking toward the enactment of the Bryan policy.[1] Lansing's own words adequately describe their reception:

The Senate resolution, introduced by Senator Gore of Oklahoma, prohibited the issuance of passports to American citizens taking passage on vessels of the Allies, and denied protection by this government to any American who took such passage without a passport. The House resolution, fathered by Mr. McLemore, of Texas, provided for the issuance of a warning to Americans not to travel on armed commercial vessels of belligerent nationality. During the latter part of February these two resolutions were hotly debated in Congress and in the press and, while the supporters of the resolutions were vociferous, the strong opposition of the President, of the Administration leaders in both Houses, and of a large majority of the newspapers throughout the country swept aside the demands of those who urged the adoption of this policy of humiliation. The Senate resolution came to a vote on March third and resulted in its defeat by sixty-eight to fourteen; and on the seventh the McLemore resolution was rejected in the House by a two to one majority.[2]

The Lusitania

EARLY in April, 1915, certain German diplomats and sympathizers decided to issue a warning to American citizens against traveling through the war zone on vessels of the enemies of Germany. This decision was prompted by the fact that the American authorities had refused to issue such a warning despite Secretary Bryan's well-founded realization, which he could have fortified by legal argument, that American citizens took the risk of belligerent location and were not entitled to American protection when their vessel was attacked by its enemy. The German Embassy in Washington, therefore, prepared a notice for newspaper publication, warning American citizens that vessels flying the flag of Great

---

[1] 64th Cong., 1st Sess., S. 3033, S. 3034. See also the following: S. J. Res. 73, S. J. Res. 74, S. Con. Res., 14; H. Res. 143, H. Res. 147 (The McLemore Resolution).

[2] Lansing, *op. cit.*, p. 116. See also Millis, *op. cit.*, pp. 255–280.

Britain or her allies were liable to destruction in the waters adjacent to the British Isles and that travelers on such ships were there at their own risk.[3] The notice was dated April 22, but for some reason it did not appear until Saturday, May 1, the day when the British Cunard liner *Lusitania* sailed from New York for Liverpool. It seems that the notice was not directed against any particular ship. The *Lusitania*, the circumstances of whose construction have already been recited,[4] was torpedoed on May 7 off the southern coast of Ireland. She sank within eighteen minutes, carrying down 1198 persons — among them 128 American citizens.[5]

The sinking of a great passenger liner with so large a loss of life naturally created a sensation. In the light of the views that had already been expressed in Washington in connection with the sinking of belligerent merchantmen, armed and unarmed, and the administration's failure to distinguish between Americans lost on American ships and those lost on belligerent ships — as well as the fact that the orders given to British merchant ships to ram submarines and conduct hostile operations against them were either unknown to the Department of State or were ignored — it is not surprising that the *Lusitania* case brought into much sharper focus the positions that had been assumed in the proposed *Falaba* note.[6] The American officials did not stop long to inquire or note whether the *Lusitania* was armed, whether she carried munitions, what orders the captain had had, whether the Americans on board had assumed any risks, how the ship had been handled; nor were they concerned with the fact that it was a British ship they were seeking to defend from the activity of

[3] "The notice seemed necessary because the Department of State had refused to warn American citizens of their risks." The notice also appeared on Saturday, May 8, 1915. Bernstorff, *My Three Years in America* (1920), pp. 131, 139 and *infra*, p. 159.

[4] *Supra*, p. 92.

[5] Report of Secretary of State Hughes, March 31, 1922, S. Doc. 176, 67th Cong., 2d Sess., p. 2.

[6] *Supra*, p. 134.

its enemy. In fact, they were unconcerned with any of the many other considerations which subsequent years and a large literature, both official and unofficial,[7] have disclosed as indispensable to an understanding of the case.

No complete analysis can be attempted here, but some of the salient facts will indicate that it was by no means so clear a case as to justify another " strict accountability " note.

While the Germans offered to pay,[8] and have paid, damages to the families of the American citizens who were drowned,[9] they have never admitted the illegality of the sinking, and there is a considerable opinion now, even in British circles, that the sinking was justified as a war measure.[10] Had the administration of 1915 exercised that calm deliberation which the President had enjoined on the nation, and had it sought the advice of competent lawyers not controlled by political sympathies, it might have arrived at a

[7] In addition to the wartime authorities already cited, see the following: Official Report by Lord Mersey, June 17, 1915 [Cd. 8022], in 1915 *Parliamentary Papers,* Reports, 1914–16, XXVII, 451; *Proceedings in Camera,* etc. [Cd. 381] 1919 *Parliamentary Papers,* Reports, XXV, 469 (supplementary to Cd. 8022); Carlton Savage, *Policy of the United States toward Maritime Commerce in War,* II, 1914–18 (Department of State Publication No. 835, Government Printing Office, 1936); *For. Rel.,* 1915, Suppl., *passim; For. Rel.,* 1916, Suppl., *passim;* S. Doc. No. 176, 67th Cong., 2d Sess.; *The Lusitania* (1918) 251 Fed. 715; Corbett and Newboldt, *Naval Operations* (1921) II, *passim;* Gibson and Prendergast, *op. cit.,* p. 40 *et seq.;* Fayle, *op. cit.,* II; Dudley Field Malone Report, published in part in *New York World,* Dec. 4, 1922, p. 1, and in complete form in Savage, *op. cit.,* II, Doc. No. 96, pp. 332–340; D. F. Malone, Letter in *The Nation,* Jan. 3, 1923, p. 15; O. G. Villard: " The True Story of the *Lusitania," The American Mercury,* No. 137 (May, 1935), 41; C. E. Lauriat, Jr., *The Lusitania's Last Voyage* (1915); *Report of Robert Bonynge, Agent for the U. S. before the Mixed Claims Commission, U. S. and Germany* (Government Printing Office, 1934); and the accounts in the newspapers of the time. One of the most comprehensive and impartial studies of the case is that by Thomas A. Bailey, " The Sinking of the *Lusitania," American Historical Review,* XLI (Oct. 1935), 54–73. See also the brief but illuminating discussions of the sinking in Bemis, *op. cit.,* pp. 609–610, and *Journal of the Royal United Service Institution,* May, 1936 (Speech of the Earl of Cork and Orrery), pp. 276–277.

[8] Feb. 16, 1916, *For. Rel.,* 1916, Suppl., p. 171.

[9] Awards of Mixed Claims Commission, $2,214,050.00. Bonynge's Report (Government Printing Office, 1934), p. 18.

[10] See comment of Admiral the Earl of Cork and Orrery, *infra,* p. 163.

more constructive decision and one less costly to the United States.

President Wilson's close advisers either advocated war or considered it inevitable. Colonel House cabled the President to force the issue with Germany so as to obtain an absolute assurance that such an act would not be repeated, otherwise to declare war.[1] He even showed that telegram to Mr. Balfour.[2] Mr. Page seems to have regarded the sinking of the *Lusitania* as a godsend for his war policy.[3] It dawned upon Mr. Lansing that the war was one for democracy against autocracy.[4] Ray Stannard Baker thinks that about May 1 Wilson himself had begun to be swayed by the demands of Page and House for war.[5] Mr. Tumulty reports the President as agreeing with Sir Edward Grey that " England is fighting our fight," and he added, " I shall not . . . place obstacles in her way." [6] Other prominent men, Ex-President Roosevelt, Senator Lodge, Brand Whitlock, Herbert Hoover, and Minister Egan in Copenhagen all felt that war was either necessary or unavoidable.[7] But public opinion was not in accord with this view.

Ambassador von Bernstorff advised his Foreign Office to express regret at the loss of American lives and to restrict the activities of the submarine. On May 10 the German Government expressed its " deepest sympathy at the loss of American lives." [8] At the same time, it placed responsibility on the Brit-

---

[1] Seymour, *op. cit.*, I, pp. 432–434, 438. House added: "We can no longer remain neutral spectators." He regarded war as "inevitable" and thought it would break out in a month. Hendrick, *op. cit.*, II, 2.

[2] Seymour, *op. cit.*, I, 438.

[3] *Supra*, p. 66. Page urged war on Wilson "to give us standing and influence when the reorganization of the world must begin." Hendrick, *op. cit.*, II, 5. To Bryan he said that the " United States must declare war or forfeit European respect." *For. Rel.*, 1915, Suppl., pp. 385–386, May 8, 1915.

[4] Lansing, *op. cit.*, p. 19.

[5] Baker, *op. cit.*, V, 328. Mr. Baker says that about May 1, 1915, Wilson ceased to be "neutral in thought."

[6] Tumulty, *Woodrow Wilson*, p. 231.

[7] Citations in Grattan, pp. 297–299.

[8] *For. Rel.*, 1915, Suppl., p. 387.

ish Government which, by preventing the importation of food-stuffs and raw materials for the civilian population, had forced Germany to resort to retaliatory measures. The American proposal of trading food importations for the abandonment of the submarine, had not only been flatly refused by England, but the British Government had responded by tightening the " measures of blockade " — doubtless a reference to the Order in Council of March 11, 1915. The German authorities also referred to the armaments carried by British merchantmen and to their repeated attempts to ram German submarines, a practice which made visit and search impossible. The English press, they stated, had admitted that the *Lusitania* was armed — a charge which the evidence leaves in serious doubt — and called attention to the munitions and contraband carried by the ship.

The position taken by the United States on the *Lusitania* case ultimately determined American intervention, the outcome of the war, and the fate of Europe. Bryan, who earnestly wanted to keep the United States out of the war, adopted the view that " England has been using our citizens to protect her munitions." [9] Lansing, however, favored an uncompromising attitude. He had already expressed the opinion that American citizens had the right to travel unendangered on British ships, and this conviction led him to believe in the invulnerability of his present advice. In addition his apparent belief that war was inevitable, if not indeed desirable, made him less cautious in challenging the German position than should have been the case.

The President wished to be deliberate and sound. Fearing the overwrought emotions of his colleagues, he prepared the first *Lusitania* note himself. Mr. Tumulty suggests that the

---

[9] Statement, May 7, 1915, *Memoirs of Bryan,* p. 421. To the President he wrote, May 9, 1915, that " Germany has a right to prevent contraband going to the Allies and a ship carrying contraband should not rely upon passengers to protect her from attack." Baker, *op. cit.,* V, 333.

realization that public opinion did not favor war exercised a restraining influence on the President.[10]

The note of May 13, which was read to the Cabinet before its dispatch, reiterated the declaration of February 10 that the destruction of " unarmed " merchant ships without visit and search was legally unjustifiable and thereupon undertook again to hold Germany to " strict accountability." It then proceeded, in effect, to outlaw the submarine by suggesting the practical impossibility of its observing the elementary principles of international law concerning visit and search; it denied the adequacy of the German Embassy's warning of May 1 as a substitute for visit and search, and demanded a disavowal of the sinking and reparation so far as that was possible, together with assurance against a recurrence of an act " so obviously subversive of the principles of warfare." [1]

Secretary Garrison considered the note so uncompromising that he thought war would follow. The President realized that diplomatic relations might be severed, but argued that this had happened before without hostilities resulting.[2] Bryan, fearing war, sought to neutralize the bellicose effect of the note by suggesting a simultaneous protest against the objectionable conduct of the Allies.[3] He pointed out that the note to Germany was much sharper than the remonstrances directed to Great Britain. And it lacked any intimation that the settlement could be postponed until after the war, a view to which the President had seemed inclined earlier in May. Once again Bryan reasserted that the action the United States was condemning as illegal had been taken in retaliation for illegal British action which we tolerated. He emphasized the fact that American passengers were on British ships carrying contraband and that the American flag had been misused. He also proposed a supplementary statement to Germany that

[10] Tumulty, *op. cit.*, pp. 233–234.
[1] *For. Rel.*, 1915, Suppl., p. 393; Baker, *op. cit.*, V, 337.
[2] Baker, *op. cit.*, V, 338.
[3] *Idem*, pp. 338–339.

"strict accountability" did not mean immediate accountability but an ultimate settlement.

Wilson showed at first some disposition to heed Bryan's advice concerning the supplementary statement.[4] Lansing and others were of a different mind, however, with the result that the idea was abandoned,[5] the President consoling himself with the hope that Germany would respond "in a spirit of accommodation."[6] Disappointed at this turn of events, Bryan still hoped to mitigate the effect of the American note through a separate protest against Great Britain's measures of blockade and some action to restrain Americans from traveling on British ships.[7] Lansing, however, persuaded the President that it would be incompatible with dignity and honor thus to restrain American travelers. Wilson's speeches at that time reflect this attitude; he believed he was speaking for a "moral principle." "The force of America," he said, "is the force of moral principle . . . There is nothing else that she loves, and there is nothing else for which she will contend."[8] The crusade was beginning.

Bryan, still trying to hold the scales even, now fell back on his last resort — an effort to persuade the President to send England a protest against the illegal "blockade." While he did not disguise his preference for a warning against Americans' taking passage on belligerent ships, in deference to the President's views, he "turned to this as the only immediate remedy."[9] He got encouragement from an unexpected quarter. Colonel House at this time actually believed that he could obtain from Great Britain a voluntary concession to permit foodstuffs to enter Germany, and the President, strangely,

[4] On the ground that it was "designed merely to allay American public feeling which was hostile to war." *Idem*, p. 340.

[5] *Idem*, p. 341.

[6] *Idem*, p. 340.

[7] *Idem*, p. 341.

[8] Address, May 17, 1915, *Public Papers of Woodrow Wilson*, III, 330–332.

[9] Letter, May 16, 1915; Baker, *op. cit.*, V, 344.

seems to have shared House's belief.[10] Not unnaturally, House soon discovered that there was no basis for his optimism.

Meanwhile Wilson had cabled Colonel House " that it will presently become necessary, for the sake of diplomatic consistency and to satisfy our public, to address a note to Great Britain about the unnecessary and unwarranted interruption of our legitimate trade with neutral ports." [1] He thought it would be a brilliant stroke on England's part for her to " relieve this situation, and so put Germany wholly in the wrong . . . It would be a small price to pay for cessation of submarine outrages." [2] This hardly sounds like a " champion " of neutrality. For the sake of " diplomatic consistency and to satisfy our public," he suggests that a protest will become necessary which, if heeded, would " put Germany wholly in the wrong." He must have felt that if Britain did not yield, Germany was not " wholly in the wrong."

Great Britain did not feel the need of yielding to an American protest which, she must have realized, would scarcely be backed up. Nevertheless, Sir Edward Grey entered into desultory conversations with House. On the one hand, the British demanded the abandonment of gas warfare as well as submarine attacks, and on the other, they indicated an unwillingness to free anything but foodstuffs. This failed to satisfy the President. He desired freedom for all noncontraband shipments to neutral ports and challenged the validity of the " blockade " and its effect on American rights. But he did not press the issue.

Although he had supported the various compromises and reciprocal concessions proposed to both belligerents in 1914 and 1915 in order to restrict their respective excesses and impositions against neutrals, Wilson now, for some unknown reason, thought there was a danger in seeming to admit a connection between our disputes with one government and those

[10] *Ibid.*   [1] May 18, 1915, *idem*, p. 345.   [2] *Ibid.*

with the other. Evidently he did not appreciate the fact that the excesses of the one were connected by the belligerents themselves with the excesses of the other in their progressive campaigns of retaliation, and that a neutral could not, while professing neutrality, take an uncompromising attitude toward the one while tolerating the other.[3] On these subjects there was a blind spot in the President's mind. Thus, he cabled Colonel House on May 20, 1915, that the admission of a connection between the German and British violations would be tantamount to negotiating a bargain to obtain from either of them a concession of our undoubted rights on the high seas. ". . . The rights we claim from it [each belligerent] have no connection which we can recognize with what we claim from the other, . . . we must insist on our rights from each without regard to what the other does or does not do." [4]

This attitude seems fatally unrealistic. It could not, in fact, be consistently maintained, even had it been sound. The proffered compromises of February 20, 1915,[5] May 20, 1915,[6] and January 18, 1916,[7] were necessarily bargains, as are most negotiated settlements of conflicting claims. But the supposition that there was no connection between the excesses of the two belligerents or between a neutral's attitudes toward each belligerent, may explain why the President thought that one belligerent could be held to rigid observance of old rules in the face of new conditions, whereas the other could be excused, although conditions involving neutral trade were not new.[8] Apparently he did not feel that this antithesis might challenge American neutrality, a consideration which impressed Bryan deeply. Wilson hoped by negotiations through

[3] Lansing claims to have understood this. See his memorandum of May 3, 1915, published in the *New York Times*, Jan. 31, 1937, magazine section.

[4] Baker, V, *op. cit.*, pp. 345–346.

[5] *For. Rel.*, 1915, Suppl., p. 119.

[6] Seymour, *op. cit.*, I, 446.

[7] *Supra*, p. 103.

[8] *Infra*, p. 199.

Colonel House and Page to avoid that note to Great Britain which Bryan demanded. Both House and Page urged delay until receipt of the German reply to the *Lusitania* note and until the British Government had answered the American note of March 30, 1915. As a result, no comprehensive protest was sent to Great Britain until the long note of October 21, 1915.[9]

The genuinely neutral Mr. Bryan still hoped for a protest to Great Britain which would temper the dangerous possibilities arising out of the first *Lusitania* note, with the policy of which he disagreed. He realized the force of Mr. Wilson's statement of February 19, 1915, made in another connection, that " ' vigorous ' protests are apt to be regarded as logically leading to action." [10] He felt that the *Lusitania* note was too " vigorous."

The German reply of May 31 increased Mr. Bryan's apprehensions. Instead of meeting the President's demands it suggested that certain facts in the *Lusitania* case might have escaped the attention of the United States Government, namely: the *Lusitania* was an auxiliary cruiser, and was transporting Canadian troops; she had guns on board and carried munitions, but for the explosion of which — and there probably was a second explosion — the ship would not have sunk so rapidly and the passengers would in all probability have been saved. Furthermore, it pointed out that the misuse of neutral flags was designed to confuse submarine commanders, and that British merchant vessels had instructions to destroy German submarines by ramming or gunfire, thus precluding visit and search. The note suggested, therefore, that these questions of fact be examined before the diplomatic controversy was continued.[1]

The British Ambassador at once notified the Department that the *Lusitania* had carried no guns,[2] but was silent as to

---

[9] *Infra*, p. 207.   [1] *For. Rel.*, 1915, Suppl., p. 419.
[10] Baker, *op. cit.*, V, 257.   [2] *Idem*, p. 422.

the other charges. The German contention that the vessel carried Canadian troops seems untrue.

Although Germany had suggested that cases involving neutral vessels such as the *Cushing* and the *Gulflight* would be dealt with individually and indemnities paid where the facts justified payment, it gave no intimation that submarine warfare against enemy vessels would be abandoned. This irritated the President and many of the Cabinet, for it was not a prompt compliance with the President's demands.

Forthwith, the President prepared a reply. His draft was read to the Cabinet on June 1. Its intransigent attitude and the strong approval accorded it by several members of the Cabinet elicited from Bryan the charge that they were " pro-Ally." Wilson, resenting this, took the opportunity to rule out any new note to Great Britain on interference with neutral trade.[3] His action foreshadowed Bryan's resignation a few days later.

The second *Lusitania* note of June 9 took a position which was not sound in law and was practically certain to lead to trouble. Germany was informed that " nothing but actual forcible resistance or continued efforts to escape by flight when ordered to stop for the purpose of visit on the part of the merchantman has ever been held to forfeit the lives of her passengers or crew." [4] This was poor law and was hardly the result of considered research. It contemplated the existence of two conditions, both of which were absent in 1915. First, it assumed that all merchant ships were completely unarmed, and not that some were armed; second, as observed by Lansing, it assumed that surface vessels were the only warships afloat, the basis of the old rule.[5] Now, however, when some belligerent vessels were armed and many misused neutral flags, all vessels were exposed to the same danger, for a submarine could not afford to come up and inquire whether a

---

[3] Baker, *op. cit.*, p. 351.
[4] *For. Rel.*, 1915, Suppl., p. 436.

[5] *Supra*, p. 104.

particular ship was or was not equipped with guns.[6] In addition, the President overlooked the specific orders given British merchantmen to ram submarines and, if armed, to fire upon them at sight. Nor yet was Wilson correct in stating that only " forcible resistance " could justify submarine attack. Any indication of resistance, either by arming, or by traveling under instructions to attack and ram, or by accepting belligerent convoy, exposes merchant vessels to instant attack and waives the necessity for visit and search. And by 1915, Britain had armed numerous vessels and had ordered all vessels — including the *Lusitania* — to attack submarines at sight. Nor are " continued " efforts to escape necessary. Any attempt to escape justifies an attack on the escaping vessel. And finally, no one had contended, so far as appears, that the lives of passengers or crew were " forfeited " by resistance or flight. The law simply provides that those who take passage on belligerent ships expose themselves to danger and that there can be no greater immunity for such passengers or crew than for the belligerent carrier itself.

Possibly the President realized that his position was vulnerable, for he added that there were " principles of humanity " involved " which throw into the background any special circumstances of detail that may be thought to affect the case." [7] Unfortunately, the argument for humanity could not increase the legal rights of the *Lusitania* or of the passengers who had ventured into a war zone on a belligerent ship.

On the facts of the case, to which Germany called attention, the second *Lusitania* note sent by the American Government merely stated that it had enforced the United States laws in seeing that the vessel was " not armed for offensive action " or serving as a transport, or carrying a cargo prohibited by American statutes. The note considered the carriage of contraband or the possible explosion of that material as irrelevant to the sinking. It insisted on the immunity of American citi-

---

[6] *Idem.* [7] *For. Rel.*, 1915, Suppl., p. 437.

zens " as passengers on merchant ships of belligerent nationality." Contrary to the position taken by the Germans, the note added that the United States did not understand the German Government " to question those rights," or to deny " the principle that the lives of non-combatants can not . . . be put in jeopardy by the capture or destruction of an unresisting " — changed from " unarmed," in the first note [8] — " merchantman." Finally, it called upon Germany to " take sufficient precaution to ascertain whether a suspected merchantman is in fact of belligerent nationality " or was actually carrying contraband under a neutral flag.[9]

Apparently regarding the special facts and the resulting legal issues as beyond discussion, the President seems to have relied mainly upon the awful tragedy that " a great steamer, primarily and chiefly a conveyance for passengers, and carrying more than a thousand souls who had no part or lot in the conduct of the war, was torpedoed and sunk without so much as a challenge or a warning, and that men, women, and children were sent to their death in circumstances unparalleled in modern warfare." [10] The President added that the fact that " more than one hundred American citizens were among those who perished made it the duty of the United States to speak of these things," and to impress upon the German Government the grave responsibility of the United States, and " the indisputable principle upon which that responsibility rests." He then invoked that appeal which so often is the prelude to war. The United States, he said, " is contending for nothing less high and sacred than the rights of humanity."

A week had elapsed between the preparation of the note on June 1 and its dispatch on the ninth. During that time, Bryan made desperate but unsuccessful attempts to tone it down. The President having supported Lansing in his insistence that

[8] Cf. *supra*, p. 145.
[9] *For. Rel.*, 1915, Suppl., p. 438.
[10] *Idem*, pp. 436, 437.

no warning be given American citizens against traveling on belligerent ships, the best Bryan could get was an admission from the President that " we ought to take steps, as you suggest, to prevent our citizens from travelling on ships carrying munitions of war." [1] But the steps were never taken; indeed they were actually opposed, for they raised the dread fear of inconsistency with prior positions and would, so the President said, have weakened the force of the *Lusitania* note. This is an admission that his case was vulnerable.

The President being immovable in his determination to send the note, Bryan considered it necessary to resign. He felt unable to join in the note " without violating what I deem to be an obligation to my country." [2] The President thought Bryan wrong in his contentions, and, supported by the rest of the Cabinet, insisted on sending the note. Bryan was not wrong, however, and his statesmanlike departure from the Cabinet adds to his political stature. Bryan's prophecy that the position taken in the note would lead to war was unhappily vindicated. But the war was postponed in spite of the wishes of the more ardent interventionists. The country was not yet ready for war. The " process of enlightenment " [3] had only begun.

The German notes of July 8 [4] and the American reply of July 21 [5] added but little to the essentials of the controversy. The Germans blamed the submarine campaign on Britain's efforts to starve Germany and illegally to stop trade with her and contiguous neutrals, and on the necessity of saving Germany from destruction. They offered to do everything possible to spare neutral lives and shipping, and suggested several plans. A concurrent diminution in submarine sinkings tended to appease President Wilson, and led him to conclude that submarine warfare could be conducted according to his

[1] Baker, *op. cit.*, V, 355.
[2] *Idem*, p. 357.
[3] Lansing, *op. cit.*, p. 25.
[4] *For. Rel.*, 1915, Suppl., p. 463.
[5] *Idem*, p. 480.

rules and limitations. When Germany remarked that both the United States and Germany were " contending for the freedom of the seas," the President drew from this the peculiar implication that the Germans were violating the doctrine, whereas they had referred to the British. Wilson stated that the United States would " continue to contend for that freedom from whatever quarter violated, without compromise and at any cost."

The issue was thus left unsettled. But although the United States had lost its diplomatic capacity to enforce its neutral rights and the " freedom of the seas " against Great Britain, even had it so desired, its minatory attitude toward Germany [6] laid the foundation for subsequent events.

Facts and the Law Concerning the Lusitania. There is little doubt that the war spirit, both in the administration and among large groups of the people, particularly in the East, was greatly stimulated by the sinking of the *Lusitania*. Little attention was paid to the legal issues involved or to the fact that there might possibly be two sides to the case. It must have been apparent to all concerned, however, as it clearly was to Mr. Bryan, that the first *Lusitania* note was in the nature of an ultimatum from which, unless good luck intervened, there was only one exit. It was, therefore, extremely important that the United States, at every stage of the discussion, be absolutely right both on the facts and on the law. Thus, it is unfortunate that the sagacious advice of Governor Baldwin of Connecticut, among others, that the matter be arbitrated, was not adopted. That the Bryan " cooling-off " treaties could have been successful may be doubted, for while the Germans relaxed the intensity of their submarine campaign in order to avoid embroiling the United States — even agreeing after the *Sussex* case not to attack unarmed ships of their enemies [7] — the outcome, in the light of the differential

---

[6] Baker, *op. cit.*, p. 367, note 4.
[7] *For. Rel.*, 1916, Suppl., pp. 257, 259.

American attitudes toward the two belligerents, was all but inevitable.

Certain inquiries concerning the *Lusitania* were as necessary then as they are now before any judgment can be passed. In the first place, was the vessel armed? Although the evidence still favors the view that she was unarmed, there are certain indications which cast doubt upon that conclusion.

Officially, it has been maintained that the *Lusitania* did not carry guns. The first official statement to this effect was that of Ambassador Spring-Rice, in accordance with instructions from Sir Edward Grey, on May 31, 1915.[8] The British Ambassador categorically denied that the *Lusitania* had been armed " at any time during the war." This was evidently inspired by the charge, contained in the German reply to the first *Lusitania* note, that the vessel carried masked guns.[9]

Chief reliance in support of the view that the vessel was unarmed, however, is usually placed on the Report of the Mersey investigation of June 17, 1915; [10] here also is a flat denial of the charge. This was the source on which Judge Mayer relied in the proceedings for a limitation of the liability of the owners,[1] and the report has since then been followed without discussion by many writers.[2] The supposed distinction between " offensive " and " defensive " arms was preserved by the United States in its second *Lusitania* note: " It was its [America's] duty to see to it that the *Lusitania* was *not armed for offensive action, . . .* and it performed that duty . . . It is able, therefore, to assure the Imperial German Government that it has been misinformed." [3] Why was it necessary to make the qualification, " for offensive action "? The question was, did she carry arms at all?

---

[8] Spring-Rice to Bryan, *For. Rel.,* 1915, Suppl., p. 422.

[9] *Idem,* p. 419.

[10] Gibson and Prendergast, *The German Submarine War,* 1914–18 (1931), p. 30.

[1] 251 Fed., p. 715 (1918).

[2] Cf. Corbett and Newboldt, *Naval Operations* (1921), II, 394.

[3] *For. Rel.,* 1915, Suppl., pp. 436, 437. (Italics supplied.)

Now for the evidence on the other side. Lacking official confirmation, it is admittedly scrappy and circumstantial. It may be summed up briefly under the following seven points:

(a) The *Lusitania* was constructed in 1907 with specially reinforced emplacements for twelve six-inch quick-firing guns, located, according to the diagrams, as follows: four on the bow, two on the stern and three along each side of the shelter deck — i.e., *the deck immediately below the promenade deck.*[4]

(b) Under a private agreement with the Admiralty, entered into in 1903, Cunard vessels were placed in a special status; they were either " regularly commissioned merchant cruisers "[5] or were specially prepared to serve as troop transports.[6]

(c) It was a part of the British policy to arm merchant ships as a protection against German liners converted into cruisers.[7]

(d) On June 18, 1913, Cunard officials " acknowledged " that the liner was " being equipped with high power naval rifles in conformity with England's new policy of arming passenger boats."[8] This statement does not appear to have been retracted or refuted.

(e) Both the *Lusitania* and the *Mauretania* were listed as " Armed Merchantmen " in the *British Naval Pocket Book for 1914.*[9]

---

[4] *Engineering,* LXXXIV, 135, and appended deck plans (Plate XXXIII, Figs. 32 and 33); Bailey, *op. cit.,* p. 57. The *Mauretania* was similarly equipped. *Engineering,* LXXXIV, 609, and appended deck plans (Plate C, Figs. 52 and 53).

[5] Winston Churchill (March 26, 1913), *Parliamentary Deb.,* 5th ser., L, 1777.

[6] Fayle, *Seaborne Trade* (1923), II, 41.

[7] Winston Churchill (March 26, 1913, and March 17, 1914), *Parliamentary Deb.,* 5th ser., L, 1777, and LIX, 1914.

[8] Dispatch by *Tribune* correspondent; *New York Tribune,* June 19, 1913, p. 1; also quoted in H. E. Barnes, *Genesis of the World War* (1927 ed.), pp. 615 ff.

[9] Bailey, *op. cit.,* p. 58.

(f) The American reply to the German charge that the vessel was equipped with masked guns, specified that the liner " was not armed for offensive action." Were the last three words redundant or were they significant?

(g) Nothing of the foregoing is directly refuted in the Malone Report presently to be examined.

The possible existence of masked guns has been suggested, i.e., they may have been hidden behind temporary partitions or other flimsy structures. Mr. Dudley Field Malone, in his official capacity as Collector of Customs of the Port of New York, made an inspection of the vessel just before its departure from New York on its ill-fated trip. He did not observe any mounted or masked guns at that time. The language of his report, however, is interesting. After submitting affidavits from a number of his subordinates to the effect that they had not observed any guns on the vessel, Mr. Malone added:

In addition, I, myself, boarded the steamship *Lusitania* on the morning of May 1, 1915, within one hour of the time of her actual departure and, after an inspection of her open bow deck and open stern deck, I can testify to my own personal knowledge that there were no guns of any character, mounted or unmounted, masked or unmasked — on the said bow or stern decks, *or the open promenade deck,* around which I walked on the ship.[10]

Reference to the deck plans of the vessel during construction indicates that for armament inspection Mr. Malone was one deck too high. That he knew of the gun emplacements, however, is indicated by the fact that in another portion of his report he states:

. . . I beg to state that the *Lusitania,* in her construction, was so built that certain sections were reinforced, and in her structure at certain points, bases were laid for mounting guns of 6-inch calibre. The said bases were riveted to the steel structure of the ship but were entirely covered over at all times by the wooden planking

[10] Savage, *op. cit.,* II, 332, 333.

of the decks. The reason why the deck of the *Lusitania* was built with provision for guns was that if the Admiralty should call the *Lusitania* from the merchant service to the service of the British Navy, she would be more readily adaptable for naval purposes. Consequently, if any guns had been mounted, or there was any intention to mount guns on the *Lusitania on her open bow or open stern deck,* these guns would have been mounted on the stable gun bases provided for the purposes, and not upon any blocks or blocking or other alleged paraphernalia for this purpose. *This statement is merely made to indicate the improbable character of any testimony which states that any guns were mounted on the bow or stern of the Lusitania on wooden blocks or blocking.*[1] (Italics supplied.)

The limitations attached to this statement, while possibly not intended to qualify the Collector's conviction that the vessel was unarmed, nevertheless do not determine the issue.

None of the foregoing circumstantial evidence is conclusive. On the balance, the evidence still indicates that the *Lusitania* was not armed. Perhaps certainty on the point will never be attained without the aid of deep-sea divers.

Several other factors connected with the sinking merit at least passing mention. The vessel was a belligerent ship and was carrying munitions as well as passengers. Yet even Secretary Bryan was astonished to learn on the day after the sinking that munitions were included in the cargo.[2]

The most detailed description of these munitions appears to be that given in the Malone Report. It is there stated that the cargo contained 5,468 cases of ammunition, 4,200 cases of which contained powder, the remainder consisting principally of shrapnel shells not yet loaded.[3] The ultimate consignee of the 4,200 cases of loaded cartridges was the British Government. The powder content of this shipment was ap-

[1] *New York World,* Dec. 4, 1922, pp. 1, 2, col. 3. Savage, *op. cit., II,* 332, 338.
[2] *Memoirs of William Jennings Bryan* (New York, 1925), p. 421; Baker, *op. cit.,* V, 332.
[3] Savage, *op. cit.,* II, 332 *et seq.;* Bailey, *op. cit.,* p. 61.

proximately 5 pounds per case, or 10½ tons in all. A summary of the manifest, as given by Dr. Savage,[4] shows these 4,200 cases as the most valuable single item in the entire cargo.

Another factor, often overlooked, is that Captain Turner of the *Lusitania* had received the various notices sent by the Admiralty to all British vessels regarding the proper maneuvering should a submarine be sighted.[5] This fact was stressed at the time by the German authorities:

The Imperial Government furthermore has the honor to direct the particular attention of the American Government to the fact that the British Admiralty by a secret instruction of February of this year [1915] advised the British merchant marine not only to seek protection behind neutral flags and markings but even when so disguised to attack German submarines by ramming them. High rewards have been offered by the British Government as a special incentive for the destruction of the submarines by merchant vessels and such rewards have already been paid out.[6]

Next, Germany had given preliminary and actual notice that she would do everything in her power to stop all shipping within the war zone. Preliminary, in the " War Zone " declaration of February 4, 1915, operative two weeks later,[7] and in the specific notice dated April 22, 1915, which the German Ambassador said he had neglected to insert in the New York newspapers of Saturday, April 24,[8] but which did appear in those of May 1,[9] the morning the vessel sailed, as well as in those of the following Saturday.[10] Actual, in that, from the inception of the submarine campaign on February 18, 1915, until the following May 1, ninety merchant vessels, mostly British, were sunk in the war zone through which

---

[4] Savage, *op. cit.*, II, 332, 339. It is valued at $152,400. Bailey states that half the cargo was for military use. *Loc. cit.*

[5] *Proceedings in Camera, supra*, p. 155; Bemis, *Diplomatic History* (New York, 1936), p. 610; Millis, *The Road to War*, p. 163.

[6] German note of May 28, 1915, *For. Rel.*, 1915, Suppl., p. 419; Savage, *op. cit.*, II, Doc. No. 93, pp. 327, 329.

[7] *For. Rel.*, 1915, Suppl., pp. 95–97.

[8] Villard, *op. cit.*, *The American Mercury*, No. 137, pp. 41, 43.

[9] *New York Times*, May 1, 1915, p. 19, col. 7.

[10] *Idem*, May 8, 1915, p. 21, col. 8.

the *Lusitania* was to travel.[1] It is noteworthy that the American passengers on the *Lusitania* had had ample opportunity to transfer to the American steamer *New York* of the American Line, sailing two hours later, and carrying no munitions.[2]

Investigators of the problem have called attention to a variety of circumstances which lead to the conclusion that Captain Turner of the *Lusitania* was either extremely careless or was navigating the vessel according to orders.[3] The government failed to supply a convoy; the Captain slowed down the vessel instead of going full speed; he remained in the regular course instead of following an irregular route; he failed to zigzag, as instructed; he turned the vessel just in time to receive the torpedo. Although he was in possession of special wireless messages apprising him of the presence of submarines, which a day before had sunk two steamers in that vicinity, he was apparently not alert to his dangers. On the stand, he was vague about his specific instructions. The first report of the Wreck Commissioner — the Mersey Report of June 17, 1915 — was in many circles regarded as a palpable whitewash, not a genuine investigation. The secret proceedings of the investigation were not made public until 1919. There is a good deal about the case to arouse question.

Lansing's reactions to the German warning appearing in the May 1 newspapers have recently been made public. On May 9 he wrote Secretary Bryan that:

[1] *M. S. Losses* (1919); *New York Times,* May 8, 1915, p. 5, cols. 3–4; Bailey, *op. cit.,* p. 66, note 44.

[2] Bailey, *op. cit.,* p. 67. Several prominent Americans, including Ambassador Gerard, Vice-President Marshall, A. Mitchell Palmer, and some Senators expressed the view that a few Americans ought not for selfish ends to have been allowed to risk the welfare of their country. *New York Times,* May 9, May 11, 1915. *For. Rel.,* 1915, Suppl., p. 461; cited by Bailey, *op. cit.,* p. 67.

[3] Bemis, S. F., *Diplomatic History of the United States* (1936), p. 610; Bailey, *op. cit.,* pp. 70–72.

It is my opinion in view of the facts that it would cause general public condemnation and indignant criticism in this country, if the Government should attempt now to avoid vigorous action by asserting that the Americans drowned by the torpedoing of the *Lusitania* were blamable in having taken passage on that vessel. They had the right to rely on the note of February 10th, and they had the right to expect a warning from this Government, if it considered that it could not support them if they took risks by going abroad on British vessels.[4]

On May 10 Lansing wrote a memorandum for the State Department in which, after characterizing the German Ambassador's notice as " an act of insolence," he concluded:

If the warning had been delivered to this Government, it would have been compelled to decide whether it should be made public. It had no opportunity to do this. It did, however, have opportunity to advise the American people to heed the warning. This it did not do. It ignored the warning, and by remaining silent gave the impression that the warning might be ignored.[5]

This very human unwillingness of the administration to admit that it had made a mistake in its basic decisions and would not now run the risk of appearing to be inconsistent, was fully appreciated by President Wilson. On May 11, he wrote Bryan:

Mr. Lansing's argument seems to me unanswerable. Even if it were just to take the position that a warning that an unlawful and outrageous thing would be done might operate as an exemption from responsibility on the part of those who issued it, so far as our citizens were concerned, it is now too late to take it. We

---

[4] Savage, *op. cit.*, II, Doc. No. 77, pp. 309, 310.

[5] Savage, *op. cit.*, II, Doc. No. 80, pp. 311, 313. As evidence that emotional reactions often depend on prior mental attitudes, the difference between Lansing's and Bryan's conception of the German warning may be noted: Lansing characterized the warning as " an impertinent act, which would warrant summary action if it was expedient," and concluded that " everything seems to point to a determined effort to affront this government and force it to an open rupture of diplomatic relations." Baker, *op. cit.*, V, 325. Bryan thought the German warning a " fortunate thing . . . evidence of a friendly desire to evade anything that might raise a question between Germany and the United States." *Ibid.*

defined our position at the outset and cannot alter it, — at any rate so far as affects the past.[6]

Yet, had the administration announced on May 1 its intention to protect the *Lusitania* against submarine attack, such action would doubtless have been regarded as an intervention in the war.

It has already been observed that President Wilson, just before dispatching the second *Lusitania* note, was " inclined to think that we ought to take steps, as you [Bryan] suggest, to prevent our citizens from travelling on ships carrying munitions of war, and I shall seek to find the legal way to do it." [7] Yet the way he sought was a way which would not " hopelessly weaken our protest " to Germany.[8] Rather than adopt the simple method of warning American citizens off belligerent ships, especially munition ships, he continued to insist on their absolute immunity, even on British armed ships. In substance, the situation was this: the President conceded Bryan to be right, but would not publicly make the admission because it would indicate weakness in the American position. Thus, by refusing to lift a warning voice against the daily increasing risk, the administration was encouraging American citizens to travel on such ships — even, in effect, encouraging the British to hire Americans in their crews. And to all intents and purposes, the administration guaranteed to protect these citizens, apparently oblivious of the fact, notwithstanding Wilson's admission to Bryan, that its legal position was unsustainable. In any event, President Wilson seemed to think a warning might have proved ineffectual: ". . . the danger is already fully known, and those who do not refrain because of the danger will not, in all probability refrain because we request them to do so. . . ." [9]

[6] Savage, *op. cit.*, II, Doc. No. 83, pp. 314–315.
[7] Baker, *op. cit.*, V, 355.
[8] *Ibid.*
[9] Wilson to Bryan, May 14, 1915, Bryan's *Memoirs,* p. 403; Baker, *op. cit.*, V, 341–342. Wilson also expressed his aversion to warning American

There remained nothing for Bryan to do but resign, as previous positions were reaffirmed in further ultimata to Germany. It was this drifting into war — and insistence upon it — that Millis has so forcefully depicted.[10] This was the policy of persevering in blunders, of issuing ultimata in defense of British ships, of refusing to take obvious precautions at home when such action was imperative. The policy was stimulated throughout by an unneutral bias, doubtless accentuated by the shock of the novelty of submarine attacks on merchant ships.

No attempt will be made to weigh the expediency or morality of the *Lusitania's* sinking. It proved to be a political blunder of the first order, which the diplomacy of the American Government aggravated.

Nevertheless, one observation is permissible. That the *Lusitania* case does not affect all authorities in the same way as it did the Wilson administration in 1915 is evident from the comments of a British Admiral, lately in command of the Home Fleet, the Earl of Cork and Orrery, formerly Sir William Boyle. Speaking before the Royal United Service Institution in 1936, he said:

. . . If you look back at the late war, you will remember that the great advantage which the allies had over the enemy . . . lay in the British Merchant Marine; yet we held up our hands in horror when the Germans sank our ships, although every ship they sank meant a reduction in the great forces that we had to use against them. Very often we condemned this action of the enemy on the ground that there were non-combatants and women and children in the ships. . . . If women and children choose to travel in ships in a war area, they must take what they get. It is

citizens off belligerent ships, because " it weakens the effect of our saying to Germany that we mean to support our citizens in the exercise of their right to travel both on our ships and on belligerent." The President possibly never realized that he had received excessively bad legal advice.

[10] *The Road to War, passim.*

a very cowardly thing for us to try to defend our merchant ships by this plea.

As our ships went to sea to win the war for us, I cannot see myself . . . that the Germans were so very wrong in sinking them. Take the case of the " Lusitania ": there was a great ship which could carry 10,000 troops to the front in one voyage as her sisters did to Gallipoli. The Germans sank her, and surely to some extent they could plead that they were justified and that it was a fair and legitimate operation of war, in spite of pre-War conventions on the subject.[1]

But the American Government had entrenched itself in the partisan attitude of holding Germany to " strict accountability " for submarine attacks against British vessels, the illegality of which was by no means clear, while yielding with ever fainter protests to the British impositions. The partiality which Bryan had criticized became an irrevocable policy under which neutrality was gradually submerged. The administration in effect fought the British case against the submarine, and entangled itself in the bargain. It lost, by its position, all opportunity to obtain relaxation of British illegalities. American intervention in the war was thereby foreordained. Mr. Page, and probably others, found in the *Lusitania* less reason for regret than opportunity for intervention, for Mr. Page expressed the cheerful hope that another *Lusitania* might be sunk [2] and thus awaken America to the revealed duty that it must fight at the side of the Allies to save civilization.

After the Lusitania

WHILE there were no major passenger sinkings between May 7 when the *Lusitania* went down and July 21 when the

[1] Speech before the Royal United Service Institution in London on Feb. 5, 1936, *Journal*, May, 1936, pp. 276–277.

[2] Page to House, July 21, 1915, Hendrick, *op. cit.*, II, 26. Sir Edward Grey was disappointed that the crisis had passed without producing intervention, and considered such restraint an impairment of American influence. Grey to House, June 6, 1915, Seymour, *op. cit.*, II, 54.

last *Lusitania* note was dispatched by the United States, the respite was temporary only. Without acknowledging the change in policy to foreign countries, it seems that the German civil authorities had induced the naval authorities to avoid the sinking without warning of large passenger vessels. Yet on August 19, 1915, the British White Star Liner *Arabic* was sunk without warning. This was contrary to orders, the Germans claimed. Two American lives were lost. Lansing had informed Bernstorff on July 21, 1915, that war would eventuate if any more American lives were lost.[3] Bernstorff now feared an immediate rupture and advised a conciliatory response to the American protest. House wished to sever relations immediately. The cause of the *Arabic's* sinking was not at once clear, but Bernstorff stated that the loss of American lives was contrary to German intentions and, in advance of an investigation of the facts, expressed his sympathy.

In Germany the dispute between civil and naval authorities continued, unabated, the former claiming that American intervention must be avoided, the latter that restraints on the submarine were preventing them from ending the war.

The issue had been so framed by the American *Lusitania* note of July 21, 1915, that a failure to restrain the submarine, even against enemy vessels, would doubtless have caused a break with the United States. However, public opinion in the United States at that time — a period marked by further invasions of neutral rights by Great Britain, such as making cotton absolute contraband — was not, in spite of the propaganda, as yet conditioned for war. The Germans were thus in an acute dilemma and so was the Wilson administration. The situation was saved by assurances that the submarine would continue to be restrained. On September 1 Bernstorff announced to Lansing that liners would not be sunk without warning and without providing for the safety of the

---

[3] Bernstorff, *My Three Years in America*, pp. 140–146.

lives of noncombatants, providing the vessels did not resist or try to escape.[4] The recurrence of an *Arabic* incident was considered out of the question.[5] It was stated that the submarine commander who sank the *Arabic* was convinced that the ship intended to ram the submarine, and indemnity was offered for the American lives lost.

But sinkings of the British steamship *Persia* and the Italian steamship *Ancona* in the fall of 1915, the one by German and the other by Austrian submarines, again intensified the situation.[6] In January, 1916, came the Lansing proposal to the Allies for the disarmament of merchantmen as a condition of further protest against submarine warfare. The President's subsequent withdrawal from that sound position has already been noted.[7]

With things in this state of suspension, the submarine issue was actively revived by the torpedoing, without warning, on March 24, of the unarmed French Channel steamer *Sussex*. Again Colonel House announced that war was inevitable.[8] No American lives were lost, but a few Americans were injured. Lansing advised an immediate severance of diplomatic relations.[9] Several of Wilson's ambassadors prepared to come home.

A very sharp note was thereupon sent to Germany which pointed the course of future events. It took the categorical position that submarine attacks on an enemy's commerce are " utterly incompatible with the principles of humanity, the long established and incontrovertible rights of neutrals and the sacred immunities of non-combatants." [10] In this respect

---

[4] *For. Rel.*, 1915, Suppl., pp. 530–531. The German Ambassador filed a memorandum Jan. 7, 1916, restating the restrictions that had been placed on submarine commanders. *For. Rel.*, 1916, pp. 144–145.

[5] *Idem*, pp. 560–561.

[6] *For. Rel.*, 1915, Suppl., pp. 611, 646, 655–658.

[7] *Supra*, p. 122.

[8] Seymour, *op. cit.*, II, 225–226.

[9] *Idem*, p. 227.

[10] *For. Rel.*, 1916, Suppl., pp. 232–234.

it reiterated the pronouncements of earlier notes but hardly improved their legal correctness. The note ended with another ultimatum stating that unless the German Government should immediately abandon its methods of submarine warfare against passenger and freight ships, the United States would sever diplomatic relations.

The tension was temporarily relieved by the German reluctance to risk drawing America in. They made a new and far-reaching commitment to restrain the use of the submarine as a commerce destroyer. The Germans even asked Ambassador Gerard whether they might reserve the right to sink armed merchantmen at sight. They were given to understand, however, that the President demanded that submarines conform entirely to the rules governing surface vessels. They acquiesced, expressing the hope that the President would exert his efforts to bring about peace.[1] They promised in the note of May 4, 1916, that " in accordance with the general principles of visit and search and destruction of merchant vessels recognized by international law, such vessels, both within and without the area declared as naval war zone, shall not be sunk without warning and without saving human lives, unless these ships attempt to escape or offer resistance." [2] The note added, however, that if the United States should be unable to obtain from Great Britain a respect for " the rules of international law universally recognized before the war," as laid down by the United States in notes to the British Government of December 28, 1914, and November 5, 1915, so that " the laws of humanity might be followed by all belligerent nations, . . . the German Government would then be facing a new situation in which it must reserve [to] itself complete liberty of decision." [3]

While this was regarded as a complete victory by Colonel

---

[1] Gerard, *My Four Years in Germany*, p. 324 *et seq.*
[2] *For. Rel.*, 1916, Suppl., pp. 257–259.
[3] *Ibid.*

House and the President, Mr. Wilson declined to accept the qualification at the end of the German note that Germany would reserve its freedom of action if the United States could not persuade the British to modify their illegalities. Reasserting the position taken in the note of February 10, 1915, and in the *Lusitania* note of May 13, 1915, he stated that he

cannot for a moment entertain, much less discuss, a suggestion that respect by German naval authorities for the rights of citizens of the United States upon the high seas should in any way or in the slightest degree be made contingent upon the conduct of any other government affecting the rights of neutrals and non-combatants. Responsibility in such matters is single, not joint; absolute, not relative.[4]

This persistent refusal of President Wilson to see that there was a relation between the British irregularities and the German submarine warfare is probably the crux of American involvement. The position taken was obviously unsustainable, for it is a neutral's duty to hold the scales even and to favor neither side. No one had more strongly insisted upon this than President Wilson himself in his proclamation of neutrality and in his speeches at the beginning of the war. Yet his actions took a different course. His refusal to hold Great Britain to account and his inability to win a single concession from her were compensated by a determined and unyielding attitude toward Germany. That hostility was not pressed to the point of war, however, even though it was contemplated by the administration as early as 1915, until American public opinion in the Middle and Far West could be prepared for that final step.

Although Germany had on several occasions claimed that it was sacrificing its right to conduct submarine warfare against enemy shipping, in accordance with its notice of February 4, 1915, and that it was yielding its rights in order

[4] *For. Rel.*, 1916, Suppl., p. 263.

to conciliate the United States, the unmistakable promise to conduct submarine warfare according to the rules governing surface vessels, as the President had demanded, doubtless served to convince Mr. Wilson that his peremptory demand was legally flawless. But it was not. At this time Allied merchant vessels were arming with increasing frequency and a regular warfare against submarines with armed and disguised merchantmen was under way. Under such circumstances, to demand that passengers and crew be saved before merchantmen could be sunk was to invite the submarine to commit suicide or at the very least to impair greatly its utility as a weapon against British commerce. It is not surprising, then, that Colonel House had called Grey's attention to this service which the United States was rendering to Britain.[5]

Germany's agreement to continue the restrictions on the submarine, on condition that the United States succeed in getting Great Britain to abide by the rules of international law and enable Germany to trade with neutrals in foodstuffs and raw materials, merely repeated the position taken in earlier notes. The President's refusal to accept the condition reflected the administration's policy to make no further demands in this direction upon Great Britain — the last protest had been sent on October 21, 1915, after cotton was made contraband — and acceptance would have conflicted with the President's unfortunate view that the violations by each belligerent of neutral rights were distinct affairs and that this country was privileged to take a different attitude toward each without thereby impairing American neutrality. A tacit acknowledgment of this error may be found in the fact that he rested the discrimination between the two belligerents on the difference between the loss of life and the loss of property. But even here the distinction is less con-

[5] Seymour, *op. cit.*, II, 72.

vincing than it seems. The loss of life occurred primarily among American seamen or passengers on British or Allied merchantmen, where they were under the protection of the British or Allied flag under which they voluntarily sailed, and not under the protection of the United States. So far as concerns the loss of property, we know that subsequent administrations failed to collect substantial damages from Great Britain, and have placed serious obstacles in the path of claimants to the limited funds left in American hands under the Executive agreement of May 19, 1927, to compensate the sufferers.[6] So the last justification for the discrimination disappears, leaving the bare and all too perceptible fact that the administration did not really desire to remain neutral after the middle of 1915. Various influences gradually converged to produce that policy, and in September, 1916, two months before the November election with its slogan, " He kept us out of war," we find the President saying, " The business of neutrality is over." [7]

All parties doubtless realized that the precarious submarine truce could hardly last. In May, 1916, Colonel House had informed Bernstorff that the United States could do nothing to mitigate the British " blockade." [8] Germany placed its entire hopes on an early peace which might avoid the showdown, and made several tentative moves for peace through President Wilson and then, on December 12, 1916, directly. But Great Britain was adamant, doubtless comprehending that the German demands were due to the relentless pressure exerted by the " measures of blockade " and the war of attrition, which the Allies could stand much better than Germany.

The President's own efforts at mediation in December,

[6] *Infra,* p. 282.

[7] Dodd and Baker, *Public Papers of Woodrow Wilson,* II, 376, 381.

[8] Bernstorff's statement, *German Official Documents Relating to the World War,* I, 234; Grattan, *op. cit.,* p. 342.

1916, postponed until then owing to the November election, fell on barren soil in England, for his influence now was limited, as Page had earlier suggested, to his expected aid as a belligerent. His helpfulness as a mediator was hardly desired. Notwithstanding the election slogan, the country was subjected to unremitting Allied and home propaganda for intervention. Only the necessary occasion was lacking to set off the dynamite. Yet the President continued to speak as if he were a mediator and would not engage in the war, for on January 22, 1917, he made his famous " Peace without victory " speech.[9]

On January 31, 1917, the bombshell burst. Germany, unsuccessful in bringing the belligerents to a discussion of peace, and with her population demanding a cutting of the Gordian knot by drastic action, took the desperate step of announcing that the Allies' insistence on the continuation of the war gave back to Germany her " freedom of action " reserved in the *Sussex* note of May 4, 1916. After February 1, 1917, " all navigation, that of neutrals included," was forbidden in the war zone around the British Isles, with certain exceptions, which she was willing to negotiate, for passenger vessels. The whole series of American ultimata was put to the test. It had either to be backed up or withdrawn. On February 3, 1917, diplomatic relations with Germany were severed.

On that day the President went before Congress and reviewed the diplomatic correspondence which had led to the break. He emphasized again his reply to the German condition attached to the *Sussex* note: that the United States " cannot for a moment entertain, much less discuss, a suggestion that respect by German naval authorities for the rights of citizens of the United States upon the high seas should in any way or in the slightest degree be made contingent upon the conduct of any other Government affecting the rights of neu-

[9] Scott, ed., *President Wilson's Foreign Policy*, pp. 245, 249.

trals and non-combatants." [1] Although he informed Congress that diplomatic relations were severed, he still gave the impression that he thought hostilities might be avoided. The justification for this hope is not easy to perceive.

On February 26, 1917, the President hit upon the idea of arming American merchant vessels as had been done in 1798 against French depredations on American commerce. Possibly realizing that this might immediately result in war, and advised that Congress must give the authority for such arming, he informed Congress that two American vessels had been sunk, one carrying foodstuffs consigned to a London firm, the other carrying lemon box staves to Palermo; that American shipping had been tied up by the war zone decree and the promise of ruthless submarine warfare. He therefore requested authority to arm our neutral vessels. Yet, strangely, he expressed the devout hope that it would not be necessary to put armed forces into action on the ground that the " American people do not desire it." He still maintained that he was " the friend of peace " and stated his determination " to preserve it for America so long as I am able. I am not now proposing or contemplating war or any steps that need lead to it." [2]

Congress declined to give him the power requested because of a Senate filibuster in which twelve Senators participated. These were the Twelve Wilful Men who, for venturing to exercise their constitutional privilege to oppose the President, were pilloried by the administration. But their effort to resist war was futile. Denied the power by Congress, the President decided to proceed without it, and stated in his Inaugural Address of March 5,[3] " we have been obliged to arm ourselves. . . . We stand firm in armed neutrality." But he now admitted that " we may even be drawn on, by circumstances, not by our own purpose or desire, to a more active assertion of our rights as we see them and a more im-

[1] *Supra*, p. 168.   [2] Scott, *op. cit.*, p. 265.   [3] *Idem*, p. 270.

mediate association with the great struggle itself." In that speech he again expressed his devotion to the freedom of the seas " for the use of all peoples, under rules set up by common agreement and consent."

At first, arms were provided for American neutral vessels but no United States naval officers were placed in charge. Here, the President was running a great risk. These neutral vessels were undertaking to fire on belligerents, a privilege not open to neutrals. The bedlam of the times, and the belief that submarine warfare as then conducted was without legal justification, possibly tempered the thoroughness with which the question of legality was examined. But on advice from competent authority that the arming of neutral ships under such circumstances constituted piracy and left the neutral without a recognized place in law, the United States Government on March 20, 1917, assumed official responsibility for the firing of guns and put naval men in charge of them. Under these circumstances firing would be a public act and to that extent regular. But it would be an act of war.

On April 2, 1917, the President appeared before Congress and demanded recognition of the state of war thrust upon the United States by the acts of Germany. He rejected the German plea of retaliation and claimed that submarines were " impossible to employ as it [Germany] is employing them without throwing to the winds all scruples of humanity or of respect for the understandings that were supposed to underlie the intercourse of the world. . . . The present German submarine warfare against commerce is a warfare against mankind . . . a war against all nations." He added that the ships of other and friendly neutral nations had likewise been sunk. " The challenge is to all mankind. Each nation must decide for itself how it will meet it. . . . Our motive will not be revenge or the victorious assertion of the physical might of the nation, but only the vindication of right, of hu-

man right, of which we are only a single champion. . . .
Armed neutrality, it now appears, is impracticable." Submarines as commerce destroyers " are in effect outlaws," apparently because " it is impossible to defend ships against their attacks as the law of nations has assumed that merchantmen would defend themselves against privateers or cruisers, visible craft giving chase upon the open sea." That is, because submarines were different from surface vessels and because armed merchantmen could not defend themselves against them as they could against privateers or surface cruisers — the antithesis of Lansing's argument of January 18, 1916 — submarines were outlaws. This is a legal proposition somewhat difficult to defend. The defense is made even more difficult by the President's statement, reiterating the British position, that " it is common prudence in such circumstances, grim necessity indeed, to endeavor to destroy them before they have shown their own intention. They must be dealt with upon sight, if dealt with at all." [4] He added that " the wrongs against which we now array ourselves are no common wrongs. They cut to the very roots of human life."

After pointing out that full coöperation, military and financial, with the Allied governments was necessary, including the " extension to those Governments of the most liberal financial credits, in order that our resources may so far as possible be added to theirs," he pictured the great adventure as a crusade for peace. He said:

Our object now, as then, is to vindicate the principles of peace and justice in the life of the world as against selfish and autocratic power and to set up amongst the really free and self-governed peoples of the world such a concert of purpose and of action as will henceforth insure the observance of those principles. Neutrality is no longer feasible or desirable where the peace of the world is involved . . . We have seen the last of neutrality in such circumstances. We are at the beginning of an age in which it will be insisted that the same standards of conduct and of responsibil-

[4] Scott, *op. cit.*, pp. 276–278. Cf. *supra*, p. 94.

ity for wrong done shall be observed among nations and their governments that are observed among the individual citizens of civilized states.[5]

Thus neutrality ended for the United States.

Freedom of the Seas. Among the laudable objectives of the peace sought by Colonel House was an agreement by belligerents to respect the freedom of the seas.[6] In February, 1915, Grey and Tyrrell appeared to support the idea. First conceived as an immunity for all private property, it was later whittled down by Grey to a vague formula promising a possible convention, after the war, to respect the traditional rights of neutrals, if Germany entered " some League of Nations where she would give and accept the same security against war as did other nations." [7] This was not especially hopeful, and even House lost interest in his proposal after the sinking of the *Lusitania* and his own mental commitment to enlisting the United States in the war.[8] In the fall of 1915, Britain feared that this " freedom of the seas " would " strike the weapon of sea power out of British hands." [9] Her coolness to freedom of the seas was covered by professed enthusiasm for a postwar organization to insure compulsory observance of the rules of sea law; this idea House embraced and with it converted Wilson to the belief that Great Britain favored the freedom of the seas.[10] Wilson in 1916 and early 1917 made frequent demands for sea freedom and an association of nations to enforce it.[1] He grasped the nettle firmly.

[5] *Idem,* p. 281.

[6] Seymour, *op. cit.,* I, 369–374, 401, 411, 425 *et seq.,* 446 *et. seq.* Cf. House, " The Freedom of the Seas," *Contemporary Review* (April, 1928), p. 416.

[7] Seymour, *op. cit.,* II, 87, 89, 425, 426.

[8] Seymour, *op. cit.,* I, 453.

[9] Seymour, *op. cit.,* II, 79, 80.

[10] Seymour, *op. cit.,* I, 117. But Lloyd George was definitely opposed, *idem,* p. 129.

[1] Seymour, *op. cit.,* III, 327; *For. Rel.,* 1916, Suppl., p. 41; Wilson, *Works,* III, 188; *idem,* p. 303; *For. Rel.,* 1917, Suppl. I, 24, 26, 29.

In the Second of his Fourteen Points of January, 1918, Wilson demanded " absolute freedom of navigation," by which House says he meant complete immunity from capture. Both anticipated British agreement, because of the qualification that " the seas might be closed by international action in order to enforce international covenants." [2] The British press response was not friendly, although labor organizations supported it. Lloyd George expressed doubt as to the meaning of " freedom of the seas," professing to think it meant freedom for submarines, in which case the government was against it.[3] As we know, at the time of the Armistice, Britain refused to accept the Second Point.[4] Although Wilson had bravely refused to " consent to take part in the negotiations of a peace which does not include freedom of the seas," [5] he not only did take part, but found excuses for British obstinacy and his own surrender. He was ready to " fully and sympathetically recognize the exceptional position and necessities of Great Britain with regard to the use of the seas for defence both at home and throughout the Empire and also realize that freedom of the seas needs careful definition." [6] Colonel House still kept up a show of resistance to retrieve for the future what had been surrendered by the Wilson administration during the war and again in the Armistice negotiations.[7] But this did not last long.[8] If the League consoled them for their defeat, the fact remains that the boast

[2] Seymour, *op. cit.*, III, 327.

[3] *For. Rel.*, 1918, Suppl. I, 72, 78.

[4] Seymour, *op. cit.*, IV, 152 *et seq.; For. Rel.*, 1918, Suppl. I, 351, 365. Germany had accepted it in 1917 and again during the pre-Armistice negotiations. *For. Rel.*, 1917, Suppl. I, 98; also Austria, *idem*, pp. 162, 165. German acceptance of Point 2, *For. Rel.*, 1918, Suppl. I, 27, 41, 53, 258, 304, 314, 357.

[5] *Idem*, p. 423. Cf. *idem*, pp. 425–437 and Seymour, *op. cit.*, IV, 161–174.

[6] *For. Rel.*, 1918, Suppl. I, 427, 428.

[7] Seymour, *op. cit.*, IV, 180–181, 183–185; *For. Rel.*, 1918, Suppl. I, 448, 456, 461.

[8] When Balfour stated that Britain needed her " power to help right wrongs," as she had just done, House replied that she could use her navy under the League. Seymour, IV, 255. Thus, House also yielded the American case.

that the United States would " continue to contend for that freedom from whatever quarter violated, without compromise and at any cost," [9] had been sadly punctured.

A Belligerent Ship Is Belligerent Territory

THE firmness of the Wilson administration in protecting British ships from attacks of German submarines because of the presence on board of American citizens was based on the belief that they were defending the rights of humanity, a justification considered so overwhelming that legal considerations received inadequate attention. It has already been observed that the position of the administration in attributing a peaceful character to armed merchantmen was legally unsustainable.[10] Equally unsound was the view that the United States had the privilege or was called upon to guarantee the safety of belligerent merchantmen, because American citizens were so reckless as to risk their lives by taking passage or serving on them.

Had the *Deutschland*,[1] a commercial submarine, carried an American passenger, it is not to be supposed that the Department of State would have claimed the right to protect him from unheralded attacks by the British. The United States found that the *Deutschland* was an unarmed merchant vessel and, as such, entitled to the privileges attaching to that classification.[2] Norway also expressly exempted commercial submarines [3] from its prohibition against cruising or

[9] *Supra*, p. 154.

[10] *Supra*, p. 88.

[1] For an account of this submarine, see Navy Department, Office of Naval Records and Library, Historical Section, Publication No. 1, *German Submarine Activities on the Atlantic Coast of the United States and Canada* (Government Printing Office, 1920), pp. 15–18. See also Millis, *op. cit.*, pp. 327 ff.

[2] Polk to Gerard, July 17, 1916, *For. Rel.*, 1916, Suppl., p. 768.

[3] P. G. Vigness, *The Neutrality of Norway in the World War*, Stanford University Publications in History, Economics, and Political Science, Vol. IV, No. 1, p. 104.

lingering in territorial waters by " submarine crafts equipped for usages of war." [4] Sweden did likewise.[1] Can it be, then, that the traveler on an unarmed commercial submarine — a slow craft, as innocuous as it is vulnerable — should be treated less considerately than his colleague on the much speedier and safer surface vessel?

The proper rule is that neither is entitled to invoke American intervention on his behalf. Both take the risks of their locations and must seek their protection from the flag of the vessel on which they take passage. This is not a new rule, nor one fabricated for the occasion. To quote John Bassett Moore:

It is a fundamental principle that ships on the high seas are under the protection of the country to which they belong and are for jurisdictional purposes treated as part of its territory. It was on this ground that we resisted the British claim of impressment; and the British, in asserting that claim, admitted the soundness of the principle, declaring that they went no further than to claim that if, when in the exercise of the belligerent right of visit and search, they recognized any person aboard as a British seaman, they might take him. The same jurisdictional principle was the foundation of the rule " free ships, free goods," which was eventually incorporated in the Declaration of Paris in 1856. It is also the basis of jurisdiction of criminal offenses on the high seas; they are justiciable only in the courts of the country to which the ship belongs.[2]

This same principle was recognized by the United States, Great Britain, and Spain in the case of the *Virginius* in 1873.[3] There, Spanish authorities illegally seized on the high seas a vessel carrying the American flag and under American registry. The registry was subsequently shown to have been

---

[4] Proclamation of Oct. 13, 1916, quoted from Vigness, *op. cit.*, p. 89, citing *Oversigt* (1920) II, 5.

[1] Vigness, *op. cit.*, p. 92.

[2] John Bassett Moore, Statement at Hearings on S. 3474, Committee on Foreign Relations, U. S. Senate, 74th Cong., 20th Sess. (Jan. 10–Feb. 5, 1936), p. 185. With regard to impressment see Moore, *Digest*, II, 987–1001.

[3] *Idem*, p. 967.

fraudulently procured, but that was an issue involving only
the United States and the owner of the *Virginius*. After bringing the vessel into Santiago de Cuba, the Spanish authorities
staged a summary trial and shot fifty-three members of the
expedition — among them, nineteen British subjects. The
resulting British claim against Spain — for which compensation was duly made — involved, however, no complaint
about the illegality of the seizure of the vessel on the high
seas, or of any feature of the proceedings other than the summary nature of the subsequent execution on land. That was
a move not justified by imminent necessity as a measure of
self-defense: ". . . it was the duty of the Spanish authorities to prosecute the offenders in proper form of law, and to
have instituted regular proceedings on a definite charge before the execution of the prisoners." [4] But in all questions
relating to the vessel while on the high seas, the British citizens were expected to seek their protection from the state
whose flag the *Virginius* flew.

The celebrated *Trent* [5] affair, involving the Northern attempt to take Mason and Slidell, Confederate diplomats, off
a British ship, is another outstanding example of the application of the rule. Recognizing that the same basic principle
was at stake as in the impressment controversy, Secretary
Seward announced:

If I decide this case in favor of my own Government, I must dis-
allow its most cherished principles, and reverse and forever abandon its essential policy. The country can not afford the sacrifice.
If I maintain those principles, and adhere to that policy, I must
surrender the case itself. It will be seen, therefore, that this Government could not deny the justice of the claim presented to us
in this respect upon its merits. We are asked to do to the British
nation just what we have always insisted all nations ought to
do to us.[6]

[4] Hall, *International Law* (4th ed.), p. 279; quoted in Moore, *Digest*, II,
903.

[5] Moore, *Digest*, VII, 768–778, also 626–629; *idem*, II, 1000–1001.

[6] Mr. Seward, Secretary of State, to Lord Lyons, Dec. 26, 1861, *Br. and
For. State Papers*, LV, 628, 638; quoted in Moore, *Digest*, VII, 626, 629.

An analogous case came before the United States Supreme Court in the case of *In Re Ross*.[7] There, a British subject, enrolled as a seaman on an American vessel, committed murder in the harbor of Yokohama. At that time (1880), the United States exercised extraterritorial jurisdiction over its citizens in Japan by virtue of the Treaty of 1857. In passing upon the jurisdiction of the American Consular Court in Japan to try and sentence the culprit, the United States Supreme Court, speaking through Mr. Justice Field, held that " while he was an enlisted seaman on the American vessel, which floated the American flag, he was, within the meaning of the statute and the treaty, an American, under the protection and subject to the laws of the United States equally with the seaman who was native born." [8]

Again, in prosecuting the claim of Shields, a British seaman on an American vessel who had been brutally assaulted by Valparaiso police, the State Department in its representations to Chile not only recognized but insisted upon this same rule.[9]

In the celebrated case of the British merchantman, *Nereide*, the neutral passenger and cargo owner, Mr. Pinto, by wrapping himself in the Spanish flag, could not have mitigated the danger of his position. If the *Nereide* had been sunk, the cargo lost, and Pinto killed during the resistance, no representation or claim on the part of Spain would have been recognized. He was on an armed British, i.e., enemy, ship that offered resistance to capture. In that position and during the resistance, he was on no better footing than the actively hostile British crew. Any other rule would have been absurd.

While enemy merchantmen may legitimately resist capture — that is, may resist without subjecting themselves to the charge of being franc-tireurs or pirates that would be visited

[7] 140 U. S. 453 (1891).
[8] *Idem*, p. 479.
[9] *Shields (U. S.)* v. *Chile*, Aug. 7, 1892, Moore, *Arb.*, III, 2557–2559. Cf. Borchard, *The Diplomatic Protection of Citizens Abroad*, p. 477.

upon resisting neutrals — by so doing, they render themselves liable to be fired on and sunk by the belligerent warship. The same rule applies also to flight. And, naturally, all property and persons on board such a resisting ship take the risks of their location. As Chief Justice Marshall pointed out with respect to the *Nereide:* " She conveys neutral property which does not engage in her warlike equipments, or in any employment she may make of them; which is put on board solely for the purpose of *transportation, and which encounters the hazard incident to its situation."* [10] (Italics supplied.)

Should the enemy vessel surrender after resistance or flight and subsequently be brought into port for adjudication, the neutral cargo and passengers that contributed in no way to the arming of, or resistance by, the vessel are *then* regarded as divorced from their erstwhile carrier for purposes of adjudication as prize or treatment as prisoners of war.

During the first few months of the World War, this issue was again presented to the United States when German, or allegedly German, passengers were removed from American vessels on the high seas by French cruisers.[1] Secretary Bryan immediately took up the cudgels. He cabled:

Also point out that independent of any question of Piepenbrink's American citizenship, this Government insists that his removal from an American vessel on the high seas was without legal justification . . . there is no justification in international law for the removal of an enemy subject from a neutral vessel on the high seas bound to a neutral port, even if he could properly be regarded as a military person.[2]

As authority, he cited diplomatic correspondence showing both French and English insistence on this rule in the *Trent* case.

[10] The *Nereide* (1815), 9 Cranch 388, pp. 430–431.

[1] *For. Rel.,* 1915, Suppl., pp. 744–755.

[2] Bryan to Page, March 2, 1915, telegram No. 1209; included in telegram of March 2, 1915, Bryan to Sharp, *For. Rel.,* 1915, Suppl., pp. 747–748.

When, during 1916, a British destroyer removed thirty-eight Germans, Austrians, and Turks from the American vessel *China* while on the high seas, Lansing himself invoked the rule. He insisted in that case that the American flag covered these alien passengers, and demanded their immediate release. Great Britain sought to enter into discussions as to the status of some of the kidnaped persons (i.e., whether they were reservists); but Lansing denied the validity of any supposed extenuation and effected their release.[3]

It should thus be abundantly clear that, for purposes of jurisdiction, a vessel on the high seas is subject exclusively to the law of the nation to which, or to whose citizens, she belongs. In the eyes of the law, she is considered as part of that nation's territory for all jurisdictional purposes.[4] The reason for this fundamental postulate of international law is intimately connected with America's historic position in regard to the freedom of the seas.

The modern doctrine that " free ships make free goods," i.e., that neutral ships cover with immunity from capture even enemy goods on board[5] (except contraband), was evolved out of the acceptance of the contention of authorities like Hübner and Galiani in the eighteenth century that a neutral ship at sea was part of the territory of that neutral and under its exclusive jurisdiction.[6] This became an admitted principle of international law.

As was stated by the Permanent Court of International Justice in the *Lotus* case: " A corollary of the principle of the freedom of the seas is that a ship on the high seas is assimilated to the territory of the State the flag of which it flies, for,

[3] *For. Rel.*, 1916, Suppl., pp. 630–679.

[4] Moore, *op. cit.*, I, 930 *et seq.*, and authorities there cited; *The Lotus* (1927), *P. C. I. J.*, ser. A, No. 10.

[5] For this doctrine the United States has contended ever since the Continental Congress of 1776; Great Britain finally accepted it in the Declaration of Paris, 1856.

[6] Butler and Maccoby, *The Development of International Law* (London, 1928), pp. 262–263.

just as in its own territory, that State exercises its authority upon it, and no other State may do so." [7]

It is thus apparent that the first American protest on submarines of February 10, 1915, with its challenging " strict accountability," was founded on the false premise that the United States was privileged to speak not only for American vessels and their personnel, but also on behalf of American citizens on Allied and other vessels. No other neutral country appears to have fallen into this error. As we shall see, all the Northern neutrals of Europe suffered far greater losses than the United States both in men and in ships, but did not commit themselves to views that could not be legally sustained and that invited war.

Of the 194 American lives lost on Allied ships, fifty were seamen, who from time immemorial have been regarded as an integral part of their ship and subject to its jurisdiction alone. The Allied governments, in the light of the American stand, soon appreciated the political value of carrying Americans in the crew of their ships. American passengers were probably equally welcome. Professor Bemis has even voiced the suspicion that the *Sussex* may possibly have invited submarine attack.[8] Yet the American notes made no distinction in principle between Allied, neutral, and American ships, between armed and unarmed ships, between contraband carriers and innocent vessels.

Throughout the controversy, the administration's position was as unsound as its defense was eloquent.

Submarines and the Law

DAVID BUSHNELL during the American Revolution, and Robert Fulton during the Napoleonic Wars, were probably the first to experiment with undersea warships.[9] Their prod-

---

[7] *The Lotus* (1927), *P. C. I. J.*, ser. A, No. 10, p. 25.
[8] Bemis, *Diplomatic History*, p. 610.
[9] See, for example, the following: Lieutenant Colonel H. L. Abbott

ucts were admittedly crude, but they laid a foundation for later developments. While submarines were employed during the American Civil War, it was the French — and an Englishman named Whitehead — who really brought the new vessel to something approximating its modern form. Mr. Whitehead achieved fame primarily for developing the torpedo that bears his name — a weapon that was promptly adopted by most of the major naval powers. The French attained remarkable proficiency during the last quarter of the nineteenth century in submarine manufacture — interestingly enough, because of their desire for protection from the overpowering British Navy.

Admiral Aube, just before assuming the office of French Minister of Marine in 1886, had stressed the inadequacy of French coastal defenses. Cocking an apprehensive eye at the British Navy and merchant marine, he espoused the submarine as France's answer. A portion of one of his many utterances on the subject is worthy of reproduction:

Tomorrow war breaks out. An autonomous torpedo-boat — two officers, twelve crew — has encountered one of these merchant ships, carrier of a cargo more valuable than the most luxurious Spanish galleons. The crew and passengers of this vessel number several hundred. Is the torpedo-boat going to make known its presence to the master of the merchantman, to hail him, [to declare] that he can be sunk and that as a result he will be made prisoner — himself, his crew and his passengers — in short, that he is platonically under the control of a prize crew and that, as such, he must betake himself to the nearest French port? To such a declaration, comparable in folly to the chivalrous " *A vous, Messieurs les Anglais* " of Fontenoy, the captain of the steamship would reply with well-directed cannon fire which would send the torpedo-boat, its crew, and its chivalrous captain to the bottom; then, tranquilly, the ship would pursue its briefly interrupted

(U. S. Army Engineering Corps), *The Beginning of Modern Submarine Warfare* (1881); H. C. Fyfe, *Submarine Warfare* (1907); O. Guileneuc, *Dreadnought or Submersible?* (1916); Paul Fontin, *Les sous-marins et L'Angleterre* (1902); Captain R. B. P. Castex, *Synthèse de la guerre sous-marine* (1920).

voyage. Rather, the torpedo-boat will follow, invisibly and at a distance, the steamer it has encountered; after nightfall, silently and easily, it will send to the depths steamship, cargo, crew and passengers. With a clear conscience and a feeling of great satisfaction, the captain of the torpedo-boat will then continue his cruise.[10]

That was written in 1885 by an eminent French naval authority. Shortly thereafter, as Minister of Marine, he inaugurated an intensive program of submarine construction and experimentation. Other powers were not slow to follow his lead. The United States Navy entered the field prior to the turn of the century and Great Britain immediately followed suit. About 1903 Germany started constructing undersea boats, perfecting still further the basic American invention, with its French improvements.[1] Naval men realized that the submarine was a mere extension of the old torpedo-boat, except that it fired its torpedo while submerged.

Torpedo-boats and submarines had already made a place for themselves when the first Hague Conference met in 1899. Although experience has made clear that an effective weapon has never been successfully outlawed — despite the fact that its first appearance causes an outcry against its use, as was the case with the invention of gunpowder — the delegates of Great Britain, Germany, Russia, Japan, Italy, and Denmark, at the Hague Conference were willing to ban submarines,

[10] Admiral T. Aube, " Défense nationale," p. 12 (translation). This article, dated Dec. 5, 1885, is in Henry Mager, *Atlas Colonial* (1886) ; it is available in Harvard University Library.

This issue flared up in the Washington Conference of 1921. Captain Castex of the French General Staff had in 1920 defended the German use of the submarine in 1915–17 as " absolutely justified " and " absolutely correct." (*Synthèse de la guerre sous-marine*.) He expressed pleasure at the opportunity thus afforded to overthrow the naval power of England. Lord Lee acrimoniously resented this suggestion, coming from an authorized French source (*Proceedings,* pp. 652–656). Admiral de Bon, the French delegate, invoking the eternal friendship of France for England, hastened to repudiate Captain Castex (*idem,* p. 658).

[1] " A Short History of German Submarine Design "; appearing as Appendix II in Gibson and Prendergast, *op. cit.,* pp. 340–350.

provided all the nations concurred. The representatives of France, Austria-Hungary, and smaller powers like the Netherlands, Turkey, Sweden, Norway, and Siam, however, opposed their abolition on the ground that they were a protection to the weak. The French delegate thought they had an " eminently defensive object." The United States through its delegate, Captain Mahan, reserved its opinion on the subject.[2]

The following table shows the subsequent international rivalry in this new field:

Submarines	1908 [3]	1914 [4]	1934 [5]
England	68	75	66
France	60	76	108
Germany	2	32	—
United States	12	47	93

These figures are illuminating, even though many of the early vessels were small experimental craft. To indict the submarine *per se* merely because of its ability to travel under water, was not realistic.[6] This Sir Edward Grey did, in 1916, in his protest against the merchant submarine *Deutschland's* admission into United States waters. Sir Edward did not think that the rules of international law governing surface vessels ought to be applied to a device which he consid-

[2] Meetings of May 31 and June 5, 1899, of the Second Subcommittee, *Conférence internationale de la paix* (18 *mai*–29 *juillet*, 1899), (The Hague, 1899), Part II, p. 86 *et seq.*

[3] Gibson and Prendergast, *op. cit.*, p. 346.

[4] F. T. Jane, *Fighting Ships*, 1914 and 1934. Vessels ordered or under construction are included in these figures. Cf. 1936 figures in Hubbard, " Future Uses of Submarines," *U. S. Naval Institute Proceedings*, Dec., 1936, p. 1721.

[5] *Idem.*

[6] *For. Rel.*, 1916, Suppl., p. 769. See also Millis, *op. cit.*, p. 328. See Appendix A; also Appendix E. Cf. Dr. L. Isserlis, " Shipping Statistics," *Manchester Guardian Commercial*, Reconstruction in Europe, Sec. II, pp. 94–97 (May 18, 1922). See Resolutions of Washington Conference, *Conference on the Limitation of Armament, Washington, November 12, 1921–February 6, 1922* (Government Printing Office, 1922), pp. 267, 695, 711, 1607.

ered beyond the pale of international law. In his memorandum he said:

From the point of view of sea power so much depends both now and in the future upon the way in which submarines are to be treated in international law that it seems impossible to leave the controversy at the stage where the United States Government are disposed to let it rest.

The first point to be established is that international law ought not to transfer without modification to submarines, rules and regulations which work fairly well as regards surface vessels. If this be once conceded we may hope to have an international code drawn up which might meet conditions of naval warfare . . .[7]

At the Washington Conference of 1921, Elihu Root also came to the conclusion that the submarine was incapable of complying with the rules of international law governing surface vessels. He pointed out that a submarine could not regularly accost merchantmen and summon them to stop for visit and search, remove the crew and passengers on board, and take them into a place of safety — which he seemed to believe fundamental rules of warfare — and therefore held that not the rules but the submarine must cease.[8]

But while both Grey and Root were correct in their premise that the submarine — like the airplane — was a new fact, the conclusion does not follow that the old rules should not be applied to it where possible or that it is outlawed because it is unable to comply with some of the old rules. This is not the way law has grown through the ages, for the law adjusts itself to human activities; it does not create them.

It was equally unrealistic for American officials, especially the naval experts, to fail to devise a common-sense plan for the submarine's reception into the scheme of things as soon as it became apparent that Germany had perfected this weapon and was able to use it against British commerce. A continental country with a long coast line has no reason to frown upon the submarine. Islands dependent upon oversea supplies for their living have good reason to wish the submarine outlawed.

Postwar Developments. By the Treaty of Versailles, Germany was prohibited from building any submarines. She was also obliged to turn her existing submarines over to the Allied governments, but not for destruction. France received fifty of them. At the Peace Conference the representatives of the United States agreed with the British that the submarine had no peaceful uses and were willing to see them abolished. President Wilson " hoped the time would come when they would be contrary to international law." [9] Lloyd George said that " it would be better to destroy as many of these pests as possible." [10]

But although the outlawry of the submarine has been a consistent British policy it was frustrated by the position of France and other Powers. A provision was included in the treaty for the criminal trial of certain submarine commanders who had sunk hospital ships and in other ways violated rules of war.[1] This denunciation of submarines, this justifying of passions aroused by the war, gave rise to a powerful propaganda for their abolition. In the United States, the position that had been adopted by the government during the war was considered unquestionable. Both these interests converged, in the Washington Conference on the Limitation of Armaments of 1921 — attended by the United States, Great Britain, Japan, France and Italy — to produce resolutions justifying the British and American objection to the submarine as a commerce destroyer. Lord Lee of Fareham made a valiant argument for the total abolition of the submarine.

[9] Baker, *Woodrow Wilson and World Settlement* (New York, 1922), I, 417–418.
[10] *Ibid.*
[1] A few were ultimately tried in Leipzig, with varying results. Cf. German War Trials, " Report of Proceedings before the Supreme Court in Leipzig," *A. J. I. L.*, XVI (1922), 628.

Elihu Root, for the American delegation, did not go so far, but proposed a resolution confirming the validity of the American war attitude.[2]

Lord Lee called the submarine " a weapon of murder and piracy, involving the drowning of noncombatants; [3] an instrument " in violation of all laws, both human and Divine." [4] It was " the negation of humanity, chivalry and civilization itself." [5] " Was there to be one rule for Germany and another rule for the rest of the world? " [6] To the French argument that the submarine was the " legitimate weapon of the weaker Powers and was an effective and economical means of defense for an extensive coast line and for maritime communications," [7] he answered that it was an aggressive weapon against innocent merchantmen, but was relatively ineffective against warships, which alone it could legitimately attack. To the argument that it was a " cheap method of warfare " he replied, " Surely this Conference did not desire to make war cheap? When war had been cheap it had been almost continuous." [8] He reiterated at several points that Great Britain in demanding the abolition of the submarine was actuated by no selfish motives [9] — an argument that Lord Balfour reinforced — but was speaking for all humanity. Finally and magnanimously, he offered to scrap the entire British submarine fleet.[10]

The French Government was impervious to these persuasive arguments, as was the Italian. After paying full tribute to the humanitarian solicitude of the British Govern-

[2] In 1928 Secretary Kellogg announced the willingness of the United States to sign a treaty " prohibiting the use of the submarine entirely." Kenworthy and Young, *Freedom of the Seas* (London, 1929), p. 184.

[3] *Proceedings, op. cit.*, p. 484.

[4] *Idem*, p. 480.

[5] *Ibid.*

[6] *Idem*, p. 480.

[7] *Idem*, p. 476.

[8] *Idem*, p. 482.

[9] *Ibid.*

[10] *Idem*, p. 484.

ment, a sentiment in which the French entirely shared, the French delegate argued " that the submarine is the only weapon which at present permits a nation scantily supplied with capital ships to defend itself at sea." For France, therefore, the submarine is " an essential means of preserving her independence which she can not give up." [1] The Italian delegate denied the assertion of Lord Lee that " submarines were not an efficient means of defense." [2] The Japanese argued that " submarines in their legitimate employment were no more atrocious than poison gas or air bombs." [3]

The French had indicated their belief that it was possible " to reconcile the use of submarines with the laws of humanity," [4] so the Conference set itself the task of defining a formula for such humanitarian employment. The delegates had been embarrassed occasionally by the inconsistency between their uniform denunciations of Germany's submarine warfare and the manifest insistence of France and Italy that they intended to rely upon it for their own defense against superior navies. Hence the compromise on limiting the functions of the submarine to the rules of visit and search governing surface vessels; hence the guileless dodging of the question of armament on merchantmen, an issue which the 1916 administration had realized lay at the crux of the problem. The American delegation to the 1921 Conference ran away from this vital question by submitting a memorandum advocating that " laws should also be made which prohibited the use of false flags and *offensive* arming of merchant vessels." [5] This was a lame and impotent evasion, as we have seen.[6] The distinction between offensive and defensive weapons is metaphysical at best, and in relation to submarines, any armament on merchantmen is calculated to be fatal to the

---

[1] *Proceedings, op. cit.*, p. 486.
[2] *Idem*, p. 488.
[3] *Idem*, p. 490. Cf. General Sir Henry Thuillier in *Journal of the Royal United Service Inst.*, May, 1936, p. 273.
[4] *Idem*, p. 488.
[5] *Idem*, p. 496. (Italics supplied.)
[6] *Supra*, p. 88.

submarine. The conclusions reached by the Conference, although they never came into force for lack of unanimous ratification,[7] were largely vitiated at the outset because they failed to deal with the immemorial and well-established distinction between armed and unarmed merchantmen.

The Conference purported to regard as " an established part of international law " that a belligerent must determine by visit and search the liability of a merchant vessel to seizure; that it may not be attacked unless it refuses to heed the summons to stop or obey an order issued after seizure; [8] nor must it be destroyed, except possibly as the outcome of such an attack,[9] unless passengers and crew have been removed to a place of safety.[10] This admits the traditional legitimacy of destroying enemy or neutral prizes when there is no opportunity to supply a prize crew or take them in for prize adjudication, but it pretty effectively cripples the submarine. Submarines cannot take many passengers on board, and even if they did, the passengers would be exposed to the greatest danger, for the submarine could be attacked at sight; this was true even as to surface captors, as Sir Edward Grey recognized in 1908 in his instructions to the British delegation at the London Conference.[1] What is a " place of safety " was not defined until the Naval Conference of 1930 but during the war the United States contended that lifeboats did not satisfy this requirement.[2]

The Washington Resolutions, however, provided that submarines were not exempted from ordinary rules governing

---

[7] The resolutions were ratified by the United States, Great Britain, Japan, and Italy, but not by France.

[8] *Proceedings, op. cit.,* p. 1607; Mori, *op. cit.,* pp. 121, 175.

[9] Cf. Italian caveat, *Proceedings,* p. 686.

[10] Without undertaking to analyze these rules, they do not even represent the law as to surface vessels, for a neutral vessel can only be given orders to proceed to a belligerent port if there is suspicion of violating the well-known belligerent rights.

[1] Cf. John Bassett Moore in *Harvard Law Review* (1937), L, 441–442.

[2] The Germans agreed, during the War, that lifeboats would be considered " safe " only when general conditions, weather, sea, and proximity of the coasts afforded absolute certainty that port would be reached.

surface vessels, and that if they could not comply, the merchant vessel must be permitted to proceed unmolested. All other " civilized " Powers were invited to express their assent. Further, to give the stamp of approval to the Versailles attitudes of the Allied Powers at the Conference, the resolutions provided that any member of the naval personnel who shall violate any of these rules whether or not acting under his government's orders shall be liable to be punished " as if for an act of piracy " in any country laying hands on him. Some of the conferees had qualms about the practicality of such a provision, but it was adopted, possibly with the realization that ratification might not follow.

Finally, the Conference recognized the " practical impossibility of using submarines as commerce destroyers, without violating, as they were violated in the recent war of 1914–18, the requirements universally accepted by civilized nations for the protection of the lives of neutrals and noncombatants." Thereupon, use of the submarine as a commerce destroyer was outlawed among those states represented at the Conference, and an invitation was addressed to all other nations to join the renunciation. The suggestion, sometimes advanced, that this represented the already existing law of nations lacks justification; and as new legislation it lacks ratification as a Convention. Nor was it adhered to by any other Powers.

The inconclusive character of the Washington Conference Resolutions led to a new attempt to incorporate into law the outlawry of the submarine as a commerce destroyer. At the London Naval Conference of 1930, attended by Great Britain, the United States, Japan, France, and Italy, Article 22 of the treaty undertook to accept as established rules of international law the requirement that submarines must conform to the rules governing surface vessels:

In particular, except in case of persistent refusal to stop on being duly summoned, or of active resistance to visit or search, a warship, whether surface vessel or submarine boat, may not sink or render incapable of navigation a merchant vessel without having first placed passengers, crew and ship's papers in a place of safety. For this purpose the ship's boats are not regarded as a place of safety unless the safety of the passengers and crew is assured, in the existing sea and weather conditions, by the proximity of land or the presence of another vessel which is in a position to take them on board.[3]

The high contracting parties invite all other powers to express their assent to the above rules.[4]

As stated by Commander Hazlett,[5] these limitations on the use of submarines reduce their effectiveness against shipping to " almost nil." While insular Powers doubtless would desire that, Commander Hazlett remarks that the United States has again sacrificed a solid advantage " for the sake of an ethereal ideal." [6] He adds: ". . . a weapon potent against our possible naval adversaries but to which we ourselves are largely immune is at hand; to so tie our hands with treaties that we are unable logically to prepare it or readily to grasp it would appear to verge on blind folly." [7]

It is highly doubtful whether the London rules ever constituted international law. Their acceptance by some of the principal maritime Powers, however, may lead to that result. But even here, it is well to remember that treaties which do not reflect the mores, such as the Kellogg Pact, are likely to become dead letters. The faith of the Powers in their renunciation of certain uses of the submarine — the legality of which is now recognized — will probably be tested by their willingness to refrain from arming their merchantmen. The failure to make allowances for the effects of arming merchant-

---

[3] These rules came into force for the United States, Great Britain, and Japan. *Proceedings of the London Conference,* 1930, Conference ser., No. 6 (Washington, 1931), Art. 24 (2), p. 219.

[4] Hazlett, " Submarines and the London Treaty," *U. S. Naval Inst. Proc.,* p. 1691.

[5] *Idem.*

[6] *Idem.*

[7] *Idem.*

men gives all the resolutions a touch of unreality.[8] As Commander Hazlett says, to France the submarine " is much less of a threat than a promise." [9] The London Naval Conference dropped into limbo the attempt to characterize as pirates submarine commanders who sink merchant vessels in disregard of the rules announced.

The resolutions of the London Conference of 1930 were to last only until December 31, 1936. In 1935, a new Conference was therefore called to deal with the possibility of continuing an agreed limitation on armaments. Only slight success was achieved in this respect,[10] but the three signatory Powers, the United States, Great Britain and Japan, agreed to continue in force the provisions of Article 22 of the 1930 Treaty [1] on submarines. France and Italy announced in 1936 their acceptance of the two rules of the 1930 London Treaty.[2] Whether this will have a practical effect in universalizing the proposed rules and whether, although having both moral and legal value, they will be enforced even among the signatory Powers is open to question. Informed naval opinion seems to doubt it.[3] We have already referred to General Sir Henry F.

[8] In May, 1936, the British Government announced its intention to arm Cunard White Star liners with six-inch guns. *New York Times,* May 24, 1936, Part I, p. 30, col. 3.

[9] " Submarines and the London Treaty," *U. S. Naval Inst. Proc.,* p. 1690. See the criticism of the French position in Commander Carlyon Bellairs, *The Naval Conference and After* (London, 1931), p. 37.

[10] London Conference of 1936. Dept. of State Conference Series No. 24.

[1] Procès-Verbal, Nov. 6, 1936, *Treaty Information Bulletin 86,* p. 35.

[2] *Ibid.* Other countries were invited to adhere. The German, Soviet Russian, Belgian, and Greek Governments are reported to have given their assent. *New York Times,* Feb. 23, 1937. Such a provision was included in the Havana Convention of 1928 on Maritime Neutrality, Treaty Series 845, Art. 1. This has been ratified by United States, Bolivia, Haiti, Dominican Republic, and Nicaragua.

[3] Lieutenant J. C. Hubbard, " Future Uses of Submarines," *U. S. Naval Inst. Proc.* (Dec., 1936): " It is probable that this type will always be retained, and that the fullest possible use of it will be made in future wars " (p. 1721). Commander Hazlett says: " Is there any doubt, then, that future wars will also see the use of submarines as in the last war rather than in accord with the Treaty of London — and based on German precedent? " *Loc. cit.,* p. 1691.

Thuillier's remarks before the Royal United Service Institution in February, 1936, suggesting that the element of surprise in submarine attack aroused undue hostility and that the enemy's war methods, if successful, are more likely to be considered inhumane than one's own methods.[4] The General added:

To come back to submarines: it is argued that submarine attack on *merchant* vessels is inhumane since it violates an old and excellent sea custom that non-combatants should be taken off in safety. Submarines cannot take off passengers and crew, and there were occasions in the late war when these were set adrift in open boats. There were also cases when they were not even given that option but were sunk without any attempt at rescue. This was certainly very inhumane. But is it more so than to bombard a town with heavy artillery, regardless of the civilians and the women and children in it? — a practice which has prevailed for centuries, and no one makes any protest against it. Is it more inhumane than blockading a besieged town and starving the civilian inhabitants, including women and children? Is it more inhumane than cutting off the food supply of the whole of Germany and Austria, knowing full well that those countries could not produce sufficient food and milk for their own population? Is it more inhumane than continuing that blockade for eighteen months after the armistice? All war is terribly inhumane. It is very splendid of our Navy to have kept up its chivalrous custom of ensuring the safety of civilians at sea right into the XXth century, but their less sensitive comrades on land have for long been in the habit of firing at railway trains or into towns without asking any questions about who are in them. We are more or less accustomed to these forms of inhumanity, but to send a few people adrift in open boats is a form which was new to us and so excited our horror and anger.[5]

Visit and search were not invented for the benefit of passengers or crew. Visit arose because of the misuse of flags; it was intended for the benefit of neutral, not enemy, vessels. When the sinking of prizes was regularized, a provision for

[4] *Supra,* p. 112.
[5] General Sir Henry F. Thuillier, in *Journal of the Royal United Service Institution,* May, 1936, p. 267.

safety of human life became an incident. It was never the reason for the practice of visit and search, as President Wilson seemed to assume.

Whether " war zones " can be tolerated, thus formally changing the rules of close blockade, or whether legal blockade of countries having submarines is practicable, are still debatable questions; as yet war zones cannot be said to have the authority of law and neutrals cannot be obliged to surrender their freedom to use the high seas because of belligerent whim. But if the safety of passengers is really desired, that can be arranged as it was in the Boer War between Great Britain as a belligerent and Germany as a neutral, by exempting certain passenger ships under the neutral flag on condition that they do not carry contraband, an arrangement which it would have been easy to effectuate in the late war but for the inflexible views of the American administration as to the impropriety of the use of the submarine even against enemy vessels. But if, as the eager efforts of the British Government would indicate, the devastating effects of the submarine on British merchant vessels lies at the root of the British objection to their employment as commerce destroyers, why is not consideration given to the time-honored American principle of the immunity from capture of all private property at sea. That was incorporated in the treaty between the United States and Prussia of 1785, and has been reiterated by Congress in numerous resolutions ever since.[6] In the submarine and the airplane may be the counterweight to British objections to

[6] Moore, *Digest*, VII, 461 *et seq.;* and recent Walsh amendment, *Cong. Rec.*, LXX (Jan. 28, 1929), 2344. When peace seemed possible in Feb., 1915, Colonel House records Grey and Tyrrell as both favoring a treaty by which " merchant shipping of whatever nature, belligerent or neutral, would be immune." Seymour, *op. cit.*, I, 369. On February 11, 1915, Sir William Tyrrell had told Colonel House that " Great Britain recognized that the submarine had changed the status of maritime warfare and in the future Great Britain would be better protected by such a policy [recognizing the immunity of private property at sea] than she has been in the past by maintaining an overwhelming navy." Seymour, *op. cit.*, I, 369–370.

abolishing war on the commerce of the enemy. In the middle of the nineteenth century, England indicated some disposition to modify that mode of warfare, but Palmerston, after approving such a proposal, later overruled it.[7] Now there is a special incentive for abandoning that ancient practice which did so much to make large navies necessary. Britain would have an advantage in giving up what heretofore has seemed a preferred position incidental to a large navy and a large merchant fleet. The small navy and the small merchant fleet have by the process of invention been afforded a compensatory advantage. The time for reciprocal concessions, now really in the interests of human progress and the limitation of the horrors of war, may have arrived.

[7] Butler and Maccoby, *Development of International Law* (London, 1928), pp. 277–278.

IV.

THE BRITISH " BLOCKADE " OF WESTERN EUROPE

IN Part I, reference has been made to the gradually increasing restrictions placed by Great Britain in 1914 on trade between the United States, on the one hand, and the Scandinavian countries and Holland on the other, in the belief that goods going to those neutrals might find their way into Germany. In this way what was called a " blockade "[8] of Western Europe was established. The British censored every trans-Atlantic shipment to Northern Europe without reference to the limitations of international law on blockade and contraband. Although the United States had withdrawn its request that England conform to the Declaration of London of October 22, 1914, the British Government nevertheless issued Orders in Council from time to time which still carried in the title the words " Declaration of London." But the modifications of the Declaration imposed by the Orders in Council made it a mere shadow of the original. In July, 1916, even the name " Declaration of London " was dropped; before that date the distinction between goods conditionally contraband and goods absolutely contraband was formally abolished. The distinction, however, had ceased to have great importance in English courts, for the Order in Council of March 11, 1915, by prohibiting all [9] trade with neutrals ex-

---

[8] In the case of the *Hakan*, Lloyd's List, June 9, 1916, Mr. Balloch of counsel referred to the blockade, when " The President [of the Prize Court] interrupted to say that what was called a blockade was not a blockade at all, except for journalistic and political purposes." Moore, *Principles of American Diplomacy* (2d ed., 1918), pp. 78–79, note.

[9] Consul General Skinner to Secretary of State, July 9, 1915, *For. Rel.,* 1915, Suppl., p. 479. On Aug. 16, Sir Edward Grey undertook to show that the United States had derived equal or more profit from the trade with the Northern neutrals than had Great Britain, *idem,* pp. 511, 514.

cept that which Great Britain conducted or to which she consented, and by regarding all goods conditionally contraband destined to Holland or to Scandinavia as in fact destined to Germany unless proof to the contrary was afforded, had already put an end, for British belligerent purposes, to the time-honored distinction.

The willingness of the United States, however, to condone and tolerate the British violations, which were conditioned upon no new facts, geographical or scientific, and were illegal beyond the possibility of doubt, was evidenced as early as August, 1914. Reference has already been made to the effort to obtain British adherence to the Declaration of London and to the helpful assistance rendered to Spring-Rice by Colonel House and Mr. Lansing in assuring American acquiescence in the Order in Council of August 20, 1914, which had already made inroads on the privilege of neutrals to trade with other neutrals in goods conditionally contraband, including foodstuffs.[1] But for the protest from large groups of the American people who had not yet realized that Great Britain was engaged in a crusade for righteousness, it is doubtful whether the Department of State would have taken as much pains as it did to point out the injuries done to the United States and its citizens by the British " measures of blockade."

The note of protest sent by the United States to Great Britain on December 26, 1914, complained against the large number of vessels with American cargoes destined to neutral countries which had been seized on the high seas and detained in British ports. This protest was denatured of all effectiveness, however, by the concession that the British interference with American trade could not be supported " unless such interference is manifestly an imperative necessity to protect their [British] national safety, and then only to the extent that it is a necessity." [2] Inasmuch as apparently the

---

[1] *Supra*, p. 62.   [2] *Supra*, p. 34.

only check upon the British right to be the judge of this necessity was the appeal to " the deep sense of justice of the British Nation," the American admonition had the effect of a tacit, if not express, acquiescence in the illegal measures. In 1915 the Lord Chancellor, Viscount Haldane, could properly remark, with conscious or unconscious irony, " We have necessity on our side; you have the law — what is left of it — on your side: we'll not seriously quarrel." [3]

A show of opposition to the British measures had to be maintained in order to placate that part of American opinion which had an interest in neutrality or which opposed British impositions.[4] On February 10, 1915, came the American protest against the German declaration of submarine warfare on enemy vessels which contained the President's " strict accountability " phrase. On that same day, under Mr. Bryan's urging, a protest was sent to Great Britain against the misuse of the American flag on British vessels, which induces Mr. Baker to say that Mr. Lansing used the opportunity to " make the Germans believe we were equally strict with Great Britain." [5]

The American protest of December, 1914, which Mr. Baker characterizes as a defense of the British measures, was finally answered by Great Britain on February 12, 1915. The argument was, first, that the increase of American trade with the neutral countries contiguous to Germany indicated that this was an indirect trade with Germany which had to be controlled, for the bulk of the increase was regarded as unwarranted and subject to interference, an allegation purported to be proved by statistics which themselves were open to serious question. Second, it was argued that the radical change in the means of transportation — presumably railroads and trucks — made the application of the doctrine of

[3] Baker, op. cit., V, 263.
[4] Cf. Trimble, " Violations of Maritime Law by the Allied Powers during the World War," A. J. I. L., XXIV (1930), 26–49.
[5] For. Rel., 1915, Suppl., p. 100; Baker, op. cit., V, 249.

continuous voyage or transport an absolute necessity, although the British must have known that railroads or trucks were not exactly new; and finally, the Foreign Office relied upon the Civil War precedents, which the Secretary of State's letter of January 20, 1915, to Senator Stone had presented as something of a justification for the British excesses.[6]

Finally the British Foreign Office, in justification of the seizure of foodstuffs destined to neutral countries whence they might reach Germany, advanced the argument, quite like that of 1793 with respect to France, that the enemy government had taken control of the food supplies, that the distinction between the civilian population and the armed forces had disappeared, and that the tremendous organization of the enemy country for war proved that everything would be consumed by the military, if military exigencies required it.[7] A comparison of Britain's note of 1793 to the United States with that of 1915 is illuminating.[8] The difference lies in the

---

[6] We have already adverted, *supra*, p. 69, to the inapplicability of the analogy. The British doubtless perceived from the complaisant protest of Dec. 26 that a change in their methods or compliance with the *pro forma* protest was hardly expected.

[7] *For. Rel.*, 1915, Suppl., p. 324.

[8] *1793 British note* ([a])

" The actual situation of France is notoriously such, as to lead to the employing this mode of distressing her by the joint operations of the different powers engaged in the war; and the reasoning which in these authors, applies to *all* cases of this sort, is certainly much more applicable to the *present* case, in which the distress results from the unusual mode of war employed by the enemy himself, in having armed almost the whole laboring class of the French

1915 British note ([b])

" Another circumstance which is now coming to light is that an elaborate machinery has been organized by the enemy for the supply of foodstuffs for the use of the German army from overseas. . . .

" The reason for drawing a distinction between foodstuffs intended for the civil population and those for the armed forces or enemy Government disappears when the distinction between the civil population and the armed forces itself

([a]) Minister Hammond to the American Secretary of State, Sept. 12, 1793, American State Papers, I, *For. Rel.*, p. 240; Moore, *Digest*, VII, 676–677.

([b]) The British Foreign Secretary to Ambassador Page, Feb. 10, 1915, *For. Rel.*, 1915, Suppl., pp. 324, 332. Cf. Jessup, *Neutrality*, IV, 60, who also employs the deadly parallel.

American attitudes of 1793 and 1915. Whereas Jefferson refused to concede the legality of making foodstuffs contraband, even when destined to French ports, and obtained heavy damages in the arbitrations under Article 7 of the Jay Treaty of 1794,[9] the Wilson administration was unable or unwilling to defend its even more unassailable position as to neutral destinations, and the American shippers and cargoowners imposed upon, or their insurers, are to this day practically unrecompensed.

In the defeat of the United States in the debate with the British Foreign Office, Messrs. Page and House played a prominent role. There is no evidence that the President at this time was not serious in his defense of American neutral rights against Allied impositions, but he left much of the negotiation, involving largely legal questions, to Mr. Lansing. Even if Mr. Lansing had been a powerful gladiator for the interests of American traders, he would have been under a great handicap by reason of the interposition of Page and House to nullify his efforts. Mr. Baker is not without justification in saying that Page was " actually playing the game of the British " and that Colonel House was " being used by

nation, for the purpose of *commencing* and supporting hostilities against all the governments of Europe; but this reasoning is most of all applicable to the circumstances of a trade, which is now in a great measure entirely carried on by the actually ruling party of France itself, and which is therefore no longer to be regarded as a mercantile speculation of individuals, but as an immediate operation of the very persons who have declared war, and are now carrying it on against Great Britain."

disappears.

" In any country in which there exists such a tremendous organization for war as now obtains in Germany there is no clear division between those whom the Government is responsible for feeding and those whom it is not. Experience shows that the power to requisition will be used to the fullest extent in order to make sure that the [wants] of the military are supplied, and however much goods may be imported for civil use it is by the military that they will be consumed if military exigencies require it, especially now that the German Government have taken control of all the foodstuffs in the country."

[9] Moore, *Arb.*, I, 299 *et seq.*; Moore, *Adjudications*, IV, *passim.*

the Allies as a pawn." [10] Men who are distinguished mainly
by their efforts to uplift the world very often surrender the
interests of their country and are the ready tools of those who
know precisely what they want. Mr. Lansing suggests in his
Memoirs that our cause for protest against the Allied measures was greater than against those of Germany,[1] for the
American case against Germany centered primarily in the use
of the submarines, whereas the Allied measures controlled all
aspects of American trade, not only with Europe but, through
the black list, with other parts of the world.

The British response to the German submarine note of
February 4, 1915, was the Order in Council of March 11,
practically prohibiting all trade with Germany. On March 1,
Mr. Asquith, Prime Minister, had announced in Parliament
that the British efforts to exert economic pressure on Germany would not be allowed " to be strangled in a network of
juridical niceties." [2]

The Order in Council of March 11, 1915,[3] had prohibited
any cargoes' going through, even though they had sailed in
complete conformity with the unauthorized British prescription as to named consignees and other conditions, unless
they were consigned to an organization set up by the Allied
governments in each of the neutral countries, an organization
which would guarantee that the goods received would be used
in the neutral country and would not go to Germany. Even
compliance with this requirement did not save all neutral
ships or cargoes.[4]

That Order in Council, elicited from the Department of
State a long protest dated March 30, 1915.[5] It was again a
statement of the law governing blockades and made clear
what the British, of course, well knew, that their Order in
Council bore no relation to a legal blockade. The British
note communicating the order had intimated that prize courts

[10] Baker, *op. cit.*, V, 261.
[1] Lansing, *Memoirs*, p. 110.
[2] Grattan, *op. cit.*, p. 226.
[3] *For. Rel.*, 1915, Suppl., p. 144.
[4] The *Noordam* [1919] P. 57.
[5] *For. Rel.*, 1915, Suppl., p. 152.

would have a wide discretion in dealing with the trade of neutrals and would facilitate claims, and that the Executive had power to mitigate the order. The American State Department noted this possibility of ameliorations with gratification.[6] But these yielded no returns. The order was enforced by the prize courts with unusual expansiveness, condemning not only goods sent to Scandinavia and Holland which might have reached Germany by evasion of the export embargoes of the neutrals, but also goods which might replace other goods that could be sent out from the neutral stock of Holland or Scandinavia.[7] Goods consigned to the Netherlands Oversea Trust, the designated consignee of the British Government, were condemned if the suspicion was entertained that they might, by evasion, reach a person in Holland who might send them to Germany if he could get them.[8] Goods in the raw state were condemned on their way to neutral ports if it was thought that they could be manufactured into goods which in turn might reach Germany.[9] Such things had been unheard of theretofore and were contrary to the fundamental principles of international law.

Page had urged the President to postpone any protest against Britain's " proposed blockade of Germany." Even Colonel House remarks that Page's efforts constituted the " strongest sort of pro-British argument." [10]

On May 7 the *Lusitania* was sunk. This afforded Sir Edward Grey an opportunity to delay his reply to the American protest of March 30. After a preliminary acknowledgment of June 17, the reply came on July 24.[1] It relied to a considerable extent on the violation of the recognized rules of civilized warfare by Germany and on Lord Bryce's collection

---

[6] *For. Rel.*, 1915, Suppl., p. 154.
[7] Cf. The *Baron Stjernblad* [1918] A. C. 173; The *Bonna* [1918] P. 123.
[8] The *Noordam* [1919] P. 57.
[9] The *Baron Stjernblad* [1918] A. C. 173.
[10] Seymour, *op. cit.*, I, 456, March 4, 1915.
[1] *For. Rel.*, 1915, Suppl., p. 168.

of atrocities in Belgium, on the poisoning of wells in German Southwest Africa, on the use of poison gas against the troops in Flanders, and on the sinking of the *Lusitania*. Sir Edward stated that as he read the American note, it did not question the British necessity for taking all steps open to Great Britain to cripple the enemy's trade, but it questioned solely the legitimacy of the particular measures adopted. Grey indicated that the British felt privileged to stop cargo going to neutral ports if they thought it was ultimately destined to Germany, and relied upon the United States' acknowledgment that " great changes . . . have occurred in the conditions and means of naval warfare since the rules hitherto governing legal blockade were formulated "; he appreciated the American recognition that " the former close blockade with its cordon of ships . . . is no longer practicable in the face of an enemy possessing the means . . . to make an effective defense by the use of submarines, mines and aircraft." The issue, as Sir Edward conceived it, came down to the question whether the measures, to quote the American protest, " conform to the spirit and principles of the essence of the rules of war," and he expressed his contentment with the application of this criterion to the British measures, which after careful consideration he found unassailable. He cited the Civil War cases; and to the suggestion that no experts approved what the British were doing, he replied that " writers merely deal with existing rules rather than offer suggestions for their adaptation to altered circumstances," and cited publicists' criticisms of the *Springbok* case during the Civil War.[2] The note ended with the statement that the British were interfering with no goods with which they could not interfere were they destined to German ports — which was scarcely a support for the legality of the action. It denied that the " blockade " embraced neutral ports and coasts, but undertook to justify the gradual expansion of the contraband

[2] *Supra*, p. 69.

lists to permit seizures of nonmilitary goods by the nature of the war and the enemy. The note even suggested a doubt whether the Declaration of Paris applied as between the United States and Great Britain, but frankly admitted that the British purpose was to intercept all commerce between Germany and the outside world.

In August, 1915, cotton was placed on the list of absolute contraband. This aroused great protest in Congress, especially from Southern senators. To resist the resulting pressure, the administration had to send notes of remonstrance; but its heart was not in them. To Senator Simmons of North Carolina, President Wilson expressed his reluctance to " press our neutral claims both against Germany and Great Britain at one and the same time and so make our situation more nearly impossible." [3] The President stated as his belief that the British position was altering in our favor — but evidence of this was not readily apparent.[4] Spring-Rice sought to meet the objections of the South by suggesting the purchase of large quantities of cotton at ten cents a pound.[5] When this rumor reached the German Ambassador he offered to buy a larger quantity than the British at the full market price, if the United States could get it through to Germany. Wilson thought this an insult, " a palpable bribe — to the Southern planters." [6] As Baker says, " We were quite willing to discuss proposals with the British which became reprehensible when suggested by the Germans. The intense and bitter feeling engendered by the war, inflamed by propaganda, was spreading in America." [7] Baker explains the irritations of the summer of 1915 by remarking that this must have been due to Grey's vacation because " the British . . . displayed less than their usual sureness of touch in managing us." [8] What has already been said indicates the soundness of this conclusion, for the

[3] Baker, *op. cit.*, V, 367.
[4] *Ibid.*
[5] Seymour, *op. cit.*, II, 60.

[6] Hendrick, *op. cit.*, I, 378–379.
[7] Baker, *op. cit.*, V, 378.
[8] *Idem*, p. 366.

American notes were not as serious as they seemed, were in part compounded with British approval, and were intended largely for home consumption. Wilson opposed " ' vigorous ' protests " to Great Britain — because they were " apt to be regarded as logically leading to action." [9] But as in the case of Germany he contemplated action, there was naturally no objection to " ' vigorous ' protests." [10] No such words as " strict accountability " can be found in the protests to Great Britain, although Secretary Garrison recommended them to the President on March 20, 1915.[1]

Reference has already been made to the entreaty of Secretary Bryan to hold the scales even at the time of the *Lusitania* crisis by protesting to Great Britain against the illegal restrictions on American trade with neutrals. Although Wilson found no good way to put Bryan off during his incumbency, when Bryan left the Department in June, 1915, all thought of another note of protest disappeared. As Wilson said, he did not wish to protest to both belligerents at the same time.

No reply to the British note of July, 1915, was dispatched until October 21, 1915.[2] That note was a sound legal argument reviewing the whole prior protest against the illegal extensions of contraband and blockade, against the unlawful practice of diverting ships from the high seas into British ports to search for evidence, statistical and inferential, that the cargo might reach Germany; against the long detentions of vessels, injuring American trade; against the condemnation of goods which ultimately were resold by British merchants to neutral countries; against the enlargement of Brit-

[9] Baker, *op. cit.*, V, 257.

[10] Elihu Root's criticism of the Wilson administration in the New York Republican convention, Feb. 15, 1916, for not following up its strong protests was premature. *New York Times*, Feb. 16, 1916. Had he known that House was then preparing an agreement with Grey looking to American intervention, his criticism would probably have been tempered. Wilson had to respect the reluctance of the American public to enter the war.

[1] Baker, *op. cit.*, V, 260.

[2] *For. Rel.*, 1915, Suppl., p. 578.

ish trade with neutrals from which American shipments were barred; against the abuses of the prize court in its rules of evidence, and the resulting improper condemnations. It listed in an appendix the many steamers which had been detained or condemned by the British in execution of their policy. It characterized the blockade as " ineffective, illegal and indefensible." But by that time Mr. Lansing was already committed to war and had stated that we would not take a course " that would seriously endanger our friendly relations with Great Britain, France, or Russia." [3] Spring-Rice had been consulted about the note and had been assured that it was merely formal. He had advised his government that the reason for the note's being sent was the necessity for a good showing before Congress met, and he had added that the controversy was " a juridical discussion." [4] As already observed, Mr. Lansing admits that the notes " were long and exhaustive treatises not designed to accomplish a settlement, but to assure a continuance of the controversies, leaving the questions unsettled, which was necessary in order to leave this country free to act and even to act illegally when it entered the war." [5]

Thus the American Secretary of State, while leaving the country and Congress under the impression that he was defending American neutral rights under international law, privately recorded the fact that he was not only seeking to protect Great Britain against the legitimate complaints of the United States, but was also keeping the way open to enter the War on the side of Great Britain, and thereafter to commit the very same illegal acts against which he was supposed to be protesting. Surely unneutrality had made unconscionable strides when an American Secretary of State was willing deliberately, though privately, to confess:

Sympathetic as I felt toward the Allies and convinced that we would in the end join with them against the autocratic govern-

---

[3] Seymour, *op. cit.*, II, 70.   [5] Lansing, *op. cit.*, p. 128.
[4] *Supra*, p. 39.

ments of the Central Empires, I saw with apprehension the tide
of resentment against Great Britain rising higher and higher in
this country. It was becoming increasingly difficult to avoid bringing the controversies between our two governments to a head and
to keep from assuming positions which went beyond the field of
discussion. I did all that I could to prolong the disputes by preparing, or having prepared, long and detailed replies, and in-
troducing technical and controversial matters in the hope that
before the extended interchange of arguments came to an end something would happen to change the current of American public
opinion or to make the American people perceive that German
absolutism was a menace to their liberties and to democratic institutions everywhere. Fortunately this hope and effort were not
in vain. Germany did the very thing which she should not have
done. The tide of sentiment in the United States turned, and it
was possible to prevent a widespread demand being made that
the Allied Powers be " brought to book " without further delay
for their illegal treatment of our commerce.[6]

He adds further:

Sifted down to the bare facts the position was this: Great Britain
insisted that Germany should conform her conduct of naval warfare to the strict letter of the rules of international law, and resented even a suggestion that there should be any variation of
the rules to make them reasonably applicable to new conditions.
On the other hand, Great Britain was herself repeatedly departing
from the rules of international law on the plea that new conditions
compelled her to do so, and even showed resentment because the
United States refused to recognize her right to ignore or modify
the rules whenever she thought it necessary to do so. Briefly, the
British Government wished international law enforced when they
believed that it worked to the advantage of Great Britain and
wished the law modified when the change would benefit Great
Britain. There is no doubt that the good relations between the
United States and Great Britain would have been seriously jeopardized by this unreasonable attitude, which seems unworthy of
British statesmanship, except for the fact that British violations
of law affected American property while the German violations
affected American lives.[7]

[6] *Idem*, pp. 111–112.   [7] *Idem*, pp. 110–111.

The British replied on April 24, 1916, to the American note of October 21, 1915. The reply was delivered in Washington at the time when the *Sussex* controversy with Germany was at its height.[8] It undertook to justify the change made in blockade and contraband and in prize court procedure by alleging that new conditions had arisen, by showing statistically that the neutral countries were receiving so much more than they had theretofore that the balance must be going to Germany. They failed in replying to admit the charge that because the measures were retaliatory they were therefore illegal, although Professor Brierly of Oxford today finds it difficult to reconcile the British retaliatory orders with legal principles.[9] The note ended somewhat ironically with the statement: " His Majesty's Government have noted with sincere satisfaction the intimation contained in the concluding passages of the United States note of the intention of the United States to undertake the task of championing the integrity of neutral rights." [10] Nor did they diminish the impression of genial contempt which this sentence embodies by advancing the assumption that the championing of neutral rights had reference to the unprovoked invasion of Belgium, to the alleged atrocities committed there, and to the submarine warfare. The note expressed His Majesty's Government's welcome of any combination of neutral nations under the leadership of the United States which would exert an effective influence to prevent the violation of neutral rights, adding that His Majesty's Government could not believe that Great Britain or its Allies had much to fear from such a combination.

The black list of July, 1916, which undertook to bar the trade of American firms with firms on the black list in any part of the world, aroused considerable irritation in Wash-

[8] *For. Rel.*, 1916, Suppl., p. 368.
[9] *Law Quarterly Review*, LI (Jan., 1935), 26.
[10] *For. Rel.*, 1916, Suppl., p. 380.

ington, but as in the case of all other impositions, it was submitted to, notwithstanding the mild form of reprisal permitted to the President in the Revenue Act of September 8, 1916, but never employed.[1] Indeed the United States yielded to the British black list at a time when Canada, then fighting in the war, refused to submit to it. Not until after the United States entered the war did the Canadians enact their own black list; when the United States entered, it enlarged the British list.

Sir Eyre Crowe in his famous memorandum of January 1, 1907,[2] spoke of the British necessity for preponderance of sea power, but intelligently remarked that such preponderance, if abused, would arouse feelings of resentment throughout the world, and so must be exercised with the utmost benevolence and a minimum of provocation. That wise injunction was thrown to the winds in 1914–17, and abuses were practiced which seem likely in time to produce a widespread reaction against the British monopoly of sea power and its assumption of exemption from customary rules of law.

[1] Bemis, *Diplomatic History of the United States* (New York, 1936), pp. 588–589.

[2] Gooch and Temperley, *British Documents on the Origins of the War, 1898–1914*, III (1928), 397.

AMERICAN LIVES LOST
On Belligerent Vessels

D URING the early part of 1915, the British instructions to merchantmen were put to their first practical application. " One vessel, the small collier *Thordis*, during heavy weather on the 28th [February, 1915], rammed a submarine off Beachy Head; Berlin admitted that she had injured the U-boat; the latter had, however, safely regained port." [3] Before the end of March, it was announced in the press that the *Thordis* had received a reward of £660 for this gallant action.[4]

For some reason the Washington administration seems to have remained in ignorance for an unduly protracted period of the British instructions — officially issued on February 10, 1915, and unofficially, on February 6. Thus, it is interesting to note both the dates and the direction of the following cables:

April 12, 1915; Bryan to Page:

Please inform us whether any order has been issued giving reward to merchant vessels which ram submarines and whether merchant vessels are trained to combat with submarines.[5]

April 13, 1915; Page to Bryan:

When the so-called submarine blockade was instituted rewards were offered publicly by private persons and organizations to merchant vessels for sinking German submarines. Claims for these rewards have been put in by several ships.

There is no record that the Government has offered such rewards but the press states that the steamer Thordis has received a

---

[3] Gibson and Prendergast, *op. cit.*, p. 32.
[4] *London Times,* March 30, 1915, p. 12, col. 2.
[5] *For. Rel.*, 1915, Suppl., pp. 365–366.

sum of money from the Admiralty for sinking an enemy submarine.

The Admiralty has issued instructions to merchant vessels as how to best avoid attack by submarines but I know of no instructions having been issued to merchant vessels with regard to attacking submarines.[6]

One of the remarkable things about Mr. Page's response to Secretary Bryan's query is its final paragraph. The British Government had instructed its merchantmen " how to best avoid attack by submarines," but had not instructed them " with regard to attacking submarines." This supposed distinction conveyed no real information. On the contrary, it resurrected the specious concept of " offensive " and " defensive " armaments and tactics so sedulously pressed in 1914 and apparently believed in by Lansing.

One other fact may be noted before taking up the consideration of American lives lost on belligerent vessels. Berlin knew of the British ramming tactics. In addition, the Germans were aware — from practical experience — of the arming of British merchantmen. On March 12, 1915, the British armed steamer *Atalanta* had been stopped and set on fire. Slightly over a month later the British steamer *La Roserina* had successfully driven off a submarine by its gunfire.[7]

The situation would thus appear to have been as follows: The British were carrying on their " defensive " tactics under instructions from the Admiralty; the Germans knew of these tactics; and the American State Department was being advised by its Ambassador that " I know of no instructions having been issued to merchant vessels with regard to attacking submarines."

In addition, the American " strict accountability " note had been dispatched on February 10, 1915. The British North Sea " military area " declaration had evoked no neutral pro-

[6] *Idem*, p. 368.
[7] Gibson and Prendergast, *op. cit.*, pp. 33, 37; Fayle, *Seaborne Trade* (1923), II, 35.

test from the United States, notwithstanding requests from the Scandinavian Governments. The armed merchantmen errors had crystallized,[8] and no distinction was drawn between American passengers on belligerent and on American vessels.

Of the thirty-five American lives lost during 1915 on foreign ships, in addition to those on the *Lusitania,* twenty-one men were killed when the *Armenian,* a British mule transport chartered by the Admiralty and " engaged on Admiralty business," [9] was shelled by a submarine. The facts of the case, as given by the official British historian, warrant repetition:

. . . a submarine was sighted on the port bow, about three miles away, steaming towards the *Armenian* on the surface. As the British ship, though unarmed, had a speed of 14-½ knots, Captain Irickey decided to make a fight for it.
He accordingly headed for the submarine with the intention of ramming her. The enemy, however, opened fire.[10]

The vessel carried no passengers according to the Admiralty; " Americans lost therefore appear to be members of crew." [11] Moreover, " all loss of life appears to have occurred from the gunfire and not from ships company having to take the boats." [1] These American muleteers were, then, not only employed on a British ship that actively attacked a submarine, but they were also in the British Government service. They were no more entitled to American protection than the members of the Lafayette Escadrille.

When the British steamer *Iberian* tried to escape and was shelled on July 30, an American muleteer, already in bad physical condition through " a protracted course of dissipa-

---

[8] *Supra,* p. 106.
[9] Page to Lansing, June 30, 1915, *For. Rel.,* 1915, Suppl., p. 457. Cf. also, same to same, July 10, 1915, *idem,* p. 463.
[10] Hurd, *op. cit.,* II, 9.
[11] Page to Lansing, June 30, 1915, *For. Rel.,* 1915, Suppl., p. 457.
[1] Page to Lansing, July 3, 1915, *idem,* pp. 458–459.

tion at Manchester," died from the shock.[2] Three weeks later, two Americans were lost in the torpedoing of the British liner *Arabic*;[3] Germany subsequently disavowed this sinking and offered an indemnity.[4]

The extent of American losses incurred in the sinking of the Italian steamer *Ancona* in the early part of November is somewhat uncertain. Shortly after the disaster, the American Ambassador in Italy cabled that apparently twenty-seven Americans had been killed.[5] Subsequent correspondence with Rome, however, reduced this by two thirds: " Twelve Americans known to have been aboard Ancona . . . Of the foregoing, only three are known to survive . . ."[6] Even this may not be accurate, but it appears to be all the official information available. It is somewhat curious to find Lansing subsequently stating that " about twenty " Americans perished in this disaster.[7] The sinking was disavowed by Austria-Hungary and indemnities were offered before the end of the year.

The British steamer *Persia*, sunk on December 30, 1915, is sometimes charged with two American casualties, but on the basis of official records, it is apparent that only one American fatality occurred: " P. and O. liner *Persia* carrying 4.7 gun sunk . . . December thirtieth . . . Two American citizens aboard. Charles H. Grant . . . is safe Alexandria. Robert Ney McNeely . . . most probably lost."[8]

It is worthy of note that it was apparently the *Persia* sinking which stirred Lansing into his attempt to " get out from under " the September, 1914, ruling on armed merchantmen.

[2] Consul Frost to Lansing, July 31, 1915, *idem*, pp. 510–511.

[3] *Idem*, p. 518.

[4] Oct. 5, 1915, *idem*, p. 560.

[5] *Idem*, p. 611; *New York Times*, Nov. 11, 1915, p. 1, col. 5.

[6] *For. Rel.*, 1915, Suppl., p. 646; *New York Times*, Nov. 15, 1915, p. 1; *New York Times*, Nov. 18, 1915, p. 2, col. 5.

[7] Lansing, *Memoirs*, p. 88.

[8] Consul Garrels to Lansing, Jan. 1, 1916, Department of State, " Diplomatic Correspondence," *European War, No. 4*, p. 131. See also *New York Times*, Jan. 3, 1916, p. 1, col. 5.

He wrote President Wilson on the second day of the new year: " The fact that the vessel was carrying a 4.7 gun raises a question which, it seems to me, we ought to settle." [9] The miscarriage of his subsequent proposal of January 18, 1916,[10] to the Entente Powers has already received sufficient comment.

In all, 163 American lives were lost during 1915 on belligerent ships [1] — including the 22 in the crews of the *Armenian* and the *Iberian* — as a direct or indirect result of the submarine campaign. This figure was increased to 176 by the end of 1916 — and stood at that number on February 3, 1917, when diplomatic relations with Germany were severed.

On March 23, 1916, the " horse-ship *Englishman*," carrying " several Americans," was sunk. Although it is not clear from the published correspondence how many of these " several " were killed, a list published by the Department of State in 1918 [2] placed the loss at six — a figure that will have to be accepted here, although that list has been found to be inaccurate in several cases. The official British account of the sinking shows that the vessel tried to escape from a submarine that had signaled it to stop; the submarine then gave chase and commenced firing her gun. In all, ten of the crew were lost, most of them when shots hit the davits of some lifeboats " causing the boats to fall into the water, together with about thirty men. The ship was then stopped . . ." [3]

Consul Frost reported the horse-transport *Marina*, sunk on October 28, as ". . . mounting 4.7 gun . . . Fifty-one Americans aboard; forty-five safe." [4] Germany refrained

---

[9] Lansing to Wilson, Jan. 2, 1916, Savage, *op. cit.*, II, Doc. No. 149, p. 430.

[10] Lansing to Wilson, Jan. 17, 1916, Savage, *op. cit.*, II, Doc. No. 155, pp. 440, 441. Cf. *supra*, p. 103.

[1] See comment following the tabulations in Appendix C.

[2] *European War, No. 4*, pp. 300–301.

[3] Hurd, *op. cit.*, II, 302.

[4] *European War, No. 4*, pp. 258, 259. Cf. also *idem*, pp. 312, 320.

from remarking on the fact that the vessel was armed " as it did not wish to reopen the discussion of the question of defensive and offensive armament." [5] One other American citizen was killed when the Italian horse-transport *Palermo* was sunk on the second of December.[6]

The total American losses on belligerent vessels through February 2, 1917, amounted to 141 passengers and 35 sailors or hostlers (21 of whom were enrolled on a vessel admittedly in the service of the British Admiralty).

The year 1916 also marked the peak of American solicitousness for the lives of travelers on belligerent vessels. When the French channel boat *Sussex* was torpedoed on March 24,[7] no Americans were lost,[8] although several were injured. Washington's direct threat to sever relations with Germany at that time [9] resulted in the so-called " *Sussex* pledge." [10]

The United States was the only nation that could have commanded the attention of the Entente Powers in any efforts to humanize — and, perhaps, even to end — the warfare on both sides. Sir Edward Grey saw this clearly. In one place he characterizes the United States as " in a sense the trustee for the right of weaker neutrals." [1] In describing the British blockade measures, he states: " the United States was the formidable and vital difficulty " in making them airtight. Referring to President Wilson's too long delayed proposal for a conference in the latter part of 1916, Sir Edward remarked, when viewing events in retrospect:

[5] Grew (Chargé in Germany) to Lansing, Nov. 27, 1916, *idem,* p. 313.

[6] *For. Rel.,* 1916, Suppl., p. 323.

[7] Page to Lansing, March 25, 1916, *For. Rel.,* 1916, Suppl., p. 214.

[8] Report to Assistant Naval Attaché Smith to Ambassador Sharp, March 30, 1916, *A. J. I. L.,* X, Special Suppl. (1916), pp. 230, 231.

[9] " The *Sussex* Note," Lansing to Gerard, April 18, 1916, *For. Rel.,* 1916, Suppl., pp. 232–234.

[10] Gerard to Lansing, May 4, 1916, *For. Rel.,* 1916, Suppl., pp. 257–260, *supra,* p. 167.

[1] Grey, *Twenty-five Years* (1925), II, 110.

If she [Germany] had accepted the Wilson policy, and was ready to agree to a Conference, the Allies could not have refused. They were dependent on American supplies; they could not have risked the ill-will of the Government of the United States, still less a *rapprochement* between the United States and Germany.[2]

It seems rather clear that the American officials could — had they so wished — have exerted considerable pressure to induce Great Britain to abide by established rules of international law with regard to her " measures of blockade." [3] The Germans asked no more in return for their curtailment of the submarine.

During the period of the " overt act " (February 3 to April 6, 1917), seventeen American lives were lost on British ships, ten on the *Vedamore* which ". . . carried one gun in stern . . . Crew contained 15 Filipinos of whom 8 drowned, 1 died of exposure . . . and 2 American negroes, of whom 1 drowned." [4] Again, these were sailors enrolled on a British vessel — this one admittedly armed. The same is true of the " American colored fireman " who lost his life in the sinking of the armed horse-transport *Crispin*.[5]

Three Americans perished on February 25 in the sinking of the *Laconia*, another armed [6] British steamship. Two of this number were passengers,[7] and the other a negro member of the crew.[8] The other three Americans killed during this period were also members of the crews of British vessels: two on the *Galgorm Castle* [9] and one on the *Eavestone*.[10] The lat-

---

[2] Grey, *Twenty-five Years* (1925), II, p. 135.

[3] So called in Sir Edward Grey's note of March 15, 1915, *For. Rel.*, 1915, Suppl., p. 143.

[4] Page to Lansing, Feb. 13, 1917, *For. Rel.*, 1917, Suppl. I, pp. 130–131.

[5] *Idem*, pp. 189–190, 194.

[6] *European War, No. 4*, pp. 285–286; *M. S. Losses* (1919), p. 34.

[7] Consul Washington to Lansing, Feb. 27, 1917, *For. Rel.*, 1917, Suppl. I, p. 151.

[8] See *European War, No. 4*, pp. 290–291; *New York Times*, March 4, 1917, Part I, p. 6, col. 3.

[9] *For. Rel.*, 1917, Suppl. I, p. 156.

[10] *Idem*, p. 144.

ter was sunk while endeavoring to escape from a submarine on the very day relations with Germany were broken.

Two other American lives were lost during this same period: one a passenger on the French troop-transport *Athos,* the other a fireman on the Norwegian *Sjostad.* Both cases deserve some comment. In neither case is it certain whether mine or torpedo caused the sinking.[1] Perhaps the most complete exposition of the *Athos* case is that given in the following press dispatches:

Paris, Feb. 23. — The French steamer Athos, carrying Senegalese troops and colonial laborers, has been torpedoed in the Mediterranean Sea.

The torpedoing occurred despite the fact that the Athos was escorted by the French torpedo boat destroyers Mameluk and Enseigne Henry . . .

Washington, Feb. 23. — A paraphrase of the dispatch given out at the State Department follows:

" Robert Allen Haden, Presbyterian missionary stationed at Soochow, China, perished when the French liner Athos was torpedoed . . . on the 17th inst. . . ."

The report of Consul Keblinger is the first news received here of the sinking of the Athos. It was admitted that if the ship was employed as a transport for troops, as reported, the enemy [*sic*] had a right to sink it without warning.

Officials did not regard the attack on the Athos as the " overt act " referred to by President Wilson in his address to Congress. . .[2]

The operative factors connected with the sinking of the *Sjostad* are equally interesting. According to Consul Osborne:

Norwegian steamer *Sjostad* . . . sunk 28th . . . either torpedoed or mined; 17 in crew; 9 missing and believed drowned, comprising . . . 1 American named Smith . . . shipped as fireman . . . Eight survivors fell in sea; rescued by French torpedo boats,

[1] *European War, No. 4,* pp. 300–301.
[2] *New York Times,* Feb. 24, 1917, p. 1, col. 7.

which had convoyed Sjostad, and brought to Havre.[3] (Italics supplied.)

To sum up these losses: 144 passengers and 50 sailors — 194 American citizens — had been lost on belligerent vessels, of whom 128, or approximately two thirds, were *Lusitania* victims. Of the remaining 66 casualties, 50 were enrolled as crew, 21 of them on a vessel engaged in Admiralty service; 17 seamen and 3 passengers were on board vessels admitted to have been armed, and another passenger was on a convoyed troop-ship. Thirty of the non-*Lusitania* losses, moreover, occurred when the belligerent vessels attempted either to resist or to escape.

This entire group of 195 have certainly made a place for themselves in history. Not, however, because these deaths should have been made a reason for war. That was pointed out by Bryan, Gerard, Gore, Stone, La Follette, McLemore, and other members of a very select group in public life at that time. These men were gifted with the sense to perceive, and the courage to proclaim, that the persistent refusals to caution American citizens against traveling on such belligerent ships could have but one outcome.

On American Vessels

THE foregoing criticisms do not, of course, apply to America's position with regard to losses on American vessels. In protesting these, the State Department was not only within its legal rights, but was also merely complying with its duty. But, unhappily, the record does not indicate the issuance of ultimata with regard to losses on American ships. The reason for that becomes clear as soon as one attempts to analyze the American losses.[4]

[3] Consul Osborne to Lansing, March 1, 1917, *For. Rel.,* 1917, Suppl. I, p. 155.

[4] Tabulations of American losses on American ships will be found in Appendix A.

Until the break in diplomatic relations with Germany on February 3, 1917, only three lives had been lost on American vessels. These were all on the *Gulflight* which was torpedoed on May 1, 1915, the very day the *Lusitania* sailed from New York. The vessel did not sink, but was towed in. Several facts about the case immediately came to light. In confirmation of press reports that appeared on May 3,[5] Page cabled Lansing four days later that the torpedoing took place shortly after noon: " Wireless Operator Short and Seaman Charpenta jumped overboard and were drowned . . . Captain Gunter died during night, coroner's inquest determines cause of death as heart failure." [6]

The American protest to Germany over this attack was incorporated in the first *Lusitania* note in the following terms:

The sinking of the British passenger steamer *Falaba* by a German submarine on March 28, through which Leon C. Thrasher, an American citizen, was drowned; the attack on April 28 on the American vessel *Cushing* by a German aeroplane; the torpedoing on May 1 of the American vessel *Gulflight* by a German submarine, as a result of which two or more American citizens met their death; and, finally, the torpedoing and sinking of the steamship *Lusitania*, constitute a series of events which the Government of the United States has observed with growing concern, distress, and amazement.[7]

Then followed the " strict accountability " ultimatum against the " intentional or incidental " infringement by Germany ". . . of the rights of American ship-masters or of American citizens bound on lawful errands as passengers on merchant ships of belligerent nationality; . . ." [8] Finally, Germany was called upon to abandon the use of the submarine against all merchant vessels, belligerent as well as neutral.

Now this indiscriminate bunching of belligerent and neu-

[5] *London Times*, May 3, 1915, p. 15, col. 3; *idem*, May 6, 1915, p. 5, col. 3.

[6] Page to Lansing, May 7, 1915, " Diplomatic Correspondence," *A. J. I. L.*, XI, Special Suppl. (1917), pp. 76, 77.

[7] *For. Rel.*, 1915, Suppl., p. 393.

[8] *Idem*, p. 394.

tral vessels, with the emphasis placed on the *Lusitania*, showed unfamiliarity with the basic legal distinction between the two classes of claims. The German reply of May 28,[9] and the supplemental notes,[1] however, made a sharp distinction between the two; for the injuries arising on the two American vessels apologies and compensation were quickly offered.

In the case of the *Cushing*, the damage had been slight. As reported by Minister Van Dyke to Secretary Bryan on April 30: " Three bombs dropped, one struck ship causing damage but no life lost." [2] It was subsequently determined that the vessel had been improperly marked.[3] The damage, if any, appears to have been so slight that Ambassador Gerard reported: " No damage had been made." [4] Moreover, the Germans " very much regretted that the attack had been made " and " hoped it would be regarded as an unfortunate, unintentional accident."

The *Gulflight* case, being the only American submarine casualty involving loss of life prior to March 16, 1917, deserves more particular attention. Once more, it is somewhat surprising to note that the first mention of the attack in the diplomatic correspondence seems to have been on May 3 in a cable, from Bryan to Page, requesting details.[5] And yet the attack had been reported to the London papers that morning. Moreover, it was Bryan again who, three days later, cabled Page for verification of information given the State Department by the owners, the Gulf Refining Company, to the effect that this tanker had been torpedoed without warning " while following British patrol boats to Bishop." [6] This information was confirmed by Page on the following day, May 7.[7] On the tenth, Page cabled again, the published para-

---

[9] *For. Rel.*, 1915, Suppl., p. 419.
[1] *Idem*, p. 431.
[2] *For. Rel.*, 1915, Suppl., p. 378.
[3] *Idem*, pp. 431, 440.
[4] *Idem*, p. 440.
[5] *For. Rel.*, 1915, Suppl., p. 378.
[6] Bryan to Page, May 6, 1915, *idem*, p. 381.
[7] *European War, No. 4*, p. 224.

phrase of his cable reading: " Mr. Page reports that it appears that Captain of *Gulflight* complied, without raising any question, with the signals of British patrol boats to proceed under their convoy. Further inquiries are being made of British Admiralty." [8]

A week later came the explanation for this *prima facie* case of belligerent naval convoy — a procedure whose legal effects have already been discussed. When hailed by the naval patrols, ". . . the late Captain Gunther of *Gulflight* . . . in replying that the ship was bound to Rouen, asked when he could secure a French pilot. The reply of the patrol boat was that he could not get one there and directed the *Gulflight* to follow the patrols to the Bishop Rock." [9] Hence the German submarine commander's explanation that he was misled by these facts and so attacked the vessel without previous warning.[10] Nevertheless, the German Government expressed its regrets ". . . concerning this incident and declares itself ready to furnish full recompense for the damage thereby sustained by American citizens." [1]

The really important feature of this case lies in the matter of dates. A week prior to the dispatch of the *Lusitania* note of May 13, the administration had good cause to believe that there might be extenuating circumstances in connection with the *Gulflight* sinking. Communications were exchanged between the State Department and London, and confirmation of these rumors was received on May 7 — six days before the sinking was protested. It was then definitely known that the vessel had been under belligerent naval convoy! Furthermore, in a note dated May 9, Germany had fully disclaimed any intention of injuring neutral vessels that " have been guilty of no hostile act."

[8] Page to Lansing, May 10, 1915 (paraphrase), " Diplomatic Correspondence," *A. J. I. L.*, XI, Special Suppl. (1917), 78.

[9] *For. Rel.*, 1915, Suppl., p. 397.

[10] Gerard to Bryan, June 1, 1915, *idem*, p. 431; *idem*, pp. 439–441.

[1] *Idem*, p. 431.

Should a neutral ship, nevertheless, come to harm through German submarines or aircraft on account of an unfortunate [mistake] in the . . . zone of naval warfare, the German Government will unreservedly recognize its responsibility therefor. In such a case it will afford damages without first instituting a prize court action.[2]

To sum up: To all intents and purposes, the *Gulflight* was under belligerent naval convoy, thus sacrificing her neutral status and subjecting her to instant attack. Knowing these facts, and also that Germany was pledged " unreservedly " to rectify any mistakes affecting neutrals, the State Department joined a protest in this case with the *Lusitania* ultimatum. In accordance with her pledge, Germany apologized and offered " full recompense," a course of action that was acknowledged by the State Department " with gratification." [3]

Meanwhile, another American vessel, the *Nebraskan,* had been struck by a torpedo on the evening of May 25, but was able to make port; " no lives reported lost." [4] The vessel, under charter to the British White Star Line,[5] was seemingly without any illumination to show its ultimate American ownership. No protest seems to have been made, but apologies and compensation were duly offered by Germany [6] in response to the American inquiry.

On July 25, 1915, the American ship *Leelanaw* was stopped by a German submarine, visited and searched, and her cargo found to consist of goods absolutely contraband consigned to an English port. The vessel was sunk after the crew had taken to the boats; these were then towed some fifty miles by the submarine in order to assure the crew's safe arrival ashore.[7] No American protest was made with regard to this

---

[2] Gerard to Bryan, *For. Rel.,* 1915, Suppl., p. 387.

[3] The second *Lusitania* note, Lansing to Gerard, June 9, 1915, *idem,* p. 431.

[4] Page to Bryan, undated, received May 26, 1915, *idem,* p. 414.

[5] Washington (Consul at Liverpool) to Bryan, May 28, 1915, *idem,* p. 418. See also the telegram of June 2, 1915 (Bryan to Gerard, *idem,* p. 430), requesting German information about the attack.

[6] Gerard to Lansing, July 12, 1915, *idem,* pp. 468–469.

[7] *For. Rel.,* 1915, Suppl., pp. 486, 487, 607–608.

action, the question at issue between the two governments
with respect to the case being, as in the similar case of the
William P. Frye,[8] the mode in which compensation to American interests should be assessed [9] under Article 13 of the
Prussian-American Treaty of 1799 [10] abolishing confiscation.

The *Frye* case, which elicited lengthy discussions on this
issue,[1] involved a sailing vessel stopped on the high seas by
the German cruiser, *Prinz Eitel Friedrich,* on January 27,
1915. Its cargo of wheat, conditionally contraband, was consigned " to order " at fortified British naval bases. After the
crew had been removed to safety aboard the raider, the vessel was sunk on the following day.

Several little-appreciated points are thus brought out
clearly. It was not the treatment accorded American vessels
by the submarine that prompted the government to issue ultimata, nor was it the loss of lives on American vessels. It was
the logical, but legally untenable, extension of a 1914 blunder
that led to the strange warping of the doctrine of freedom
of the seas whereby the United States undertook to protect
Americans traveling, of their own volition, on the ships of
Germany's enemies — ships that had been ordered to risk
themselves and their cargoes, human and material, by resort
to force; ships that sacrificed their immunities as peaceful
merchantmen. Oddly enough, this position was taken at a
time when the United States was successfully maintaining
against France and Great Britain (in the Piepenbrink and
China cases) the rule that the flag of the vessel covers its
passengers on the high seas.

Ambassador Gerard called this situation to Lansing's attention while Germany was drafting a reply to the second
Lusitania note:

[8] *Idem,* p. 341.
[9] Lansing to Gerard, Nov. 30, 1915, *For. Rel.,* 1915, Suppl., p. 620.
[10] Malloy, II, 1486, 1490. Although this treaty expired in 1810, the
provisions of Article 13 (and other articles) were revived by Article 12
of the Prussian-American Treaty of May 1, 1828 (Malloy, II, 1496, 1499).
[1] *For. Rel.,* 1915, Suppl., and 1916, Suppl., *passim.*

The only change made in present alleged international law is that English can not hire Americans to travel on English ships carrying arms and so complicate American-German relations if these ships are sunk without notice. The safety of American passengers desiring to cross the ocean even on English ships is provided for [i.e., on condition that " America shall obtain guarantees that these belligerent ships do not carry contraband of war, are not armed, and will not ram submarines "]. Anyway, when Americans have reasonable opportunity to cross the ocean why should we enter a great war because some American wants to cross on a ship where he can have a private bathroom or because Americans may be hired to protect by their presence cargoes of ammunition? On land no American sitting on an ammunition wagon could prevent its being fired on on its way to the front and England made land rules applicable to the sea when she set the example of declaring part of the open sea war territory; nor can English passenger ships sailing with orders to ram submarines and often armed be put quite in the category of altogether peaceful merchantmen.[2]

Undoubtedly, Gerard was regarded as having succumbed to German propaganda; in his reply of July 8, Lansing stated:

The President is determined not to surrender or compromise in any way *the rights* of the United States or of its citizens as neutrals or enter into discussion which might be construed into such surrender or compromise . . . You may add that this Government is willing to consider and discuss any proposal or suggestion which is reasonable and practicable to discuss unless its purpose is to curtail *the clear and established rights* of the United States or of its citizens.[3] (Italics supplied.)

It is of no little interest to note, however, that Gerard had already expressed himself on this score on May 15, when he wrote: ". . . you say that the United States will not omit any act necessary to maintain *the rights which you have claimed* for the United States and its citizens." [4] The distinction, although subtle, is apposite. Gerard was not blinded into

[2] Gerard to Lansing, July 5, 1915, *For. Rel.,* 1915, Suppl., p. 461.
[3] Lansing to Gerard, *idem,* p. 462.
[4] Gerard to Lansing, *idem,* p. 396. (Italics supplied.)

mistaking claims for *rights*. But the Ambassador's advice came too late.

It was not until four days after the President, by Executive Order of March 12, 1917, authorized the arming of American merchant ships [5] — the Senate, by inaction, having refused to give legislative sanction to the step [6] — and a week after he had called a special session of Congress for April 16, 1917,[7] that the next loss of life on an American vessel occurred. The *Vigilancia* was torpedoed on March 16. Fifteen lives were lost in the sinking, six of them American citizens: " Fifteen crew drowned in launching boats; of these 6 were Americans, 5 Spanish, 2 Greeks, 1 Peruvian, 1 Venezuelan." [8]

In the three weeks that elapsed from then until the declaration of war on April 6, 1917, forty-nine more lives, nineteen of them American citizens, were lost on two American vessels. It is interesting to examine these figures. On the day that Wilson advanced the date for the special session of Congress from the sixteenth to the second of April,[1] the tanker *Healdton* was sunk by a submarine with the loss of twenty-one lives, seven of them American citizens.[2]

Ten days later, during the night of April 1 — the eve of

[5] *New York Times,* March 13, 1917, p. 1, col. 3.

[6] *Supra,* p. 172.

[7] *New York Times,* March 10, 1917, p. 1, cols. 3, 6.

[8] *For. Rel.,* 1917, Suppl. I, p. 182. The *London Times* stated that seven of those lost were Americans (March 20, 1917, p. 5, col. 1).

[1] Proclaimed March 21, 1917, *New York Times,* March 22, 1917.

[2] *For. Rel.,* 1917, Suppl. I, p. 185; *New York Times,* March 24, 1917, p. 1, col. 5. The figures given in the Navy Department report show twenty lives lost in the sinking; one other, however, is reported to have died later as the result of injuries and exposure (*For. Rel.,* 1917, Suppl. I, pp. 183, 185). The outside figure of twenty-one has therefore been adopted for this sinking. Dr. Savage has evidently omitted this exposure victim (Savage, *op. cit.,* II, 85, 596), for, basing his statement on Lansing's 1917 letter to Senator Pomerene, he adopts twenty as the loss of life on this tanker; as a result his total for the 1914–17 period of American neutrality is less by one than the figures used in the text.

President Wilson's request for a declaration of war — the armed American freighter *Aztec* sank after an explosion with the loss of twenty-eight persons.[3] Probably not more than twelve of these were American citizens, one of the latter being a U. S. Navy gunner. This was the first American armed merchantman to be sunk; it mounted two guns and carried a complement of eleven Navy gunners under the command of Lieutenant Gresham, U.S.N.[4] The origin of the explosion appears to be uncertain; after investigation, Ambassador Sharp intimated that it may have been caused by a mine,[5] a possibility that is given support by the fact that the explosion occurred well forward. The Navy Department, however, has listed it as a torpedo casualty;[6] that classification has been followed here.

It is interesting to note that, of the *Aztec's* regular crew of thirty-nine, seventeen (including the captain) were American citizens.[7] By comparing the list of the American members of the crew[8] with the list of those saved in the same boat with Lieutenant Gresham,[9] it would appear that not more than eleven of the seventeen Americans were lost. This figure has been used in the tabulations. It should be noted, however, that this number may have been as low as six, since there were five survivors, other than Lieutenant Gresham's companions, of whose nationality it is almost impossible to be certain. The foregoing figures refer to the regular crew; they do not include the one naval gunner who, separated from

[3] Report of Ambassador Sharp to the Department of State, *New York Times*, April 9, 1917, p. 20, col. 1.

[4] *New York Times*, April 3, 1917, p. 1, col. 1; *idem*, April 4, 1917, p. 4; *London Times*, April 4, 1917, p. 8, col. 4.

[5] Report to the Department of State, *New York Times*, April 6, 1917, p. 3, col. 1.

[6] Navy Department, Historical Section, *American Ship Casualties of the World War* (Government Printing Office, 1923). In the Mixed Claims Commission the Germans disclaimed knowledge of the source of the *Aztec's* explosion, but submitted to an award without conceding liability.

[7] *New York Times*, April 3, 1917, p. 24, col. 3.

[8] *Ibid*.

[9] *Idem*, April 30, 1917, p. 6, col. 4.

his companions, was among the first of the many gallant members of the American armed forces soon to sacrifice their lives.

In all, then, sixty-six seamen and one gunner were killed on four American vessels between August, 1914, and April 6, 1917.

The three lost in 1915 on the *Gulflight* while under belligerent convoy, however, were not entitled to any American protection, as Lansing must have fully realized at the time. They had, wittingly or unwittingly, given up the protection of the neutral flag and had placed themselves and their vessel under the armed protection of one of the belligerents. While such convoy lasted, their sole source of protection lay in the two British patrol boats — irrespective of what flag their own vessel was flying. Any indemnity in this case which the United States may have succeeded in getting from Germany under the threat of the *Lusitania* ultimatum must clearly be regarded as a windfall; it was not legally due.

Thus, the legal situation on February 3, 1917, was this: no one entitled to American protection had lost his life through the German submarine campaign. That may be an unpalatable statement, but it is none the less the fact. And it was not until the period of watchful waiting for an " overt act " was a month and a half old that anyone legally entitled to American protection lost his life. Of the sixty-four in this category killed during the next three weeks, twenty-five were American citizens; the other thirty-nine were of foreign nationality. Although these foreigners were clearly entitled to American protection, it is probably an inadvertence to find the Department of State sponsoring the following statement in the year 1936: " At the time Congress convened [April 2, 1917], *sixty-six American citizens* had been killed as a result of submarine attacks on American vessels . . ."[10]

[10] Savage, *op. cit.*, II, 85. (Italics supplied.)

Comparative Figures

THE foregoing pages have been devoted to an analysis of American casualties of the period from the outbreak of war in Europe to the American declaration of war against Germany. It may not be without interest now to examine the comparative figures of various neutral nations as regards wartime shipping losses, both human and material.[1]

Lives. Including the case of the *Gulflight*, 67 lives were lost on American vessels between August 4, 1914, and April 6, 1917, as a result of German submarine activities. Added to this total might be the 4 killed, one a Spanish stoker, as a result of mine explosions in February, 1915.[2] Since it is obviously impossible to state with any degree of accuracy which of the belligerents was responsible for these mine casualties, they have arbitrarily been attributed to German mines by most writers.[3] But the startling fact is that, of this total of 71 dead, 64, or 90 per cent, were lost between March 16, 1917, and April 6, 1917, i.e., during the last three weeks of armed expectancy preliminary to the declaration of war. Including the 194 lives lost on *belligerent* merchant ships, and the one lost on a foreign neutral vessel, America's total loss of life, wherever situated, on April 6, 1917, amounted to 266 — including the forty foreigners on American vessels, for whom America was responsible.

A recent government publication states that in addition to the lives lost on American vessels, " one hundred seventy-seven " Americans had been killed " on foreign vessels " up to April 2, 1917 — a total of 243.[4] As authority for this

[1] Cf. Appendices.

[2] The fatalities occurred in Feb., 1915; on the nineteenth of that month, a Spanish stoker was " frozen and buried at sea " after the *Evelyn* struck a mine (*For. Rel.*, 1915, Suppl., p. 339), and on the twenty-second, three more persons were lost on the *Carib* (*idem*, p. 339).

[3] Cf. however, J. K. Turner, *Shall It Be Again?*, p. 101.

[4] Savage, *op. cit.*, II, 85. On March 31, 1917 (i.e., without the eleven

figure, a footnote reference [5] is made to a letter of November 26, 1917, from Lansing to Senator Pomerene in which the Secretary inclosed a table showing the 177 figure as of April 6, 1917. Since that table has not been made public, it is impossible to verify this total. Several places have been indicated in the text where there appears to have been some doubt as to the number of Americans lost, e.g., in the *Ancona* and *Englishman* cases.

With respect to the lives lost on American vessels during the period of neutrality, however, the figure of seventy-one does not appear to be open to question. From then until November 11, 1918, 398 more lives were lost — 31 as the result of mines — on American merchantmen, making a total for the entire war period of 469 killed (including the 35 mine casualties) on American ships.[6] If those lost on belligerent vessels during the period of neutrality be added, the total would stand at 664; these cannot properly be included, however, in a comparative study as no other country has done so or has even published such losses — which is in itself an eloquent commentary.

In comparison with the foregoing, the official Norwegian records show that by February 1, 1917 — two days before America broke off relations with Germany — 247 lives had been lost *on Norwegian vessels*. This was over thirty-five times the comparable American figures (submarines plus mines), and 64 more than America's combined losses on national *and belligerent* ships. Of these Norwegian losses, 50 were directly attributable to German submarines, 80 to mines (nationality unknown), and 117 to explosions caused either by mines or torpedoes.

on the *Aztec*) Lansing had said 225 American citizens were killed; *For. Rel.*, 1917, Suppl., p. 191.

[5] *Idem*, p. 596, note 90.

[6] Compiled from the Navy Department publication, *American Ship Casualties of the World War* (1923). Eleven more lost their lives as the result of mine explosions between the date of the Armistice and July 2, 1921.

During February, March, and the first five days of April, 1917, 243 more men were lost — 141 by submarine action, 2 because of mines, and 100 from undetermined explosions. By April 6, 1917, Norwegian casualties thus totaled 490, or practically seven times the comparable American figure on the date of the declaration of war, and almost double the total American casualties, including those on belligerent vessels.

For the whole period of the war, 1,139 lives were lost on Norwegian vessels through the actions of the belligerents; added to these must be 23 lost through mine explosions in December, 1918, making a total directly attributable to the war of 1,162. These were apportioned as follows: submarine action, 456; mines, 128; undetermined explosions, 571. The figures do not include, however, losses of 943 on vessels that completely disappeared.[7] Solely on the basis of the verified wartime losses on national merchant and fishing vessels, Norway lost almost two and one-half times as many lives as did America during its combined periods of thirty-one months of neutrality and nineteen and a half months of belligerency.

No such detailed statistics for the other European neutrals seem to have been made public. Of the figures that are available, a few merit consideration for comparative purposes. In 1915 alone, Sweden lost 113 lives on national ships,[1] and in the following year, 49 more. Although the figures for 1914 are not available, it is probable that they brought the total for the three years up to, if not over 200. The total loss of life, 1914–18, on Swedish vessels has been estimated to approximate 800.[2]

---

[7] This figure is given by W. Keilhau, *Norway and the World War,* "Economic and Social History of the World War" (Carnegie Endowment, 1930), pp. 360 ff.

[1] The Swedish figures, except where otherwise indicated, are taken from E. T. Heckscher and K. Bergendal, *Sweden in the World War, passim,* "Economic and Social History of the World War" (Carnegie Endowment, 1930).

[2] *Idem,* p. 28.

In the case of Denmark, no yearly figures are available, but the total loss of life on national vessels during the war is given as 698.[3] A very approximate working figure of 225 for the period up to 1917 may be arrived at by comparison of the ship and tonnage losses, each of which showed approximately one third of the total war losses as occurring prior to 1917.

These Scandinavian figures, it must be emphasized, are based on losses incurred *on national vessels*. That very fact is indicative, it would seem, of recognition by these countries of the rule of law that the flag of the vessel, and not the nationality of crew or passengers, is the operative factor. The same principle was followed by Great Britain; in her official report of merchant shipping losses, all lives lost while traveling under the British flag are listed without comment.[4] For example, under the *Lusitania,* the report lists 1,198 deaths, the total number that perished in that disaster.[5] The U. S. Navy Department likewise adhered to the same rule in publishing the schedule of American losses;[6] only American ships were included, and, with regard to those, all lives lost thereon were lumped together without any effort at classification according to nationality, race, color, or creed.

Ships and Tons. The losses in tonnage are also of some interest. As has been shown, at the time America adopted its intransigent attitude toward the submarine, not a single American vessel had been sunk by that novel weapon, and only one, the *Gulflight,* had been damaged, under extenuating circumstances. In addition, one sailing ship of 3,374 gross tons had been captured and sunk by a German raider, and three ships, totaling 7,372 gross tons, had been lost on mines.

[3] E. Cohn, *Denmark in the Great War,* abridged from the Danish by K. Vedel-Petersen, " Economic and Social History of the World War " (Carnegie Endowment, 1930), p. 508. Unless otherwise specified, the Danish figures are from this source.

[4] *M. S. Losses* (1919).

[5] *Idem,* p. 6.

[6] Navy Department, *American Ship Casualties,* (1923).

Up to the break in diplomatic relations, 6 ships, totaling 20,866 gross tons had been sunk,[1] and one had been surrendered (1,571 gross tons). Four American ships had also been damaged by surface craft and submarines — one of these, the *Rebecca Palmer,* having suffered " about two hundred dollars damage "[2] from gunfire while traveling through the War Zone with no flag flying. Mine losses increased these totals to 12 ships of 34,007 gross tons lost (including one surrendered), and 7 damaged. Nine more were sunk during the period of armed expectancy, so that when war was declared American losses amounted to 21 ships, totaling 70,424 gross tons, plus 7 vessels damaged.

By November 11, 1918, these figures had jumped to 146 lost (339,240 gross tons) and 23 damaged. The figures as of July 2, 1921, showed total war losses of 152 American merchant vessels sunk (361,022 gross tons) and 24 ships damaged.

Norway, whose merchant shipping losses were second only to those of Great Britain, presents a striking contrast. By April 6, 1917, she had lost 433 ships, totaling 625,999 gross tons. On a percentage basis, when America declared war its losses in ships amounted to 4.8 per cent of Norway's, and in tonnage to 11.2 per cent.

By November 11, 1918, after America had been actively participating in the war for over nineteen months, these percentages had increased to 17.7 per cent for ships and 27.6 per cent for tonnage. Norway's losses on that date amounted to 826 ships of 1,230,546 gross tons. In addition, 30 Norwegian vessels were damaged, and 67 ships of 60,380 gross tons disappeared without trace.[3]

---

[1] The inclusion of one of these, the *Lanao*, is perhaps questionable; Germany contended it was a British vessel. See *For. Rel.*, 1916, Suppl., p. 324.

[2] Consul Washington to Lansing, Dec. 22, 1916, *European War, No. 4*, pp. 277, 278.

[3] The number and tonnage of vessels that disappeared taken from Keilhau, *op. cit.*, p. 360; all others from the official *Rapports de mer.*

The Swedish statistics are few. In 1915, 59, and in 1916, 31 Swedish vessels were lost, or a total for the two years of 90 as against America's 11. This differential would probably not be as large, however, on a tonnage basis, since many of the Swedish ships were small.

For the whole period of the war, Sweden's tonnage losses amounted to 201,276 gross tons [4] (or, roughly, 60 per cent of America's losses for the combined periods of neutrality *and belligerency*. On the same basis, the Netherlands is reported to have lost 211,969 gross tons, and Spain, 168,491 gross tons.[5] These would amount to 60 per cent and 50 per cent, respectively, of the composite American 1914–18 figure.

Up to January 1, 1917, Denmark lost 86 vessels with a total tonnage of 56,700 gross tons or almost twice the comparable American tonnage losses of 30,864 gross tons. For the entire war period, Danish losses totaled 269 vessels of 243,707 gross tons.[6]

It is thus apparent that the northern neutrals of Europe suffered much more than the United States from belligerent excesses, but wisely realized that war did not afford a remedy. Early in the war, when a common stand of the neutrals might have been helpful in preventing excesses, the United States declined its coöperation. The northern neutrals were imposed upon by both belligerents; so was the United States. The distinction between loss of life and loss of property, invoked to justify war with Germany, did not seem to many a sufficient cause for war. Liberals and moralists were then enlisted by the argument — based mainly on imagination, it must be conceded — that this was a fight for a new world, of the forces of light against the forces of darkness.

---

[4] Fayle, *op. cit.*, III, 466.
[5] *Ibid.*
[6] Fayle, *op. cit.*, III, 466. This would equal 72 per cent of the American figure. These are the same figures shown in Salter, *Allied Shipping Control*. Cf. Cohn, *op. cit.*, p. 508; Turlington, *op. cit.*, III, 224.

VI.

" A PARTNERSHIP OF DEMOCRATIC NATIONS "

THUS the crusade for peace and democracy was launched. All nations were to be democratic nations, for " a steadfast concert for peace can never be maintained except by a partnership of democratic nations." [7] Just how the disintegrating effects of a war were to produce peace and democracy, President Wilson did not explain. There was to be plenty of time in which the impossibility of attaining such goals by means of war was to be demonstrated. In the War Address, the League of Nations was also announced, including the word Covenant. It was, indeed, to become a " League of Honor." [1]

In such company there was no place for neutrals. Motivated by a desire, for a variety of reasons, to insure Allied victory, grounded on the iniquity of submarine warfare, and justified as a crusade against autocracy and for the establishment of permanent peace through a League of Nations, peace by war and incantation received its spiritual birth.

But the President had not come to these conclusions suddenly. As early as August 6, 1914, the indignation of Harvard's ex-President Eliot at the invasion of Belgium persuaded him to suggest to Wilson a sort of League of Nations, " a combination of the British Empire, the United States, France, Japan, Italy and Russia, in offensive and defensive alliance to rebuke and punish Austria-Hungary and Germany for the outrages they are now committing." [2] This overwhelming use of force was justified as " an effective international police method suitable to the present crimes, and the probable

---

[7] War Address, April 2, 1917.   [2] Baker, *op. cit.*, V, 69.
[1] *Idem.*

issues of the future," replacing the outworn " balance of power." This force was to lead to " the future establishment and maintenance of federal relations and peace among the nations of Europe," with the consequent reduction of the burden of competitive armaments which was stifling social progress. The President appropriately considered it " a momentous proposal." It was momentous in the sense that it contemplated a fundamental break by the United States with its policy of not participating in European wars. It was less momentous than curious, however, in its comprehension of international relations and in its assumption that by a great war a new state of federal relations could be accomplished. It also conceived that bizarre figure which has afflicted the world ever since, the Crusader bearing fire and brimstone in one hand and sweet-scented lavender in the other. World war for peace, democracy and a new order thus began its preposterous career.

The theory of justifying American entrance into war as an agency for peace did not die with President Eliot's letter. President Wilson's aspirations for a new world order had been indicated on several occasions, and those who wished to draw him into the war did not fail to emphasize that note. Mr. Page's comment from London after the *Lusitania* tragedy was typical: " We live in hope that the United States will come in as the only chance to give us standing and influence when the reorganization of the world must begin." [3] Colonel House supported his frequent demands on the President to enter the war with the argument that it would enable him to participate in preparing the League of Nations.[4] Sir Edward Grey in 1915 had enticed House with the attractive prospect of a League of Nations to enforce peace.[5]

Those who wish to study the origin of wars can find in the

---

[3] Hendrick, *op. cit.*, II, 5.
[4] Seymour, *op. cit.*, I, 365, 425; II, 82 *et seq.*
[5] *Idem*, p. 425.

President's rhetorical flights an exposition of the type of conviction and emotional dedication for which throughout all history millions of men have been slain. The depth of the misunderstanding implicit in his phrases can only be plumbed in the light of time and in the misery they produced. Intellectual training is valueless before lofty emotions that obscure realities in the name of the Higher Morality, and achieve mainly irresponsibility, if not, indeed, hallucinations. But such is the nature of man that he easily succumbs to a conviction of his own superiority and righteousness and the inferiority and malevolence of those who disagree with him. So long as man remains man, passion is not difficult to arouse and nations are readily stirred to crusades. The feeble so-called peace machinery of recent years does not even touch the surface of the problem; that lies in the history of humankind.

The dedication to war as a means to noble ends was a compound of various subconscious drives, which had to be rationalized. This paradox is largely responsible for the confusion which marks the current " peace movement." It explains the belief that coercion among nations can produce pacification, that war, if justified by moral ends, can produce a satisfactory or prolonged peace. The departure from American tradition which intervention in a European war involved has resulted in injury not only to the United States but to the rest of the world as well. " World service " is an expression of good intentions, but hardly a reliable inspiration to practical achievement. It has cost the United States that confidence in its foreign policy which marked its earlier history, it has exposed the country to the propaganda of alien groups seeking to enlist it in foreign struggles, ideological or material, and has induced the country to espouse so-called " neutrality " policies which endanger its peace and its future. Confusion of mind and policy begets an instinctive resort to force, and the most noticeable outcome of the demand for peace by coercion is an astronomical, competitive increase in armaments in nearly all countries, the consequences of which are helplessly and anxiously envisaged by every participant. These, among other unpleasant phenomena, are the identifiable results of America's departure from its traditional neutrality. By picturing this departure from fundamentals as a virtue, we are in danger of perpetuating the error until unneutrality and permanent alliances become the new national creed. To this end, a great part of the postwar drives for so-called " peace " is, consciously or unconsciously, directed.

PART III
SANCTIONS *v.* NEUTRALITY

I.

THE "ENFORCEMENT OF PEACE" BY SANCTIONS

THE Peace Conference of 1919 was dominated by two conflicting points of view, Clemenceau's desire for an old-fashioned Punic peace and Wilson's demand for a new world order. These aims were patently irreconcilable, but the impossible was attempted. During the war the Allies had said nothing which committed them to Wilson's idealistic peace aims and he had said nothing concerning their secret treaties. Their minds had not met except on the one objective of defeating Germany. Thus, at the first reference to the secret treaties at the Peace Conference, President Wilson said, " As the United States of America were not bound by any of the [secret] treaties in question, they are quite ready to approve a settlement on a basis of facts." [6] While it is true that the United States was not bound by the treaties, it is equally true that it had used the full force of American arms in order that these secret engagements might be written into the Treaty of Versailles.[7] This had not been realized in Washington. Lansing admitted before the Foreign Relations Committee of the Senate on August 6, 1919, that while he knew something of the secret Treaty of London of 1916 regarding promises to Italy, he had no knowledge of the other secret treaties.[8]

[6] Baker, *Woodrow Wilson and World Settlement* (New York, 1922), I, 45.
[7] Baker, *op. cit.*, I, 25 *et seq.*
[8] Hearings 190, quoted in Baker, *op. cit.*, I, 33. As to Wilson's unfamiliarity with the secret treaties, see *supra*, p. 47.

Even Colonel House had no great interest in the secret treaties because, as Baker says, " It seemed to him more important to win the war than to know what was to be done with the victory." [9]

President Wilson had reiterated that the United States had " no selfish ends to serve " but was to become a servant of mankind.[1] He had also said, " We cannot stultify our position by accepting any spoils of war." [2] We wanted nothing and got it. America's Allies appreciated the unselfishness and made good use of it. They also were fighting for justice, but as Baker says, " Justice never meant the same things to France, Great Britain, Japan and the United States, and still does not." [3]

Of the Fourteen Points and the Four Principles,[4] the Allied governments took what they could use and discarded the rest. But Wilson still hoped that in the League of Nations he had obtained an instrument to cure the defects he had perceived in the peace treaties; in Article 19 of the Covenant he found a hope that changes could be effected when they proved necessary. Perhaps he did not adequately observe that there might be differences of opinion as to when changes were necessary; that the nation asked to make sacrifices might be unenthusiastic.

Clemenceau and other gentlemen of the old school found it difficult to understand Wilson. So also did the keener liberals. One celebrated critic is reported to have said, " I admire and appreciate the principles of President Wilson; but I cannot understand how anyone who has his eyes open for a moment believes in their realization." [5] At first some of

---

[9] Baker, *op. cit.*, I, 34.

[1] Baker, *op. cit.*, I, 91; *President Wilson's Foreign Policy*, p. 379.

[2] Confidential memorandum on disposition of German and Austrian vessels of war, Baker, *op. cit.*, III, 198, 199.

[3] *Idem*, II, 107.

[4] Wilson Speeches, *President Wilson's Foreign Policy*, pp. 354–364.

[5] George Brandes, as quoted by William C. Dreher in *The Nation;* Baker, *op. cit.*, I, 87.

the principal Allies were suspicious of the League proposal. But when they found that they could not only appease Wilson and win his support for the substance of the peace treaties but also continue to rely upon the combined might of the war Allies, reinforced by some other nations, they became warm League supporters.

Thus the League began its career with conflicting views of its functions. Wilson thought of it as ameliorating, Clemenceau and his hardy followers as guaranteeing the peace treaties. While it may charitably be said that in 1919 it was not clear which of these ideas would win out, the passage of time has resolved any doubt. As Walter Duranty observed: " The settlement was imposed by force and maintained by military power and a system of alliances." [6] The " disentangling alliance " became extremely entangling. Military alliances were at once concluded among certain League members, although the League theory of " collective security " is definitely opposed to separate military alliances. But while the facts reflected the real political conditions, lip service was paid to the " collective " theory and the phrase.

It is doubtless true that the American objection to the ratification of the Treaty of Versailles lay less in the terms of that treaty, the effects of which few could understand, than in the League of Nations, to the creation of which President Wilson had devoted his major energies. Articles 10 and 16 of the Covenant were regarded as requiring the United States to guarantee the territorial integrity of the members of the League, by sanctions and military force, against any act of " aggression."

However, the League had definite functions to perform. Article 8 of the Covenant looked to a progressive disarmament, of which German disarmament was to be the first step. Pressed to action by genuine pacifists and by the groups that

[6] Quoted in Bradley, *Can We Stay Out of War?* (1935), p. 26. Cf. Professor Langer in *Polity*, Feb. 13, 1936, p. 10.

had placed their faith in the new method of "enforcing peace," a Conference on the Limitation of Armaments was called in 1932. Again the assumption was made that enlightened ways of international life could be produced in disregard of underlying conflicting interests and policies. It did not take long to discover that the Conference should more accurately have been called a Conference for the Rearmament of the World. The failures of the League in Manchuria, in the Chaco, in Ethiopia, did not merely evidence the weakness of a young organization, but disclosed the unsoundness of the theory on which it was built and its fundamental inconsistency with the ways of international life. And unhappily some of the useful administrative and nonpolitical services that the League can perform and the opportunities for conciliation which a genuine league of equals could employ are lost in that grave disparity.

The resolution of conflicting interests and the sense of trusteeship for the peace of Europe which marked the Congress of Vienna were not in evidence at Versailles, nor have they been since then. Signor Grandi can hardly be charged with exaggeration when he told the Council of the League of Nations, March 18, 1936: "Almost . . . twenty years after arms were laid down, Europe finds herself in a situation which the gloomiest pessimists would not have dared to predict."

The Psychology of Enforcing Peace

It is a matter of profound regret that the organized peace movement, far from affording a defense against the forces of reaction which have brought the world to its present state, has encouraged them by misconceiving and oversimplifying the nature of the problem, by giving it a moral aspect, and by playing into the hands of those who desired at all cost to maintain their military supremacy and to make no effective concessions for general pacification. The disarma-

ment of the Great Lakes is due to the fact that the United
States and Great Britain determined in the Treaty of Ghent
to live thereafter at peace. Such an elementary principle was
not perceptible at Versailles in 1919. But the adherents of
the American peace movement, as the late Frank Simonds
observed, have not manifested notable interest in those normal accommodations which are an indispensable part of civilized life, nor have they indicated any clear perception of the
drift of the world since 1919 or of the causes of that drift.
On the contrary, they have devoted their energies to the
conclusion of pacts and more pacts until, as one wit has put
it, we suffer today from pactomania. Mr. Frank Simonds
wrote:

So utterly have the leaders of the American peace movement identified their cause with that of the League that both the fortunes of
the movement and their own prestige are now inextricably bound
up with the fate of the latter.[7]

By lending support to the mechanical devices designed to
hold down the European status quo and by clamoring for
combined force to suppress an aggressor, the professional
" peace " societies in this country have permitted a kind of
adolescent idealism to be used in behalf of military policies
which were anything but conducive to peace and were at all
times injurious to the United States.

The fallacies of thinking which have thus, by a natural
progression, converted the peace movement into an engine
of war are not difficult to analyze. They are largely psychological and philosophical. In the first place, the forces that
make for international relations, involving millions of people,
are dynamic. They have historical, economic and psychological roots which defy permanent control by any legal
document, however lofty its inspiration. Negotiation, on
practical considerations of common sense and decency, re-

[7] " The Humpty-Dumpty of Geneva," *Saturday Evening Post*, CCVIII
(Oct. 5, 1935), 5. Cf. Seymour, *American Neutrality*, pp. 168–180.

mains the only way of relieving maladjustments. Again, the whole conception of " aggressor " is a delusion and a betrayer of reason in a world such as this. When the term, moreover, is identified with certain selected Powers as congenitally aggressive, it is likely to arouse uncontrollable resentments and to poison international relations. Furthermore, the analogy between the internal relations of a state to its citizens and the international relations of states among themselves is unsound and misleading. The systems are fundamentally different. A state does not permit its own citizens to determine the amount of armaments they may possess; it subjects them to the control of law by making frequent changes in legislation in an effort to meet the exigencies and disequilibriums of daily life. But in the international world, there is no legislature, no common superior, each member is independent and the judge of its policies, military and economic; unfair competition is the order of the day and any scheme of physical control of a nation's actions cannot survive withdrawal of its voluntary consent. Law has only a limited scope. And neither its importance nor its scope is enlarged by the attempt to characterize as " international law " treaties imposed under duress or out of harmony with the current mores, with the resulting threat of moral obloquy and outlawry, if not war, which is visited upon the violator. Such " writing up of international paper," as Harold Nicolson calls it, resembles the prohibitions of the Eighteenth Amendment. Both invite breach and disobedience and weaken respect for all law. A treaty to be reliable must rest on voluntary consent, and must serve the interests of both parties. No other treaty can long survive.

Finally, the assumption that you can " enforce peace " without creating the psychology of war, without inciting war, is hazardous in the extreme. The first essential of a peace movement should be to pacify. To threaten, to boycott, to coerce, is not to pacify. Hamilton and Madison knew better than to incorporate into a scheme of federation a plan for coercing member states, even in such a natural union as the American. Madison remarked that " the practicability of making laws, with coercive sanctions, for the States as political bodies, had been exploded on all hands." [8] Hamilton characterized it as " one of the maddest projects ever devised," certain to lead to war. " A project of this kind," said he, " is little less romantic than the monster-taming spirit attributed to the fabulous heroes and demi-gods of antiquity." [9] The new theory rests on the false assumption that the supposed aggressors will become contrite or will promptly surrender.

These ideas, associated with the supposition that we now have an excellent " organization " for peace which was formerly lacking, draw sustenance from the extraordinary view that the system of international relations which prevailed before 1914 was " international anarchy," and that what we now have represents " law and order." Perhaps it is not unnatural, therefore, that the evangelism of the " new order " is directed toward a disparagement of the international law which sustained the " old order " — that it indiscriminately characterizes " war " as a common-law crime and would deprive the laws of war of all legal standing, that it regards neutrality as " immoral," if not " illegal," and insists that collective intervention and force will, or should, alone assure " peace."

War is an affliction to which humanity will be exposed as long as the causes are not checked. Rarely have the causes been so virulent as at present; and it hardly seems useful therapeutics to exhort against the symptoms, armies and armaments, while leaving the causes untouched. To provoke deep-seated resentments and then to denounce their open manifestation seems a strange conception of a road to peace. Provocations are permitted; only resentments are taboo.

[8] Constitutional Convention, July 14, 1787, M. Farrand, *Records of the Federal Convention*, II, 8–9.
[9] Scott, ed., *Federalist*, No. 16, Part I (1894), 90.

But there are other objections to the recent idealization of boycotts and embargoes as promoters of peace. The whole philosophy of boycotts and embargoes is ruinous to normal relations between human beings, and among larger groups is likely to be particularly exasperating. It is calculated to embitter, enrage, and ultimately lead to violence. Jefferson, in a worthy cause, undertook to embargo our trade with France and Great Britain in 1807, and the principal result was revolt and disorder at home.

In the long view sanctions are equally unfortunate. No device could so greatly stimulate self-sufficiency and autarchy. Under the fear of boycotts every country will seek to make itself as independent as possible, militarily and economically, of other countries. Whether it considers sanctions practical or not, it will, with certain possible outstanding exceptions, never know when it may be selected as the guilty nation and must be prepared to survive alone. This does not make for tranquillity but for fear and hysteria. In this atmosphere international trade is likely to evaporate; concomitantly, the incentive to acquire raw materials under a nation's own control grows irresistibly. Thus the threat of potential sanctions stimulates the urge for conquest.[10]

The Attack on Neutrality

In his address asking Congress to declare war on April 2, 1917, President Wilson had said: " Neutrality is no longer possible or desirable when the peace of the world and the liberty of the peoples is at stake."

This summons to world war in the name of peace is reflected in the League Covenant. The Carnegie Endowment for International Peace, Division of Intercourse and Education, keeps up the good work. It enlightens the world by asserting

[10] See further objections to sanctions in John Fischer Williams, " The Reform of the Covenant of the League," *Hungarian Quarterly*, II, 195; Lord Lothian, *supra*, p. 52; H. Rowan-Robinson, *op. cit.*, p. 192.

that " for a moral government and a moral people there can
be no neutrality when the issue is between one who breaks
his given word and one who keeps it." " Neutrality " represents an " insidious attack " upon " the foundations of prosperity and peace." [1]

The theory of the Covenant that a war or threat of war
anywhere is a matter of concern to the entire world, and that
the combined force of all the " peace-loving " nations must
be directed against any disturber of the peace, necessarily
excludes the conception of neutrality. There is no place left
for him who wishes to stand aside. Thus, disinterestedness,
nonparticipation and impartiality are by definition ruled out.

This reversion to medieval conceptions which were failures in their own time was acclaimed as evidence of progress.
Yet, while it overlooked practically every important factor
in international relations, it enlisted the support of influential groups, some of whom saw in the late war the prototype
of their yearning for a League of Nations to enforce peace.
The collective action of 1917 was the ideal of the collective
action of the League.[2]

The intimate association between the World War crusade
to end war and the postwar system of enforcing peace is
exemplified in the economic and military sanctions provided
for in Article 16 of the Covenant. Leaving aside the post-
Armistice blockade of Germany, Mr. Turlington, in his recent
book, expresses the opinion that Article 16 finds its origin in
the devices employed during the war to bring both neutrals
and nonneutrals under the control of the belligerents. Speaking of that period, he says:

. . . It also provided many object lessons in the use of essentially nonforcible economic devices in the repression of conduct
deemed to be inimical to the welfare of the international community.

[1] *Annual Report of the Carnegie Endowment, 1936,* pp. 5–6; *New York
Times,* March 1, 1937, p. 10.

[2] *Supra,* p. 51.

This is indicated by the use which committees of the League of Nations made of these precedents, when engaged in elaborating plans for the application of sanctions under Article 16 of the Covenant.[3]

As it was necessary in 1917 to end American neutrality to enable the United States to participate in that system of collective security which reached its apotheosis at Versailles, so now again it becomes necessary to condemn and denounce American neutrality as an obstacle to participation in similar collective effort. Thus we find David Hunter Miller saying, " Certainly in theory this neutrality of modern international law is ended by the Covenant so far as the members of the League *inter se* are concerned . . ."[4]

Professor Ehrlich of Poland says: " There is in my opinion no neutrality under the regime of Article 16 of the covenant . . . nor under the regime of the Briand-Kellogg Pact."[5] A recent appointee to the so-called World Court has remarked: ". . . I was much struck with the treatment of neutrality in M. Politis' recent volume. ' Considered as an institution,' he says, ' neutrality is the product of international anarchy.' "[6]

From the multifarious pronouncements in similar vein, the following excerpts have been culled:

. . . I think neutrality is doomed. Little by little we are coming to the theory, so well stated by President Wilson, that in a war of principle neutrality is unconscionable. . . .[7]

. . . Members of the League can not be neutral, but must take effective action to safeguard the peace and if war develops must give moral, if not physical, support to the victim of aggression as there defined, and to the police forces which go to his assistance.[8]

[3] Turlington, *Neutrality*, III, 152.
[4] i.e., against a covenant-breaking state. *The Drafting of the Covenant*, I, 432.
[5] Ehrlich, *Collective Security*, International Studies Conference, 1936, p. 437.
[6] Hudson, *Proceedings of Amer. Soc. of Int. Law*, 1935, p. 44.
[7] Whitton, *Proceedings*, 1930, p. 109.
[8] Wright, *idem*, pp. 86–87.

But the whole purpose of my argument was to improve the Kellogg Pact and make something out of it.

In principle and ideal I think it is one of the greatest steps we have ever taken in history, but I want to make it useful; and I propose doing that by eliminating neutrality and combining the efforts of all against the aggressor state or against the lawbreaker.[9]

It [neutrality] is " an ancient and now useless theory." [10]

Neutrality is the negation of law and order. Neutrality is a denial of the principle of collective responsibility upon which any system of international law must rest. Neutrality is contrary to the fundamental conceptions of law which have prevailed between man and man in every civilized State and prevailed between State and State in the United States.[1]

I cannot see that we can have any international law in this world if we are going to have neutrality. . . . Neutrality must go as a legal conception.[2]

As late as 1929, even the British Foreign Office under the Labor government seems to have been under the impression that neutrality had been abolished, for in an official document it is said: " As between Members of the League there can be no neutral rights, because there can be no neutrals." [3]

Inasmuch as the United States did not join the League of Nations, so that this country cannot use Article 16 of the Covenant to crush an aggressor, the same purpose, it is maintained, can be accomplished under the Kellogg Pact. Hence the Kellogg Pact has become featured as another device for breaking down American neutrality. According to Professor Clyde Eagleton:

. . . The only way to maintain peace and respect for law and treaty rights is by collective action; and such action is incompatible with neutrality. The Kellogg Pact will be respected only if we deliber-

[9] Eagleton, *idem*, p. 113.
[10] *Idem*, 1935, p. 133.
[1] Fenwick, *Proceedings*, 1936, p. 149.
[2] *Idem*, 1933, p. 55.
[3] Great Britain, Foreign Office, *Memorandum on the Optional Clause of the Statute of the Permanent Court* (Miscellaneous, No. 12 [1929]), p. 10.

ately and strongly take sides against the violator of the Pact; and this can only be done effectively in conjunction with the other signatories of the Pact, acting through an established machinery.[4]

Mr. Warren, as a matter of fact, last night disposed of the factual side of the law of neutrality, and showed that actually there can be, or there is, no law of neutrality today. From the moral point of view, I shall have to dispose of that for myself by saying summarily that neutrality as a principle is immoral.[5]

Mr. Politis, a pillar of the Temple of Peace at Geneva, in his recent book *Neutrality and Peace,* announces that: " In law, neutrality has therefore ceased to be an institution. But the law is here in advance of habits, beliefs and facts." [6]

These assaults on neutrality emanating from well-known students of international relations are not cited invidiously. Their authors are men with splendid emotions. They exemplify a school of thought which was inspired either by the Great War or by the League or by both to believe that for any country, but especially the United States, to preserve neutrality in other people's wars is impractical or barbarous. In justice to them it should be said that they had hoped the mere threat of preponderant holy force would discourage any potential aggressor and cause it to cease and desist; thus, by preventing the outbreak of war, neutrality would become academic.[7] It was not adequately appreciated that peace-enforcing national armaments might be used for purposes whose holiness might be disputed and even debated by war.[8]

Undoubtedly the prevention of war has an attraction incapable of exaggeration. But, although the world has been dealing with that problem a long time, threats of war or starvation had not heretofore been expected to produce paci-

[4] Eagleton, *Proceedings,* 1935, p. 133.
[5] Eagleton, *idem,* 1933, p. 163.
[6] *La Neutralité et la paix* (1935), p. 179. Professor George Scelle states that " neutrality is destined to disappear." *Collective Security,* p. 25. Cf. Jessup (*idem,* p. 425), denying that neutrality is outmoded.
[7] Stimson, *Proceedings,* 1935, pp. 121, 126, 129.
[8] Cf. J. B. Moore, *New York Sun,* Dec. 10, 1935, p. 24.

fication. The new doctors failed to supply confidence in the
efficacy of the new prescription. For the sake of the theory
and the hope we were expected to abandon the experience of
centuries which had enabled some nations at least occasionally
to enjoy the blessings of peace.[9]

Professor Beard has wisely commented upon the seductive phrases by which war masquerades as " coöperation for
peace." He has remarked:

> To say that one favors " American cooperation in every effort to
> build alternatives to war " is, in my opinion, merely using words,
> unless one is prepared at the same time to demand the employment
> of American military and naval power in making effective any rules
> of peace agreed upon. To take part in talking without taking part
> in the coercion necessary to make talking prevail is, in my view,
> both futile and perilous. If our efforts to right historic wrongs and
> bring peace and reason to Europe in 1917–1919 have not taught
> American citizens anything, no words of mine can add to their
> education.[10]

Numerous distinguished laymen have recently given
expression to the thought that there is no such thing as
neutrality.[1] What they probably mean is that the equal operation of neutral duties upon the belligerents is difficult or impossible to achieve. But the law never conceived neutrality in
any such sense. It merely means that the neutral state must
not intentionally hold the scales uneven or exhibit partisanship. It is not the neutral's duty or privilege to equalize the
handicaps of a belligerent arising out of geographical or other
physical considerations.

The suggestion, from whatever source derived, that neu-

---

[9] Some of the more alert proponents of these new theories have admitted their failure. *Ibid.* " Now, fifteen years afterwards, these hopes seem
to have crumbled to ashes in our hands." Stimson, *Democracy and Nationalism
in Europe* (Princeton University Press, 1934), p. 2. Rowan-Robinson, *Sanctions Begone, a Plea and a Plan for the Reform of the League* (London, 1936),
passim.

[10] *Forum,* Feb., 1937, p. 90.

[1] Baruch, *New York Times,* Jan. 29, 1936; Arthur Krock, *idem,* Dec. 26,
1936; Senator Connolly, reported *idem,* Feb. 21, 1937.

trality is immoral, outmoded or impractical, has done the law much harm and by that very token has promoted militant hysteria and disorder and an accompanying deterioration of international relations.

The Weakening of " Collective Security "

IN 1921 certain fears began to afflict the members of the League that they might be bound by the conclusions of the Council to undertake economic and military sanctions, and if they refused that they might be charged with violating the Covenant. To make certain that this would not happen, the original theory of Article 16 was modified, for instead of the collective decision of the Council or Assembly proclaiming the aggressor after a hearing, the Amendment of 1921, adopted by the Assembly but not yet universally ratified, provides that each state is to be the judge of the question whether an aggression has been committed [2] and of what it will contribute in the way of sanctions.

While the original system was unworkable and could only have added to the terrors of force as a governing agent for the world, the new system has the practical advantage of enabling each League member to undertake hostilities against the nation it dislikes and to refuse to undertake hostilities against an ally or group of favored nations. But this implicitly does away with any such collective system as was originally planned; it abolishes that which the theorists for the most part still praise and extol. The new individualization of punishment invites, even necessitates, a system of alliance and counteralliance.

Several speakers at the International Studies Conference on Collective Security in 1935 pointed out the paradox involved in a system of collective action against the aggressor

---

[2] It also provides: " The Council shall give an opinion whether or not a breach of the Covenant has taken place." Lauterpacht, *Collective Security,* p. 412.

which forbids " nations to resort to war for the defense of their own interests, that is, for the causes which affect them the most deeply, and to make it, on the contrary, their duty to throw themselves into the struggle to ensure the respect of abstract rules which have no roots in their sentiments, their beliefs or their passions." [3] Mr. Coppola, a member of the Conference, remarked:

It is undeniable that, since the war, this myth of *security*, this vaguely-outlined nightmare, has disturbed and distorted political intelligence throughout the world and especially in Europe; that it is a paralysing burden on European politics; and that it thus constitutes one of the greatest obstacles to the establishment in the world, and especially in Europe, of a veritable peace, that is to say, a peace not only diplomatic and legal, but political and psychological as well. [4]

The " New Neutrality "

WITH the concession that each country was to be the judge of the question whether a momentarily unpopular nation should be stigmatized as an aggressor or not, and that this might result in divergent judgments and impair the whole theory that it was easy to pick an aggressor, members of the League began to speculate on what would happen to neutrality. Those who did not choose to pick the aggressor or to inflict punishment would naturally have to remain neutral, a fact which punctured the theory that neutrality was immoral. So we find a new theory arising to bridge this difficulty. The new device of the peace engineers provided that the nation declining to participate in sanctions would nevertheless not regard both belligerents alike but would discriminate against the nation that had been selected by its fellow members as the aggressor. This may be called a sport from the original theory; it was calculated to enable a nation to

[3] " Final Report," *Collective Security*, p. 444.
[4] Coppola, *Collective Security*, International Studies Conference, pp. 144–145.

remain out of the *posse comitatus* while yet clearly and effectively indicating its displeasure with the aggressor. American supporters of the " taking of sides " theory were equal to the occasion:

. . . I say that because I want to see the law so changed that it never can be said again that a neutral is under a legal obligation to accord the same measure of treatment to a belligerent who in the opinion of the neutral is an aggressor that he accords to one who in his opinion is a victim of an aggression.[5]

. . . Then I should say that in the present anarchic situation, in which each state can judge for itself the right or the wrong of the cause, the United States also ought to assume her responsibility in determining the right or wrong of the cause, even if it is an insufficient judgment, and take sides for what she thinks is the right.[6]

The Swiss view that a small nation might lose its independent life by a hostile attitude [7] made it necessary to admit that there must be differences among the nations in their obligations to enforce the Covenant. Perhaps that explains why some of the European nations are now arming so heavily, as is stated, to fulfil their League obligations.[8] Yet it hardly helps to lighten the burden that the people of a peace-loving nation are asked to bear.

But differential " neutrality " has brought new problems to those who would save the world by pacts. This new neutrality no longer implies impartiality but authorizes and legalizes partiality or the " right to discriminate against the aggressor without thereby disregarding the rules of international law in the matter of neutrality." [9] In this way, it is assumed, the collective system can be reconciled with " qualified neutrality." Admittedly this is " a weak collective sys-

[5] Garner, *Proceedings*, 1933, pp. 148–149.
[6] Eagleton, *Proceedings*, 1931, p. 222. Cf. President Wilson's statement, April 20, 1915: " no nation is fit to sit in judgment upon any other nation." Scott, ed., *op. cit.*, p. 85.
[7] Schindler, *Collective Security*, pp. 424–425.
[8] Bradley, *op. cit.*, p. 27.
[9] Lauterpacht, *Collective Security*, p. 418.

tem," [10] but international idealists are now grateful for small favors.

The qualified or benevolent neutrality is justified as having historical roots. In one sense this is true. It was a phenomenon of the primitive period before neutrals were assured of their right to remain out of foreign wars, when in order to survive they had by alliances and favors to pick the winning side in wars in which they had no direct concern. Dr. de la Pradelle has remarked:

A new institution has been born: a relative, benevolent, attenuated, differential or partial neutrality, tending toward the setting up of an ideal system of sanctions, which would be characterised by the disappearance of neutrality, and which already has gone considerably beyond the traditional regime formulated in 1907. If this evolution is in contradiction with the positive law of The Hague, it finds, however, support and important and solid precedents in the theoretical and practical history of neutrality.[1]

The theological principle of the " just war " has been revived in order to explain this reversion to medievalism. Although qualified neutrality was always a dangerous flirtation with war, and, despite the fact that the theory of the " just war " never did work,[2] qualified neutrality is now advocated for the United States.

We are given new wine in old bottles, and it is admittedly intoxicating. Judging from recent experience, however, it is slightly sour. After having first been abolished completely, neutrality is now admitted to have a large role to play in cases where the aggressor cannot be picked or under the toler-

[10] *Idem,* pp. 413, 415.

[1] De la Pradelle, " The Evolution of Neutrality," *Collective Security,* pp. 408.

[2] On partial neutrality, see also Bourquin, " Final Report," *Collective Security,* p. 455.

" The idea of neutrality . . . is visibly transformed. . . . You have kept the word but have given it a different meaning." Cassin, *idem,* p. 439.

" It is no longer the neutrality of 1912 or 1913, it is a totally different neutrality which does not observe the traditional principles." Ehrlich, *idem,* p. 437.

ated wars of Article 15 of the Covenant. But even in the untolerated wars in which an aggressor is picked, the nations that do not choose to judge can still remain neutral while yet discriminating between aggressor and aggressee.

This is called the " new neutrality." [3] Quite in the current tradition, it makes confusion worse confounded. One of the virtues of neutrality is the fact that it requires candor and honesty.[4] The new system requires neither and permits gross acts of hostility under the guise of nonparticipation. And the neutral peoples are led to believe that they can thus escape the consequences of hostility and participation. Concurrent economic unneutrality and military neutrality are a paradox. Not altogether to lose connection with legal terms while in fact flouting them, the new school undertakes to apply to its discriminatory system the worthy name of " neutrality." So, to our collection of paradoxes we now add this: unneutrality masquerading in the name of neutrality. We have spoken of the burdens imposed upon war to achieve peace by waging more war. We now have new burdens cast upon neutrality to support discrimination and hostility, again in the name of a peaceful order.

A special place in this system is reserved for the United States. The Kellogg Pact is the instrument for America's enlistment in the good work. Based on the notion of Article 11 that a war anywhere in the world is an attack on all nations, and on the professed world-wide interdependence of economic and social interests,[5] it is argued that the United States must regard a violation of the Kellogg Pact — we shall assume here that it can be violated — as a legal wrong inflicted upon the United States which must be adequately resented. Although this conflicts with the Senate's distinct understanding of the nature of the American obligation as

[3] Cf. John Bassett Moore, " The New Isolation," *A. J. I. L.*, XXVII (1933), 607, 622 *et seq.*

[4] *Supra*, p. 6.

[5] " Final Report," *Collective Security*, p. 446.

merely a self-denying ordinance neither requiring nor permitting action to penalize a violation,[6] the effort of the sanctionist school of thought has nevertheless been unremitting to bring about American intervention.

Professor Fenwick has remarked:

. . . The Kellogg Pact was, it appeared to many persons, a great advance upon the Covenant of the League of Nations with its sanction of force and its possibilities of entanglement, and America had now done her duty in her own more efficient way.

Mr. Stimson's address makes it clear that the Department of State regards the Pact as putting an end to the traditional doctrine of neutrality, " the duty of a neutral to maintain impartiality between two belligerents." This is in itself a great gain in the development of international law; for it indicates that the pledges of the Pact are regarded by the United States not merely as expressing the renunciation of war as an instrument of its own national policy, but as indicating a concern as to the observance of the Pact by other states and an intention to depart from its traditional attitude of neutrality should others be guilty of a breach of the Pact.[7]

Professor Quincy Wright of Chicago has recently made the following pronouncement:

Withdraw Aid from Aggressor. The objection that discrimination between aggressors on the one hand and victims of aggression or sanctioning powers on the other is contrary to international law has no weight. The Pact of Paris, binding all important states, is the important international law in this connection, and a state which has gone to war in violation of its provisions has clearly violated a right of the United States entitling the latter to undertake discriminatory measures by way of reprisal. The national policy based on this assumption specifically stated by Ambassador Norman Davis at the Disarmament Conference on May 22, 1933, must eventually find a place in American legislation dealing with the situation of foreign war. Probably the term neutrality in this connection should be abandoned, for the objective is not impartiality but keeping the country out of war.[8]

[6] *Infra,* p. 295.
[7] Editorial Comment, " The Implication of Consultation," " Pact of Paris," [Charles G.] Fenwick, *A. J. I. L.,* XXVI (Oct., 1932), 787.
[8] Wright, in *Polity,* Feb., 1936, p. 8, col. 2.

On another occasion, he remarked:

By ratifying the Kellogg Pact the United States gave up the rights of neutral trade with violators of the Pact and was relieved of the duties of neutrality for the benefit of such States, and furthermore that in every future war one or more of the belligerents would inevitably be a violator of the Pact.[9]

Professor McNair of Cambridge has interpreted a breach of the Kellogg Pact not as obliging all states to depart from their neutral attitude but as permitting them to do so. He added, " It may be that in so doing they would commit breaches of the traditional law of neutrality, but their justification for so doing would be the fact that they are doing it in return for a legal wrong inflicted upon them." [10] Others have assumed that at least the Kellogg Pact forbids the signatories to aid a violator by supplying it with munitions while presumably permitting such assistance of nonviolators.[1]

The final report of the Committee on Collective Security of the International Studies Conference at London in 1935 sought to appease the American fear of being drawn into war on such a plausible justification by saying:

Neutrality, in their [American] eyes, means essentially the possibility of remaining far from the field of battle. Is it not then possible to devise for them a form of collaboration whose nature and characteristics would protect them against this risk? A distinction between measures which, directly or indirectly, imply participation in hostilities and those which can be taken without such participation — here lies, perhaps, the road along which the solution of this problem may best be sought.[2]

Professor Lauterpacht of London approved the proposal that the United States conclude " agreements authorizing the parties to discriminate, when neutral, against the other sig-

[9] Wright, *Proceedings*, 1930, p. 84.
[10] McNair, *Collective Security*, pp. 435–436.
[1] Cassin, *idem*, p. 439.
[2] " Final Report," *Collective Security*, p. 455. Cf. " Introductory Report," p. 27.

natories resorting to war contrary to the provisions of the Briand-Kellogg Pact." [3] Possibly the provision in most of the executive trade agreements by which the United States reserves the privilege " in exceptional circumstances " of embargoing, besides arms, ammunition, and implements of war, other commodities " needed in war," or " other military supplies," carries out this suggestion.

Yet the realization that differential or discriminatory neutrality, or economic unneutrality as it was called by one commentator,[4] involved military danger led to the proposal of some jurists [5] that before applying economic sanctions the neutral states should " conclude defensive alliances to protect themselves against the risk of an attack by the state which has violated the Covenant." [6] This would certainly be a wise precaution, for it is obvious that discriminatory neutrality, if such a contradiction be possible, is an act of war.

The Aggressor

It has already been indicated that serious doubts prevailed even among the devotees of collective security as to what made a state an aggressor; who was to determine the aggression; and what was to be done about it. The only sense in which agreement on the meaning of aggression may be said to have been reached is contained in some of the bilateral nonaggression pacts concluded between various potential enemies in Europe. The Soviet Government in various treaties has undertaken to give a definition of the kinds of aggression which are to be prohibited by the nonaggression pacts it has concluded. These are as follows:

(a) a declaration of war;

(b) invasion without declaration;

(c) bombardment of territory or attack on naval or air forces;

[3] Lauterpacht, *idem,* pp. 417–418.
[4] Schindler, *idem,* p. 423.
[5] *Idem,* p. 423.
[6] *Idem,* p. 423.

(d) landing of armed forces without permission of the government, etc.;

(e) establishment of a naval blockade.

The pacts then list various acts or grounds which are not to be deemed a " justification for attack." [7]

How effective such definitions are only time can tell. When the Locarno Pact of 1925 provided for a mutual guaranty against " unprovoked " aggression, the word " unprovoked " constituted an escape clause enabling each party to reserve its complete freedom in determining whether to intervene or not in support of its guaranty. The Soviet nonaggression pacts may be welcomed as *modi vivendi* which effect temporary stabilization.

The " Final Report " of the International Studies Conference indicated some of the difficulties involved in defining aggression. The purpose of the definition, it was conceded, was to decide when a country " resorts to war " in violation of Article 11 of the Covenant. But it was admitted that this was a mechanical formula because " first, it takes into consideration only acts of violence which shall have been actually committed, thus excluding everything which precedes the explosion of force, everything relative to provocation and to the preparation of the aggression; secondly, it sets up, among the five aggressive acts enumerated in the formula, a hierarchy based on the chronological order in which they are committed." [8] The artificiality of making the fate of nations depend upon a sporadic act without reference to its background or provocation was pointed out by several of the members at the Conference.[9]

The impossibility of securing an official determination of

[7] Soviet Declaration submitted to Disarmament Conference, Feb. 6, 1933, *International Conciliation*, No. 292 (Sept. 1933), 65.

[8] " The State shall be considered the aggressor which will have been the first to commit one of the following acts . . ." Bourquin, " Final Report," *Collective Security*, pp. 452–453.

[9] *Idem*, pp. 453–454.

the aggressor as a fundamental condition of the operation of
the system did not escape the Conference. The final report
recognized that " unless the aggressor is determined . . .
it is impossible to bring into play the mechanism of sanctions." [10] M. Bourquin in the Report indicates these difficulties by contrasting the collective decision of a central body,
the Council of the League, with a system leaving each state
to be the judge of the question, as provided in the 1921
amendment. He says:

Finally it must not be forgotten that the determination of the
aggressor raises one last question of the greatest practical importance: who is to make this determination? Is it to be left to each
State to decide the question, at the risk of arriving at incoherent
results? Or is this mission to be entrusted to an international authority? In the latter case, what is this authority to be, and under
what voting regulations will it be authorised to take its decision?
Is it possible to believe that in the present state of affairs, Governments will agree to acquiesce, in so important a matter, in a majority
decision, which might be contrary to their most important interests
and to their most cherished convictions? To state these questions
is enough to make us realize the extremely complicated nature of
the problem; and it must be admitted that we are far from seeing
a solution of this problem which is at once practical and fully
satisfactory.[1]

Ever mindful of America, the " Final Report " admits also
that the determination of " aggression " implies some action,
military or economic, and hence discrimination between the
belligerents; it then expresses its doubt as to whether such
discrimination can be deemed consistent with neutrality and
asks how far it may go without involving the discriminator in
war.[2]

For many years the British Government is supposed to

[10] *Idem*, p. 452.
[1] *Idem*, p. 454. Cf. Zimmern, *The League of Nations and the Rule of Law*
(1936), on the " hue and cry " theory, and Professor Wolfers' penetrating review, *Yale Law Journal*, XLVI, 727.
[2] Final Report, *Collective Security*, p. 454.

have made impossible an automatic functioning of the new system by refusing to adopt the Geneva Protocol of 1924 involving definitions of what constituted a " resort to war " or an act of " aggression." Sir Austen Chamberlain thought " it will be a trap for the innocent and a signpost for the guilty." This was deplored by all good believers in the collective system to such an extent that finally, in 1932, Great Britain was persuaded to present to the Disarmament Conference a definition of aggression differing only slightly from that of the Soviet treaties.[3] But even these efforts have not solved the problem. It seems impossible to agree on what is a " resort to war." Thus, Professor Eagleton asks, " What is war? " and adds: " All these steps we are discussing go back to that same question. As long as you admit that a state has the right to make its own decisions in all these matters, then you are not going to get anywhere." [4] This question of what constitutes a " resort to war " and whether an act of force or reprisal, like Mussolini's bombing of Corfu, is one has baffled many an international conference and student of these matters.[5]

This much has been said on this metaphysical subject in order to expose not only its futility but its great danger to the United States. It is not unfair to assume that much of this effort to define an aggressor and to determine what signatories of the Covenant and of the Kellogg Pact may do has been undertaken to facilitate the entrance of the United States into the " collective security " system — a short cut to the next European war. Were it not for this fact, the activities of the intelligent men who participate in these efforts would be meaningless. The United States Government has contributed to this effort at its own ensnarement by offering

[3] See Part I of the draft convention submitted by the United Kingdom, *League of Nations Documents*, X (1933), 2.

[4] Eagleton, *Proceedings*, 1932, p. 131.

[5] " War and Peace," *A. J. I. L.*, XXVII (1933), 114–117.

its own definition of " aggression " at the time of the so-
called Disarmament Conference, when Mr. Norman Davis, as
delegate of the United States, proposed a formula for American coöperation which included the suggestion that " the
simplest and most accurate definition of an aggressor is one
whose armed forces are found on alien soil in violation of
treaties." [6] One treaty in mind was doubtless the Kellogg
Pact, and possibly the then recent invasion of Manchuria
inspired the definition. The suggestion that a nation which
does not cease firing at the command of Geneva shall be
deemed an aggressor is as impractical as all the others, for
the restraint might under certain circumstances invite national and collective suicide. The enemy might not stop at
the same time. Yet this was the basis for the condemnation of
Paraguay by the League in the Chaco War, an attempt which
added no laurels to the efficiency of the new system of gen-
erating peace.

Not only is the meaning of " aggressor " elusive,[7] since it
is impossible to define the objective criteria on which the
validity of an overt act may depend, but the very effort to
pick him is calculated to promote distrust among nations.
Their resulting policies may encourage hostilities in which
all parties, aggressor, aggressee, and *posse comitatus* will
feel a moral justification for their respective efforts at making their own ideas and forces prevail. The assurance of help
in suppressing an unpopular nation is an encouragement to
war, for it discourages that sense of responsibility which had
heretofore acted as a brake on violence. It might tempt those
who wish to crush an " aggressor " to provoke him into
overt acts. On the assumption that the effort is honest, the
system requires such speed of determination on the part of
third countries that the decision must necessarily be reached

[6] *New York Times,* May 23, 1933; Press Releases, May 27, 1933, p. 390.
[7] See article, " The Slippery Aggressor," in *The World Tomorrow,* June,
1930.

of copper, oil, trucks, tractors, scrap iron and scrap steel should not be made to either belligerent affected only Italy, for Ethiopia had seldom, if ever, imported any of these commodities from the United States.

Satisfaction is even derived by believers in the system of " enforcing peace " from the arms embargo against both belligerents, for, it is argued, if the United States refuses to sell arms to either belligerent, whereas the members of the League refuse to sell to the aggressor only, the latter would find itself deprived of military equipment.[10]

This advocacy of coercion as a cure for war, the new war to end war, naturally culminates in the demand that violence be fought by violence, fire with fire, war with war.[1] We are solemnly informed that war can only be stopped by war and an aggressive nation can only be stopped by the use of force. But as the repression of war by force can only involve another and greater war, it is not clear how the cure will help the patient. The peace of the cemetery marks the end of that trail.

These various justifications for substituting discrimination for impartiality have advanced not the cause of peace but the cause of confusion. The attempts to break with history and to find brand new methods of coercing nations into obedience have not had the hoped-for results. They have, however, had the effect of preventing any genuine discussion of pacification and appeasement, the indispensable conditions of any peace; for the notion entertained by numerous governments that they would have other countries at their disposal to help enforce their will — and especially the 1919 treaties of peace — has tended to make it seem unnecessary for them to concede anything at all to the dissatisfied nations. The

[10] De la Pradelle, *Collective Security*, International Studies Conference, pp. 409–411, quoting Mr. Eagleton. J. P. Chamberlain, *International Conciliation*, No. 251 (1929), 281.

[1] Eagleton, in speech before Foreign Policy Association, March 7, 1936; *New York Times*, March 8, 1936, p. 26, col. 1.

lamentable state of Europe is a direct result of that obstinacy.

The Depression in Sanctions

BEFORE analyzing further the consequences of the disintegrating conception of sanctions, we ought to mention briefly the growing appreciation that neutrality, after all, is not " a thing of the past " but has a large sphere of operation left. Above all, we should note the fact that practice has, during recent years, reaffirmed the continued vigor of the legal conception of neutrality.

Although apparently it was at first assumed not only by President Wilson, but also by many others, that the Covenant of the League had abolished war and with it neutrality, it did not take long to discover that even within the artificial mechanism of the Covenant a good deal of room was left for permitted wars. After the 1921 recommendations for the amendment of Article 16, it was found that war was still allowable because the Council's function as the sole agency to determine whether a state had gone to war contrary to the Covenant had been reduced to the status of a suggestion or recommendation. Each nation could now determine whether a war was just or unjust. Thus the system of sanctions became a method for bringing pressure to bear on a disfavored state by a partial alliance, which dangerously risks, as Captain Eden discovered in 1935, the inauguration of a general war.

The conclusion is inescapable that the " new neutrality " of coercion, having on several occasions proved its utter futility, has become moribund and no longer deserves serious consideration. All that is left of it is an old-fashioned military alliance. The United States is the special object of European solicitude in this respect and in the name of " world service " [2] seems readily susceptible. In fact, the rhetorical

---

[2] President Wilson said in May, 1914: "A war of aggression is not a war in which it is a proud thing to die, but a war of service is a thing in which it is a proud thing to die." *President Wilson's Foreign Policy*, p. 40.

devotion of American government officials to the Kellogg Pact conveniently holds open the " service " door.

The possible scope of the principle of collective security has by attrition been reduced to microscopic proportions. As Mark Twain says in another connection in *Tom Sawyer*, it " narrows down the company of the elect to a body too small to be worth saving." The practical impossibility of a unanimous agreement on the identification of the aggressor, each nation's individual privilege of selection, the opportunities for disagreement, the political motives for a judgment, the privilege of indifference — all shrink the system to little more than a theory, discredited by experience. But the admission that traditional neutrality is unimpaired even under the supposed obligations of Article 16,[3] and a fortiori is untouched when an agreement on an aggressor proves impracticable — the gap in the Covenant — reduces the scheme to a chimera. Even the professed hope that some day the world may be thus governed presupposes a fundamental change in the system of sovereign states. The assumption that peoples and nations can be moved about like the pawns on a chessboard and that they will obey some centralized command underlies these theories of international control. But they do not correspond with the facts. No further explanation is needed, although many are available, as to why the plan crumbles at the touch.

Practice in Sanctions

IN the case of Manchuria in 1931 the United States took the lead in provoking the League of Nations to action. On its face, the Japanese invasion looked like an unjustified act. Those particularly who had little familiarity with the history of the Far East and who had great faith in the powers of

[3] " In the very place where it ought logically to have given way before the obligation of guaranty and sanctions." De la Pradelle, *Collective Security*, pp. 404–406.

coercion at once sprang to the ramparts to proclaim in the name of the Kellogg Pact and the League Covenant another Holy War on the infidel. The administration in Washington began to send admonitions to Japan and only the refusal of Great Britain to have anything to do with the adventure prevented an intervention which might have become a major war.[4]

China naturally resorted to the League of Nations with the hope of obtaining outside assistance. Great Britain co-operated to the extent of fostering the creation of the Lytton Commission which made a long report disclosing that there were distinctly two sides to the issue, running far back into history. Historians can present many reasons why Japan invaded Manchuria. Manchuria had been won from Russia in the Russo-Japanese War and had been returned to Chinese control at the request of the Great Powers whose conflicts of interest in China have probably been the main reason for China's survival as a nation. The " territorial integrity " of China which had been so eloquently discussed at Geneva and incorporated as a term of the Nine-Power Pact, was largely a figment of the imagination, although imagination is no deterrent to war. On February 27, 1933, Sir John Simon, British Foreign Secretary, announced, to the chagrin of the more ardent enforcers of peace, that Great Britain was neutral in the war then raging between China and Japan.[5] He said: ". . . There is one great difference between 1914 and now, and it is this: in no circumstances will this Government authorise this country to be a party to the struggle." The League found it impracticable to take any action on the Lytton Report other than to censure Japan. But the investigation of the Commission, while not obstructed by the Japanese Government, profoundly irritated the Japanese people, enabled the military party to attain

[4] Stimson, *The Far Eastern Crisis* (1936), *passim*.
[5] 275 *Parliamentary Deb.*, 5th ser., col. 59.

greater influence, and promoted the policy of nationalism and expansion in Japan in a way that probably no internal stimulus could have accomplished. The Lytton Report and the League's condemnation led to the withdrawal of Japan from the League, to the declaration of a sort of Eastern Asiatic Monroe Doctrine — which the Lansing-Ishii Agreement of 1918 had already fostered — and helped to demonstrate that outside pressure on a state provokes excessive nationalism.

In the case of the Bolivian-Paraguayan War for the Chaco, commendable efforts at mediation were made by the American neutrals, and when they failed to accomplish anything the League stepped in. This long-standing boundary dispute had been smoldering for years before it finally burst into armed action. It would be difficult, and perhaps futile, to determine who made the first armed move. The suggestion, so popular in certain circles, that the one who fires the first shot is the aggressor is too casual and superficial. The law does not require that the threatened person await the overt act of his antagonist before he fires; Italy pointed this out when she replied to Turkey's suggestion that the aggressor in the Mediterranean would be the nation that fired the first shot.[6]

Paraguay, which surprisingly displayed all the marks of a victor by penetrating deeply into the Chaco territory, declined to heed the League injunction to cease and desist, although Bolivia, apparently losing the war, was quite ready to comply. Thereupon Paraguay was pronounced the aggressor and sanctions were ordered,[7] including an arms embargo against Paraguay alone. This proved ineffective because of smuggling, evasion and lack of coöperation among the League Powers. Paraguay, however, left the League of Nations. The American neutrals were persuaded that League

[6] Rowan-Robinson, *op. cit.*, p. 37.
[7] League of Nations, C. 186, M. 75, 1934, VII (May 12, 1934), 12.

methods were inappropriate to ending the controversy. After another year of war a new American effort at mediation proved more successful.[8]

In the Abyssinian dispute, the League made its greatest effort and achieved its most striking failure. France and Italy had worked out a *modus vivendi* in January, 1935, indicating France's acquiescence in Italy's expansion in Africa. Great Britain, however, took the lead in exerting pressure on Italy to prevent the invasion and annexation of Ethiopia. Italy and Great Britain had signed two treaties covering their respective spheres of interest in the event of the dissolution of Ethiopia. The impending incursion of Italy early in 1935 threatened these treaties.

In January, 1935, Abyssinia appealed to the League under Article 11 of the Covenant, because of the clash with Italian soldiers at Wal Wal and the alleged uncertainty of the boundary between Ethiopia and Somaliland. In February Italy began to send troops. An attempted arbitration, resulting in a report exonerating both parties, proved interesting rather than helpful. The British Government offered certain concessions to Italy and others to Abyssinia.

In the meantime, Lord Robert Cecil and the friends of the League of Nations had organized a campaign in England, to which the Labor party gave its support, to secure approval of the policy of the League in enforcing peace by sanctions. Failure of the negotiations with Italy made certain members of the British Cabinet believe that sanctions were now called for. How far Britain's national interest was integrated with the coercion of Italy by the League we need not stop to inquire. Britain dispatched a fleet to the Mediterranean and made alliances with various Mediterranean Powers. A diplomatic contest then began between Italy on the one hand and

---

[8] On the ineffectiveness of the Paraguayan sanctions, see Kain, " The Chaco Dispute and the Peace System," *Pol. Sci. Quarterly*, L (1935), 321–335.

Great Britain and the League of Nations on the other. In October, 1935, the invasion of Ethiopia began. A Coördination Committee of League Powers was organized to determine how sanctions could be coöperatively applied.

The United States went as far as it could to help these League sanctions, as will be explained later; but without consulting the United States, Great Britain in December worked out the Hoare-Laval Agreement giving Italy enlarged rights in Ethiopia, with some additional territory. This aroused the moral indignation of the sanctionists in England and in other countries, and ended in the repudiation of the deal and the resignation of Sir Samuel Hoare as Foreign Secretary. There are indications that Mussolini was inclined to accept the Hoare-Laval Agreement; but with its defeat the war proceeded. The British fleet was in dangerous proximity to the Italian fleet while the conquest of Abyssinia went on. Rather than risk war with Italy the British Government abjectly withdrew from its advanced position, and reduced its fleet in the Mediterranean. Mussolini captured Addis Ababa and announced the annexation of Abyssinia. He suspended his attendance on the meetings of the League until the delegates of Ethiopia were expelled. Great Britain and France took the lead in proposing this expulsion of Ethiopia from the League, and while the small Powers have temporarily delayed this move of *Realpolitik*, it will doubtless come in due course. The annexation of Ethiopia has now been tacitly recognized by Great Britain, France, and other countries, and the capital for the exploitation of Ethiopia will doubtless be found in England. Those sanctionists who would not accept the practical solutions of the Hoare-Laval Agreement and considered it a betrayal of Ethiopia and the League must assume a heavy share of responsibility for the killing of thousands of innocent people, for the extinction of independent Ethiopia, for the humiliating retreat of Great Britain, for grave injury to the League of Nations, for the practical collapse

of the whole theory of sanctions, and for the furious rearmament of England.

Numerous explanations have been supplied as to why
sanctions against Italy failed, although no more plausible case
for their application could be conceived. But the limpidity
of the theoretical case does not conceal its practical complexity. As already observed, one of the difficulties of all
mechanistic schemes for allaying international conflicts is
their oversimplification of conditions that do not admit of
clear delineation. Sanctions against Italy were applied unequally by different Powers, for sanctions cut both ways.
They often affect the sanctioner as much as the sanctionee,
and not all nations are able or willing to make the necessary
sacrifices. The result has been a widespread admission of
the futility of sanctions and an insistent demand for the
reform of the League.

In the main sanctions have failed because they lack any
sensible foundation. As the Abyssinian episode indicated,
economic sanctions against a great Power are not likely to
extend over a long period and can be made effective only by
military action, which brings us back to the old dilemma of
the war to end war. Yet the policy continues to have its strong
advocates among the more indomitable theorists. No League
such as these idealists conceive is possible unless the sovereignty of its constituent members is terminated by their disarmament and the surrender of their independence. Inasmuch as the world is not ready for this, the present League
can have no more power than its constituent members are
willing to supply.

Yet the coercive activities of the League have been not
innocuous but extremely harmful. For the United States,
therefore, to undertake indirectly to support the League of
Nations in its enforcement of peace is merely an indirect
method of supporting certain Powers in the League of Na-

tions in their European policies. As Mr. Coudert, the well-known New York lawyer, has stated:

The only possibility of avoiding war is through coöperation. The failure of the Naval Limitations Conference, by reason of the intransigent attitude of Japan, makes the time particularly opportune for strengthening that Anglo-American coöperation which can do so much for the maintenance of general peace.[9]

Apart from the evidences of international " coöperation " in the enforcement of peace which we have noted, the nations of the world have given little evidence of their intention to abandon neutrality as a conception or as a practice. In 1919, Canada gave notice that it would have nothing to do with the Graeco-Turkish War, and Great Britain, who helped to incite it, also decided to remain neutral. In 1922 and 1923, the Conference on Radio and Aircraft in Time of War considered the rules of neutrality to be still in force. In 1923, the Permanent Court of International Justice decided the famous *Wimbledon* case, involving Germany's power to close the Kiel Canal at the time of the Polish-Russian War of 1920, on the authority of the established rules of neutrality. The nations of the American continent declared their neutrality at the time of the Chaco War between Bolivia and Paraguay.[10] In 1928, the Havana Convention on Maritime Neutrality was adopted affirming the neutral duties of impartiality; the convention was ratified by the United States in 1932. In 1933, the Argentine Anti-War Pact adopted at Rio de Janiero enjoined on neutrals a " solidary attitude " in defense of neutrality. The treaty was ratified by the United States in 1934 and by several European nations, including members of the League. The United States Senate, in February, 1934, amended a discriminatory arms embargo resolution to provide that any prohibition of sale or export

[9] Coudert, *Proceedings,* 1935, p. 24.
[10] See G. G. Wilson's editorial, " War and Neutrality," *A. J. I. L.,* XXVII (July, 1933), 724–725.

of munitions should apply impartially to both belligerents. The Chaco arms embargo of the United States and the Neutrality statutes of August, 1935, and February, 1936, each provided that embargoes on arms and munitions should apply to both belligerents impartially. No country has repealed its neutrality legislation.

Thus, it would seem that in spite of the powerful propaganda on behalf of the policy of sanctions, a propaganda which finally resulted in an effort to apply them, neutrality has still retained its hold on the practical world. Belgium's return to neutrality may be evidence that it is now stronger than ever, as being the only known method with an established basis in legality to keep countries out of war. The theory that peace-loving nations could combine against an aggressor has demonstrated its impracticability, but its spirit persists in the attempt to mold American policy into new forms, making use of the popular devotion to neutrality but changing its purpose and effect.

II.

DEMANDS FOR UNNEUTRALITY —
1922–1933

HAVING been precipitated into a European war for the establishment of a new world order, the United States found great difficulty in extricating itself. Although the Treaty of Versailles came into force on January 10, 1920, fourteen months after the Armistice, the United States remained at war for another twenty-three months. The failure to ratify the Treaty of Versailles was, of course, a contributing factor.[1] Formal peace was not declared by the United States until the Knox-Porter Resolution of July 2, 1921, was adopted, and was not conclusively established until the ratification of the Treaty of Berlin on November 11, 1921. Inasmuch as the existence of a state of war had been declared by a Congressional Resolution on April 6, 1917, it is not apparent why a simple resolution repealing the declaration of war would not have brought the country back to a state of peace.

The issue is not academic because between the Armistice and July 2, 1921, the Alien Property Custodian seized some of his choicest bits of alien property, including the 4,500 German patents which became the object of the Chemical Foundation transaction. This alien property, which was sequestrated under an express commitment of President Wilson promising that private property would be respected in accordance with the rules of international law, was subsequently held as a kind of pledge for the repayment by the German Government of the war claims of United States citizens. At the present time, twenty years after its seizure, 20 per cent of

[1] On July 14, 1919, trade with Germany had been restored by Executive Order.

the property has not yet been returned to its owners.[2] These sequestrations are but one instance of the contaminations that American policy suffered by association with the European war, establishing precedents which for the indefinite future are likely to be highly injurious to the United States.

It was perhaps only an accident that so many of those who favored American association with the League of Nations were among those who had most strongly supported the entrance of the United States into the European war. These groups had become firmly convinced that the way to peace lay in taking the right side. This was called internationalism, although the devices themselves operated with centrifugal force to drive nations apart and to promote violent nationalism. But the nationalism it mainly fostered was not that of the United States.

After the Washington Naval Conference of 1922 and during the comparative lull in Europe due to the exhaustion of the war, the promotion of the League of Nations was associated with the promised goal of disarmament.

Although Article 8 of the Covenant of the League had suggested that the private manufacture of munitions and implements of war was open to grave objections, and that the Council was to advise how these evils could be obliterated with due regard to the interests of nonmanufacturing countries,[3] very little was effectively done about the problem until the Traffic in Arms Convention of 1925,[4] ratified by the United States in 1935. While several nations, especially since the Crimean War, had prohibited their citizens as neutrals from shipping arms and sometimes contraband of war to belligerents, international law, as already observed, had permitted such traffic to neutrals. Indeed, strong arguments were presented in support of this practice on the ground that the

[2] Cf. Editorial, " Reprisals on Private Property," *A. J. I. L.*, XXX (Jan., 1936), 108–113.

[3] Paragraph 5.

[4] The St. Germain Convention of 1919 was rejected by the United States.

denial of the right to purchase arms when needed would stimulate the establishment of national munitions industries and would lead to the excessive accumulation of arms in time of peace. Mr. Lansing had stated these reasons to Austria-Hungary on August 12, 1915, in response to Austria's protest against the unilateral supply of arms and ammunition to the Allied governments by the United States:

The principles of international law, the practice of nations, the national safety of the United States and other nations without great military and naval establishments, the prevention of increased armies and navies, the adoption of peaceful methods for the adjustment of international differences, and, finally, neutrality itself, are opposed to the prohibition by a neutral nation of the exportation of arms, ammunition, or other munitions of war to belligerent powers during the progress of the war.[5]

The unsuccessful St. Germain Convention on Traffic in Arms of 1919 had undertaken to prohibit the export of arms and ammunition except for the use of the signatory governments — which was apparently a method for excluding non-signatories from receiving arms in any war in which they might be engaged. The 1925 Traffic in Arms Convention provides that in time of war the prohibition on arms shipments to belligerents shall be lifted.[6] For the rest the purpose of this convention was the statistical control of the arms traffic so as to make publicly known any undue accumulation of arms by any state.[7]

Arms embargoes were not new to this country. In 1912 and 1922, the United States had adopted two important arms embargo resolutions, designed especially to prevent the export of arms to nations in civil war on this continent and in

[5] *For. Rel.*, 1915, Suppl., p. 798.

[6] The question might arise whether the arms embargo provided by the 1935 Neutrality Act and continued in force by the 1936 Act will be deemed to violate this treaty.

[7] Chamberlain, " The Embargo Resolutions and Neutrality," *International Conciliation,* No. 151 (June, 1929), 271. On the control of manufacture, the nations are in serious disagreement.

China. While the resolutions did not specifically make a distinction between constituent governments and rebels, their intention was to prevent the supply of arms to rebels and, with minor exceptions in the case of the Huerta and other governments in Mexico, they have been so applied by the United States.[8]

In 1927, during the negotiations preliminary to the Kellogg-Briand Pact, Representative Burton of Ohio introduced a resolution defining American policy as prohibiting " the export of arms, munitions and war material to any country engaged in a war of aggression against another, in violation of a treaty, convention, or any other arrangement providing for recourse to peaceful means for the settlement of international differences."

The Burton Resolution was so clearly unneutral that it aroused loud protests. As a result, Representative Burton introduced on January 25, 1928, a new resolution providing that " the policy of the United States shall consist in forbidding the export of arms, munitions, or war material to any nation engaged in war with another nation." Although this resolution looked definitely toward the neutrality of the United States in providing that both belligerents must be treated alike, it was opposed both by League advocates and by the Secretaries of War and Navy who believed that the armed forces of the United States depended upon the private manufacture of munitions and did not wish to see the munitions industry impaired.

After 1933, the investigations of the Nye Committee into the munitions industry and the bankers, and the general belief that an embargo on arms from the United States would exert restraint on war abroad and at the same time save the neutrality of the United States, stimulated the adoption of the policy of the Burton Resolution as part of the permanent

---

[8] Chamberlain, *loc. cit.*, pp. 275–277; Williams, *American Diplomacy* (1936), p. 385.

neutrality legislation of the United States. Whether it will remain permanent is open to question.

The Neutrality Claims Against Great Britain — Executive Agreement of May 19, 1927

BOTH President Wilson and Secretary Lansing had indicated on several occasions that the German submarine attack upon American lives required immediate vindication even to the extent of war, whereas the property losses caused by the Allies could await money compensation at the end of the war.[9] The intimation was that American demands for the immense property losses, estimated at $100,000,000, would be presented to the Allied governments after the war; in fact, on several occasions American officials stated that the country's entrance into the war in 1917 had not constituted a waiver of American neutral rights [10] or of the demands for compensation for their violation. This question having come up in Congress at various times in the form of resolutions and in debate, the administration finally undertook in 1926 to deal with the problem actively. A study of the American claims for property losses was undertaken in the Department of State under the direction of Under-Secretary Olds; Mr. Phenix, his assistant, was charged with a mission to London to negotiate a method of settlement.

The result is interesting. Great Britain paid the United States nothing, but graciously left in American hands a sum of $1,500,000 which the United States had conceded to be due for services rendered by Great Britain to the American Navy in Europe in 1917 and 1918. The British were also willing to

[9] Cf. Lansing's statement on property losses, *Memoirs,* p. 110; Wilson's speech, Sept. 2, 1916, Scott, ed., *op. cit.,* pp. 237–238, and address, April 2, 1917, that property losses could be paid for; and Newton D. Baker, *Foreign Affairs,* Oct., 1936, p. 86.

[10] See *For. Rel.,* 1917, Suppl. II, pp. 865, 866; *idem,* pp. 875, 876; *idem,* 1918, Suppl. I, Vol. II, 934. Cf. Morrisey, " The United States and the Rights of Neutrals, 1917–1918," *A. J. I. L.,* XXXI (Jan., 1937), 17–30.

leave here the amount of a claim against the United States, the validity of which the United States had not admitted, variously estimated to amount to an additional $4,000,000. It was decided by the Executive agreement of May 19, 1927, that the United States might distribute these sums to the owners of meritorious American claims who had gone to the British prize courts and been defeated, or whom, by virtue of the equitable nature of the claim, the Department of State might excuse from such recourse.[1]

Inasmuch as few of the claimants would feel disposed to undertake the great expense of litigating in a British prize court for the practically impossible purpose of getting a decision to the effect that an Order in Council was illegal,[2] the agreement served, if rigidly applied, to kill off the American claims. The exception of " equitable " claims opened the door to State Department discretion which, on the whole, has been used against the American claimants, for the agreement had the remarkable effect of placing the State Department in the position of a defender of the British measures. Claimants against the limited sum placed at American disposal for distribution have encountered, not a willingness, but a decided reluctance on the part of the Department of State to admit the British violations of neutral rights — even though those violations were within the precise terms of the protests of Secretary Lansing in his note of October 21, 1915. The sums to be distributed under the agreement might have afforded an opportunity for the State Department to write strong opinions in defense of the law and of neutral

---

[1] Those claims were to be paid " which the Government of the United States regards as meritorious and in which the claimants have exhausted their legal remedies in British courts, in which no legal remedy is open to them, or in respect of which for other reasons the equitable construction of the present agreement calls for a settlement " (Art. 3).

[2] The Orders in Council of March 11, 1915, and Feb. 16, 1917, the retaliatory orders under which most of the illegal seizures were made, were sustained by the British courts in the *Stigstad* [1919] A. C. 279 and the *Leonora* [1919] A. C. 974.

rights for the guidance of Congress. These would have been useful; they would at least have supported Secretary Lansing's protests of October 21, 1915, and would have been a caveat for the future.

In fairness, it should be said that on two or three occasions the Department, realizing that it occupied the position of judge and defendant at one and the same time, has conceded the propriety of an arbitration between the claimant and the Department. On the whole, however, the entrance of the United States into the war on the side of Great Britain, notwithstanding the reservation of American neutral rights, has been nearly as effective in killing off American neutral claims as was entrance into the War of 1812 as an enemy of Great Britain.

But that was not all. Participation in the war had a further effect. Great Britain had endeavored to justify her extraordinary measures in throttling neutral trade on the ground of reprisal against Germany, thereby implicitly admitting them to be illegal under international law. Now, however, she took advantage of American submissiveness to provide openly in the agreement that she reserved the right to do the same thing again in any future war; and the United States reserved its right to protest.[3] This agreement to disagree indicated, however, the existence of a fundamental difference between Great Britain and the United States with respect to the rights of neutrals. Such a situation could not but arouse apprehension in informed circles.[4]

The settlement was accomplished in the form of an Executive agreement, rather than a treaty, presumably on the as-

[3] "That the right of each government to maintain in the future such position as it may deem appropriate with respect to the legality or illegality under international law of measures such as those giving rise to [the neutrality] claims is fully reserved, it being specifically understood that the juridical position of neither government is prejudiced by the present arrangement."

[4] Cf. "The Neutrality Claims against Great Britain," *A. J. I. L.*, XXI (1927), 764.

sumption that the United States was gaining something of value and giving up nothing. A sacrifice customarily would have required Senate consent. Moreover, a treaty would have given rise to a serious debate in the Senate.

Thus, in spite of the wartime promises that American neutral claims against the Allies would be vindicated, in practical effect they have been all but abandoned. And worse yet, the future rights of neutrals have been jeopardized. The postwar disparagement of neutrality may be credited with another achievement.

Borah Resolution for the Restatement of Rules of Maritime War

As a result of this difference between Great Britain and the United States on the rules of maritime law, now raised to the status of a formal disagreement, Senator Borah attempted to find a solution for the problem. In February, 1928, he introduced a resolution [5] calling for a restatement of the rules of maritime law. Since the rules embodied in the Hague Conventions and in the Declaration of London had been violated in important respects during the war, and since the limitation of armaments and the orderly conduct of international relations are obviously dependent upon relative certainty in the rules of law, the Senator urged that an agreement on the rules governing the conduct of belligerents and neutrals should precede the meeting of the Conference on the Limitation of Naval Armaments, then scheduled for 1931.

Contrary to the common experience after former wars, there had developed after the late war a disposition not to discuss the issues created by the British " measures of blockade " and similar illegal impairments of the rights of neutrals. The fundamental nature of these problems, however,

[5] S. Res. 157, 70th Cong., 1st Sess., *Cong. Rec.*, LXIX (Feb. 21, 1928), 3421.

made it impossible to ignore them for long. Neither the Naval Conference of 1927 between Great Britain, the United States, and Japan, nor the Executive agreement of May 19, 1927, just discussed, had allayed any of the differences on the rules of law or naval policy. Lord Wemyss had even explained to the House of Commons that Britain's demand for a large cruiser fleet, which had broken up the 1927 Conference, was designed not merely to protect commerce between Great Britain and other nations, but also to prevent commerce between Great Britain's enemies and third states.

Inasmuch as the United States may be said to consider its normal position that of a neutral, it is evident that it has a genuine interest in the maintenance of the rules of law and in opposing claims based upon belligerent interest alone.

The assumed freedom of a belligerent to dispose of neutral commerce as its interest dictates is likely to prove unreliable and precarious even for a belligerent, for it encourages a general increase in naval armaments and the concomitant temptation to use them. More security is likely to be obtained from an international agreement on the rules of law at sea than from any implicit or explicit assertion of the supremacy of necessity over law. Such were the considerations behind the resolution.

Despite all that, however, the Borah Resolution was vigorously opposed by advocates of the League of Nations, because it dared to recognize the possibility of future war and because it looked forward to neutrality. In 1928 there was still a widespread belief that war had been exorcised. Hence there was opposition to the suggestion that it ought to be regulated.

Professor Manley Hudson argued that the proposal to restate the law of neutrality was contrary to Articles 11 and 16 of the Covenant of the League. " The provisions of the Covenant . . . constitute an attempt to realize President Wilson's statement that the ' day of neutrality is past.' "

" Apart from the United States," he said, " all others of the Powers chiefly interested in using sea power — France, Great Britain, Italy and Japan — are committed to the Covenant." Mr. Hudson added that these nations " are committed to the attempt to say that a war is a matter of general interest, and that in cases of pronounced aggression no body of sea law is to restrain attempts to overcome the aggressor." Thereupon he asked:

Is the United States to maintain a contrary thesis? Are we to insist on behalf of ourselves and other states, that the old law of neutrality which gave us such difficulty during the war, must be observed in the future? If not, are we prepared to join in some recognition of common action which other states may take against the aggressor? Only in this latter case, which finds no statement in Senator Borah's resolution, can a fruitful collaboration of the leading maritime powers be envisaged. If the United States should insist on a continuation of the pre-war law of neutrality, while all other naval powers are insisting upon its revision in the light of covenant obligations, there would seem to be little basis for an international conference or for any attempt at recodification.[6]

Apart from the manifold difficulties of securing " common action " against that amorphous entity, the " aggressor," the intimation that no law should stand in the way of the League's efforts to overcome aggression is very questionable. The suggestion that the end justifies the means is not uncommon among moralists. The desired end was obviously to insure American " coöperation " with the League Powers in their coercive enterprises. And even internationalized force — assuming it to be possible — should be employed under definite rules of " sea law " or any other law, for order is not achieved without law. It would be unfortunate for the League if it were to be associated in the public mind with open advocacy of lawlessness.

The popular impression which the defenders of short cuts

6 Manley O. Hudson, *New York Times*, March 11, 1928.

to salvation have sedulously purveyed, to the effect that war cannot be regulated because it is pure violence, that its regulation prevents the development of a law of peace, that unlimited war will shorten wars, and that the laws of war are always violated [7] is refuted by history. No earlier age cultivated such misconceptions. If they had, Western civilization would very likely have disappeared long before this. Wars have been effectively regulated in the past and because of that fact civilization has been able to proceed in spite of the blight. The indications are strong that the lifting of restrictions upon war would make for pure chaos. Far from shortening wars, such action would make even temporary peace problematical. All laws are occasionally violated, but we live by them, nevertheless. An increasing popular respect for law marks the development of the Western mind and a weakening of that respect will mark its deterioration. The press reports of violence necessarily excite more comment than law observance, which is not news. But it is too bad that professed strivers for peace should be among the major opponents of the regulation of war, as they are of the principle of neutrality. Fortunately no governments have followed their advice. There is, indeed, no reason why the regulation of war and the cultivation of methods for ameliorating the causes of strife cannot go along together. The suggestion of an inconsistency between them is an instance of the confusion created by the movement for enforcing peace by violence.

Thomas Baty, the learned English international lawyer, has said: " Unless war is to be replaced by unchecked violence, masquerading under the name of ' self-defense ' or ' federal execution,' neutrality with its rights and obligations cannot be regarded as out of date." [8]

John Bassett Moore, whose practical contributions to al-

[7] Cf. J. L. Kunz, " Plus de lois de la guerre? " *Revue gén. de droit int. pub.*, XLI (1934), 26–27, who condemns these assumptions.

[8] Baty, " The Future of Prize Law and the Freedom of the Seas," *Journal of Comparative Legislation*, XIII (1931), 3rd ser., 181.

laying strife may be numbered among the signal achievements of the United States, has warned that

if while we await the capitulation of war to a declaration of its
illegality, we spurn the present opportunity to work with all our
might for the preservation and advancement of that system of
law which, recording from age to age the slow progress of humanity,
has established the distinction between combatants and non-
combatants, enjoined the humane treatment of captives, limited
the destruction and confiscation of property, enlarged the bounds
of commercial freedom, and furnished the rules of decision by which
international courts have in countless cases determined grave disputes and stilled the voice of strife, we shall only draw upon our
generation the bitter fate portrayed by Milton in the solemn lines:

> " Alas! from what high hope to what relapse
> Unlooked for we are fallen." [9]

The Borah Resolution was not adopted.

The Kellogg-Briand Pact

THE Kellogg-Briand Pact opened up a new chapter in the
attack on American neutrality. Promoted by those who desired to have the United States participate in the system of
collective security,[10] it enlisted by clever strategy the support of the League's severe critic, Senator Borah, who had
favored the outlawry of war. With the League out of the
way, the movement gained headway. Fired by the enthusiasm of a considerable group, it advocated a somewhat new
credo: the belief that human habits and institutions could be
changed by a determination to abandon them; dueling was
cited as an instance of such change in the mores. Inasmuch
as the two complementary articles of the Kellogg Pact contemplated the renunciation of war as an instrument of national policy and the submission of all disputes to pacific

[9] J. B. Moore, *International Law and Some Current Illusions*, pp. 36–37.
[10] Shotwell, " War as an Instrument of National Policy (New York, 1929)
passim; D. H. Miller, *The Pact of Paris* (New York, 1928), p. 7 *et seq.;*
Steed, *Vital Peace* (New York, 1936), p. 188.

settlement, it seemed to many persons that at last the cure for that social disease called " war " had been found.

The origin of the negotiations between the United States and other Powers leading to the conclusion of this Pact is well known. Beginning with an expression of good-will in M. Briand's note of April 6, 1927, the tenth anniversary of the entry of the United States into the war, France expressed a willingness to conclude a bilateral treaty renouncing war between the two nations. Negotiations developed rapidly. On June 20, the French Foreign Minister presented the draft of a treaty embodying his proposal; it provided for condemnation of " recourse to war " and renounced war between France and the United States as an " instrument of their national policy." Settlement of disputes was never to be sought " except by pacific means." But Mr. Kellogg was doubtful of the bilateral feature of the plan, which he thought might be misunderstood to be a treaty of alliance. On December 28, 1927, therefore, he proposed to the French Ambassador the extension of the proposed declaration to all the principal Powers.

The French press was critical. France, it was maintained, had obligations to the League of Nations and could not contract these new engagements. But criticism was quickly silenced by the publication of the French reply undertaking to renounce " wars of aggression." This gave a new turn to the negotiations.

While the State Department did not comment officially, officers of the Department pointed out that the term " aggression " changed the entire meaning of the proposal and rendered it unacceptable to the United States. In this position the State Department seems to have had the support of much of the American press. Editorially it was agreed that " renunciation of aggressive war " was too intricate an expression to define and that the French interpolation of this qualification left Mr. Kellogg's proposal denatured of its vital part and therefore meaningless. As Mr. Kellogg pointed out, the first French note of June 20, 1927, had not been limited to wars of aggression.

Considerable correspondence took place in the early part of 1928 as to the construction to be given to the proposed treaty. In a note of February 27, explaining his objection to qualifications of the obligation to renounce war, Mr. Kellogg stated:

The ideal which inspires the effort so sincerely and so hopefully put forward by your [the French] Government and mine is arresting and appealing just because of its purity and simplicity; and I cannot avoid the feeling that if governments should publicly acknowledge that they can only deal with this ideal in a technical spirit and must insist on the adoption of reservations impairing, if not utterly destroying, the true significance of their common endeavors, they would be in effect only recording their impotence, to the keen disappointment of mankind in general.

The same thought was expressed in Mr. Kellogg's speech to the Council on Foreign Relations on March 15, 1928. He said:

It seems to me that any attempt to define the word " aggression," and by exceptions and qualifications to stipulate when nations are justified in going to war with one another, would greatly weaken the effect of any treaty such as that under consideration and virtually destroy its positive value as a " guaranty of peace."

Subsequent negotiations, however, disclose the unfortunate fact that these very nullifying exceptions and qualifications have actually found their way into the treaty as it is now generally construed.

The French Government maintained that the Pact must be interpreted so as not to bar the right of legitimate defense, or the performance of obligations under the Covenant of the League of Nations, under the treaties of Locarno, or under its treaties of alliance with various Allies — for some unexplainable reason called treaties of neutrality. The Pact, it was said, was to become ineffective if violated by one nation. Moreover, it was to be signed by every state before it became effective for any state. With the exception of this last reservation, Secretary Kellogg agreed to this interpretation of the French Government in his speech before the American Society of International Law on April 28, 1928. He incorporated his interpretation of the reservations as to self-defense, wars under the League Covenant, under the treaties of Locarno, and certain undefined " neutrality " treaties, in a note of June 28, to the Powers, some fifteen in number, adding that " none of these governments has expressed any dissent from the above-quoted construction."

On May 19, Great Britain accepted the American proposal in principle. Sir Austen Chamberlain expressed his government's assent to the reservations made by France, and then proceeded to a new one:

There are certain regions of the world, the welfare and integrity of which constitute a special and vital interest for our peace and safety. His Majesty's Government have been at pains to make it clear in the past that interference with these regions cannot be suffered. Their protection against attack is to the British Empire a measure of self-defense. It must be clearly understood that *His Majesty's Government in Great Britain accept the new treaty upon the distinct understanding that it does not prejudice their freedom of action in this respect.* The Government of the United States have comparable interests, any disregard of which by a foreign Power they have declared they would regard as an unfriendly act. (Italics supplied.)

The words in italics were reiterated by the British on July 18, 1928. The Pact was signed with appropriate ceremonies on August 27, 1928.

Mr. Kellogg's original proposal had contained an unconditional renunciation of war. As qualified by the French and British interpretations, however, the treaty constituted no renunciation or outlawry of war at all. When we look at the exceptions we observe that they inferentially sanction all wars of self-defense — each party to be the exclusive and unreviewable judge of what is self-defense — wars under the League Covenant, under the Locarno treaties, and under the French treaties of alliance.

Considering the breadth of these qualifications or interpretations, it would be difficult to conceive of any wars that nations have fought within the past century, or are likely to fight in the future, that cannot be accommodated under them. Far from being an outlawry of war, they constitute the most definite sanction of specific wars that has ever been promulgated. In the past, war had been considered something like a disease — neither legal nor illegal. Now by a world treaty, practically all wars obtained the stamp of official approval. The mere renunciation of war in the abstract in the first article of the treaty could have but little scope for application in view of the wars in the concrete sanctioned by the accompanying interpretations of the treaty.

Again, it will be noticed that the United States specifically recognized the British claim to use war as an instrument of national policy in certain undefined " regions of the world," and to regard any " interference " by anybody, including the United States, as a cause for war. When the United States at the first Hague Conference secured recognition for the Monroe Doctrine, it was regarded as a striking achievement of American diplomacy. But the Monroe Doctrine has geographical limits known to everybody. To this new British claim — which other nations may also advance on their own behalf — there are no geographical limits. The vague and expansive terms of the British prerogative cover any part of the world in which Britain has " a special and vital interest." No such broad claim to the right to make war had ever before been recognized.

But the most extraordinary feature of this Pact still remains to be mentioned. It will have been noticed that the United States recognized the legality of League wars and

Locarno wars. As Europe correctly seemed to assume, the United States was now bound by League decisions as to " aggressors " and by League policy generally, but without any opportunity to take part in the deliberations leading to League conclusions. The United States, indeed, recognized by this treaty the legal right of the League to make war against any nation.

The new contract began with diverse interpretations of its obligations, for European views left no doubt that Europe regarded the treaty as a means of involving the United States in European politics. And the United States was entangled in the most dangerous way; it was bound by decisions made in its absence, because the recognition of the French and British reservations, now made the authoritative interpretation of the treaty by all the signatories, was a commitment for the United States. Its hands were tied, not theirs. But for the subsequent disintegration of the war-making powers of the League, it might in theory have been safer for the United States openly to join the League of Nations and obtain the privilege of taking part in deliberations which could have such important consequences. In this way it might have been able to prevent undesirable conclusions and have used its bargaining power to obtain occasional benefits instead of only war.

Nor is the meaning of the Pact doubtful. Whether the exchange of notes which embodied the understanding by the signatories of the obligations they were then contracting be called reservations, conditions, interpretations, or whatnot, it constitutes the official explanation of the meaning assigned to the vague terms of the Kellogg Pact, " that uncertain formulation of a nebulous doctrine." [1]

And M. Briand left no doubt of his view that the supposed renunciation of war would never interfere with the full

---

[1] Professor Rappard of Geneva, " Small States in the League of Nations," *Pol. Sci. Quarterly*, XLIX (1934), 554, 571.

application of Article 16 of the Covenant of the League. M. Paul-Boncour has reported [2] that M. Briand regarded the Pact as, above all, a means to draw the United States into the machinery of the League of Nations. He argued that it could hardly be imagined that when an aggressor " had torn up the Covenant " and the sanctions of Article 16 had been set in motion, the United States, instigator of the Pact, would remain indifferent to its violation and would fail to " throw into the duel " for peace the weight and power of America.

When reporting out the Pact, the Senate Committee on Foreign Relations met the objection that had been raised to the effect that it had committed the United States to the use of force by an expressed declaration that the treaty was to be a self-denying ordinance only; it was not to carry " teeth," and under no circumstances was it to be enforced.[2a] But the ink had hardly dried on the signatures before the movement began for associating the United States with enforcement.

The provision found in Article 11 of the Covenant was employed to prove that a war anywhere affected the entire world, and that a war in violation of the Kellogg Pact would require the United States to take action against the treaty-breaker. Not only had this view no substantial foundation in law, but it was directly contrary to the Senate understanding with which the Pact was consummated.

Yet the idea continued to command support in the highest quarters in this country. A means had been discovered whereby the United States might be wrenched from its neutrality and made a participant in the enforcement of peace against aggressors. The term " violator of a treaty " was now substituted for the somewhat objectionable term " aggressor." It was argued that it would be unconscionable for the United States to treat violator and violated alike and

[2] *New York Times,* April 10, 1932.
[2a] *Cong. Rec.,* LXX (Jan. 15, 1929), 1730.

that to supply a violator with arms and munitions would be to make the United States his accomplice.

Hence Senator Capper was persuaded to introduce in February, 1929, a resolution calling for the prohibition of the export of " arms and munitions and implements or other articles for use in war " to any country which the President declared to have violated the Kellogg Pact. The Capper Resolution declared it as American policy " that the nationals of the United States should not be protected by their government in giving aid and comfort to a nation which has committed a breach of the Kellogg Pact," and the President was requested to enter into negotiations with other governments to secure similar action.[3]

A considerable propaganda was released behind the Capper Resolution and in the confusion as to where American interests lay, it might have been adopted but for the turn of events in Europe and Asia during 1930 and 1931.

Believers in the policy of taking sides in foreign disputes have made of the Kellogg Pact the cornerstone of their campaign. We have already had occasion to observe the demand for implementing it with " teeth." Not a few professors contended that " the Kellogg Pact will be respected only if we deliberately and strongly take sides against the violator of the Pact." [4] It was regarded as " a great advance upon the Covenant of the League of Nations." [5] But its value for punitive purposes was said to depend upon its use " effectively in conjunction with the other signatories of the Pact, acting through an established machinery." [6] It was lauded

---

[3] Another Capper Resolution of 1932 provided for an arms and commercial embargo on the aggressor, if other nations in conference and the President determined that a breach of the Pact had occurred. This foreshadowed the Norman Davis commitment of 1933, *infra*, p. 300. B. H. Williams, *American Diplomacy* (1936), p. 335.

[4] Eagleton, *Proceedings*, 1935, p. 133.

[5] Fenwick, " The Implication of Consultation," " The Pact of Paris," *A. J. I. L.*, XXVI (Oct., 1932), 787.

[6] Eagleton, *Proceedings*, 1935, p. 133.

not merely as expressing a renunciation of war by the United States, " but as indicating a concern as to the observance of the Pact by other states and an intention to depart from its traditional attitude of neutrality should others be guilty of a breach of the Pact." [7] Indeed, the interventionist school of thought considered the Kellogg Pact to have revolutionized American policy and international law as well. As it was deemed to authorize discrimination between aggressors on the one hand, and the victims of aggression and the sanctioning Powers on the other, it was hailed as now formally " entitling the United States to undertake discriminatory measures by way of reprisal." [8] It became for the moralists an inspired opportunity for regenerating the world by violence.

But the temptations of the Kellogg Pact have enticed others than academicians. Relying on the facile assumption that the Pact had really outlawed war and violence, and indulging the unfounded belief that it was the privilege of the United States to determine whether a fellow signatory had violated it and thereupon to admonish, if not to chastise him, more than one Secretary of State has launched reprimands and expressions of obloquy against foreign countries because they have not observed the legal and moral standards which it was supposed the Kellogg Pact had established. Secretary of State Stimson invoked the Kellogg Pact in 1929 as the justification for his admonition to Soviet Russia in its dispute with the Manchurian Government arising out of the Chinese Eastern Railway. The sharp reply of the Soviets resenting the interference was not very encouraging. Again the Pact was invoked as a basis for the Secretary's complaint against Japan for invading Manchuria. Fortunately the British Government was more impervious than the United States to moral considerations. When finally Sir John Simon announced in the House of Commons, on February 27, 1933,

[7] Fenwick, *op. cit.*, p. 787.
[8] Wright, *Polity*, Feb., 1936, p. 8, col. 2.

that " under no circumstances will this government authorize this country to be a party to the conflict," the ardor for
American intervention diminished perceptibly.

But the supposed prohibitions and injunctions of the Kellogg Pact stimulated a widespread movement in the United
States for boycotts, embargoes, and other hostile measures
against Japan. Harsh language was employed on both sides.
America may well be grateful to the British Government for
declining to be persuaded to support an adventure which
might have had the most dire results for all countries concerned. Secretary Hull invoked the Pact in the indirect chastisement of Italy contained in his reply of July, 1935, to the
protest of the Emperor of Ethiopia, and his reply of October 5, 1935, to the League of Nations' request for coöperation in the Ethiopian conflict.

A penetrating commentator, Mr. Lincoln Colcord, has described as follows the functions of the Kellogg Pact:

Propagandized as a treaty for world peace, the Kellogg-Briand
pact in reality proposed as the price of peace the perpetuation of
the Treaty of Versailles. Thus it was based on errors which it did
nothing to correct. It did not conform to the immediate self-interest
of all its signatories, or to the ultimate self-interest of any of them.
Hence it was destined to fall apart almost of its own weight the
moment a strong national self-interest reared its head in any particular quarter. This moment came when Japan, in fulfillment of
what she felt to be her national destiny, decided to occupy Manchuria.

The point is that the Kellogg-Briand treaty should never have
been written or signed, since it represented no cogent agreement in
world relations. Such a treaty, like a bad law that does not have the
support of public opinion, is merely written to be broken. To insist
that treaties like this should be sustained by all their signatories in
the face of strong national trends, or that their abrogation by any
signatory under the pressure of such a trend is an act of national
dishonor, is to deal with world relations in terms of romance rather
than realism.[9]

[9] *New York Herald Tribune*, March 20, 1936.

The Consultative Pact

SHORTLY after the Kellogg Pact was ratified, a movement was initiated from Geneva to draw the United States into a " consultative pact " to determine what should be done about its enforcement. At the London Conference of 1930, the head of the American delegation displayed some sympathy for the idea. Two years later, at the " Disarmament " Conference, acceptance by the United States of such a Pact was made a prominent condition of the French promise to consider any limitation of armaments. Quite naturally, this enlisted the ardent support in the United States of those who wished to associate this country with the Geneva schemes for dealing with old-world aggressors.

" Consultation " must be understood in its connotations. When associated with a purpose to select an aggressor and take common action against him to " enforce peace," it is necessarily not a platonic gesture, but a prelude to war. That is how the term is understood in Europe. The fact that both Democratic and Republican campaign platforms of 1932 approved the idea of a consultative pact indicates how far the United States has drifted from its traditions and how susceptible it is to allurements for foreign military engagements. The promise to " consult " appears innocuous enough, but the now common method of drawing the United States into dangerous commitments is to employ simple, innocent, and attractive words the implications of which many Americans who use them often fail to comprehend. The consultative pact is almost certain to be followed by " understandings," and those understandings would be likely to involve the United States deeply in the morass of European feuds. It was Lansdowne's " consultative pact " — known in 1904 by its old-fashioned name " entente " — which committed the British people to France and, by departing from the " splendid isolation " of Salisbury, made the European war practically certain. Its very vagueness was perhaps its most pernicious characteristic, for it deceived not only the British people, but their antagonists as well, and, far from avoiding, encouraged the coming war. An open military alliance would be less dangerous than these nebulous commitments, which blow simultaneously hot and cold.

As John Bassett Moore has remarked:

Agreements are interpreted according to the subject matter. A reduction in armaments in consideration of a " consultative pact " would necessarily indicate as the subject of consultation the number of men, of ships and of aircraft that should be contributed in order to supply the place of what had been given up . . . The commitment of the United States to such a " consultative pact " as is desired at Geneva would, I believe, constitute the gravest danger to which the country has ever been exposed, a danger involving our very independence. It seems to be thought that we are an easy mark, and I say this not in any spirit of reproach. We all are human. Lambs are killed by men as well as by lions, but lambs are especially appetizing to the cultivated tastes of the old and polished European nations.[10]

The Norman Davis Commitment at Geneva, 1933

THE 1932 Geneva Conference on the Limitation of Armaments had by May, 1933, plodded its weary way for fifteen months, spurred on by the hopes of enthusiasts for disarmament and the promises of the League Covenant, but retarded by the reluctance of several highly armed powers to believe that a limitation of armaments was meant for them. At the same time the occasion was used to importune the United States to help preserve the peace of Europe by committing itself to aid the " right " side. The campaign took various forms and the prolonged extension of the Conference may in part be explained by the patient effort to work a commitment out of the United States which might be helpful to certain powers. In the United States, the long delay evoked various

[10] " An Appeal to Reason," *Foreign Affairs*, July, 1933, p. 27.

unofficial suggestions, such as a remission of the Allied debt in return for disarmament. Finally, the administration was persuaded to permit Mr. Norman Davis, its delegate to the Conference, to make, in return for some undesignated limitation of armament, the following engagement:

We are willing to consult other states in case of a threat to peace with a view to averting a conflict. Further than that, in the event that the states in conference determine that a state has been guilty of a breach of peace in violation of its international obligations and take measures against a violator, then, if we concur in the judgment rendered as to the responsible and guilty party, we will refrain from any action tending to defeat such collective effort which the states may thus make to restore peace.[1]

It is surprising that in return some concession to American desires for the limitation of armaments was not made. Probably only a slight symbol of good intentions in the form of a few divisions or guns would have served the purpose. But the extent of the willingness of the United States Government at that time to coöperate with Geneva in the " enforcement of peace," is not without interest. In the first place, the " consultative pact " was revived, and as already observed, consultation for the purpose of determining who is an aggressor can have only one result. If, moreover, the " states in conference " — now no longer the equivalent of a unanimous League of Nations — should decide that a state has violated its international obligations and take measures against a violator — the Kellogg Pact euphemism for " aggressor " — the United States, if it concurred in the judgment as to the guilty party, would refrain from action tending to defeat the collective effort of the states in conference to restore peace. League supporters appreciated that this was a commitment to support the League of Nations at the expense of American neutrality[2] and that it would expose the United States

---

[1] Hearings on S. 3474, Committee on Foreign Relations, U. S. Senate, 74th Cong., 2d Sess., p. 201; *New York Times*, May 23, 1933.

[2] Wright, *Polity*, Feb., 1936, p. 8.

to the charge and the dangers of taking sides in a foreign war.

The Norman Davis proposal did not meet a very favorable reception in this country, but it indicated an extraordinary desire to coöperate with the League of Nations in the enforcement of peace without openly joining the League. The charge frequently made that the United States would of necessity be bound by decisions made at Geneva was ostensibly tempered by the provision that the application of the obligations assumed by the Davis commitment would depend upon the United States' concurring in the Geneva finding. It does not seem likely that in practice there would have been serious difference of opinion in that respect. It is also apparent that refraining from any action tending to defeat a " collective effort " is a participation in that " collective effort " by unneutral discrimination.[3] It was generally understood that the Johnson amendment to the Arms Embargo Resolution of 1933 [4] had as its effect " to qualify, if not partly to nullify, the pronouncement on the abandonment of neutrality made . . . at Geneva by Norman H. Davis." [5]

The Doctrine of Nonrecognition

AND now we have a final pearl for the necklace — spurious like the others. The doctrine of nonrecognition of annexations has lately been advocated and practiced as a further sanction against disapproved " aggressions." But this contributes very little to peace. Change is natural. Until we find a way of making changes amicably, the nonamicable method cannot be successfully outlawed. The principle of prescription, designed to confirm as valid a long-established state of

[3] Cf. a most illuminating letter by Lincoln Colcord to the *New York Herald Tribune*, January 4, 1936.

[4] Insuring its impartial application, *infra*, p. 311.

[5] *New York Times*, May 28, 1933. Senator Pittman, Chairman of the Foreign Relations Committee, also expressed his disagreement with the Norman Davis proposal. Hearings on S. Bill No. 3474, *op. cit.* p. 201.

things, however accomplished, has been called an unwritten statute of repose. Both law and life frown upon long-continued uncertainty. A country refusing to recognize a fact must either content itself with making faces or must fight. Little satisfaction can be derived from either alternative.

The effort to have the United States " enforce peace " in other parts of the world has thus taken various forms. All of them implied a departure from the obligations of neutrality. They exerted a powerful influence, however, in molding the neutrality legislation of recent years in the direction of unneutrality. A brief recital of that struggle between the interventionists and the neutrals for satisfactory legislation will indicate the conflict of policies.

III.

THE LEGISLATIVE STRUGGLE

The Arms Embargo of 1933

EARLY in 1933 when the failure of the League to solve the Manchurian problem had become evident, Senator Borah, as Chairman of the Foreign Relations Committee, was persuaded to introduce a resolution patterned after the Embargo Acts of 1912 and 1922. Those earlier resolutions permitted the President to embargo the shipment of arms to any Latin-American country or to any country in which the United States exercised extraterritorial jurisdiction, when he believed that such an embargo would promote the termination of domestic violence and the re-establishment of peace in those countries.

This Borah Resolution provided that whenever the President finds

that in any part of the world conditions exist such that the shipment of arms or munitions of war from countries which produce these commodities may promote or encourage the employment of force in the course of a dispute or conflict between nations, and, *after securing the cooperation of such governments as the President deems necessary,* he makes proclamation thereof, it shall be unlawful to export or sell for export, except under such limitations and regulations as the President prescribes, any arms or munitions of war from any place in the United States *to such country or countries as he may designate,* until otherwise ordered by the President or by Congress.[6]

Probably this resolution emanated from the Department of State, then in the midst of the effort to reprimand Japan. The resolution differed from those of 1912 and 1922 in its applicability to international wars and not merely to domestic

[6] Italics supplied. S. J. Res. 229, 72d Cong., 2d Sess. *Cong. Rec.,* LXXVI, 2096.

insurrections, in its contemplating the possibility of " securing the cooperation of such governments as the President
deems necessary," and more particularly in its permitting the
President in his discretion to apply the embargo " to such
country or countries as he may designate."

It is doubtful whether the implications of these clauses
were fully realized at the time, for the resolution passed the
Senate by unanimous consent just nine days after its introduction.[7] It is not even certain that those who drafted the
resolution appreciated the connotations of the discretionary
power to act unneutrally which it embodied. But when their
attention was called to this possibility, they insisted tena-
ciously upon that very feature of the bill.

Senator Bingham of Connecticut, who had not been present when the resolution was passed, moved for reconsideration and got a favorable vote. He then opposed the resolution
and sought backing for his stand. The Department of State,
on the other hand, undertook to counteract Mr. Bingham's
opposition by writing to a Connecticut industrialist to persuade Mr. Bingham to yield. The Senator had previously
been informed (by one of the authors of this book) that the
purpose of the resolution was sound and proper, provided,
however, that the arms embargo in question was not so applied as to operate upon only one of the countries at war, a
proceeding which would have resulted in a serious form of
unneutrality with all its concomitant dangers.

To meet this objection the Department of State submitted
to the House Committee on Foreign Affairs, then considering
the resolution, the following memorandum:

ARMS EMBARGO RESOLUTION AND NEUTRALITY

The resolution authorizes the President to join other countries
in a refusal to ship arms whenever the shipment would promote
war. The argument is made that action taken under this would

[7] S. J. Res., 229, adopted January 19, 1933.

sacrifice American neutrality and so involve us. The fact is that the developments of the past few years show that there is little or no practical danger involved and that the discussion is based on almost medieval conditions which modern experience and realities have almost wholly replaced. The following points should be noted:

First — The Joint Resolution of 1922 providing for an embargo in cases of domestic violence in this hemisphere and in China has been employed with great effect and negligible friction. Nearly all the opportunities for antagonistic sentiment, for charges of non-neutrality and for the expression of that resentment against our commerce or other agencies of the American people occur as much in the field of civil strife within a country as they do in foreign wars. Our experience has shown that the refusal of the United States to allow munitions to revolutionists has never provoked serious resentment among the adherents of the revolutionaries and has substantially stabilized conditions in the smaller countries and prevented a number of incipient revolts. The moral approval of a policy against the shipment of munitions has been so marked that even where there has been sympathy with the revolting elements, the friction has been negligible.

Second — In the case of a war between two foreign countries, the embargo would not of course be employed unless there was general cooperation and united opinion among the principal world powers who could supply munitions. If there was no developed public opinion or international attitude, it is obvious that the employment of the measure by this country would be fruitless and improper. If there was public opinion and general world concern leading to cooperation, one of two conditions would exist —

(a) The world would cooperate in refusing supplies to both nations. This would certainly involve no breach of neutrality by the United States as the movement would be general and the nations united in a common front;

(b) There might be a situation in which as a result of investigation and consultation on a large scale there was a clear definition agreed upon by all the cooperating powers that one side or the other was the aggressor. It is becoming evident in recent years that this condition is much easier to realize than used to be believed. The worldwide publicity afforded since the Great War on every international incident and army movement, and the means of investigation by international commissions which is rapidly gaining ground, all show that there are situations today in which there can be a general verdict far beyond previous anticipation. The verdict of the

League of Nations on this point, for example, as shown by recent events is a perfectly practicable procedure. If the League or any other comprehensive group of important states had mutually arrived at such a verdict, the participation of the United States in a general arms embargo would be not merely practical and sound but practically necessary to preserve our national dignity and standing as a peaceful nation.

Third — Much of the old conception of neutrality as a possibility is gone in the modern world if large nations are involved in war. We were unable in spite of the most earnest efforts to maintain neutrality in the World War. Today nearly all the world except the United States and Russia are members of the League of Nations and so closely bound by agreements in the Covenant and other treaties that real neutrality in a large scale war is almost impossible. War today involves blockade and the commerce of the neutral is as much under fire as are the participants.

Fourth — The view that a neutral is obligated to sell arms to a belligerent is generally criticized by modern writers. Access is always unequal (as in the case of the Allies and Germany to the United States in the World War) and impartiality never really results. Disarmament agreements have already complicated the problem. There is a general feeling among writers on international law that the rule of impartiality in supplying arms, if it ever was generally accepted, is subject to criticism. There never was a right in the belligerent to buy arms. (Hyde criticizes the view in " International Law," p. 868 and Oppenheim in his " International Law " says the sale of arms to a belligerent is dictated by greed and will disappear with better standards of public morality, p. 350.)

It seems unnecessary to comment at any length on the Memorandum. Its good intentions are apparent, but its views were not perceptibly realistic when it held that a new day had now arrived, that neutrality was obsolescent, that it was now comparatively easy to pick an aggressor, that the League of Nations would pick the guilty nation, and that if the League or any other comprehensive group of states had arrived at such a verdict the participation of the United States in a general arms embargo would be not merely practical but necessary to preserve our national dignity as a peaceful nation.

While Senator Borah was not sure that the resolution would be abused in the way its language permitted, he nevertheless did not press it to passage again, and the session closed without further action upon it.

On the advent of the new administration, President Roosevelt took over this Hoover policy and had the original resolution reintroduced. Extended Hearings were held before the House Committee on Foreign Affairs, in which the Republicans objected that the bill adopted the League policy of discrimination against aggressors and permitted the Executive to employ hostile embargoes unneutrally. In the Hearings we find the following quotation from a letter written by Lord Robert Cecil to the *London Times*:

On Jan. 11 the Democratic President-elect of the United States, Mr. Roosevelt, said:

" I have long been in favor of the use of embargoes on arms to belligerent nations, especially to nations which are guilty of making an attack on other nations . . . that is, against aggressor nations."

Just a month later there was published in Washington a memorandum by the Republican Secretary of State, Mr. Stimson, addressed to the Foreign Affairs Committee of Congress. It was in support of a resolution authorizing the President to associate with other nations in an arms embargo against belligerent nations, and it included the following statement:

" If the League of Nations or any other comprehensive group of important States had mutually arrived at such a verdict — that is, a verdict that one of the belligerent nations was the aggressor — the participation of the United States in a general arms embargo would be not merely practical and sound, but practically necessary to preserve our national dignity and standing as a peaceful nation.

" These very important pronouncements make it clear that both parties in the United States stand for participation in an arms embargo against an aggressor State and that the Republican Secretary of State declares that in this connection a decision by the League of Nations as to which is the aggressor is, for practical purposes, conclusive." [8]

[8] Hearings on H. J. Res. 93, Committee on Foreign Relations, House of Representatives, 73rd Cong., 1st Sess. (March 28, 1933), pp. 24–25.

The Hearings had brought to sharp issue the advocates of
American neutrality and the advocates of intervention against
aggressors. That issue reappeared in every subsequent " Neutrality " bill, until the field was partly preëmpted by a third
school which wished so firmly to insulate the United States
against foreign war that they demanded a mandatory prohibition of the export of munitions, of loans to belligerents,
of the American ownership of any commodities after shipment from the United States to a belligerent destination —
the " cash and carry " plan — of the carriage of goods conditionally contraband by American vessels, and of the sailing
of American citizens on belligerent vessels.

In opposing the Arms Embargo Resolution, with its possibility of Executive discrimination against aggressors and its
unilateral application to one belligerent only, John Bassett
Moore had advised the House Committee, in part, as follows:

. . . The pending resolution is, I do not hesitate to affirm, opposed
to the settled policy and the highest interests of the United States
and also to the provisions of our Federal Constitution. If adopted,
it would enable the President (1) to make international engagements of the most far-reaching kind at his will, without the advice
and consent of the Senate, and (2) to carry us into war without the
prerequisite constitutional declaration of war by Congress. Perhaps
it may be answered that by the proposed resolution the Senate
would voluntarily abdicate its constitutional powers regarding international engagements, and that the Congress would likewise
abdicate its constitutional powers regarding the declaration of war.
This argument might be accepted if the Senate and the Congress
could constitutionally divest themselves of their constitutional powers and commit everything to the Executive. But, as they were unwilling to do this during the so-called World War, when it was
proposed to give the President complete dictatorial powers, I can
only suppose that the present extraordinary agitation is due to the
misleading and somewhat deafening clamor of those who, in the
name of peace, would confer upon the President an unlimited right
to engage in hostilities. I refrain from saying an unlimited right to
make war only out of deference to the profound and learned authorities who assure us that war can be abolished either by calling it

peace or by refraining from calling it war. This is, I may remark, a favorite notion with those who demand that the Kellogg pact shall be equipped with " teeth " in order that it may masticate alleged " aggressors " and otherwise benignantly bite and gnaw its way to universal peace and concord. Unfortunately, there are many who appear to have been infected with these confused notions, which have been so industriously propagated in the United States. But, judged by the course of the principal members of the League of Nations during the past ten years, and by their attitude toward the hostilities lately in progress in the Far East and elsewhere, such notions appear never to have had any real charm for the responsible authorities of the countries which would have been required to make the chief sacrifices in blood, in treasure, and in tears. To say this is not to impeach their wisdom or their sincerity. It may merely indicate that, having had enough of war, they long for real peace and an opportunity to recuperate.

Should the proposed measure become a law, no gift of prophecy is required to foretell what will follow. Groups moved by interest, or swayed, consciously or unconsciously, by propaganda, will clamor at the White House and at the Department of State for the un-neutral application of the ban in favor of those whom they like or approve and against those whom they dislike or disapprove. We are assured that we may trust our authorities to resist such importunities, and to refrain from doing things that would involve the country in trouble. In other words, we are told that our authorities may be relied upon to refuse to exercise the powers so sweepingly conferred upon them. This is indeed a singular argument. Couched in the language of irresponsibility, it is not only self-stultifying but also unjust. The burdens and cares resting, especially at the present juncture, upon those who administer our affairs, are already grave and harassing enough without imposing upon them the pastime of playing with war. Within the terms of the pending resolution, our Government would be asked to set itself up in rash and arrogant judgment upon the acts of other nations and on the merits of their conflicts, with a view to give or to permit military aid to one as against another. Before committing ourselves to this presumptuous program, spun of the wild and flimsy fantasy that, when nations fall out and fight, the question of the " aggressor," which still baffles students even of ancient wars, lies upon the surface of things, and may be readily, safely, and justly determined by outsiders, of whose freedom from individual interest or bias there is no guarantee, we should reflect upon the fact that, had such a notion heretofore prevailed, we might and in all probability should ourselves have been the victim of it.[9]

But the bill was finally passed by the House on April 17, 1933.[10]

When the resolution went over to the Senate, Senators Johnson and Borah took the lead in protesting its unneutral features before the Foreign Relations Committee. After consultation with advisers, Senator Johnson proposed an amendment to the resolution to the effect that " any prohibition of export, or of sale for export, proclaimed under this resolution shall apply impartially to all the parties to the dispute or conflict to which it refers."

This amendment appears to have been approved by the administration. It was thereupon adopted by the Committee and unanimously passed the Senate on February 28, 1934. Neutrality had been temporarily saved.

But when the amended resolution was returned to the House for its concurrence, some change in the administration view seems to have occurred, for consent to the Senate amendment was now declined. The result was that no bill was passed.

The Chaco Embargo

In May, 1934, after the Chaco War had proved not to be susceptible to settlement either by the American neutrals or the League of Nations, the President asked Congress for authority to place an arms embargo on both belligerents, and

[9] Letter of John Bassett Moore addressed on March 27, 1933, to the Hon. Hamilton Fish, Jr., submitted at Foreign Affairs Committee Hearing on March 28, 1933, printed in the House of Representatives document presenting the Minority Views to accompany H. J. Res. 93. H. Report 22, Part II, pp. 5–9, 73rd Cong., 1st Sess.

[10] H. J. Res. 93 H. Report 22, Part I, 73rd Cong., 1st Sess. Minority Report of Hamilton Fish, *idem*, Part II. Debate began April 13, 1933, *Cong. Rec.*, LXXVII, 1683 *et seq.* Cf. Speech of Representative Frear, p. 1686 *et seq.*, S. Rep., 101, 73rd Cong., 1st Sess. (May 29, 1933).

promptly received it.[1] The measure was noteworthy because it departed from the taking-of-sides theory, despite the fact that Paraguay had been declared the aggressor by the League, and adopted the demand of defenders of American neutrality for impartial treatment of both belligerents.

Prosecutions for violation of the Chaco Embargo Resolution were subsequently begun against certain exporters of airplanes. In defense the exporters pleaded the unconstitutionality of the resolution, which permitted the application of the embargo " if the President finds " that an arms embargo " may contribute to the reëstablishment of peace between those countries." They claimed that it delegated too much legislative power and too broad a discretion to the President. The United States District Court agreed with them.[2] The Court concluded that the penalties of a criminal statute could not constitutionally be made dependent upon a mere expression by the President that in his opinion such a measure " may contribute to the reëstablishment of peace."

The United States Supreme Court, however, on December 21, 1936,[3] a month after the election which had returned the President with an overwhelming majority, reversed the District Court and held that in the field of foreign affairs the President should be permitted liberal discretion because of his intimate and often secret knowledge of what was happening. Congress, therefore, could legitimately leave the enforcement of policies to his personal opinion of their probable success. Justice Sutherland, speaking for the Court, somewhat overdid the argument by citing indiscriminately instances in which embargoes had in the past been authorized for hostile purposes or for purposes of conservation, as either retaliatory or defensive measures.

It is obvious that embargoes for warlike purposes, includ-

---

[1] H. J. Res. 347, 48 Stats. 811 (May 28, 1934). Revoked Nov. 14, 1935.

[2] *U. S.* v. *Curtiss Wright Export Corporation*, decided March 24, 1936, reargument April 6, 1936, 14 Fed. Sup. 230.

[3] 57 S. Ct. 216.

ing embargoes by way of reprisal designed to insure respect for American rights, as in the case of the limited war with France of 1798 and in the case of Jefferson's and Madison's embargoes, are of a character involving the President's war power as Commander-in-Chief, and in that relation his hands must not be tied. On the other hand, an embargo to conserve American resources or to preserve American neutrality is of quite a different nature. The latter objective requires the observance of the strictest safeguards in order to prevent an unequal application of the embargo and does not justify the conclusion that Congress could vest in the President an unlimited power to determine what commodities were to be embargoed and when. Yet the Curtiss-Wright opinion has been used by advocates of Executive discretion as justifying the policy, not merely the constitutionality, of the widest Executive discretion in the application of embargoes for " neutrality " in foreign wars.

Re-affirmation of Neutrality — The Neutrality Resolution of 1935

THE gathering clouds of war in Europe incidental to the German and the Japanese departure from Geneva, the complete failure of the so-called Disarmament Conference, the denunciation by Germany of various parts of the Versailles Treaty, and the growing bitterness among European nations, re-aroused in this country an interest in American neutrality which even the advocates of the theory of punishing aggressors had to take into account. This school of thought rationalized its disappointment at the impartiality of the Chaco Embargo by the explanation that Washington was coöperating with Geneva.

In the meantime, however, another movement gained headway which influenced subsequent American legislation. In April, 1934, the Senate had authorized the investigation of the munitions industry of the United States by a committee headed by Senator Nye of North Dakota. This committee was motivated by a genuine desire to keep the United States out of European wars and to demonstrate that the munitions industry and banking interests had in some way conspired to force the United States into the European war in 1917. It charged itself also with the duty of " taking the profits out of war." Munition makers had been the subject of numerous books and articles indicating their possible interest in the fomenting of wars, a charge to which the activities of a Mr. William Shearer at the Geneva Naval Conference of 1927 lent some support. The Hearings before the Nye Committee, begun in September, 1934, have a very considerable value and deserve more study than they thus far appear to have received.[4]

Important as the work of the committee was (despite its inability to obtain access to some of the confidential information in the Department of State relating to the war), it is doubtful whether the Committee proved the thesis that munition makers and bankers forced the United States into war. Neither group wrote the administration notes of 1914, 1915, and 1916 which placed the United States Government in a position from which it felt itself unable to retreat, a position that a neutral government should never have taken. Many elements in the country supported American entrance into war, and bankers among other people may well have been pleased to have the United States Treasury assume the further obligations for financing the Allied cause, to which the American public was becoming reluctant to lend more money.

The several purposes of the Nye Committee — the maintenance of American isolation from a potential foreign war, the avoidance of those policies which had led the United States into the last war, the control of the munitions industry, and

---

[4] Hearings on S. Res. 206, 73rd Cong., thirty-five parts to date, Mar., 1937; and S. Rep. 944, 1st Sess., in seven parts.

the policy of taking the profits out of war — led the Committee to make various legislative proposals.

As a result, the main feature of the Neutrality Act of August 31, 1935, was a mandatory embargo on " arms, ammunition and implements of war," strictly defined by the Arms Traffic Convention of 1925 to include little else besides lethal weapons. It also provided for setting up a national munitions control board which would regulate and supervise the export of munitions and implements of war from the United States by a registration and license system. The resolution further provided — and Secretary Bryan must have nudged President Wilson as they watched the proceedings from the Elysian fields — that American citizens take passage on belligerent vessels at their own risk.[5] Submarines of a foreign nation might not enter American ports or territorial waters, if the President so proclaimed,[6] and American ports could not be used as a base for supplying men or cargo to any belligerent warship at sea.[7] This resolution, passed in the closing days of the 73rd Congress, was to remain in force until February 29, 1936, before which date new legislation was contemplated.

There is evidence that although the August, 1935, Resolution was signed by the President, it did not fully meet his approval. He criticized the inflexible provisions of the embargo and urged that in the light of unforeseeable situations he should have discretion in coöperating with peacefully

[5] But this was made dependent on a presidential proclamation, and under such regulations as the President might prescribe.

[6] The conditions of the prohibition were a presidential finding that this was conducive to American peace or security or the protection of American commercial interests. But the President could relax the prohibition by rules and regulations. It is not clear whether the resolution applied equally to armed and unarmed submarines, belligerent or neutral.

[7] The Germans had violated this rule of international law in 1914 by supplying coal from American ports to German raiders at sea, giving false destinations in the clearance papers. This practice was stopped by Executive Order under authority of the joint resolution of March 4, 1915. *For. Rel.*, 1915, Suppl., p. 851.

minded governments in order to promote peace. In signing the resolution the President stated:

The latter section [arms embargo] terminates at the end of February, 1936. This Section requires further and more complete consideration between now and that date. Here again the objective is wholly good. It is the policy of this government to avoid being drawn into wars between other nations, but it is a fact that no Congress and no executive can foresee all possible future situations. History is filled with unforeseeable situations that call for some flexibility of action. It is conceivable that situations may arise in which the wholly inflexible provisions might drag us into war instead of keeping us out. The policy of the Government is definitely committed to the maintenance of peace and the avoidance of any entanglements which would lead us into conflict. At the same time it is the policy of the Government by every peaceful means and without entanglement to cooperate with other similarly minded governments to promote peace.[8]

While it is undoubtedly true that history is filled with unforeseeable situations, it is not possible to apply arms embargoes discriminatorily or flexibly without inviting all the risks of actual unneutrality. And it was unneutrality that the resolution was designed to avoid and prevent. In the light of the consistent demand for a policy enabling the United States to coöperate with other nations in punishing aggressors, a demand which the committee had considered, the whole purpose of the resolution was to make certain that the embargo would be applied against both belligerents without discrimination. If, on the other hand, the President had in mind the possibility that it would be undesirable to apply the embargo against all the belligerents in any particular war, he would also be departing from the express intention of the resolution, which was to make the arms embargo mandatory in the event of any foreign war. It is not possible to tell which aspect of the embargo the President was objecting to — its applicability to all belligerents or its mandatory im-

[8] Press Releases, XIII (Aug. 31, 1935), 162–163.

position in every war. And just how the inflexible provisions could drag us into war he did not explain.

Perhaps the President did not realize that a discretionary arms embargo would expose him to the importunities of those who believe that it is a practical peace policy to help a favored nation and hurt the disfavored. If the arms embargo injured the favored nation they would urge the President not to proclaim it; if it helped, they would be silent. And it is far easier to exert influence on the Executive than on Congress. Less propaganda is required.

Inasmuch as embargoes are usually hostile acts, the grant of discretion to the President and the opportunity for unneutrality involved would transfer to the President the power actually to make war. Wars rarely break out without prior unfriendly acts; a discriminatory arms embargo could readily provoke open hostilities. Just as dangerous, as we shall see, was the demand made on Congress in 1936 to give the President discretionary power to impose commodity embargoes. Even the power to apply arms and commodity embargoes to both belligerents would not preclude unneutrality if the President has the power to choose the commodities to go on the embargo list, for commodities can be selected whose lack would hurt one belligerent more than the other. And if that happened, the handicapped belligerent would be certain to regard the discrimination as intentional.

Italian-Ethiopian Embargo

IN October, 1935, the Italians entered upon the war that had for a year been threatened against Ethiopia. The League declared Italy to be the aggressor (October 9, 1935) and appointed a Committee to bring about coördination in the application of sanctions, which were to become effective November 18, 1935. Difficulties at once arose, notably between Great Britain and France. The common phenomenon of Great Powers proving unable to agree on any major policy became at once apparent. The difference served at least to limit the scope of the sanctions. Each day a Geneva dispatch to the *New York Times* informed the American public of the changing list of commodities which it was proposed to embargo against Italy. Imports from Italy were in the main banned. Loans and credits to Italy were prohibited.[9] Besides armaments, transport animals, rubber, bauxite, aluminum, iron ore and scrap iron, nickel and various ores used for steel-making, tin and tin ores were embargoed.

On October 5 the President ruled that Americans traded with, and traveled on the ships of, belligerents at their own risk.[1] The injunction against general trade was unauthorized, but was hailed by advocates of the League of Nations as an abandonment of the freedom of the seas, a doctrine which unfortunately they seem to believe is a detriment to peace. It became apparent, too, that inasmuch as practically the only trade between the United States and the belligerents was with Italy and the only belligerent ships on which Americans could take passage were Italian, the administration's request operated to handicap Italy alone.[2] And it was made very clear that it was the sanctionists' desire to discourage trade with Italy. On October 10 the Secretary of State reinforced the President's proclamation by supporting embargoes as well as by further discountenancing American trade with the belligerents.[3]

On October 26 Secretary Hull addressed the President of the Committee of Coördination of the League of Nations, expressing " sympathetic interest " with " the individual or concerted efforts of other nations to preserve peace or to localize or shorten the duration of war." This was generally,

[9] A description of the sanctions is found in Professor M. J. Bonn's article, " How Sanctions Failed," *Foreign Affairs,* XV (Jan., 1937), 350.

[1] Press Releases, XIII (Oct. 5, 1935), 251, 256.

[2] *New York Times,* Oct. 7, 1935, p. 1, col. 5.

[3] Press Releases, XIII, pp. 303–304.

and probably correctly, interpreted to express sympathy with the policy of suppressing Italy.[4] On October 30 the President issued a further warning against " transactions of any character with either of the belligerent nations " except at the trader's risk. The statement was made that this restriction of trade was designed to shorten the war.[5] The Secretary of State on the same day reiterated his purpose " to discourage dealings with the two belligerent nations." [6] It was conceded that this restriction of ordinary trade was not authorized by the Neutrality Act of August 31, 1935, but it was argued that it was within the " spirit " [7] of that act and was justified " upon the further purpose not to aid in protracting the war." It was urged that trade and the profits accruing from it would be obtained " at the expense of human lives and human misery." [8] But misery is promoted not by supplying but by withholding commodities that countries at war most urgently need.

In executing its policy, the government cautioned our citizens not to trade in any commodities with either of the belligerents, although at that time even League of Nations' sanctions had not come into force and it was not then known to what materials such sanctions would apply. The injunction was accompanied by pressure on the shippers of commodities, such as oil, which eventually the League decided not to embargo at all. In his address of November 6 Secretary Hull indicated his desire for an embargo extending beyond " arms, ammunition and implements of war " as a part of our general neutrality legislation. He added that

[4] *New York Times*, Oct. 27, 1935.
[5] Press Releases, XIII (Nov. 2, 1935), 338.
[6] *Idem*, p. 339.
[7] Cf. Debate in *Cong. Rec.*, LXXX, 2270, Feb. 17, 1936.
[8] The injunction against trade in general commodities may be regarded as a violation of the 1871 commercial treaty with Italy. Malloy, I, *Treaties between the United States and Other Powers*, Arts. 6, 13, 15, p. 969. A really neutral arms embargo may now be considered an exception. See " Neutral Embargoes and Commercial Treaties," *A. J. I. L.*, XXX (July, 1936), 501.

our foreign policy would indeed be a weak one if it began or ended
with the announcement of a neutral position on the outbreak of a
foreign war. I conceive it to be our duty and in the interest of our
country and of humanity, not only to remain aloof from disputes
and conflicts with which we have no direct concern, but also to use
our influence in any appropriate way to bring about the peaceful
settlement of international differences.

He desired " a virile policy tempered with prudent caution
. . . for after all if peace obtains, problems regarding neutrality will not arise." [9]

On November 15, 1935, shortly before the League sanctions were to come officially into effect, it was announced in
Washington that the shipment to the belligerents of oil, copper, trucks, tractors, scrap iron and scrap steel — in some
respects going beyond, in others short of, the lists suggested
from Geneva — would be disapproved. Traders with Italy
were warned that they were violating American policy.[10]
American ships under mortgage to the United States Shipping
Board were required to desist from trade with the belligerents, which in effect always meant Italy alone.[1] On Novem-

[9] Press Releases XIII (Nov. 9, 1935), 367, 369. A few months earlier ex-
Secretary Stimson had stated: " Neutrality offers no certain road for keeping out of war. The only certain way to keep out of a great war is to
prevent that war from taking place, and the only hope of preventing war
or even successfully restricting it is by the earnest, intelligent, and unselfish
coöperation of the nations of the world towards that end." *Proceedings,*
1935, p. 129.

[10] The Secretary of State added, " This class of trade is directly contrary to the policy of this Government as announced in official statements of
the President and Secretary of State, as it is also contrary to the general
spirit of the recent neutrality act." Press Releases, XIII, No. 320 (Nov. 16,
1935), 382; *New York Times,* Nov. 16, 1935, p. 1. The Secretary was not
well advised on the relation between letter and spirit. The limitation of the
embargo to arms, ammunition, and implements of war, and the debates which
clearly limited that term (*Cong. Rec.,* LXXIX [Aug. 21, 1935], 13, 954; *idem,*
[Aug. 23, 1935], 14, 432; *idem,* 14, 433) make it manifest that any extension
beyond the limitations set by Congress was contrary both to the letter and
spirit of the Act of Aug. 31, 1935.

[1] The *New York Times* remarked, on Oct. 23, 1935, that the Department's
warnings against trade " would amount, of course, to virtual sanctions against
Italy, inasmuch as our trade with Ethiopia is negligible."

ber 27 the administration limited itself to requesting shippers to desist from trade in " abnormal " quantities beyond pre-war levels, but no administrative machinery was supplied for determining what that level was or for enforcing the limi-tation.

On November 30, the *New York Times'* correspondent re-ported from Geneva that the League was encouraged by the activities of the United States in enjoining American trade in " copper, trucks and tractors," because Secretary Hull had classed them as " essential war materials " on November 15. But the suggestion that " oil, copper, trucks, tractors, scrap iron and scrap steel " constitute " essential war materials " is legally unsustainable. All these commodities are used for civilian purposes. At most, they might be goods conditionally contraband only. Heretofore belligerents have issued contra-band lists; neutrals have not been keen to cut off their own trade. In all these warnings against American trade with Italy, the United States was in advance of the League of Nations,[2] enjoining trade in commodities which the League ultimately declined to control.

Possibly this government pressure on American traders would have gone on but for the fact that the news from Geneva was not encouraging. There was some dissent among League members to the Geneva policy. Sanctions were limited to a few commodities, and were administered in such a way that they could have a crippling effect on Italy only after a considerable time. Irate, Great Britain took drastic measures by enlarging its Mediterranean fleet, and the threat of a con-flict between Italy and Great Britain almost overshadowed in importance the Ethiopian War then in progress. Thus, the anti-Italian policy of Washington involved the danger of this country's becoming embroiled on Great Britain's side if

[2] See letter of President Roosevelt to Bishop Oldham, *New York Times,* Dec. 7, 1935, p. 10. On Oct. 26, 1935, Secretary Hull said that our steps were " in advance of action by other governments." *New York Times,* Oct. 27, 1935.

British-Italian hostilities developed — a serious possibility at the time.

Finally on December 12 the celebrated Hoare-Laval Agreement [3] was concluded, which would have saved everyone's face; but the " peace " advocates of England would not accept so sensible a solution. Like other moralists, they demanded righteousness in all its perfection. But the announcement of the Hoare-Laval Agreement and the manifest difficulties of the sanctions policy caused Washington to withdraw its demands on American traders, and the possible threat of a foreign war extending to America was diminished.

The manifest desire of Congress to maintain American neutrality (the same efforts were made by Congress in 1915 and 1916), combined with the experience of the Executive effort to coöperate in some fashion with the sanctions of the League of Nations against Italy, gave rise to a new turn in the program.

Tentative Redraft of the National Peace Conference

THE Neutrality Resolution of August 31, 1935, was not acceptable to believers in sanctions. Various peace societies which had identified their interest in peace with the enforcement machinery of the League of Nations had associated themselves in an unofficial body called the National Peace Conference. Shortly after the passage of the Resolution of August, 1935, they had appointed a committee to study the legislation itself and to suggest proposals for its modification at the 1936 Session of Congress. The report of this committee was published on December 26, 1935, together with a suggested redraft of the Neutrality Act.[4] A prominent feature of the redraft was the now common use of the word " neutrality " to accomplish the most unneutral purposes. Begin-

---

[3] See Rowan-Robinson, op. cit., pp. 232–236.

[4] International Conciliation, No. 316 (Jan., 1936) ; New York Times, Dec. 27, 1935.

ning with the implication that " domestic neutrality laws can have only a limited effect and must be supplemented by international agreements before the United States can be even moderately secure against war," the committee suggested that American participation in the late war was caused by a lack of international agreement as to neutral rights of trade. The implication is that the same result will again occur unless an agreement is reached on coöperation with the League of Nations. The framers of the redraft state:

The difficulties are increased by the lack of agreement regarding the effect of the Pact of Paris upon the legal status of neutrality. Similarly, there is need of international agreement defining clearly the rights and duties of the United States in cases where sanctions of the League of Nations are being applied against a State which has resorted to war in violation of the covenant. . . . The committee believes that a general treaty between the United States and other signatories of the Pact of Paris could, without dangerous concessions on either side, clarify the position of this country in the event either of war or of the application of sanctions so as to safeguard the United States against involvement in war over neutral rights and to strengthen the peace action of the League.[5]

While professing to base its proposed legislation on the now inescapable obligation of the Resolution of August, 1935, to treat all belligerents alike, the redraft nevertheless provided

an escape clause to safeguard the United States against being rigidly held to a system of embargoes under conditions which might subsequently arise, when it had become evident to Congress as well as to the President that one or more of the belligerent countries had been attacked while it remained loyal to the Kellogg-Briand Pact. The circumstance might even arise that a nation would be attacked by reason of this very loyalty as evidenced by measures of disarmament.

The redraft also took advantage of an oversight in the Resolution of 1935 by retaining the provision that the Presi-

[5] *International Conciliation*, No. 316, p. 37.

dent might embargo arms, ammunition, and implements of war not only on the outbreak of war but " during the progress of war." This opportunity for delaying the embargo might enable the Executive, it was correctly assumed, to handicap the disfavored belligerent. The redraft provided, too, that the President be empowered to embargo commodities other than arms, ammunition and implements of war at his discretion.

This redraft has been referred to merely for the purpose of indicating how many good people of this country have been persuaded that coercion and force against particular nations present a method for producing peace. The visible fact that these measures have produced nothing but disaster and an increase in armaments such as the world has never before seen leaves them unimpressed.

The Neutrality Act of February 29, 1936

THE promotion of the tentative redraft was stopped by the introduction on January 3, 1936, of what has been called the administration's, or Senator Pittman's, New Neutrality Bill.[6] While the bill did not follow the redraft, it took from it its most dangerous provision, conferring on the President the discretionary power to embargo commodities other than arms, ammunition and implements of war. We have seen the attempts that were made during the Italian-Ethiopian War to expand the concept of " arms, ammunition and implements of war " by including within it raw materials like oil and copper, and finished products like trucks and tractors, under the name " essential war materials."[7] The Hearings held before the Senate Foreign Relations Committee on the Pittman Bill disclosed a belief in high quarters that there is no logical distinction between arms and raw materials which might be used for warlike purposes.

---

[6] S. 3474, 74th Cong., 2d Sess.

[7] Hearings on S. 3474, Committee on Foreign Relations, U. S. Senate, 74th Cong., 2d Sess. (Jan. 10–Feb. 5, 1936).

Now it is a well-known fact that the distinction between lethal weapons and raw materials is based not on logic, but on the fact that neutrals have heretofore wished to limit the interferences of belligerents with their trade. Raw materials having both civilian and belligerent uses and being incapable directly of killing have not been banned by belligerents, because neutrals heretofore would not tolerate it. Now we have the extraordinary phenomenon of at least one neutral, in its desire to cripple belligerent populations on supposedly moral grounds, being willing to injure itself by foregoing trade in raw materials with belligerent governments and their populations. Happily for the world in general no country has followed the United States in these policies.

Section 4 of the 1936 bill was designed to give the President the power to restrict to the prewar level the export to any belligerent country of " certain articles or materials used in the manufacture of arms, ammunition or implements of war or in the conduct of war," if he thought that such restriction would " serve to promote the security and preserve the neutrality of the United States, or to protect the lives and commerce of nationals of the United States, or that to refrain from placing such restrictions would contribute to a prolongation or expansion of the war." These terms were broad enough to permit the President to control all American commerce as he saw fit in any foreign war. The special exception of " food or medical supplies " merely indicated how broad was the category of commodities subject to embargo. The moral purpose of using embargoes to shorten foreign wars reflected the new conception that it is a neutral's function to starve foreign peoples because they permit themselves to go to war. The picture of a neutral country as an active force exerting pressure on belligerents, and therefore influencing the outcome of a foreign war, owes its origin to the Geneva theories of coercion. In 1933, the predilection for discriminatory embargoes had been confined to arms and ammunition.

Since the Resolution of August, 1935, had made an arms embargo mandatory and impartial, the advocates of Executive discretion now shifted their demand for discretion to commodities other than arms and ammunition.

If it was desired to insulate the United States against difficulty with belligerents, the exception of foodstuffs hardly had that effect because it is around foodstuffs that some of the principal controversies between neutrals and belligerents have turned. Moreover, a limitation to normal shipments might prove damaging and unjustifiable on any rational basis, because the effect of war is to upset the domestic economy of any belligerent by increasing the demand for many articles that his war activities disable him from supplying himself. The needs of a belligerent are nothing like those of a peaceful country and the more industrialized the belligerent the greater the dislocations caused by war. Again, just as much difficulty with the belligerents can arise from a " normal " shipment as from the enlarged demands which war might create.

The commodity embargo derived sustenance from the efforts of the more extreme group in the Senate and House who were sponsoring what was called the Nye-Clark-Maverick Bill to embargo all trade beyond the prewar levels of a five-year average and to prohibit the carriage even of the permitted quantity in American ships. This group was sincerely neutral, was opposed to the peculiar theories of the League of Nations for enforcing peace, and was convinced by the investigations of the Nye Committee [8] that public loans, munition makers and banking interests had gotten the United States into the last war. The Pittman Bill's proposed embargo was milder than that demanded by the Nye group and being applicable to both belligerents it was thought to be satisfactory to the supporters of neutrality and freedom of the seas.

[8] *Supra,* p. 314.

In addition to reaffirming the provisions of the Resolution of August 31, 1935, the Pittman Bill provided for the prohibition in the United States of the purchase or sale of bonds, securities or other obligations of a belligerent country,[9] but excepted ordinary commercial credits and short-term commercial obligations. American vessels were to be prohibited from carrying arms or other commodities embargoed by the President. The President could require American citizens to assume the risk of all commercial transactions with the belligerents or with persons residing in belligerent countries. Citizens were to travel at their own risk on belligerent vessels if the President so proclaimed and no passport was to be valid for such travel. Treaties in conflict with the act were to be terminated or modified by negotiations, and the United States reserved and reaffirmed its rights under international law as it existed prior to August 1, 1914.

It was the opportunity for discretionary embargoes under Section 4 which incurred the criticisms of certain international lawyers, and in the light of the Italian-Ethiopian War, of the Italian-American population of the United States. The bill nevertheless passed the House of Representatives. When it went over to the Senate, Executive Hearings were begun before the Foreign Relations Committee at which Secretary Hull and Assistant Secretary Moore at six separate sessions were requested to explain the bill. Other qualified persons were called by the committee for the expression of their opinions. John Bassett Moore in an extensive memorandum expressed serious concern at the opportunities for Executive war-making and for damage to American commerce permitted by Section 4 of the bill.[10] So far as concerns American foreign

[9] New loans to nations now in default on their public debt to the United States Government had been banned by the Johnson Act of 1934, 48 Stats. 574, 31 U. S. Code Ann., Sec. 804a.

[10] Hearings on S. 3474, Committee on Foreign Relations, U. S. Senate, 74th Cong., 2d Sess. (Jan. 10–Feb. 5, 1936), pp. 172, 187.

trade, it was pointed out that the embargo power would expose the United States as a capricious supplier, a fact which might discourage foreigners from buying in this market even in time of peace. The quota provisions were attacked by several critics [1] because they would dislocate all foreign trade and would present administrative obstacles requiring its severe regimentation.

So far as our domestic produce and manufacture are concerned, the embargoes could easily disrupt our home markets as they did in the early 1800's and cause distress in this country. The reservation of Executive discretion in the selection of commodities and in the application of the embargoes preserved an unqualified opportunity to handicap one belligerent as against another, and was thus acclaimed by supporters of the League of Nations as a compliance with their demand for discriminatory " neutrality." [2]

---

[1] See especially Frank H. Simonds, in *New York Herald Tribune*, Jan. 13, 1936.

[2] An articulate representative of this group, Professor Quincy Wright, makes a classification of what he calls five organized pressure groups:

" (1) the isolationist neutrals following the Nye committee,

(2) the traditional neutrals advocating freedom of the seas,

(3) the interventionists urging the causes of the respective belligerents,

(4) the patriotic imperialists anxious to seize the opportunity for augmenting the territory and prestige of the United States, and

(5) the co-operationist neutrals."

Group 5 is the sanctionists who believe in suppressing aggressors as a way of peace. It is not perceived in what respect they differ from group 3. They are also probably the only group that is organized and that have financial subsidy. It is not known to whom group 4 refers.

Professor Wright bases his proposal for a discretionary " neutrality " on a platform attributed to Secretary Hull as constituting the " four pillars of a sound peace structure: "

" First, the renunciation of war as an instrument of national policy; second, a promise of nonaggression; third, consultation in the event of a threat to peace; and, fourth, noninterference on our part with such measures of constraint as may be brought against a deliberate violator of peace."

He comments further: " To carry out this policy the arms and loan embargo provided in the present neutrality act should be extended to all war materials, but the executive should be given authority to remove these embargoes, in behalf of the victim of aggression and the states assisting it, as soon as he has determined, in consultation with other states, who is the aggressor, a task which has not in practice proved especially difficult." Wright, *Forum*, Feb., 1937, p. 94. A similar, but more elaborate, program in support

The Foreign Relations Committee agreed not to press for the enactment of Section 4, the bill was set aside and a short bill adopted reaffirming with slight improvements for clarity the bill passed on August 31, 1935, but adding to it a provision for a prohibition on loans to foreign belligerents.[3]

An amendment was attached providing that the act was not to apply to an American republic engaged in war with a non-American state.[4] This committed the United States to an avowed policy of unneutrality in a war between a non-American and an American country. This new policy goes far beyond the Monroe Doctrine and amounts to the promise of an alliance of the United States with any Latin-American country which for any reason might find itself at war with a non-American country. It seems particularly unfortunate to introduce a gratuitous promise to intervene in foreign wars that might not concern the United States in a bill designed to preserve American neutrality.

The President, in signing the Resolution of 1936, reiterated his conviction that trade with the belligerents in the Italian-Ethiopian War in excess of normal peacetime quotas would result in profits not possible during peace, assist the war, and magnify its evil.[5]

It has already been observed that practically all of the provisions of the neutrality legislation of 1935 and 1936 could have been applied in 1915 or 1916 either under the statutes which Congress desired to enact or merely by Executive proclamation. An arms embargo was urged by a considerable body of opinion in Congress in 1914 and 1915 when it became apparent that the United States had become a supply station for one set of belligerents. An embargo on loans was

---

of "discretionary" legislation was prepared by Professors Shotwell and Wright on behalf of the League of Nations Association, *Cong. Rec.*, Feb. 15, 1937, p. 1494.

[3] H. J. Res. 491, Pub. Res. 74, Feb. 29, 1936.

[4] Providing the American Republic is not coöperating with a non-American state.

[5] Press Releases, XIV, No. 336 (March 7, 1936), pp. 197, 198.

enforced by Executive request in 1914, but the doors were opened through a secret reversal of this request by President Wilson.[6]

After it became apparent that the sinking of belligerent ships with American citizens on board excited American sensibilities and that the administration was taking a drastic position on these tragedies, the Gore-McLemore Resolutions sought to keep Americans off belligerent vessels. Although this was merely declaratory of an existing rule of law and was recommended to the administration by Secretary Bryan, the administration, as we have seen, not only refused to exercise its powers but vigorously opposed the enactment of such a bill. The supplying of warships at sea from American ports, of which the Germans had taken advantage, thereby making American ports a base of naval supply, was wisely stopped by Joint Resolution in March, 1915.[7] The 1935 and 1936 Acts omit all reference to armed belligerent merchantmen and the fact that they should not be admitted into American ports as innocent vessels, although actually such a prohibition requires no legislation.

Supporters of sanctions as a method for producing peace were disappointed at the fate of the Pittman Bill and at the failure to grant the President the discretion to embargo commodities other than lethal weapons. Nor has the campaign for the unneutral measures proposed subsided. Mr. Arthur Krock, who has been advocating the delegation of broad discretionary power in his column in the *New York Times*,[8] has frankly stated that the advocates of this policy do not believe in neutrality or in its practicability for the United States. He says, " There is no such thing as neutrality." What he urges, therefore, is Executive discretion " so that unneutrality (in effect) may be wisely directed." He urges this unneutrality in order that " effective discretion . . . might cancel an ad-

[6] *Supra,* p. 40.
[7] *Supra,* p. 315.
[8] December 29, 1936, and December 31, 1936.

vantage held by belligerents hostile to democratic freedom."
What he fails to realize is that the discretionary embargo
power is the equivalent of intervention in a foreign war, and
that he is asking Congress to delegate its war-making power
to the Executive, which Congress may not constitutionally
do.[9] He forgets, too, the results of another crusade for
democracy.

In most of the reciprocal trade agreements there is a provision enabling the contracting parties " in exceptional circumstances " to embargo not only arms and gold but any
other " military supplies " or materials " needed in war." [1]
This clause finds its origin in Geneva and in recent British
treaties.[2] It embodies the authority for sanctions, an authori-
zation which is not to be found in the enabling Act of June 12,
1934,[3] on which the President must rely to justify this action.
Moreover, it seems incongruous and in conflict with the official theory that commercial restrictions menace peace, to
qualify our commercial treaties so as to leave the way open
to the exercise of acts of coercion.

Buenos Aires Conference

THE Sixth Pan-American Conference which met in Havana
in 1928 drafted a long code of maritime law in time of war

[9] Cf. J. B. Moore, quoted in Minority Report on H. J. Res. 242, March 1,
1937, Rep. 320, Part II, p. 4, 75th Cong., 1st Sess.: " No one who wished
unlimited power to make war could ask for more than the authority, in his
own discretion, to impose and revoke, and to modify and adjust, embargoes
upon our foreign commerce."

[1] There are fifteen agreements now in force, and nearly all contain such
a clause.

[2] Some British commercial treaties contain provisions which permit embargoes; among others they recognize embargoes on arms and war materials
" and under exceptional circumstances, also in respect of other materials
needed in war." An alternative phrase is " all other military supplies." See
Art. 9 of the Treaty of May 12, 1927, with the Serb-Croat-Slovene Kingdom;
Art. 16 of the Treaty of March 1, 1930, with Turkey; Art. 14 of the Treaty
of August 6, 1930, with Roumania.

[3] 48 Stats. 943.

which conformed reasonably closely to the time-honored rules for the protection of neutral rights at sea. The United States ratified this Convention.[4]

Again, the Latin-American countries drafted, in 1933, what is called the Argentine Anti-War Pact, which, among other provisions, contemplated that nonparticipants in the war will adopt a " common and solidary attitude in their character as neutrals." The fact that this agreement is subject to obligations owed to the League of Nations may seem to make it slightly ambiguous, but the exception is no longer as virile as it was. Various European countries have adhered to this Anti-War Pact.[5]

In January, 1936, the Buenos Aires Conference was projected for the purpose, among others, of considering a common neutrality policy for the countries on the American continent. There was a good deal of interest in determining whether the United States would support the policy of nonintervention among American neutrals should war break out on this continent or elsewhere, or whether it would support the policy of embargoes to be placed by neutrals on their trade with belligerents, a policy which could easily be employed to affect the outcome of a foreign war. The draft submitted by the American delegation at Buenos Aires on December 7, 1936,[6] was vague; it provided in Article 7 that " individual neutral powers shall be free to impose such prohibitions and restrictions on trade and commerce between them and belligerents . . . as they may deem appropriate in the interest of their domestic policy or of international peace." Such provisions were not to be considered as violations of commercial treaties

---

[4] 47 Stats. 1989, Treaty Series, No. 845 (proclaimed May 26, 1932). The Senate made a reservation to Art. 12, Sec. 3, which applied the rules of war to armed merchantmen.

[5] European states ratifying or adhering — Bulgaria, Czechoslovakia, Norway, Roumania; American states ratifying or adhering — Argentine, Brazil, Chile, Colombia, Cuba, Dominican Republic, El Salvador, Ecuador, Guatemala, Haiti, Mexico, Nicaragua, Panama, Peru, United States, Uruguay, Venezuela.

[6] Press Releases, XV (Dec. 12, 1936), 478.

providing for reciprocal freedom of trade. Although the measures were to apply equally to all the belligerents, except as League of Nations' obligations might require partisan application, the opportunity for partiality was inherent in the proposal.

Article 8 of the United States' draft provided for a mandatory embargo on arms, ammunition and implements of war, including shipments to neutral countries from which these articles could be transshipped for the use of the belligerents. By Article 9 the flotation of loans was to be prohibited in all neutral countries. The right was to be reserved in Article 10 to add further restrictions on trade between neutrals and belligerents in commodities other than arms, ammunition and implements of war, a revival of the unadopted Section 4 of the Pittman Bill of January, 1936.

This effort to persuade neutrals on the American continent to adopt more drastic measures of " neutrality " than either the 1928 Havana Convention or the 1933 Argentine Anti-War Treaty had contemplated did not meet a hospitable reception. Even the proposal to make these embargoes optional within the domestic legislation of each country met with no favor. Apparently the Latin-American countries — consumers not producers of arms — were unwilling to support an embargo on arms and munitions. And as exporters of raw materials on which their economic life largely depends, they could hardly commit themselves to embargoes on the sinews of life, however noble the purpose. As they have but little money to lend abroad, the prohibition on loans was practically meaningless. Consequently they declined to adopt the invitation to join in embargoes in any form, rejecting even the permissive domestic legislation. Argentina, not satisfied with this negative attitude, made an express reservation to the effect that embargoes shall never include foodstuffs or raw materials, practically the main exports of Latin-America.

In other respects the Buenos Aires Conference adopted a

provision for consultation [7] (but not the suggested provisions for a Permanent Consultative Committee) among neutrals whenever war breaks out on this continent or any other. The countries involved agreed to adopt a " common and solidary attitude in their character as neutrals," and committed themselves to recommending the ratification of the Gondra Treaty of 1923 for conciliation, of the Havana Conference of 1928 for arbitration, of the Argentine Anti-War Treaty of 1933 and of the Kellogg Pact. No formal mention was apparently made by the American delegation of the one treaty really dealing with neutrality — the Havana Convention for Maritime Neutrality of 1928 — which the United States had already ratified but many others had not.

It has been said that the South American states who were members of the League of Nations, led by Mr. Saavedra Lamas, Foreign Minister of the Argentine, also objected to the provision for equality of treatment between the belligerents, claiming that their League obligations contemplated discrimination. The " escape clause " suggested by the United States for this contingency is said not to have satisfied the Latin-American predilection for inequality between an aggressor and his victim. Mr. Bruce Bliven in a recent article [8] states that while our higher officials sympathized at heart with this attitude, opinion at home both in and out of Congress was so firmly in favor of treating all belligerents alike that the hands of the United States' delegation were tied.

Whether the Buenos Aires Conference has seriously damaged genuine neutrality is as yet hard to say. In so far as it presents an occasion for coöperative diplomatic protests in defense of neutral rights, it may be welcomed, for it affords an opportunity similar to that which the United States declined in 1914. In so far as it encourages joint consideration

---

[7] This consultation, presumably through diplomatic channels, is to be limited to the furtherance of mediation, conciliation, and arbitration, and is not apparently to discuss hostile measures like embargoes or intervention.

[8] *The New Republic*, Feb. 24, 1937, p. 64.

of mediation and conciliation in a conflict arising in the Americas it may well be supported. In so far, however, as it encourages proposals for coercive action by neutrals to starve out or bring pressure upon a belligerent deemed guilty of an " unfriendly act," it may open up a field for differences in the Americas. If the League members join against an aggressor, and the United States adopts a " solidary attitude " with these American countries, the way to sanctions for the United States has been legally established. The conflict, therefore, between neutrality and unneutrality as a national policy has been brought to this continent from Europe, and as yet it is uncertain on which side the ultimate victory will lie.

The *Commercial and Financial Chronicle,* one of America's most responsible journals, comments upon what it calls " a happy escape at Buenos Aires," as follows:

It is not often that the American people have occasion to be thankful for the defeat of an Administration on a major item of its foreign policy. The refusal of the Inter-American Peace Conference at Buenos Aires to accept the draft convention regarding neutrality, consultation and other related matters which Secretary Hull submitted is, however, ground for national satisfaction. For once the Latin American Republics, led by Argentina, have not only turned down an extraordinary proposal which would have weakened rather than strengthened their position, individually as well as collectively, in the event of war, but have also, in so doing, prevented the United States from entangling itself in an agreement which at best would have been difficult to enforce, and which in any case would seriously have impaired the independence of action which every nation ought scrupulously to preserve.[9]

Spanish Civil War Embargo

EARLY in January, 1937, great excitement was aroused by the fact that a New Jersey dealer in used machinery had taken out a license to ship secondhand airplanes and parts to the Spanish Government at Madrid. A so-called Neutrality

[9] *Commercial and Financial Chronicle,* CXLI (Dec. 19, 1936), 3897.

Committee sitting at London had resolved, with problematical success, to keep arms and ammunition from both the constituent and the rebel governments in Spain. Civil wars having been unprovided for in the American neutrality legislation of 1935 and 1936, the Department of State at once sought an amendment of the law so as to cover such conflicts. In unseemly haste, and after an attempt by coast guard vessels to stop the sailing of a freighter carrying some of the airplane parts, Congress on January 9 passed the Pittman Resolution extending the prohibitions of the 1935 Act to Spain.

This was thought to be neutrality legislation. In fact, it was the precise opposite. International law required the United States to treat the elected and recognized government of Spain as the lawful government of Spain and, until the belligerency of the rebels is recognized, as the only government entitled to receive the assistance of the United States in suppressing armed insurrection. The 1912 and 1922 Congressional Resolutions had provided that whenever the President of the United States considered that arms from this country would help to promote domestic violence in American countries or China he was privileged to order an embargo. While these embargoes had not always worked effectively, and particularly in Mexico had enabled President Wilson to act unneutrally by laying and lifting embargoes against factions as his policy dictated, the fact is that in practically all instances the embargo had been applied to rebels.[10] The discouragement of revolutions was the point of President Wilson's Mobile speech of 1913.[11] International law also requires that revolutions receive no aid or comfort from the United States. A Pan-American Convention of 1928

[10] The application of the embargo " under such limitations and exceptions as the President prescribes," embodied wide Executive discretion, not always happily used, as in the embargo of 1930 against the Vargas insurgents two days before they became the government of Brazil.

[11] *President Wilson's Foreign Policy*, p. 19.

signed by the United States had forbidden the supply of arms and war material to revolutionists whose belligerency has not been recognized. During the years of the Cuban insurrection, from 1868 to 1878, and again from 1895 to 1898, the United States strictly observed its obligations to Spain and treated the rebels in such a manner as to avoid giving any offense to the Spanish Government. During the American Civil War several of the important arsenals were located in the South. Had England undertaken to embargo arms to both the North and the South, the North might have lost the war.

The Pittman Resolution on Spain reversed this legal order by placing unrecognized rebels and the constituent government on the same footing. As we shall see, the pending legislation of 1937 also deals with civil war in a somewhat curious fashion. In January, 1937, however, the belligerency of the Franco faction in Spain had not been formally recognized by the United States; but recognition of belligerency appears not to be the test for the application of the embargo. That, at least, would help to regularize the policy.

The Pittman and McReynolds Resolutions of 1937

THE expiration on May 1, 1937, of the temporary neutrality legislation of 1935 and 1936 made it necessary to propose new legislation. The chairman of the Senate Committee on Foreign Relations and his colleague of the House Committee on Foreign Affairs each introduced bills. Dominated by the demand for insulation against contacts with belligerents as manifested in the cash-and-carry plan, the Pittman Resolution adopted two provisions strikingly different from those of the legislation of 1936. Instead of barring the shipment of any excess beyond the prewar normal supply of commodities other than arms, ammunition and implements of war, the Pittman Resolution [12] provides that

[12] S. J. Res. 51, Sec. 1-A, 75th Cong., 1st Sess. (Jan. 22, 1937).

whenever the President thinks that a wider embargo is necessary, he may issue a proclamation listing " certain articles or materials " and it is thereafter unlawful for any American vessels to carry such commodities to any belligerent state or to any state for transshipment to a belligerent country. Presumably goods conditionally contraband would be included in this list, which does not even except foodstuffs or medical supplies, as did the bill of 1936.

The interesting aspects of the proposal are that a neutral now contemplates the preparation of a contraband list of its own, and its ships are forbidden to carry such contraband. The neutral enforces belligerent claims, although there is still opportunity for contesting belligerent contraband lists. No first-class Power has ever thus restricted its freedom.[1] The application by a neutral of the doctrine of continuous voyage to such goods greatly enhances the opportunity of the belligerent's controlling the sea to defeat its enemy. And carriage of the commodities placed on this list is to be confined to foreign ships, belligerent and neutral. This again is likely to favor the belligerent that controls the sea. The President has a broad discretion in determining the commodities to be placed on the embargo list, thus encountering the risk of belligerent charges of intentional discrimination. The rights of small nations, of which we heard so much in 1917, are to be further exposed to impairment or extinction at the hands of the mighty.

A further radical amendment [2] is designed to require that title to any American goods be transferred to a foreigner before they go to sea. This applies to all goods and not merely to those on an embargo list. The unembargoed goods American vessels may carry. But as the goods are now liable to be

---

[1] Since the Crimean War a number of smaller Powers which are not arms-manufacturing countries have as neutrals prohibited the export of arms and sometimes of contraband and on occasion prohibited their own ships from carrying them. These limited controls are briefly described by Woolsey, " The Munitions Trade," *Proceedings*, 1921, pp. 28–34.

[2] Section 2–B.

enemy owned, the vessel is exposed to special danger. If the purpose of the bill is to save the lives of American seamen, as Mr. Pittman contends, then, logically, American ships ought not to be allowed to carry anything to belligerents. And the practical alliance with Sea Powers which the bill establishes will create special danger for American shipping and thus defeat the major purpose of the bill — to quarantine the United States.

Section 1 of the Pittman Resolution includes civil strife in foreign countries among the conditions bringing into operation the mandatory arms embargo and the discretionary commodity embargo. But whereas in the case of international war the President is merely required to proclaim the fact of its existence for the arms embargo automatically to go into force, in civil war it comes into force only if the President finds that the " armed conflict is of such a magnitude or is being conducted under such conditions " that the export of arms, ammunition and implements of war " would threaten or endanger the peace of the United States." This is a curious provision. Apparently arms and munitions may be freely exported to a country in civil war until, perhaps by the use of arms shipped from the United States, the President thinks the war has reached certain threatening dimensions. Thereupon he may forbid the further export of arms. Obviously, this again places in the hands of the Executive the power to help one party in a civil war and to disable the other — all under the guise of neutrality. This is quite susceptible of making new enemies for the United States. It would be preferable to make the application of the embargoes provided for dependent upon the recognition of the belligerency of foreign insurgents.

Section 4 of the 1937 Pittman Resolution reincorporated the amendment of 1936 excepting American countries from all the embargoes of the bill in any war in which they may engage with a non-American state, no matter how recklessly they may have invited the war. Heretofore the United States had not considered that European hostilities against an

American republic offended the Monroe Doctrine unless the hostilities contemplated the acquisition or permanent occupation of American territory. Although the United States has recently been continentalizing the Monroe Doctrine in various Pan-American Conferences, it now seems that we promise the world that we will act unneutrally and become an ally of any Latin-American state which gets itself into war with a non-American state. If Great Britain should undertake to adopt hostile measures against an American country, the position of Canada will become interesting. The Canadian Prime Minister announced on February 19 [3] that our renunciation of the Monroe Doctrine afforded Canada an additional reason for increasing her armaments. Perhaps our repudiation of neutrality and the danger to Canada in having to choose between Great Britain and an independent neutrality in the event of a British-Latin-American war justify this further increase in Canadian armament. It is not without significance that practically every measure for the so-called maintenance of peace adopted under the specious and resounding phrases of recent years has had as its first effect a great increase in the armaments of all countries.

By Section 8 of the Pittman Resolution the President's power to restrict the entrance of submarines is extended to armed merchantmen. The presumption is that unless they are excluded they are privileged to enter American ports. Armed merchantmen, as has been shown,[4] are by law deemed to have the status of warships. This view actually requires no legislation to sustain it, and its enforcement should not depend on a presidential proclamation.

Section 9 would make it unlawful for an American citizen to travel on a belligerent vessel only after the President so proclaims. The implication is that until such proclamation is issued, the United States would protect such a citizen in his belligerent travels. This provision seems unwise, for two

---

[3] *New York Times*, Feb. 20, 1937.   [4] *Supra*, p. 102.

reasons: first, a neutral American always takes passage on belligerent vessels at his own risk and is not entitled to American protection; second, in view of the fact that by earlier provisions of the resolution American vessels are practically barred from the seas, since they cannot carry goods on the contraband list (if the President announces such a list), an American citizen may have a hard time finding an appropriate vessel to carry him. There is no reason why an American citizen should not be privileged to travel on any vessel of his choice — but if he chooses a belligerent vessel he does so at his own risk.

Section 10 contains a most unusual provision by which it is made unlawful for an American vessel engaged in commerce with a belligerent country to be armed, but only after the President issues a proclamation to that effect. This seems to imply that until the President issues such a proclamation American neutral merchant vessels may be armed. When the President in March, 1917, undertook to permit American vessels to arm, it was pointed out to the Secretary of the Treasury that they risked treatment as pirates, for neutral vessels may not engage in hostilities with belligerents. The government's undertaking responsibility for their armament dangerously risked a participation in the war. No reason is given why a provision for the armament or disarmament of neutral American merchantmen even by way of presidential discretion was included in the resolution.

The cash-and-carry provisions of the bill — cash to be paid by the foreigner before shipment — are to be enforced by an affidavit in which the American shipper renounces all claims to protection by the United States. The practicability of such a provision will remain to be demonstrated. That it is likely to impair foreign commerce seems hardly doubtful. What the domestic effect of such measures is likely to be is uncertain.

The House Foreign Affairs Committee prefers to regard

its measure as a plan to keep the country out of war rather than an attempt to maintain strict neutrality.[5] It will generally be found that provision for keeping the country out of war but without neutrality is a way of explaining and facilitating intervention in foreign struggles on the " right " side. The House Bill confers a wider discretion on the President in the matter of embargoes than does the Pittman Resolution. Operation of the cash-and-carry principle is discretionary with the President, rather than obligatory, as it is in the Senate Bill. If he issues no proclamation then the cash-and-carry principle will not come into effect, although under the House Bill as under the Senate Bill the President has discretion to proclaim an embargo list of commodities which no American vessel may carry. Fear of the incalculable effects of so revolutionary a measure persuaded the House to limit its operation to two years.

The House Committee justifies its espousal of wide discretionary powers on the ground that the President's hands should not be tied " so that it [the United States] could not use its good offices for the prevention of wars. Our influence would be gone for world peace, when we ought to be in a position to use our influence to prevent wars, not, of course, becoming allied or connected politically with any foreign Power." [6] This revival of League of Nations' aims in a neutrality bill is a further warning that discretionary and adjustable neutrality is a contradiction in terms. At least the House Committee understands this discretionary power as an opportunity to employ the influence of the United States politically " for the prevention of wars." As is more likely to be the case, however, that influence would probably be used to hasten intervention in foreign wars. The suggestion that a discretionary embargo power will be used for the

[5] *New York Times,* Feb. 25, 1937. H. Rep. 320, 75th Cong., 1st Sess., on H. J. Res. 242.
[6] Report, *op. cit.,* p. 7.

" prevention of wars " is not flattering to the intelligence of the American public.

In spite of the avowal of Senator Pittman that the freedom of the seas is not impaired, the bill makes it unnecessary for the United States to assert it. Senator Johnson characterizes the bill as the " scuttle-and-run " policy. The policy of 1914–17 is exacting its retribution. We turn from one evil and embrace new ones. How handicapped foreign countries will view a policy which makes us a supply station for the belligerent with cash and in control of the seas is an open question. War is often declared against the ally of a belligerent for no other reason than his assistance to one side. The derision of neutrality has given rise to iconoclastic measures which can only be understood in the light of the unneutral policies of 1914–17. How they will serve us remains to be seen.

But above all else, a sincere intention to remain neutral is indispensable. That cannot be legislated. In a recent public address President Roosevelt uttered a profound truth — which the experience of the late war should sear into the minds of the citizenry: " The effective maintenance of American neutrality depends today, as in the past, on the wisdom and determination of whoever at the moment occupy the offices of President and Secretary of State." [7]

[7] Address at Chautauqua, August 14, 1936, *International Conciliation*, Sept. 1936, p. 445.

IV.

SUMMARY

THIS record of American policy over the last generation has two aspects — the national and the international. Just as Great Britain turned from her traditions with the ill-fated entente with France and Russia of 1904, so the United States broke with its fundamental principles by the unprecedented decision to participate in a European war and send troops to cure Europe of nationalistic wars and autocratic governments. The results of that adventure, which have helped neither Europe nor the United States, are likely to be far-reaching. For not merely American neutrality, but American independence, may be " a thing of the past."

Our subjection began in August, 1914, and there has been little recovery from that depression. There are no longer many principles in American foreign policy. Having flouted the wisdom of those who charted America's course, we now respond easily to temptations to enforce policies formulated in other countries without our participation. The American people, having falsely been told that our effort to preserve our neutrality got us into the war, have been driven in their perplexity to heterodox measures, such as the 1937 Pittman Act, which are designed to insulate the United States from all contact with belligerent powers, but which are likely to have quite different effects.

It would have been more sensible simply to embargo arms and loans as did the 1935–36 legislation. For the rest, we should have maintained the freedom of the seas and the time-honored rights of neutrals which other nations, more confident of their capacity to stay out of wars when they wish, must now uphold. By resigning all opportunity to stand for American rights, we come close to insuring license for belligerents only.

The retreat from American traditions has been stimulated by the provocative interventionist policy of the League of Nations, whose devotees have continued to befuddle the American people with the argument that neutrality is immoral and that in a European war the United States cannot remain neutral. Without knowing the identity of the combatants or the issues of the war, we are blandly informed that the United States has no choice but to participate. The argument is humiliating to American independence which, indeed, is the inevitable victim of the assault. But it has encouraged European nations to seek to enlist us in the name of the Higher Morality in their perpetual feuds, and Kellogg Pacts open a ready door to involvement.

The attack on neutrality as a principle and a practice, so sedulously cultivated since the war, has, however, been based not only on the League cult of partisanship, but also on the contention that the law is now so uncertain that neutrals have no rights on which they can rely. It is argued that as neutrality failed to keep us out of war in 1917, unneutrality must perforce become the national policy. It has even been urged, entirely without justification, that insistence on our neutral rights brought us into the war and that escape lies in an abandonment of neutral rights. This belief is implicit in the 1937 legislation.

But the fact is that neutral rights were as clear in 1914 as was any other branch of public law, and while the law was grossly violated during the war, it has not thereby been ended or modified. American submissiveness may have temporarily weakened respect for law, but its permanent vitality is unimpaired — unless indeed unmitigated force has now become the sole arbiter of human affairs. If this book has proved anything, it should have shown that, whatever the reasons, the mind and heart of the Wilson administration were not seriously concerned with neutrality. They thought they saw in the struggle higher purposes than the simple undramatic obligation to safeguard the United States against war with all its consequences.

Repudiating the very basis of American tradition in foreign policy, some of our leaders as early as 1915 considered it in the interests of " civilization " that we should enter the war. Under this view of American interests, neutral rights were not pressed but, on the contrary, were surrendered. The submarine controversy with Germany, which was made the legal justification for war, turned on President Wilson's insistence, as a matter of National Honor, that American citizens were privileged to travel unmolested on belligerent, even armed belligerent vessels. Mr. Lansing admitted the mistake in January, 1916, yet was not allowed to withdraw from it, but on the contrary was compelled to adhere to the error until it brought its natural results. We undertook to protect British ships against attacks of their enemies, a policy never theretofore pursued by any neutral nation, a policy utterly without legal merit. On the other hand, the Allies' violations of the time-honored neutral right to trade with other neutrals were met only by paper protests, which it is now admitted lacked sincerity.

Thus the United States fell into the toils. When a strong neutral fails to stand firm on neutral rights, he betrays not only himself but all neutrals and the law as well. He assists in his own undoing. A strong neutral is the trustee for civilization in a shell-shocked world. The United States, which may justly be proud of its contributions to international law and neutrality down to 1913, has lost its eminence as a leader in the law and now turns in confusion either to coercive measures to " enforce peace " or to a timorous retreat from legitimate relations with belligerents. This renunciation is less likely to assure our peace than an intelligent administration of well-established rights under international law. For not only does the withdrawal from the defense of neutral rights encourage belligerent excesses, but the very fact that the Pittman-Nye policy of 1937 makes the resources of the United States by our own legislation available only to the belligerent that controls the sea, will probably provoke measures of retaliation which will in their turn expose us to hostilities.

Nor have the international effects of American intervention been any happier. With the psychology of Uplift which the war inspired, Mars appeared revealed as a regenerator of the souls of men and nations. There resulted the facile assumption that by a Covenant the warring nations of the world would mend their ancient ways and adopt honest measures for preventing war and punishing the unruly. But such hopes had not the slightest roots in history or experience. The creators of this idea unconsciously or deliberately blinded themselves to the harsh political facts they were establishing by the treaties of 1919. Oblivious to the disintegrating forces which the war itself had set in motion, they built themselves paper machinery for the regulation of mankind. They neglected the physical and psychological recuperation and therapy which bleeding men and nations demanded, and which alone could heal the wounds and prevent a renewal of the fratricidal strife in even more virulent form. The causes of that strife in social and economic disequilibriums were left untouched. The fundamental problem of the distribution of raw materials and markets was not even considered until 1936. The great forces moving millions of men were thought of in moral terms of righteousness versus malevolence, and schemes were devised for holding down an unhealthy status quo while the ill-informed were made to believe that all this planning was in the interests of Uplift.

The prewar system of international relations, imperfect though it was, was denounced as " international anarchy " which was to be replaced by a new world order in which right and justice alone would prevail. Yet we learn that today, even in France, all classes of the people look back to the stability of the prewar years with nostalgia. Under the system of that time at least facts were faced and long decades of peace and tranquillity blessed Europe and the world; and if war occurred, the effort of other nations was not to participate in it and assume the impossible task of acting as a judge of its merits, but by limiting its area to shorten the conflict and to exert on both parties the beneficent influence of the mediator and reconciler of grievances. Under that system, in the eighteenth and nineteenth centuries, Europe and the world achieved an advance in material and spiritual endowments probably unequaled in history. To characterize such a period and the law under which it grew, however defective, as anarchy, is sadly to depreciate the achievements of the past and, by misconceiving them, to misappraise the " new order." And this very order seems calculated to make of turmoil and chaos a vested interest and to promote crisis, fear, apprehension, and hostility as the normal way of life. The corrosion of liberalism and democracy and the intensive inflation of nationalism, political and economic, are natural corollaries of the " new order."

In spite of the quest for formulæ, there does not seem to be any short cut to peace. That is a condition which must be carefully nurtured in the soil of contentment, confidence, and mutual respect. The effort to organize collective armed intervention for peace can never achieve peace. To engender peace by the threat of force is inherently incongruous. World coöperation is to be found in ameliorating the underlying causes of friction and in the adoption of the time-honored, homely virtues of simple decency, fairness, and reconciliation of conflicting interests, in the adjustment of grievances, and in strengthening, not weakening, the rules of law. This is the type of world coöperation that is likely to produce measurable peace, and there is in it no threat to use force.

The 1919 " peace " doctrines and the machinery for carrying them into effect have been tried and found wanting. This ought now to be clear enough. There is danger in further relying upon a novel remedy conditioned upon a change in human and international relations which is nonexistent. That way can lead only to disappointment and despair. The Hague Conferences were closer to reality than the postwar machinery, and in their modest way achieved practical successes which the more ambitious demand for wholesale regeneration cannot record.

Carried away by enthusiasm for noble ends, the United States rushed to Europe in 1917 to make the world " safe for democracy," to fight a " war to end war." In that period the golden age of rhetoric and phantasy in these matters was inaugurated. But in the light of the results achieved, the enterprise must be regarded as a ghastly failure. Europe is today less peaceful in time of peace than she has ever been. The " international government " which was established at Geneva has not brought unification or political coöperation, but on the contrary has widened the rifts between the countries of the continent. The concert of Europe has rarely been less harmonious. Democracy is not in high renown and dictatorships of a kind not dreamed of in the nineteenth century mar wide areas of the landscape. Collective and individual insecurity is nearly universal.

These phenomena are not accidental. They are the result of ill-considered policies which could not have lasted as long as they have without the coöperation of the United States in giving the countries of Europe the impression that we could be counted on to do again what we had just done. The least that can now be done is to avoid similar ineptitude in the future. By intervention in European quarrels we can make the situation worse, but never better. The road prepared for us by the coercive peace machinery of Geneva, which has proved so alluring to some of our statesmen, can lead only to deeper involvement. Europe must work out its own problems; it understands them better than we ever can.

It is inevitable that the temptations to " coöperate " with the " peace-loving " nations of Europe will destroy our objectivity and neutrality and by making the United States the particular friend of some Powers make us necessarily the enemies of others. The sound advice of George Washington which opens this book was based on a profound knowledge of human nature. By cultivating friendly relations with all nations, developing with each the highest possible degree of trade, by bargaining off the international debts as part of the terrible price paid for a bitter lesson, by using the great gifts and resources which nature has placed in our keeping to set the world an example of contented living, we may again demonstrate the American capacity to manage American affairs.

There is no improvised formula to insure abstention from war and yet maintain national dignity. Neither the taking of sides nor widespread embargoes marks the road to peace. Far more important are an honest intention to remain aloof from foreign conflict, a refusal to be stampeded by unneutral propaganda, a knowledge of the law and a capacity to stand upon it, meeting emergencies and problems not romantically but wisely. The cultivation of sagacity in these matters, of detachment, of moderation, of toleration, of the spirit of live and let live, and the renunciation of the psychology and policy of " enforcing peace " by hostile measures probably present the only tangible hope for preserving peace in broad areas of the world.

V.

THE PERIOD 1937–1940

EARLIER sections of this book have indicated the departures from American neutrality and historic tradition which the war of 1914 inspired in the Wilson administration. Such departures, it has been pointed out, were unnecessary then and have been injurious to the United States and the world ever since. The so-called imperialistic stage of American expansion from 1890 to 1914 had witnessed our participation in a good many international conferences, while staking out new fields for investment; but there were no departures from the doctrine of neutrality during foreign wars. Only in recent times, when the romantic urge to " do good " abroad, without adequate comprehension of the complexity of the problems, began to affect certain sections of the American public, has intervention in foreign quarrels been promoted as a worthy policy.

The misfortunes of that policy, with its theory of " enforcing peace " upon " aggressors," and its unrelieved record of failure, humiliation and disturbing of international relations, should by 1937 have deterred American citizens from continuing to espouse it. But no. Those who believed in America's mission to save the world for this and that, those who embraced the League of Nations with such trustful devotion, still continue their advocacy of intervention in foreign quarrels in the interests of righteousness, still discountenance American neutrality in principle and in practice. It is this group which has striven to insert in the neutrality statutes of recent years presidential discretion to discriminate between belligerents, to help one belligerent against the other, to employ embargoes against " aggressors," and to manipulate American foreign policy so as to handicap disfavored nations while helping assumed friends. For this school of thought, executive discretion and executive discrimination are interchangeable terms.

While the Neutrality Acts of 1937 and 1939 had the appearance of literal and legal neutrality because they required American impartiality between belligerents, in fact the administration of those statutes has accomplished the reverse; partiality and discrimination are begetting unneutrality. Dr. Charles A. Beard has described the conflict of policy between the interventionists and the noninterventionists. He writes:

At the bottom of this discussion, however, lay diametrically opposite conceptions of American policy. One conception holds that the United States is morally responsible for the peace of Europe and the Orient, that only collective action can keep peace, that the President can always discover just who is an aggressor in any dispute, and that the United States cannot stay out of a general war if it comes. The other conception of policy denies these postulates. It holds that the United States does not have this moral responsibility and would not know how to exercise it if it did; that the one sure way to get into war is to take sides in any dispute likely to lead to an open breach; that intervention[s] in disputes in Europe or the Orient are futile unless backed by a will to war in case of a major diplomatic defeat; and that the United States can and ought to stay out of European and Oriental wars, no matter what the pretexts on which they are started and waged.[1]

In February, 1936, the administration had made strong efforts to obtain power for the President to embargo commodities other than arms, ammunition, and implements of war in quantities beyond normal peacetime quotas. This request had been challenged on the ground that in the very selection of commodities the President had power to discriminate between belligerents and thus affect the outcome of foreign wars.

The effort to obtain authority for general commodity em-

[1] *Events*, Sept., 1937, pp. 167–168.

bargoes had been induced presumably by the desire to obtain lawful authority for the extra-legal injunctions against shipment to disfavored nations of such commodities as copper, oil, trucks, tractors, scrap iron, and scrap steel, injunctions which had been issued by the Secretary of State during the Italo-Ethiopian War of 1935.[2] Inasmuch as this program contemplated an extension and expansion of the arms embargo under the Act of 1935, that embargo was not only accepted as basic but was even praised by administration spokesmen.[3] Subsequent defeat of the commodity embargo produced no noticeable wavering of confidence in the arms embargo. In his speech of August 22, 1936, at Chautauqua, President Roosevelt had applauded prohibitions on the arms traffic and on extension of credit to belligerents. Among other things he said:

The Congress of the United States has given me certain authority to provide safeguards of American neutrality in case of war.

The President of the United States, who, under our Constitution, is vested with primary authority to conduct our international relations, thus has been given new weapons with which to maintain our neutrality.

. . .

Nevertheless, if war should break out again in another continent, let us not blink the fact that we would find in this country thousands of Americans who, seeking immediate riches — fools' gold — would attempt to break down or evade our neutrality.

They would tell you — and, unfortunately, their views would get wide publicity — that if they could produce and ship this and that and the other article to belligerent nations the unemployed of America would all find work. They would tell you that if they could extend credit to warring nations that credit would be used in

[2] *Supra,* p. 320.

[3] Cf. testimony of Messrs. Hull, R. W. Moore, and Hackworth in Hearings on S. 3474, 74th Cong., 2d Sess., pp. 20, 40–41, 64, 74–75, 102, 135, 288, 293, 298.

Witnesses before the Senate Committee who expressed doubts on the practicability and long-run effects of all embargoes were unfavorably criticized. *Idem,* p. 25.

the United States to build homes and factories and pay our debts. They would tell you that America once more would capture the trade of the world.[4]

It would be hard to resist that clamor. . . . To resist the clamor of that greed, if war should come, would require the unswerving support of all Americans who love peace.

If we face the choice of profits or peace, the Nation will answer — must answer — " we choose peace." . . .

No matter how well we are supported by neutrality legislation, we must remember that no laws can be provided to cover every contingency, for it is impossible to imagine how every future event may shape itself. In spite of every possible forethought, international relations involve of necessity a vast uncharted area. In that area safe sailing will depend on the knowledge and the experience and the wisdom of those who direct our foreign policy. Peace will depend on their day-to-day decisions.

We can keep out of war if those who watch and decide have a sufficiently detailed understanding of international affairs to make certain that the small decisions of each day do not lead toward war, and if, at the same time, they possess the courage to say " no " to those who selfishly or unwisely would let us go to war.[5]

As a result, in 1937 the desirability of continuing the arms embargo as a part of permanent American policy does not appear to have been questioned by the administration. Although there are arguments against arms embargoes, these were not raised by the administration.

Moreover, the President was given the power, in the Act of 1937, to confine to foreign vessels the carrying of exports other than munitions, and to require that cash be paid for them and that title be transferred to a foreign owner, when it was found that such restrictions were " necessary to pro-

[4] Yet in demanding the repeal of the arms embargo, September 23, 1939, President Roosevelt remarked: " From a purely material point of view, what is the advantage to us in sending all manner of articles across the ocean for final processing there when we could give employment to thousands by doing it here? . . . And if abnormal profits appear in our midst even in time of peace as a result of this increase of industry, I feel certain that the subject will be adequately dealt with at the coming regular session of the Congress." *Cong. Rec.* (daily), LXXXV, 8–10.

[5] Press Releases, XV, No. 360 (Aug. 22, 1936), 167–168.

mote the security or preserve the peace of the United States or to protect the lives of citizens of the United States." It was hoped that in this way American cargoes and citizens would escape danger, but that American trade might continue, to some extent, if for cash and in foreign bottoms. The novelty of the cash-and-carry provisions persuaded Congress [6] to limit them to two years, so that they automatically expired on May 1, 1939.

This act passed the Senate and the House by overwhelming majorities; [7] Senator Pittman was so enamored of it that he dubbed it " the Peace Act of 1937." Rushed to the President by airplane, the act was signed immediately, and was forthwith implemented by proclamation — all on May 1, 1937.[8]

The Spanish Civil War

REFERENCE has already been made to the unseemly haste with which on January 9, 1937, Congress placed an arms embargo on both parties to the Spanish Civil War.[9] Yet the Executive refused to admit the existence of a war in Spain — an admission which would have entailed recognition of both parties to the war as belligerents and hence entitled to exercise belligerent rights on land and at sea. By the embargo, the administration nevertheless implicitly admitted that there were two parties to the war and that the rules of neutrality and nonintervention required that those parties be treated impartially. So America was confronted with the anomalous situation wherein on the one hand the Government admitted the existence of a war and of two warring groups between which the United States chose to be neutral, while on the other it stoutly protested that there was no war, that the

---

[6] At the initiative of Representative Shanley of Connecticut.

[7] Senate, 63 to 6; House, 373 to 13.

[8] Public Resolution No. 27, 75th Cong., 1st Sess., 50 Stats. 121 *et seq.*

[9] *Supra*, p. 336.

only government of Spain was the legitimate Government of Madrid, and that neither that Government nor the rebels were, in fact, belligerents.

This self-contradiction by the administration itself found a ready echo in the press, with resultant confusion all around. If this Government insisted on the existence of only one Spanish government — the legitimate Government of Spain — then the Franco forces were relegated to the category of rebels. It was therefore an unfriendly act, a violation of the treaty with Spain of 1902 [10] and of international obligations, for America to refuse the Spanish Government access to weapons with which to quell the rebellion. To treat the legitimate Government and the rebels on a parity was, further, an act of intervention on the side of those rebels against the legitimate Government.

On the other hand, if the Franco group was to be treated by neutrals on a parity with the legitimate Government, the inevitable implication was that a war existed between two contending groups, and that both groups were belligerents and entitled to exercise belligerent rights, as in the case of the American Civil War.

But the administration followed neither of these courses — or rather, it attempted to follow both courses at once. The result was confusion, made greater when the administration in 1938 felt itself unable to lift the arms embargo for the Loyalists, as it was pressed to do and as it perhaps wanted to, because by that time this would have been too obviously unneutral.

The only apparent explanation of the position taken by the Government lay in the fact that certain European members of the League of Nations had organized a twenty-seven-nation " Nonintervention Committee," [1] ostensibly designed

[10] Malloy, *Treaties and Conventions*, II, 1701.

[1] For a discussion of the activities of this body, see N. J. Padelford, *International Law and Diplomacy in the Spanish Civil Strife* (New York, 1939); reviewed *U. Pa. L. Rev.*, LXXXVIII (Feb., 1940), 499.

to prevent the spread of the war, and the American Government desired to coöperate with the Committee. For reasons of a practical and economic nature peculiar to Europe, this Committee had led the way in adopting the curious view of the Spanish Civil War which Washington copied. England, with extensive mining interests in the territory held by Franco's forces, was loath to classify him as a mere bandit or rebel and thereby expose British interests in that part of Spain to his wrath. Nor yet could the Government disregard British public opinion with its avowed sympathy for the legitimate Government of Spain by recognizing Franco as a belligerent. Furthermore, Britain, with extensive shipping interests in and about the Mediterranean and a " life-line " running through the Straits of Gibraltar, could not view with favor the possibility of both sides availing themselves of belligerent rights at sea — those same belligerent rights which Great Britain itself during the 1914 European war had expanded so widely at the expense of neutrals. Then, too, unrestricted trading with both parties to the war offered lucrative remuneration to British industries. And finally, while it is probable that after January, 1938, the Government of Great Britain did not look unfavorably upon the possibility of a Franco victory — provided Franco did not become a mere tool of Mussolini and Hitler — France, with its " Popular Front " Government, sympathized with the Loyalists and probably helped them.

The combination of these local European factors induced Great Britain to lead the way in organizing the so-called Nonintervention Committee, which disregarded international law but was excused in American eyes because of its announced effort to localize the conflict. The fact that Italy, Germany, and to some extent Russia, intervened in the Spanish War brought no change in the policy of the Nonintervention Committee. As early as December, 1936, Viscount Cranborne, British Under-Secretary of State for Foreign Affairs, stated to the Council of the League of Nations that the nonintervention pact was a farce,[2] while Lloyd George is credited with describing the whole nonintervention system as " the greatest and basest fraud and deception ever perpetrated by a great nation upon a weak people." [3]

Although the United States had no such practical interests in Spain as actuated the vagaries of European policy, it nevertheless followed the European example. Perhaps it was thought we were helping to " prevent war " — by imposing arms and loan embargoes on all Spain.

Later on, when Uruguay proposed that the United States join in recognizing the belligerency of both groups in Spain, the administration's reply was a polite but firm " no." Said the State Department:

The Governments of twenty-seven European nations have for many months been coöperating through the Non-Intervention Committee at London in an endeavor to prevent the internal conflict in Spain from involving the peace in Europe. While this Government has not participated in the work of this Committee, it has followed with sympathetic interest the efforts of these European nations to limit the effects of the Spanish civil strife. The Government of the United States has, moreover, in so far as the action might be consistent with its firm policy of not interfering in the internal affairs of other countries, always stood ready to support any constructive effort to promote and preserve world peace. The Non-Intervention Committee at London has not, however, as the result of its deliberations in which twenty-seven European nations have participated, decided to recognize a state of belligerency in Spain.

Therefore, while fully recognizing the high motives which have prompted Your Excellency's Government to take this initiative, and without in any way implying any judgment with respect to the merits of the proposal, my Government is confident that you will appreciate that the policy which it has consistently maintained

---

[2] " The main, melancholy, unanswerable fact is that, to all appearances, the agreement is being violated by both parties to the struggle." *Official Journal*, XVIII (Dec. 11, 1936), 11.

[3] Padelford, *op. cit.*, p. 119.

since the beginning of the Spanish conflict would preclude it from associating itself with the action proposed by the Uruguayan Government.[4]

When late in 1937 it became apparent that the arms embargo was operating to the exclusive disadvantage of the Loyalist Government, which the United States favored sentimentally and was legally obliged to accept as *the* Government of Spain, the administration was faced with a powerful movement aimed at lifting the arms embargo for the Loyalists. But the embargo was retained, on the argument that lifting it for one side would be unneutral. Lifting it for both sides might have been construed as a confession of error.[5]

The European irregularities were finally topped off by the action of the nations of the Nonintervention Committee, led again by England, in recognizing Franco's as the sole government of all territorial Spain, although the Loyalists still retained control of a respectable portion of their country.[6] At least the United States withheld that recognition until after Franco was completely in power.

Blind following of the London Committee had brought no glory to the United States. It is not strange that all reference to " civil strife " is omitted from the Neutrality Act of 1939.

Sino-Japanese War

Even before 1894, the date of the first Sino-Japanese War, China was in constant turmoil. She was a backward country, without a genuine central administration, and was therefore a ready victim of exploitation by European Powers. The Boxer Rebellion in 1900, the culmination of an antiforeign

[4] Press Releases, XVII, 194.

[5] See letter of May 12, 1938, from Secretary Hull to Senator Pittman, Press Releases, XVIII (1938), 578–579.

[6] A succinct criticism of some of the legal irregularities is to be found in Mr. Nielsen's speech of May 10, 1939, *Cong. Rec.* (daily), LXXXIV, 8624. See also Baty in *A. J. I. L.,* XXX, 377.

movement, exposed her to further encroachments. The promotion of Chinese unity was alien to the interests of the Western Powers — or so they thought — and internal strife of the war lords was not altogether discouraged.

Japan achieved maturity very late. Not until 1899 did she get rid of the extraterritorial jurisdiction of foreign consuls in dealing with their own nationals. She had been frustrated in 1895 in obtaining material benefits from her victory over China by the intervention of some of the Western Powers — England, Russia, Germany and France. She achieved little out of the Russo-Japanese War, except Korea [7] and a few minor assignments of Russian rights in China, and was talked out of Manchuria, even then largely under Russian control. The economic weakness of Japan, not her strength, drove her to emulate the Western Powers in China; this stimulated her feeling that she was discriminated against, that the prior claims of other Powers jeopardized her own interests in China, potentially the main source of Japan's raw materials and her principal market. A growing population continually sharpened the problem. By 1914, she had, through the Alliance with England and treaties with France and Russia, been woven into the anti-German front. In the War of 1914–18 Japan hoped to realize some of her ambitions for continental expansion or influence. In 1915 she presented her twenty-one demands, but even a China in turmoil was able, with Western diplomatic support, to frustrate their execution. In spite of the Lansing-Ishii Agreement of 1918, recognizing her primacy in China, Japan was denied Shantung in 1919, largely through the efforts of the United States. In 1921 she was forced back from Siberia, again by the United States. At the Washington Conference she was denied naval equality, and had to submit to the abrogation of the Anglo-Japanese alliance and of the Lansing-Ishii Agreement.

In 1927 Great Britain, smarting under the Chinese boy-

[7] Annexed in 1910.

cott, tempted Japan in vain to send an army to China to fight Chiang Kai-shek, who had Russian support. In 1930 Japan refused to submit longer to Western dictation, recovered at London her freedom of action from the 5-5-3 naval ratio, and the next year began her invasion of Manchuria, which she reorganized as the State of Manchukuo. Her ambitions in China, however, were not yet satisfied. In July, 1937, she started the large-scale attempt to bring North China under at least economic, if not political, control. The effort was not as simple as had been supposed, for in spite of Chinese disunity a strong resistance developed and the Western Powers came to the aid of the Chiang Kai-shek government. It is still an open question whether Japan can accomplish her aims of a " new order " by setting up the Wang Ching-wei government in Nanking, and whether she can by that means establish a working agreement with the Western Powers.

The " new order " in eastern Asia may weaken the political rights of the Western Powers in China, but will not necessarily damage their economic welfare. At all events, this mass movement for continental expansion is not a mere moral issue; and however unpleasant the Japanese invasion appears to Western eyes, it has deep-seated causes which defy easy analysis. It is wise therefore to reserve moral judgments. The complexity of the problem dictates neutrality.[8]

Before the Sino-Japanese War broke out in July, 1937, there was some evidence that President Roosevelt was planning a dramatic event such as an economic conference or possibly a disarmament conference. The late Lord Tweedsmuir had been ostentatiously received in Washington, Ambassadors Bullitt and Davies had returned to Washington from their European posts, Walter Runciman of the British Board of Trade was also there, while Norman Davis was conferring in London with Sir Samuel Hoare. It looked again as

[8] Cf. A. Whitney Griswold, *The Far Eastern Policy of the United States* (New York, 1938), *passim.*

if London was grooming the United States for a resumption of that moral leadership which had so often proved helpful in relieving the strains of Empire.[8a]

International relations were in ferment, but it was impossible to say whether the world was headed for conflict or conference. In June, 1937, Mr. Van Zeeland, former Belgian Premier, came to see President Roosevelt and, it was said, laid before him a plan to circumvent the Johnson Act, which excluded from our money market nations in default on debts to the United States Government. Loans by England to Germany were rumored. The United States' silver policy — accumulation at excessive cost — had drained away Chinese currency; ironically, the movement had been initiated largely by Senator Pittman, a leading advocate of chastisement of Japan. In spite of plans for the financial rehabilitation of Europe, the armament race continued.

Whatever the prospects for another world conference on disarmament or economic rehabilitation, the outbreak of the Sino-Japanese War in July, 1937, blotted them out. Beginning as a local incident at Peiping, it rapidly spread throughout North China and to Shanghai, where an enormous amount of damage was done. But the Chinese and the Japanese, for reasons of their own, did not declare war, following in that respect precedents of Europe and Asia. In all probability China did not wish to incur the embargoes of our Neutrality Act, and Japan considered it easier to make peace and to avoid charges under the Kellogg Pact if she refrained from declaring war.

This procedure had implications for the United States. The Neutrality Act of 1937 provided that whenever the President " finds " that a state of war exists he shall bring the act into force by proclamation. No proclamation was issued, however, and Senator Pittman was allowed to explain why the President could not " find " the state of war that every-

[8a] Cf. A. Whitney Griswold in *Events*, I, 325.

body else perceived. He remarked that the finding was purely discretionary with the President — hardly a logical interpretation of the statute — and that the finding might impede diplomatic negotiations looking toward peace.[9] However that may be, although the war has now been on for almost three years, the Neutrality Act has not yet been brought into force.

In the United States it was evidently assumed that invoking the act would aid Japan because she had the cash and the ships. But, in fact, the cash-and-carry plan of the 1937 Act could only be invoked at the President's discretion. True, the arms embargo, which was mandatory, would possibly have aided Japan and handicapped China, although both nations had other sources of supply. Without knowing much about the background of the war, the American public, however, had adopted an attitude of marked partiality for China and apparently approved the unneutral aid later extended to China in the form of a $25,000,000 credit from the Export-Import Bank, with a further $20,000,000 loan in prospect.[10] With respect to Japan, in July, 1938, an extra-legal "moral embargo" was placed on war materials and, subsequently, on other commodities and machinery. Thus far, the suggested embargo on raw materials has not been adopted, despite vigorous sponsorship by Senator Pittman and League of Nations groups headquartered in New York.

In the early '30's, when embargo legislation was recommended by sanctionists and interventionists, the recommendation was conditioned upon "general coöperation and united opinion among the principal Powers." Nowadays, however, since other countries have lost faith and interest in these "moral" measures of coercion, the United States is being urged to undertake them alone and to assume the sole risk and responsibility for them. To make the case worse, pro-

---

[9] *New York Times,* July 30, 1937.

[10] The Act of March 2, 1940, provides that the outstanding total shall not exceed $30,000,000. *New York Times,* March 2, 3, 1940. Part of the $25,000,000 has been repaid in tung oil and possibly tin.

ponents of such measures assume, and assure the public, that they will not lead to conflict because the resentment aroused will not or cannot find expression. They are still optimistic.

The diplomatic exchange in the Far East began in July, 1937, when Secretary Hull notified China and Japan that he hoped hostilities would be avoided. Similar representations were made by Great Britain and France. " Parallel action " had begun.

At that time, neither the Nine-Power Treaty, obliging the signatories to " respect and observe the territorial integrity and political and administrative independence of the Chinese Republic," nor the Kellogg Pact was invoked. Nor was the so-called " Open Door." [1] This is understandable because not one of these three instruments deserves serious consideration from an informed person. They are the vaguest of formulae. The Nine-Power Treaty was based on a condition contrary to fact. In 1922, China had no territorial integrity and the encroachments of many of the very signatories to the treaty had gravely impaired the political and administrative independence of the Chinese Republic. Had China been a political entity, like Japan, there would have been no such questions for a Washington Conference to deal with and fumble. In addition Russia, the party primarily aimed at in the treaty, was not a signatory, a fact which in itself would indicate its artificial character. The Kellogg-Briand Pact contained so many reservations that nothing of substance was left.[2] Later on, however, all three instruments were made the bases of interventionist policy which jeopardized the neutrality — the peace — of the United States.

In view of the sad experience of Secretary Stimson in 1932 in attempting to stop Japan in Manchuria, the administration in 1937 was more cautious. It wished to be sure that

[1] Actually, none of the countries addressed by Secretary Hay in 1899 and 1900 had conceded the " Open Door."
[2] *Supra*, p. 289.

Britain stood with it, even if a little behind it. Secretary
Hull therefore announced [3] certain fundamental principles
of international policy supported by the United States, such
as the maintenance of peace, national self-restraint, absti-
nence from force, nonintervention in other nations' internal
affairs, peaceful negotiation of differences, the observance of
treaties, and their modification by orderly processes as the
need arises, respect for the rights of others, the revitalizing
of international law, promotion of economic security and
stability, etc., with all of which the world could agree, but in
the application of which there might be differences.[4]

Secretary Eden in London preferred his predecessor's policy of 1932; he made it clear that Britain would not intervene in the Far Eastern conflict, but urged America to uphold the principles of morality.

In the first month of the Far Eastern war the administration, while not invoking the Neutrality Act, seems to have
been anxious to avoid involvement, and even took steps to
evacuate American citizens from danger zones. Yet the desire to stop " aggressors " was also strong. Although the
United States was not obligated either by Hay's notes of
1899 or 1900, by the Nine-Power Treaty, by the other Washington treaties, or by any other instrument to preserve the
territorial integrity of China — all efforts to accomplish that
had always either been prevented by the Powers or been
unsuccessful for other reasons — there nevertheless was a

[3] On July 16, 1937. Department of State, Publication No. 1079.

[4] The Portuguese Government alone had the temerity to analyze these
maxims, deprecating " the habit of entrusting the solution of grave external
problems to vague formulae." After stating that everyone agrees with " the
assertions, advices or wishes " of the Secretary, the Portuguese note adds:
" Difficulties begin only when it is sought to pass from the field of intentions
into that of action . . ." It stated that repeated affirmation of these principles by the great Powers would exert " a certain moral pressure, but will
produce rather limited practical action." The note added that states will
try to defend their soil, their economy, their currency, their workers, even if
this conflicts with general principles or engagements. It intimated that a
more profound analysis of the problems was necessary if any solution was
hoped for. Press Releases, XVII, No. 416 (Sept. 18, 1937), 229–234.

desire to bring about collective action to stop the Japanese adventure.

On August 23 Senator Pittman again explained why the Neutrality Act was not invoked; this time it was attributed to the necessity of protecting Americans in the war zone. The relevancy of the reason is not quite apparent. The other reasons alleged — absence of a declaration of war, fear of discouraging prospects for an early peace, and risk of inviting a Japanese blockade — are hardly sounder.[5] On the same day Secretary Hull made a plea to both belligerents to cease hostilities, but avoided passing judgment on the merits of their dispute; he repeated the broad principles announced in his circular note of July 16. In spite of what our interventionists called provocation, such as the Japanese blockade of *Chinese* shipping and the airplane shooting of the *British* Ambassador, America remained aloof. Even the President urged Americans to withdraw from China. Inasmuch as misdirected Chinese bombs had done much of the damage at Shanghai, and to the steamer *President Hoover*,[6] there was still a sentimental disposition to maintain neutrality.

The months of September and October, 1937, however, produced a shift in policy from neutrality to collective intervention, portrayed as a method of producing peace in the Far East. This shift was apparently induced by the intensified Japanese blockade and the bombardment of Nanking. Just as Secretary Stimson had collaborated with the League of Nations in its effort to stop Japan in Manchuria, and President Roosevelt had coöperated with the League in attempting to enforce sanctions against Italy during its conquest of Ethiopia, so now America again joined with the League when it lodged a protest against Japan.

[5] On March 17, 1938, Secretary Hull explained that the " circumstances " had not been foreseen by Congress and that " application of the law would be most likely to endanger the principal objectives which the law was designed to promote." *New York Times*, March 18, 1938. As nonintervention was the principal objective, the explanation was not very satisfying.

[6] *New York Sun*, Aug. 30, 1937, p. 1.

Once more Mr. Anthony Eden became active in his attentions to the United States; hope revived for an Anglo-American trade treaty, and officials of the two countries cooperated on treasury matters. France contributed its share by indicating a willingness to follow America's lead.[7] On September 20 the United States accepted the invitation of the League to send a nonvoting member to its Far Eastern Advisory Committee. Within a week the State Department protested twice to Japan against bombardment of noncombatants and nonmilitary areas in China, especially Nanking. Great Britain and Russia followed suit. At about the same time, the League committee adopted a resolution condemning the bombing of civilians; apparently Great Britain was feeling the pressure on her important commercial interests along the Yangtze. The press was full of atrocity stories and of a threatened British boycott against Japan.

In this way the ground was prepared for a determined effort to bring the United States and the League together in joint action. On October 4 the British delegation to the League proposed that the Far Eastern Committee summon the signatories of the Nine-Power Treaty, together with Germany and Russia, to " act on " the Sino-Japanese War. Next day the League committee pronounced Japan the " aggressor " and treaty-breaker, and invited the signatories of the Nine-Power Treaty to assemble, in company with some nonmembers.

On the same day in Chicago, President Roosevelt made what has become known as his " quarantine " speech, denouncing the " war-makers " and summoning the " peace-loving nations " to make a concerted effort to quarantine the one tenth who, he said, were intent upon war. In this effort he pledged the United States to take a part. Although America was not a party to the League Covenant, he deplored " definite violations of agreements, especially the Covenant of

[7] *New York Times*, Aug. 28, 1937, p. 4.

the League of Nations, the Briand-Kellogg Pact, and the Nine-Power Treaty." Arousing the shades of Wilsonian " idealism," the President invoked " international morality," " principles of the Prince of Peace," " world humanity," " moral consciousness," and the " heart of mankind."

. . . let no one imagine that America will escape, that it may expect mercy, that this Western Hemisphere will not be attacked and that it will continue tranquilly and peacefully to carry on the ethics and the arts of civilization.

Warming to his subject, the President next reverted to his well-known predilection for the League of Nation's theory of coercion:

. . . the peace-loving nations must make a concerted effort to uphold laws and principles on which alone peace can rest secure.

The peace-loving nations must make a concerted effort in opposition to those violations of treaties and those ignorings of humane instincts which today are creating a state of international anarchy and instability from which there is no escape through mere isolation or neutrality.

Having thus coupled the terms isolation and neutrality, as if they were synonymous, the President proceeded to the attack:

There is a solidarity and interdependence about the modern world, both technically and morally, which makes it impossible for any nation to completely isolate itself from economic and political upheavals in the rest of the world. . . . It is, therefore, a matter of vital interest and concern to the people of the United States that the sanctity of international treaties and the maintenance of international morality be restored.

Then came the passage which has earned for the speech the sobriquet of " The Quarantine Speech ":

It seems to be unfortunately true that the epidemic of world lawlessness is spreading.

When an epidemic of physical disease starts to spread, the community approves and joins in a quarantine of the patients in order to protect the health of the community against the spread of the disease.

The address closed with the ringing invocation:

America hates war. America hopes for peace. Therefore, America actively engages in the search for peace.[8]

It is scarcely surprising that also on October 5 the League of Nations committee rendered its report denouncing Japan as an aggressor [9] and convoking the Nine-Power signatories. If there was no coöperation between Washington and Geneva, there must have been telepathy.

Whether Washington's approach to intervention explains the refusal to invoke the Neutrality Act or not, the fact is that neutrality was thereafter ignored. The State Department promptly issued its unilateral judgment that Japan had violated the Nine-Power Treaty and the Kellogg Pact, and thus found itself " in general accord " with the Assembly of the League of Nations.[1] Prime Minister Chamberlain forthwith promised to back the United States in its effort to stop aggression. Senator Pittman, not to be outdone, returned to the charge and denounced Japan's " unlawful, immoral, and brutal conduct in China," and called on the world to boycott Japan. The New York Times announced in its headlines that the United States had " dropped neutrality policy to back League." [2]

[8] Press Releases, XVII, 275 ff.

[9] New York Times, Oct. 6, 1937. On October 5, Mr. Stimson wrote another letter to the Times advocating coercive action against Japan. New York Times, Oct. 7, 1937. Geneva was pleased. Idem, Oct. 8, 1937. See also Mr. Stimson's letter of Jan. 11, 1940, New York Times, Jan. 12, 1940.

[1] Press Releases, XVII, 284–285.

[2] The New York Times seems to have plumped wholeheartedly for intervention abroad. After the failure of the Brussels Conference, in an editorial of Nov. 30, 1937, entitled " America's Aloofness," it denounced those who spread abroad the conviction that the United States would remain neutral. It deplored the United States' loss of " its leadership in world affairs . . . the reason for this loss of influence is plain; treaty-breaking governments and dictators have become convinced that for no cause short of actual invasion will the United States initiate or join in any effective movement to assure world peace."

However, the " quarantine " speech met with a poor reception from the electorate. Indeed, it frightened the public into the belief that the President was contemplating another Wilsonian crusade for righteousness and that the result would again be war. Senators interested in neutrality attacked the speech, while reassuring statements were hurriedly issued from Washington. Nevertheless the administration went ahead with preparations to meet with the League Powers at Brussels, nineteen Powers convening under the misleading name of a conference of the signatories of the Nine-Power Treaty, to see what could be done about joint punitive action. Britain and France then delivered their surprise; they intimated that they would be too busy in Europe to take any active part in restoring " peace " to the Far East, but hoped that the United States would assume this burden.

On October 16 Senator Pittman went to some trouble to reconcile participation in the Brussels Conference with strict observance of neutrality. And the President issued a statement that the American delegation " will enter the Conference without any commitments on the part of this Government to other governments." [3] Yet the administration's continued denunciation of " treaty-breakers," isolation and trade barriers accompanied the expedition to Brussels.

On October 27 Japan declined to attend the meeting, and Germany immediately followed suit. Germany's diplomacy had been more clever than that of other countries in the Far East; its coöperation, as the Power most influential with Japan, was indispensable. Italy, repeatedly castigated along with Japan and Germany as wreckers of the peace, could hardly be expected to help make the Brussels meeting a success. On November 1 Mr. Eden plainly told the House of Commons that whatever action was taken in the Far East depended " essentially upon the coöperation of the United States." He stated: " I would go from Melbourne to Alaska

[3] *New York Times,* Oct. 20, 1937.

to get the United States to the conference." [4] Later, he attributed to the United States responsibility for convoking the conference. This Mr. Sumner Welles denied, admitting only our selection of Brussels for the meeting. But Edwin L. James of the *Times*, usually well informed on League diplomacy, wrote: " It is not of record that Britain, or anyone else, forced us to inspire the calling of the sad Brussels conference. It was our idea; it was our party." [5]

On November 3 the Conference opened. Mr. Norman Davis, whose forays in diplomacy seem to be cursed by unremitting failure, made a speech, reminiscent of Geneva, denouncing war and approving peace. Mediation was discussed. Soviet Russia was said to be lining up against the dictatorships. On November 4 Hitler actually offered his services as mediator to the belligerents. On the 6th Italy joined Japan and Germany in the Anti-Comintern Pact. That same day the Conference cautiously inquired whether Japan would be willing to discuss peace terms with a small number of Powers. When Japan reiterated its refusal to participate, the Conference adopted a mild reproof. Japan had maintained that she had not violated the Nine-Power Treaty and that any action proposed by the conferees should not be based on that treaty. This conclusion the resolution denied; but in spite of its mildness, Italy voted against it and the three Scandinavian delegates abstained. Only one further resolution emanated from the Conference. On November 24, eighteen of the nineteen Powers present pledged their allegiance to peace, coöperation, and the sanctity of treaties.

Thus, another effort of the United States to coöperate with the League of Nations to " enforce peace " came to a rather ignominious end. The *Herald Tribune,* in an editorial [6] en-

---

[4] *New York Times,* Nov. 21, 1937. This seems too roundabout a trip. In December, 1938, he came directly to Washington. *Infra,* p. 392.

[5] *New York Times,* Nov. 21, 1937.

[6] Nov. 17, 1937.

titled "The Miscarriage at Brussels," blamed this on "several singularly stupid moves." The first was the President's threat of a quarantine against "aggressors." The second was Anthony Eden's inadvertent admission in the House of Commons that the conference was held under a mandate from the League of Nations, a body that had already condemned Japan and that had no authority to summon either the United States or Japan to a conference of Pacific Powers. The third blunder was the invitation of eleven nations that were not parties to the Nine-Power Treaty and had no right to discuss Japan's conduct as a signatory of that Treaty.

The Department of State, however, consoled itself for the manifest failure of the Brussels Conference with a statement by the Secretary: [7]

The Conference made a substantial contribution toward keeping alive principles of world order and of respect for the pledged word. Its declarations placed a new emphasis upon the deep concern of peaceful nations over any developments that threaten the preservation of peace.

Perhaps it was the chastening experience of Brussels which persuaded the administration to handle the *Panay* incident of December, 1937, with circumspection. In this they were aided by the manifest desire of Japan not to permit trouble to arise out of the blunder of Japanese aviators in dropping bombs on an American naval vessel on the Yangtze River; in the light of the hostility toward Japan that the bombing of Nanking and the whole invasion of China had developed in Washington, it would easily have been possible to play up the *Panay* incident as a matter of "national honor." Japan promptly paid some $2,400,000, the entire bill presented by the United States, including indemnity for the sinking of some oil barges and the loss of American and Chinese lives.

[7] Address on "Our Foreign Policy" by Secretary Hull, March 17, 1938, National Press Club, Department of State, Publication No. 1146.

But later, on examination of the claims,[8] the State Department discovered that the damages had been exaggerated; it is to be expected that the excess paid the United States will be returned or credited to Japan in due course.

Aside from the *Panay,* numerous incidents arose in China during 1938 and 1939 to cause irritation in the Department of State. The American flag was mutilated by Japanese soldiers at one point, and a third Secretary of Legation had his face slapped in Nanking. The British suffered even more severely, especially at Tientsin. But as Japan indicated a desire to appease and conciliate the United States in connection with incidents which it called inevitable in time of war, American protests did not reach the dangerous stage. Claims have been filed for pecuniary compensation for any losses sustained; their validity in law is doubtful, however, in view of the fact that foreigners recovered no damages from the United States for legitimate injuries sustained during the Civil War in accordance with the general principle that neutrals in belligerent territory take the risk of their location.[9]

Education and Enlightenment

THE administration expressed its disappointment at international developments in the form of public statements which condemned all aggressors, Japan especially. Reference has already been made to the statement of Secretary Hull, circularized to all the nations, which was called " fundamental principles of international policy." [10] Inasmuch as that com-

[8] On Dec. 15, 1938, it was announced that the *Panay* claimants were angry at the delay in paying them. *New York Times,* Dec. 15, 1938.

[9] Borchard, *Diplomatic Protection of Citizens Abroad* (New York, 1915), sec. 103.

[10] July 16, 1937, Department of State, Publication No. 1079. The Council of the League of Nations hastened to approve the statement. *League of Nations Official Journal,* XVIII (1937), 922. Mr. Hull's statement and all the replies received were published as a League document, *Official Journal,* Special Suppl. No. 179 (1937).

mitted the nations to nothing, most of them subscribed to its sentiments promptly.

The fact is that probably every nation in the world has violated at one time or another every one of the prescriptions announced as the fundamental principles of international policy. Historians are not entirely lenient with United States policy in connection with the acquisition of East Florida, in connection with the Mexican War, the Spanish War, and the Panama incident of 1903, in the Caribbean, and in the invasion of Vera Cruz in 1914 when American marines in times of peace unfortunately killed nearly three hundred civilians, Mexicans and foreigners. This is not said in disparagement of principles which Mr. Hull probably applies with greater faithfulness than many another Secretary. But the United States is not immune from criticism, even for treaty violation. In 1798 Congress unilaterally abrogated the Treaty of 1778 with France. The Chinese Treaty of 1868 was violated by the Exclusion Act of 1882. In 1935 we violated the 1911 treaty with Italy; in 1937, the 1902 treaty with Spain; in 1938–39, the 1911 treaty with Japan by the imposition of " moral embargoes." The United States still holds millions of dollars' worth of German private property — much of it no longer German — from the last war, though its immunity was guaranteed by treaty and solemn presidential promise. Tariff treaties have frequently been modified by municipal statute, without so much as a by-your-leave. Secretary Gresham is said to have remarked that the United States was peculiarly prone to violate treaties.

It might even be supposed that we are rather an aggressive Power, fighting not only for ourselves on slight provocation, but protesting — if not worse — against " acts of aggression against sister nations." [1] We are not any more peace-loving than others, although we have more reason to

[1] President's address to Congress, Jan. 4, 1939, *Cong. Rec.*, LXXXIV, 74–77.

be. When Theodore Roosevelt in Milwaukee confided to his audience that he knew his fellow countrymen and that they would fight at the drop of a hat, they cheered and considered themselves complimented.

The President's restlessness under world disorder was indicated by his address to Congress of January 3, 1938. Among other things he said:

In spite of the determination of this Nation for peace, it has become clear that acts and policies of nations in other parts of the world have far-reaching effects not only upon their immediate neighbors but also on us.

. . .

But in a world of high tension and disorder, in a world where stable civilization is actually threatened, it becomes the responsibility of each nation which strives for peace at home and peace with and among others to be strong enough to assure the observance of those fundamentals of peaceful solution of conflicts which are the only ultimate basis for orderly existence.

. . .

There is a trend in the world away from the observance both of the letter and the spirit of treaties. We propose to observe, as we have in the past, our own treaty obligations; but we cannot be certain of reciprocity on the part of others.

Disregard for treaty obligations seem to have followed the surface trend away from the democratic representative form of government. It would seem, therefore, that world peace through international agreements is most safe in the hands of democratic representative governments — or, in other words, peace is most greatly jeopardized in and by those nations where democracy has been discarded or has never developed.[2]

It is an axiom of diplomacy that nations resent having their shortcomings pointed out to them. Reiterated statements that the United States bore ill will and hostility to Italy, Germany, Japan, and, more lately, Soviet Russia, have not tended to promote the peace of the world or the peace of the United States. This is the more regrettable because the sinfulness

[2] Press Releases, XVIII (Jan. 8, 1938), 31–32.

of those nations is not primarily directed toward the United States but toward others whom it seems now that the United States is obliging itself to defend.[3] The ambiguous, moralistic theory — a Geneva invention — that the use of force anywhere is of " concern " to everyone, especially the United States apparently, is an excuse for perpetual intervention. We have subscribed to and invited the perils of the League of Nations theory in their worst possible form, for we undertake now to do *alone* what the League Covenant at least provides should be done only in combination so as to limit the liabilities and risks of contributing members. It is therefore a little strange that the Secretary of State in his speech of March 17, 1938, maintained that " our Government pursues, in relation to every world area alike, a policy of noninterference, with ill will toward no nation and a sincere desire to be friendly with all." [4]

When the Secretary of State intelligently remarked on August 16, 1938,[5] " the World War left a legacy of deep-seated maladjustments within and among nations. But out of it also emerged a passionate desire among peoples everywhere for enduring peace, order and progress," he failed to indicate how the maladjustments were to be corrected. From the history of the past twenty years, we are well aware that these maladjustments were not corrected in time, but were permitted to eat their way into the very lives of people until revolution was inspired against the whole Versailles system. To meet such an upheaval — especially when it is under the direction of revolutionary extremists — by moral preachment, is a long way from practical. To identify that system and its political arrangements as " law and order " is to rub salt into open wounds.[6]

[3] See the President's address, Jan. 4, 1939. Cf. *infra*, p. 382.
[4] Department of State, Publication No. 1146.
[5] Department of State, Publication No. 1225.
[6] Cf. the penetrating criticism of this theory by Lord Lothian in the House of Lords, Feb. 24, 1938, *London Times*, Feb. 25, 1938, p. 8.

No solution to European or Asiatic maladjustments was afforded by the remark:

In common with all other nations we have, since the end of the World War, assumed a solemn obligation not to resort to force as an instrument of national policy. All this gives us a moral right to express our deep concern over the rising tide of lawlessness, the growing disregard of treaties, the increasing reversion to the use of force, and the numerous other ominous tendencies which are emerging in the sphere of international relations.[7]

Nor was confidence in the value of parallel action promoted by the statement:

The maintenance of these principles that are of concern to all nations alike cannot and should not be undertaken by any one nation alone. Prudence and common sense dictate that, where this and other nations have common interests and common objectives, we should not hesitate to exchange information and to confer with the governments of such other nations and, in dealing with the problems confronting each alike, to proceed along parallel lines — this Government retaining at all times its independence of judgment and freedom of action. For nations which seek peace to assume with respect to each other attitudes of complete aloofness would serve only to encourage, and virtually invite, on the part of other nations lawlessly inclined, policies and actions most likely to endanger peace. . . .

We have affirmed on every possible occasion and have urged upon all nations the supreme need for keeping alive and for practicing sound fundamental principles of relations among civilized nations. We have never entertained and we have not the slightest intention to entertain any such notion as the use of American armed forces for " policing the world." But we equally have not the slightest intention of reversing a tradition of a century and a half by abandoning our deep concern for, and our advocacy of, the establishment everywhere of international order under law, based upon the well-recognized principles to which I have referred. . . .

The momentous question — let me repeat — is whether the doctrine of force shall become enthroned once more and bring in its wake, inexorably, international anarchy and a relapse into bar-

---

[7] Address of March 17, 1938, Department of State, Publication No. 1146.

barism; or whether this and other peaceful nations, fervently attached to the principles which underlie international order, shall work unceasingly — singly or in coöperation with each other, as circumstances, their traditional policies and practices, and their enlightened self-interest may dictate — to promote and preserve law, order, morality, and justice as the unshakeable bases of civilized international relations. . . .[8]

These statements, which undoubtedly were well meant and reflect the benevolence of a kindly man, aroused forebodings in the minds of those who wished to keep the United States out of foreign wars.

Toward Intervention

UNEASINESS in Congress was reflected by resolutions designed to bring about the application of the Neutrality Act in the Far East. In December, 1937, the Secretary of State replied to an inquiry of Representative Case of South Dakota, as to whether or not a state of war existed in China, by asserting that the Department considered it was the chief purpose of the neutrality laws to keep the United States out of war. The reply was hardly responsive to the question. Nor was it altogether accurate for the Secretary to say on March 17, 1938, that " accordingly, exercising the discretion vested in him by the law itself, the President has refrained from putting the provisions of that law into operation." As has been suggested, the law did not give the President that discretion. The law provided that when he found a state of war to exist, then the act automatically came into force. The President refused to " find " a fact — war — which was obvious to the entire world and which does not depend on labels, declaration, admission, or recognition, bestowed either by the

[8] *Idem.* Prime Minister Chamberlain admitted in the House of Commons that " collective security " now " does not differ from the old alliance of pre-war days, which we thought we had abandoned in favor of something better." *London Times,* March 25, 1938, p. 7.

parties or by outside persons.[9] War is a fact, not merely a name. When organized armies are killing each other by the thousand, it is war — in any language.

To provide some semblance of legality for the President's continued exercise of discretion in applying the neutrality laws, an amendment was introduced in the Neutrality Act of November 4, 1939, adding a further condition for bringing the act into force; namely, that its application be "necessary to promote the security or preserve the peace of the United States or to protect the lives of citizens of the United States." That condition is so broad and uncontrollable as now really to make the invocation of the act discretionary with the President — or Congress, if the President hesitates.[1]

Fears of intervention were not allayed by the administration's powerful attack upon the Ludlow Resolution, a bill designed to insure a vote of the people before American troops could be sent to fight on foreign soil. The resolution was defeated on January 10, 1938, but only by the narrow margin of 209 to 188.[2]

Then there was Mr. Hull's statement that the United States was "deeply interested in supporting by peaceful means influences contributory to preservation and encour-

[9] The recent testimony of officials of the Department of State on the loan to Finland to the effect that when the parties do not admit that they are at war, it is optional with the United States to concede it to be war or not, as American interests might dictate, is extraordinary. (Hearings on S. 3069, Committee on Foreign Relations, U. S. Senate, 76th Cong., 3d Sess. [Jan. 31, 1940], pp. 39–41.) War's existence entails neutral obligations on nonparticipants. It is not permissible to ignore a state of war and help one side defeat the other by public loans, under or outside the Neutrality Act. Norway and Sweden took no such position as the United States. *New York Times,* Feb. 20, 1940. They declared their official neutrality — although private aid was allowed to continue.

[1] A Senate subcommittee in March, 1940, reported against invoking the act in Finland or China. *New Haven Register,* March 5, 1940.

[2] *New York Times,* Jan. 11, 1938. Cf. W. H. Shepardson, *The United States in World Affairs, 1938,* p. 156. On Jan. 8, 1940, a similar resolution was introduced by Representative Fish.

agement of orderly processes. This interest far transcends in importance the value of American trade with China or American investments in China. It transcends even the question of safeguarding the immediate welfare of American citizens in China." [3] A good many Senators felt that on the wings of this transcendentalism, where " orderly processes " take precedence over American lives, we were getting into dangerous altitudes.[4]

The *Philadelphia Record* of January 12 was led to remark, in an editorial entitled " The Marquis of Queensberry ":

His notes, letters, statements constitute a rules book that strives to bring the brutal realities of expansion, conquest and war into line with the ideals of a chivalrous Tennessee gentleman, for whose motives we have only the highest respect.

Nobody has the remotest notion of obeying the rules but apparently that doesn't matter to Mr. Hull. As long as he can write the world's moral platitudes, he cares not who makes its bombs.

That was perhaps a little harsh on Mr. Hull, who doubtless realizes how far from actual observance are his lofty principles. But there is the danger that his principles may not cope sufficiently with the psychological reasons for mass movements, and that by viewing them as moral or immoral, the Secretary overlooks their nature.

Expressions of official dissatisfaction with the neutrality

[3] Letter of Secretary Hull to Vice-President Garner, Jan. 6, 1938. *New York Times,* Jan. 11, 1938.

[4] Apprehensions were increased by Secretary Hull's statement of Sept. 10, 1938, in accepting Peru's invitation to the Lima Conference, that " the nations of the world are faced with the issue of determining whether relations shall be characterized by internal anarchy and lawlessness or by principles of fair play, justice and order under law. No nation and no government can avoid the issue; neither can any nation avoid participation, willing or not, in the responsibility of determining which course of action shall prevail." *New York Herald Tribune,* Sept. 11, 1938. The day before the President had taken the newspapers severely to task for creating the impression that he was disposed to assume moral commitments to support the democracies against the totalitarian bloc if war should come. *New York Times,* Sept. 10, 1938.

laws followed.[5] Mr. Hull criticized isolationism as an attempt "to confine all activities of our people within our own frontiers, with incalculable injury to the standard of living and the general welfare of our people, or else expose our nationals and our legitimate interests abroad to injustice or outrage wherever lawless conditions arise." [6] Washington and others among the founding fathers of American foreign policy would have been surprised at this definition of their position. So were such Senators as Borah and Johnson.

In his speech on May 28, 1939, Secretary Hull said:

There is no more disastrous illusion than the thought that a policy of national isolation would make it easier for us to solve our great domestic problems. The exact reverse is true . . .

Some argue in favor of national isolation from another point of view — namely, that by withdrawing from normal relations with other nations we can insure for ourselves freedom from risk of embroilment in war. Here again the exact reverse is true.

It is not through a policy of isolation but rather through supplementing our domestic efforts by playing our appropriate role as a member of the family of nations that we can hope to solve the problems which confront us today within our own frontiers.[6a]

So far as is known, no one in Congress had advocated such a policy of national isolation as the Secretary suggested. The only proposed withdrawal from normal relations has come from those advocating embargoes and discriminatory tariffs with which to cut down our foreign trade with countries on an executive black list. It is at least curious to have caution, self-restraint, a philosophical understanding of historical and psychological processes and of the limitations and dangers of intervention characterized as "isolation." Heretofore denunciations, name-calling, meddling, threats, embargoes, sanctions, and growing armaments had not been thought of as methods of creating peace.

[5] Cf. Report of Press Conference, April 22, 1938, *New York Times,* April 23, 1938.
[6] Department of State, Publication No. 1146.
[6a] *New York Times,* May 29, 1939.

On June 3, 1938, Secretary Hull, addressing the Tennessee Bar Association, repudiated national isolation as a means of security,[7] and a few days later Assistant Secretary Sayre remarked, " The United States cannot afford to be a cipher in this crucial period of the world's history. We must be resolute and prepared if necessary to withstand the aggression of the lawless." [8]

Not long afterwards, Senator Pittman issued his personal declaration of war against Germany, Italy, and Japan. He said,

" 1. The people of the United States do not like the Government of Japan.

" 2. The people of the United States do not like the Government of Germany.

" 3. The people of the United States, in my opinion, are against any form of dictatorial government, communistic or fascistic.

" 4. The people of the United States have the right and power to enforce morality and justice in accordance with peace treaties with us. And they will. Our government does not have to use military force and will not unless necessary." [9]

All these expressions of official opinion, whether so intended or not, were naturally interpreted as a commitment to an interventionist foreign policy.

The alarm of noninterventionists was increased by the President's address to Congress on January 4, 1939.[9a] This had all the earmarks of a proposed crusade against aggressors on behalf of religion, democracy, and good faith. His advocacy of hostile " methods short of war " was not reas-

---

[7] He considered it a " fruitful source of insecurity." Department of State, Publication No. 1190, p. 14.

[8] June 6, 1938, Department of State, Publication No. 1186, p. 3.

[9] *New York Times*, Dec. 23, 1938.

[9a] House Document No. I, 76th Cong., 1st Sess.

suring, for war always begins with a series of hostile measures short of war. Among other things, the President said:

Storms from abroad directly challenge three institutions indispensable to Americans, now as always. The first is religion. It is
the source of the other two — democracy and international good
faith. . . .

There comes a time in the affairs of men when they must prepare
to defend not their homes alone but the tenets of faith and humanity on which their churches, their governments, and their very
civilization are founded. The defense of religion, of democracy,
and of good faith among nations is all the same fight. To save one
we must now make up our minds to save all.

We have learned that God-fearing democracies of the world
which observe the sanctity of treaties and good faith in their dealings with other nations cannot safely be indifferent to international
lawlessness anywhere. They cannot forever let pass, without effective protest, acts of aggression against sister nations — acts which
automatically undermine all of us.

Obviously they must proceed along practical, peaceful lines. But
the mere fact that we rightly decline to intervene with arms to
prevent acts of aggression does not mean that we must act as if
there were no aggression at all. Words may be futile, but war is
not the only means of commanding a decent respect for the opinions of mankind. There are many methods short of war, but
stronger and more effective than mere words, of bringing home to
aggressor governments the aggregate sentiments of our own people.

There followed a secret conference on January 31, 1939,
between the President and members of the Senate Committee on Foreign Affairs, after which the rumor got out
that the President considered that America's frontier lay " in
France." While branding the rumor as a falsehood, the President gave out the following simple statement of American
policy:

Number 1: We are against any entangling alliances, obviously.

Number 2: We are in favor of the maintenance of world trade
for everybody — all nations — including ourselves.

Number 3: We are in complete sympathy with any and every
effort made to reduce or limit armaments.

Number 4: As a Nation — as American people — we are sympathetic with the peaceful maintenance of political, economic, and social independence of all nations in the world.[10]

With great respect, it may be suggested that such general statements are fairly meaningless. They become inconsistent in the face of the demands of 1938, 1939, and 1940 for an increase of several billion dollars in the Army and Navy budgets.

Big Navy

In a critical comment in the *New Republic*[1] under the title "Whom Are We Getting Ready to Fight?" John T. Flynn, an economist who sees beyond the figures, deplores the neglect of many domestic problems in the 1941 budget and emphasizes the extravagant increases in Army and Navy appropriations in the last eight budgets. Mr. Flynn gives the following figures:

1933–34	$ 640,356,000
1934–35	729,931,000
1935–36	921,684,000
1936–37	935,114,000
1937–38	1,027,841,000
1938–39	1,119,810,000
1939–40	1,734,342,253
1940–41	2,116,169,000 [2]

Numerous witnesses before the Senate Naval Affairs Committee in 1938, acting on the President's proposal for a 20 per cent increase in the Navy, pointed out that such an enormous program for naval expansion was hardly consistent with the policy of defending the home grounds against

[10] Department of State, Press Releases, XX, 99.

[1] Jan. 22, 1940, p. 115.

[2] These figures are broken down by Mr. Stone in Foreign Policy Asso., Bulletin XIX, No. 13 (Jan. 19, 1940), 4.

invaders. Dr. Beard in his testimony accused the administration of fomenting a war scare.

We are told [he said] that the Fascist goblins of Europe are about to take South America, that Mussolini will march in seven league boots across the Atlantic, through the Straits of Gibraltar, to Brazil, or that Hitler or the Mikado will do it some other way . . . This is the new racket created to herd the American people into President Roosevelt's quarantine camp.[3]

Indeed, the administration's plan for industrial mobilization and an army of four to five millions, as set forth in the May bill, is consistent only with adventures abroad. Justified as a bill to take the profits out of war, it authorizes an Executive regimentation of nearly every aspect of American life. Congressman Maverick, the President's friend, denounced it as " a blue print for fascism." And this hysterical inflation of the apparatus of belligerency comes at a time when, through the internecine strife of Europe and Asia, the United States is becoming relatively stronger, not weaker.

Dr. Beard characterized the President's policy as follows:

Hovering over the scene is the prospect of war. That President Roosevelt would struggle in the last ditch to keep the country out of foreign wars may well be doubted. He has, to be sure, expressed hostility to war. But realists in politics, while accepting the sincerity of his present intentions, take no stock in such declarations by rulers anywhere. Besides, President Roosevelt is more or less obsessed by the universal philanthropy of Woodrow Wilson. Like Wilson, he feels that America is morally bound to do good everywhere and imagines himself able to know the good in each and every case. Students of Wilson's letters and papers know that Wilson was eager to play a grand part on the world stage. That he might make himself the greatest man in all history by keeping the United States out of war never seemed to occur to him. . . .

Believing that he is under moral obligation to help decide the age-long quarrels of Europe and Asia, President Roosevelt has resisted every effort of Congress and the country to impose limits on his powers of intervention abroad. More than this. He has man-

[3] *Cong. Digest*, XIX, 91.

aged to destroy the letter and spirit of the first neutrality legislation and to acquire for himself almost dictatorial powers over American economy in relation to diplomacy and war — by the Neutrality Act of 1937. He would not have done this unless he believed that he was bound to help pass on the righteousness of foreign quarrels and intended to use all his powers, old and new, for such interventionist purposes. The policy of silence is foreign to the exuberance of his nature.[4]

Policies of hostility, coercion, and discrimination necessarily require large armies and navies. But when, in addition to the vast appropriations of 1939, a 25 per cent increase was asked for 1940, believers in nonintervention stood aghast. Admiral Stark, Chief of Naval Operations, supported his demand before the Naval Affairs Committee by politico-moral arguments concerning treaty-breakers and international faithlessness, quite unexpected in a practical Navy man. He then stated that we would have to have a Navy large enough to protect everything on this continent plus outlying possessions against a combination of " our potential enemies in both oceans," referring to Japan, Germany, Italy, and Russia as a coalition that had been mentioned before the Committee.[5] This luxury of conjuring up enemies, an indulgence which no other government could afford, may yet succeed in producing the coalition and war it invites.

Anti-Japanese Embargoes

THE irritation of the Department of State at Japan's conduct of the war found expression, as already observed, in what has been called an Executive " moral embargo." As in in the case of Ethiopia, a circular letter was issued on July 1, 1938, to arms manufacturers and exporters registered under the Neutrality Act, informing them that the Department

[4] Charles A. Beard, " Roosevelt's Place in History," *Events,* February, 1938, pp. 84–85.

[5] *New York Times,* Jan. 12, 1940.

" would with great regret issue any licenses authorizing exportation, direct or indirect, of any aircraft, aircraft armaments, aircraft engines, aircraft parts, aircraft accessories," etc., " to countries the armed forces of which are making use of airplanes for attack upon civilian populations." Two American manufacturers who for various reasons did not conform to this admonition were held up to public obloquy.[6] Again, in August, 1939, the Department announced that national interests suggested that there be " no further delivery to certain countries of plans, plants, manufacturing rights or technical information required for the production of high quality aviation gasoline." [7] The ostensible justification was that this was undertaken " with a view to conserving in this country certain technical information of strategic importance," although such shipments were apparently in order if sent to any country other than Japan. The State Department's suggestion was also said to be an extension of the policy of discouraging the sale of airplanes, equipment, etc., to countries " which are engaged in unprovoked bombing or machine gunning of civilian populations from the air." The word " unprovoked " may be significant, for favored countries could be excepted on the ground that their bombing was " provoked."

Apart from the fact that these moral embargoes have no authority in law and constitute a coercive exercise of the Executive's power over manufacturers in execution of a policy unauthorized by Congress, such embargoes, prior to January 26, 1940, openly violated the United States commercial treaty with Japan. Article 5 of the Treaty of 1911 with Japan contains the following sentence: " Nor shall any prohibition be imposed by either country on the importation or exportation of any article from or to the territories of the other which shall not equally extend to the like article

[6] Department of State, Bulletin I, 121.
[7] *Idem*, 714.

imported from or exported to any other country." Unlike the Nine-Power Treaty, a vague political treaty susceptible of political interpretation, this was part of a general commercial treaty. A discriminatory export embargo is a specific violation of this sentence of Article 5. The United States was thus in the position of violating a legal treaty in order to exert reprisals for the supposed violation of a political treaty.

Political treaties are not like contracts. No one should expect them to last indefinitely, nor can they be interpreted in the way contracts or legal provisions are interpreted. The political character of the Nine-Power Treaty has already been noted.[8] Respect for " the territorial and administrative integrity " of China conveys no distinct legal meaning. Similarly the term " Open Door " in Section 3 of the Treaty is too vague to provide the foundation for a legal case. The Nine-Power Treaty may have served the purpose of a temporary stabilization, but it could not resist the fermentation which has become indigenous to Asia in the last generation.

The Kellogg Pact is even more political than the Nine-Power Treaty, if, indeed, it has any content. The reservations embodied in the exchange of notes which interpret the treaty provide that it does not cover a war of self-defense, each party being the exclusive and unreviewable judge of the question whether it is engaged in self-defence. Japan has claimed " self-defence." That settles the legal question as to whether the Kellogg Pact is being violated.[9]

Any statesman who now invokes the Kellogg Pact stands as a self-confessed interventionist. Having no legal substance or content, that pact has become merely an incitement to intervention in the affairs of other people. It was inappropriate for the United States to take occasion to remind both the Italian and the Ethiopian Governments of

---

[8] *Supra*, p. 364.

[9] As to other limitations on the Kellogg Pact, see *supra*, p. 289 *et seq.*

their obligations under the Pact of Paris. It was equally inappropriate when in October, 1937, Washington informed Japan that it was violating the Nine-Power Treaty and the Kellogg Pact. There is no privilege in one party to a treaty to make itself its authoritative interpreter, and more especially to assume under it the power of punishment. It might as well be suggested that a party to a private contract be allowed to constitute himself the judge of whether his co-contractor was violating the contract and, without a hearing, to exert reprisals. Yet in the much more dangerous and politically surcharged field of international relations, that is what is now proposed by advocates of an embargo on raw materials against Japan. It could hardly be assumed that one party to the treaty is unbiased in characterizing as illegal steps taken by another party now under opprobrium. Quite apart from the substance of the issue, therefore, it is extraordinary to suggest that the United States shall be the exclusive judge of the propriety of the conduct of its co-contractor and, without a hearing, condemn that co-contractor to penalties.[10]

If foreign countries should take it into their heads to exert reprisals on the United States whenever American actions displeased them, and if they excused the step by alleging that we violated international law or a treaty, we should, with entire justification, feel deeply aggrieved. The procedure would not be likely to make for the peace of nations. It may be said that the period since 1919 has been extraordinarily fertile in discovering new ways to bring about antagonism among the peoples of the earth. In this category may be included Articles 10 and 16 of the League of Nations Covenant, guaranteeing the status quo and exerting sanctions

[10] Even in the field of contracts, the Supreme Court often finds that statutory encroachments on the obligation of contracts are not unconstitutional, although a layman might easily conclude that they were. Cf. The Minnesota Mortgage Moratorium case, 290 U. S. 398 (1934).

upon those who would upset it. In this category also would belong the proposals for penalties and embargoes against countries that displease.[1]

Threatened Embargo on Raw Materials. There has been a reasonably effective American embargo on arms, ammunition, and implements of war against Japan since July, 1938. To make possible further embargoes, notice was given to Japan by the Executive on July 26, 1939, that our commercial treaty with her would be terminated as of January 26, 1940. In the intervening period, the movement for a complete embargo, especially on raw materials, has been assiduously promoted by sanctionist groups. In franker days, this would have been called by its right name, " commercial war." If commercial exchanges make for peace, as the world is assured, the cutting off of a country's trade must logically be

---

[1] When Poland in time of peace (1920) seized Vilna from Lithuania, no outcry was heard in England, France, or the United States.

The Germans occupied Vilna in 1915 and held it until they retreated in November, 1918. They handed it over to the Lithuanians, who occupied it until January, 1919. At that time, the Russians drove the Lithuanians out. The Poles took the city in April, 1919, and held it until July, 1920, when they were forced to retire before Russian advances.

Under a treaty of July 12, 1920, Lithuania agreed to support Russia and in return received Vilna and other parts of Russian territory. In August, 1920, the tide of war turned in favor of Poland. On Sept. 5, 1920, Poland appealed to the League on the Vilna question. Lithuania accepted League conciliation for purposes of the dispute. Lithuania finally agreed to accept the old " Curzon line," which had been drawn on Dec. 8, 1919, by the Conference of Ambassadors and which did not give Poland Vilna. An armistice was drawn up, which was to have gone into effect on Oct. 10, 1920, but on Oct. 9, 1920, General Zeligovski occupied Vilna and claimed it and a large part of the adjacent territory for Poland.

Poland disavowed his action but accepted its results as a *fait accompli,* taking the case out of the League's hands. The League tried to force a plebiscite but could not secure Polish evacuation or the international police force necessary to supervise it. Through Hymans of Belgium as its representative it then tried to secure negotiation and settlement. This also failed and the commission lapsed January, 1922.

On Feb. 15, 1923, Poland appealed to the Conference of Ambassadors and got recognition based on the " de facto situation."

Reported in *Survey of International Affairs, 1920–1923* (Oxford University Press), pp. 251–253; cf. *For. Rel.,* 1920, III, 376 *et seq.*

a hostile act. There is undoubtedly in this country a strong emotional opposition to what Japan has been doing, although it is doubtful whether most of the protestants have attempted to analyze the forces underlying the present war. An official spokesman of Japan has recently been quoted as follows: [2] " Should Congress follow with an embargo bill — even though it only potentially authorizes an embargo — I am frank to say it would be regarded by the Japanese people as a serious affront." It would indeed be tantamount to an act of war, and the embargo would probably not stop the war in China. Japan can probably procure in England, Germany, and elsewhere anything we embargo, but we shall have made a long-time enemy out of Japan. While the embargo has been under discussion here, meetings have been held in England to increase British trade with Japan.[3]

American unneutrality, evidenced in moral embargoes and denunciations of Japan, and in a Government loan of $25,-000,000 to China — recently increased — could now easily develop into a war with Japan. That would be highly injurious to the United States and might even bring about an understanding between Russia, Japan, and China to resist the interloper.[4] The United States could become more heavily bogged in Asia than it was in Europe. The sanctions attempted against Mussolini ought not to be forgotten, for their effects [5] constitute a lesson in human psychology which present-day sanctionists are disposed to overlook.

[2] *New Haven Register,* Jan. 31, 1940.

[3] *New York Times,* Jan. 25, 1940. The unwisdom of applying an embargo against Japan is competently exposed in an article by Prof. A. Whitney Griswold " Should Japan Be Embargoed," *Asia* (Feb., 1940), p. 92. On March 28, 1940, Ambassador Craigie made a very conciliatory speech in Tokio, indicating a British-Japanese rapprochement. This gave the interventionist press great pain. Cf. *New York Times,* March 29, April 4, 1940; *New York Herald Tribune,* April 3, 1940.

[4] Constructive ideas for a new treaty with Japan are presented in Griswold, " Facing Facts About a New Japanese-American Treaty," *Asia* (Nov., 1939).

[5] *Supra,* p. 274.

Austria, Czechoslovakia, Memel, and Albania

THE tendency to intervene actively in the Far East was tempered by developments in Europe. First came the incorporation of Austria into the Reich in March, 1938. This produced more condemnation among the peace missionaries of America than in Europe. Europeans had long anticipated the move. Administration spokesmen here denounced the dictators anew. Repellent as were some of the incidents of the Austrian occupation, Austria had been placed in an economic situation where annexation to Germany was only a question of time; [6] and American denunciation could not stop further annexations. By September, Hitler had steered Chamberlain into a position where England had to accept annexation of the Sudetenland. France, a special guarantor of Czechoslovakia, tagged along to complete the puncture of Article 10 of the League Covenant. Again Chamberlain was denounced in our Eastern press, whereas among his own people generally his action was approved. Perhaps Mr. Chamberlain was slightly naïve, for he apparently believed that after Munich the rest of Czechoslovakia could be preserved. But he took no chances; Britain stepped up her production of arms and Mr. Anthony Eden was delegated to make a trip to the United States and the White House for a purpose never disclosed.

Whether Chamberlain turned from Munich because of what Eden learned in America or because of the German intention to occupy the rest of Czechoslovakia may not be known for some time. At all events, in the middle of March, 1939, German impatience to occupy Prague [7] put an end to the policy of appeasement and turned Europe to war. The

---

[6] The break-up of the Austro-Hungarian Empire and the creation of a number of small, theoretically independent states was one of the mistakes of Versailles. At least this particular one Wilson had not advised. Austria had not been allowed the means to live, and her life was always precarious.

[7] *New York Times*, March 15, 1939, p. 1.

sources of these European movements lie deep in history and in the constant play for power which characterizes European politics. The creation at Versailles of new states in eastern Europe had political motives closely associated with the balance of power. The very existence of these states was conditioned upon a weakened if not disarmed Germany. The rearmament of that country upset the foundations of Versailles and initiated a renewed struggle to change the balance of power. The fact that a certain vocal group of Americans are so prone immediately to pronounce a moral judgment on these fluctuations in European politics is disquieting. It is a mark of unsophistication and symbolizes the susceptibility of many influential Americans to foreign entanglements.[8] It was not always so.[9]

Although the United States was not a party to the treaty which guaranteed Czechoslovakia, the Under-Secretary of State felt called upon to announce " this country's condemnation " and to remark:

[8] Cf. Beard, *Giddy Minds and Foreign Quarrels* (New York, 1939).

[9] Cf. the intelligent view of European power politics and neutral states exhibited by Attorney General Caleb Cushing in 1855: " Thus, in Europe, it generally happens that war is commenced between two or three of the great powers for purposes of mutual jealousy or ambition of their own, and as to which the other states are comparatively indifferent in feeling or interest, or have conflicting interests, which impel them to remain neutral in the war. But, very soon, as the burden of the war presses on one or another of the belligerents, he, having undertaken more than he can accomplish alone, seeks to persuade or compel the neutral states to join him. Or he cannot efficiently attack his enemy, without occupying the territory or the ports of some neutral state. Or, perceiving that his own commercial resources are wasting away in the war, he looks resentfully on the prosperity of some neutral state, whose commerce flourishes at his expense. Or, jealous of the intentions of a neutral state, and fearing it may join his enemy, he seeks to anticipate such an event by crippling the military forces of such neutral state. Or, finally, becoming fatally engaged in a protracted war, until it has at length degenerated into a mere wilful contest of pride and passion, the belligerent enters upon the desperate and frantic plan of starving his adversary by cutting off all neutral commerce, the very attempt to do which is an outrage on the law of nations, and can be carried out only by the perpetration of every kind of violence and fraud on the neutral nations." 7 Op. Atty. Gen. 126, April 28, 1855, Opinion on case of the *Sitka,* given to Marcy, Secretary of State.

It is manifest that acts of wanton lawlessness and of arbitrary force are threatening world peace and the very structure of modern civilization. The imperative need for the observance of the principles advocated by this Government has been clearly demonstrated by the developments which have taken place during the past three days.[10]

Thereupon the United States refused to recognize any legal basis for the German protectorate over Bohemia and Moravia. Undeterred, however, Germany proceeded to induce Lithuania to return Memel.[1]

When Mussolini next proceeded to absorb Albania,[2] President Roosevelt became really alarmed. He issued an appeal to both Hitler and Mussolini requesting a pledge of non-aggression against some thirty-one different countries in and around Europe for a minimum period of " ten years at least — a quarter of a century, if we dare look that far ahead." [3] The plea was ill advised and of no service to the small nations of Europe, where consternation spread under the fear that they might be " guaranteed " and so dragged into the anti-German camp. Mussolini promptly disavowed aggressive intentions, while Hitler coupled derision of President Roose-

[10] Press Releases, XX, 199, 200.

[1] *New York Times,* March 23, 1939, p. 1.
Memel was governed by the French under the Treaty of Versailles. In 1922, Lithuania began to fear that the Conference of Ambassadors would rule against her claims. Therefore, in January, 1923, Lithuanian " irregulars " forced the French garrison to surrender. As the French were then preparing to invade the Ruhr, and as neither the French nor the British were willing to send considerable troops abroad, Lithuania was successful. On Feb. 16, 1923, the Conference of Ambassadors suggested terms: (1) juridical sovereignty in Lithuania; (2) Memel to be an autonomous unit; (3) freedom of transit, etc., for both Lithuania and Poland. This was finally adjusted in a treaty drawn under League auspices May 7, 1924. Poland protested without effect. *Survey of International Affairs, 1920–1923* (Oxford University Press), pp. 256–261.

[2] *New York Times,* April 8, 1939, p. 1. The Secretary of State at once denounced it as " unquestionably an additional threat to the peace of the world. . . . [it] seriously concerns all nations . . ." Press Releases, XX (April 8, 1939), 261.

[3] Press Releases, XX, 291, 293. The American Republics and Canada expressed enthusiasm for the President's message. *Idem,* XX, 323 *et seq.*

velt's plea with demands for the return of Danzig and a road across the Polish Corridor.[4] The policy of undertaking to guide the historical evolution of Europe and Asia and to characterize mass movements as moral issues again reaped its reward — ridicule. The United States of course is not competent to undertake the part of moral preceptor and is not called upon to pursue so fatuous a role. Yet in spite of all the neutrality acts, in spite of the vote against the League of Nations and against the interventionist policies reflected in that venture, these tendencies seem to have invaded the very life blood of a small but influential group whose ideas are congenial to the President. They apparently are unable to resist the moral urge to suppress " aggressors." [5]

The Neutrality Act of 1939

THE President's address to Congress of January 4, 1939, with its promise of " methods short of war " to contest the use of force in international relations, necessarily gave encouragement to the sanctionist elements. An account has already been given of the efforts of the administration between

4 Mussolini's reply, April 20, 1939, Hitler's, April 28, 1939, New York Times, April 21, 29, 1939. The replies — Hitler's reproducing an address to the Reichstag — do not appear to have been printed in the State Department Press Releases.

5 Gladstone in response to a somewhat similar temptation remarked: " Is England so uplifted in strength above every other nation, that she can with prudence advertise herself as ready to undertake the general redress of wrongs? Would not the consequence of such professions and promises be either the premature exhaustion of her means, or a collapse in the day of performance? Is any Power at this time of day warranted in assuming this comprehensive obligation? " Letter to General Grey, April 17, 1869. J. Morley, The Life of William Ewart Gladstone (New York, 1904), II, 317.

In 1938, Charles A. Beard, in the course of questioning before the House Naval Affairs Committee, remarked:

" I will say . . . that I know Americans are a great people, a very intelligent people, but I just think we are not smart enough to settle the quarrels of Europe encrusted in the blood rust of fifty centuries of warfare, but I think we might defend our civilization and have one here."

Hearing on H. R. 9218, 75th Cong., 3d Sess., p. 2189.

1928 and 1935 to secure the power to impose arms embargoes upon "aggressors," openly identified by the administration as Italy, Germany, and Japan. Before the year 1939 was out, Soviet Russia was to be added to this list of ostracized nations, for after the notable effort of Britain and France to embrace the Russian bear, he gracelessly decided to do business with Germany and therefore, after the attack on Finland, was blackballed from polite society at Geneva. Following tradition, he thereupon became the " enemy " of the United States, and moral embargoes were imposed upon him.

Several bills were introduced in Congress during January and February, 1939, to change the Neutrality Act so as to give the President wider discretion to impose embargoes on aggressors. Numerous opponents of neutrality rallied to the support of a bill sponsored by Senator Thomas of Utah which provided for an extension of the arms embargo to so-called " essential war materials " and coupled this with a provision exempting from all embargoes nations which were not found to be violating any treaty with the United States. This loophole was broad enough, under our practice of unilaterally interpreting multilateral treaties, to enable any administration so minded to embargo all exports to Germany and Japan.[6]

Senator Thomas of Utah, who fought hard for the lifting of the arms embargo, stated in a radio speech:

A neutrality that demands an impartiality calls for a dulling of every moral impulse. It insists upon erasing the line between good and evil. That is asking too much. That reduces a neutral to an unbearable impotence. A neutral has a right to stand for some-

---

[6] During the Senate Hearings, Colonel Stimson, Mrs. Louise Wright, and Professor Fenwick strongly supported the Thomas bill. See " Neutrality, Peace Legislation, and Our Foreign Policy," Hearings before the Committee on Foreign Relations, 76th Cong., 1st Sess., Parts I, III, V, VI. Mr. Fenwick, who has no use for neutrality and considers it immoral (*supra,* p. 251), was appointed by the administration in October, 1939, to represent the United States on an Inter-American Committee at Rio de Janeiro to safeguard American neutrality!

thing in the world, not for nothing. If neutrality means a crushing of world morality it is better that we take sides and fight, because fighting for a right is better than passive submission to a wrong.[7]

The Thomas Amendment found strong support among those who considered any neutrality act too rigid; they demanded " flexibility " for the President, meaning thereby the power to disregard international law and to exercise discriminatory sanctions against disfavored nations.[8] Translated into legal terms, the plea for " flexibility " in this connection is a plea for discretionary lawlessness; it substitutes discretion for law. This proposal was hailed by the group of sanctionists who profess that there is no such thing as the law of neutrality, that because it has been violated it has ceased to exist, and that because varying interpretations have been placed upon it by belligerents and neutrals it is too uncertain for practical use. Thus, a recent work by Dulles and Armstrong contains the following passage:

the legalistic conception of neutrality, and particularly of neutral rights, is based on precedents which had long been confused and weakened by the successively different and inconsistent positions which nations had taken, depending upon whether they expected to be or happened to be neutrals or belligerents . . . Final blows to many of the legal formulae of neutrality were delivered in the World War, and those which remained were further complicated by the changes in the relationship of belligerent and neutral produced by the Covenant of the League of Nations and by the Kellogg-Briand Pact . . . The popular American conception that neutrality is a clearly defined status is erroneous.[9]

This counsel lays a firm foundation for anarchy, for that very rule of unmitigated force which the interventionist professes to decry. But the intimation that there is no such thing

[7] Broadcast of Sept. 11, 1939, *Evening Star* (Washington, D. C.), p. 5.

[8] See editorial, " Revision of the Neutrality Act," by Clyde Eagleton, *A. J. I. L.*, XXXIII (1939), 119–126.

[9] Dulles and Armstrong, *Can America Stay Neutral?* (2d ed., 1939), pp. 6, 11.

as a law of neutrality is undoubtedly of great aid to those who would exterminate it; they would substitute for it presidential discretion to aid the "righteous" with the military forces of the United States. The attacks on neutrality by devotees of the League, the surrenders of neutral rights to one side by the United States in 1914–17, the disrespect for the rights of neutrals displayed by both belligerents in the present European war, have greatly weakened the power of the Scandinavian countries and other neutrals to maintain their neutrality and their peace and have gravely impaired the freedom of the seas, one of the best fruits of neutrality. While still paying lip service to neutrality, because public opinion demands it, too many high officials harbor Wilsonian visions and in the quest to right distant wrongs would again engage the United States in holy crusades. Indeed, derision of the law, not now by criminals but by romantic uplifters, is symbolic of at least profound misconceptions of international relations, if not of that impatience with legal restraints which often distinguishes crusaders.

Some Congressional support rallied behind the amendment of Representative Allen to repeal all existing neutrality legislation and rely solely upon international law.[10] As has been made clear in earlier chapters, had President Wilson's administration really desired to maintain American neutrality, special legislation would have been superfluous — and the same is true today. But since 1933, distrust of Executive manipulations of international law had apparently been mounting in the House and Senate, so that some legislation was demanded. The country had become accustomed since the Act of 1935 to the necessity of taking temptation out of the hands of an impulsive President and to the belief that certain restrictions on neutral rights were of aid in keeping the country out of war. Such restrictions today are part of

[10] The amendment was defeated by 195 to 68 in the House. See speeches on its behalf, *Cong. Rec.*, LXXXIV, 8288–8311.

the penalty for the surrenders of 1914-17, when the interests of the neutral United States were sacrificed to higher morality and the victory of one side.

In the meantime, Senator Pittman added his bit to the interventionist attack upon the neutrals by characterizing as the "policy of isolation" the demand that the United States stay out of war and refrain from "methods short of war." "Unfortunately," said the Senator, "in spite of the history of its uniform puerility, it is urged by some of our citizens — even by men and women of prominence." [1] He interpreted the policy as a method of "refraining from taking any part in world affairs," and remarked solemnly, "Czechoslovakia, under the rules of the League of Nations, practiced a policy of isolation." (Czechoslovakia, it will be remembered, had military alliances with France, Russia, the Little Entente, and, essentially, with the League Powers.) He followed the usual formula of denouncing the use of force and threat, identified with "the Governments of Germany, Italy, and Japan, three of the most powerful military governments in the world . . . absolutely controlled by arbitrary and ruthless dictators," and then said for the American people, "while they hate war, they are not afraid to die for Christianity, morality, justice and liberty . . . that we will die, however, for these things we consider worth more than life, we know." This is an inviting prospect for American youth.

Senator Pittman followed up his speech on March 20 with what he called his "Peace Act of 1939." There he anticipated most of the administration's demands for "flexibility" and foreshadowed the act which was passed on November 4. He proposed to repeal the arms embargo, put all trade on a cash-and-carry basis, and establish combat areas from which American citizens and ships were to be excluded "ex-

[1] Radio speech, "Our Foreign Policy" by Key Pittman, Feb. 20, 1939, published by *Evening Star* (Washington, D. C.), p. 1.

cept under such limitations and exceptions as the President may prescribe." In view of the fact that the cash-and-carry plan necessarily operated to the advantage of Great Britain and Japan, the Senator thoughtfully introduced on April 27 a supplemental bill to bestow upon the President power to embargo exports and imports to and from any states violating the Nine-Power Treaty.[2] Apparently, the new concept of " treaty violator " seemed easier to put over than the term " aggressor."

It was not until May 27, 1939, that the President disclosed his own proposals for legislation. This came after the rejection of his plea of April 15 to Mussolini and Hitler for a ten-year " peace." The President's recommendations, transmitted by Secretary Hull, followed the Pittman Bill fairly closely and varied from existing legislation principally in that the arms embargo was to be lifted, all trade was to be placed on a cash basis, the President was to be allowed to establish combat areas, and additional Executive discretion was to be accorded through wide rule-making powers.

The President's proposal, known as the Bloom bill, was severely attacked because, instead of restricting, it enlarged the President's discretionary powers. The limitations imposed by amendment during debate still failed to reassure the minority.[3] As amended in the House, power to find a " state of war " was to be shared with Congress, and the act was to come into force only when it affected American peace, security, or lives; the power to determine combat areas was struck from the bill, limitations were placed upon the power to manipulate the loan embargo, and a few other amendments were adopted. Despite these changes, doubt persisted as to whether, in view of the broad power of the President to offend foreign nations and to discriminate against them, these

[2] S. J. Res. 123, *Cong. Rec.,* 84, p. 6759. See also H. R. 5432, introduced March 29, 1939, to embargo export of essential raw materials to Japan, *idem,* 3501.

[3] *Cong. Rec.,* p. 10,392.

minor withdrawals of power could be effective to prevent unneutrality and intervention.

The major controversy centered around the arms embargo.
Considering the overwhelming majority by which the 1937
Act had been passed, and the administration's and Senator
Pittman's earlier praise of arms embargoes, it was now something of a feat to attack arms embargoes as immoral and unneutral. But with war clouds gathering in Europe, strong
voices were urging the United States to assist Great Britain
and France by reopening to them our market for arms, ammunition, and implements of war. It was apparent that Germany could neither get such arms across the seas nor pay
for them; possibly she did not need them. The House, however, declined to lift the arms embargo completely. Representative Vorys' amendment, adopted by a narrow vote,
lifted it only as to " implements of war," such as airplanes.

Although it was argued by administration spokesmen that
if the law was to be changed it should be done before war
broke out, for it might be unneutral to change it thereafter,
the emasculated Bloom bill was adopted by the House on
July 1; the Senate Committee, however, by a close vote of
12 to 11, decided to postpone consideration of neutrality legislation until the next session. This decision so displeased the
administration that the President sent Congress a message,[4]
attaching to it a long communication on peace and neutrality
from the Secretary of State. Mr. Hull argued that an arms
embargo was a " hazardous departure from the principle of
international law which recognizes the right of neutrals to
trade with belligerents and of belligerents to trade with neutrals." No reference was made, however, to the fact that in-

---

[4] Department of State, Bulletin I, July 15, 1939, pp. 43–47. In a Press
Conference the President condemned those who had voted to postpone as
" gamblers with the fate of one and one-half billion people," since he was
now deprived of the power to make an American move to prevent international war. The answer to this strange assertion is given by Henry S.
Fraser, *New York Herald Tribune,* Sept. 3, 1939.

ternational law leaves each nation free to adopt in peacetime
either policy — arms shipments or arms embargoes. In fact,
the Secretary argued that an arms embargo is " directly
opposed to the idea of neutrality." This seems a strange
conception, seeing that various neutrals in Europe and Latin-
America have frequently adopted arms embargoes; its justification was attempted, however, on the ground that embargoes would operate unequally between the two belligerents.
All legislation is likely to operate unequally, but that possibility has not heretofore made such legislation unneutral.
The Secretary added that one belligerent may find itself in
a position of relative advantage or disadvantage. But this is
irrelevant; as Secretary Bryan and Secretary Lansing stated
to Germany and Austria in 1915, we could not change our
legislation merely because it operated to their disadvantage.[5]
It is not the function of a neutral to compensate for geographical or physical disadvantages between belligerents.

Moreover, it was not wise from an American point of view
for the Secretary to argue that because raw materials useful
in war could be shipped under the 1937 Act, there was therefore no logical reason for banning arms, ammunition, and implements of war.[6] History and law and common sense dic-

---

[5] For. Rel., 1915, Suppl., pp. 162, 794. See Harvard Draft, comment on
Article 13, Supplement to A. J. I. L., XXXIII (July, 1939), 316, 326-328.
Ray Stannard Baker states that President Wilson was impressed by a telegram from Messrs. Coudert, Fuller, and Tracey, reading: " altering the rules
of neutrality during warfare . . . aiding the inefficiency of one belligerent
to protect its purchases of arms by forbidding all exportation of arms to the
other belligerents is an absolute violation of neutrality." Wilson, Life and
Letters, V, 188. Lansing wrote to the President, December 10, 1914: " I
think these gentlemen are entirely right. . . . Any change in our statutes by
amendment or repeal would undoubtedly benefit one or the other of the
belligerents. Whatever the purpose of the change the belligerent, whose interests were unfavorably affected, would be justified in protesting on the ground
that the legislation was for the advantage of its enemy, and, therefore, unneutral." Lansing Papers (Washington, 1940), I, 180. As a matter of fact, an
arms embargo in 1914 and 1915 would not have been unneutral because it
would have strengthened American neutrality and avoided making the
United States a supply station for one side.

[6] The Act of March 2, 1940, authorized by implication an additional
loan of $20,000,000 to Finland for " nonmilitary " supplies. But it was said

tate the distinction, for raw materials may be used for civilian purposes as well as for armies and navies. Our former policy of limiting the scope of " contraband," which will continue to be an American interest so long as the United States is a trading nation, was considerably weakened by the contention that there was little distinction between munitions and such commodities as cotton, oil, steel, and copper. Perhaps the real motive was indicated by the Secretary's statement that the arms embargo " plays into the hands of those nations which have taken the lead in building up their fighting power. It works directly against the interests of the peace-loving nations, especially those which do not possess their own munition plants." Contesting the argument that the shipment of arms is immoral, as suggested by the President in his Chautauqua speech of 1936,[7] the Secretary apparently thought such traffic perfectly moral. He concluded, therefore, that lifting the arms embargo would make less likely the outbreak of a major war — a tenuous argument at best.

To those who feared that freedom of arms shipments might weaken America's chances of staying out of war and that it would penalize disfavored belligerents, the Secretary replied:

The basis for the recommendations made is the firm intention of keeping this country from being drawn into war. If there existed any desire to assist or to injure particular foreign countries, this Government would not have been endeavoring persistently, within the limitations of our traditional policy, over a period of many years to do its utmost to avoid the outbreak of a general war . . .[8]

Perhaps the implication was that the supply of arms to one belligerent would assist in keeping this country from being

---

that this would include fuel, oil, and gasoline. Are such materials nonmilitary when intended for friends, but military when intended for countries on the Executive black list?

[7] *Supra*, p. 353.   [8] Bulletin I, 45.

drawn into war by assuring an early victory for our favorite. American efforts to avoid the outbreak of a general war could hardly have impressed even the administration as particularly effective. On the contrary, a good argument could be made to show that continued American interference in Europe and Asia has had an irritating effect on international relations.

The administration's arguments for lifting the arms embargo were convincing only on one ground, that this would aid the " democracies " in winning their then approaching war. This was consistent with the President's policy announced in his speech of January, 1939, and a plea along these lines might indeed have moved Congress to pass the President's bill early in 1939. Instead, the attempt to argue that the lifting of the arms embargo would insure America's neutrality and its abstention from war was so unconvincing as to arouse suspicion that greater intervention was contemplated. Moreover, it was noticed that Executive faith in embargoes was still strong when applied to Japan, thus putting the Government in the paradoxical position of maintaining that an arms embargo on the Atlantic made for unneutrality and war, whereas an arms embargo on the Pacific against Japan made for neutrality and peace. The fact is, of course, that, in both cases, penalties against so-called " aggressors " and assistance to favored belligerents were the major considerations in view. These required lifting the embargo for Great Britain and France, and imposition of an extra-legal " moral embargo " on Japan. It may be questioned whether this could square with the assurance that there was no intention to adopt measures whose purpose was " to assist or to injure particular nations."

Poland. Meanwhile, events in Europe were going from bad to worse. Germany's demands for the return of Danzig

were becoming sharper. When Poland viewed this as a threat
to her independence, she received a guaranty of protection
from Britain and France.[9] Germany's plan embraced, first,
a road across the Corridor, and finally, as Poland refused,
annexation of the whole Polish Corridor. While Britain and
France were seeking to enlist Soviet Russia in guaranties of
military coöperation, on August 20 the Germans concluded
a trade agreement and, a few days later, a nonaggression pact
with Russia.[10] On September 1 Germany marched into Poland and, after two days' delay, Great Britain and France
declared war on Germany.

On September 5 the President proclaimed the Neutrality
Act of 1937 in force and outlined certain duties imposed on
American citizens under international law. On October 18
he issued a proclamation barring belligerent submarines,
military and commercial, from American ports.[1] He was silent, however, as to the Allied merchantmen which were then
entering American ports heavily armed.[2] That the President
was not unaware of the implications of such armament is indicated by his detention in New York harbor of the German
liner *Bremen* for two days in late August on the ground that
if she left with arms the United States might be held responsible under the *Alabama* rule for any depredations she might
commit. In admitting Allied armed merchantmen, however,
the President revived the distinction between offensive and
defensive armament, discredited even by Secretary Lansing
on January 18, 1916,[3] by announcing that " purely defen-

---

[9] *The British War Blue Book* (New York, Farrar & Rinehart, 1939), pp.
48 *et seq.* Poland was always in an exposed state. As a buffer between Germany and Russia, endowed with the liability of the Corridor and excessive
minorities, she was a poor risk.

[10] *New York Times*, Aug. 21; *idem*, Aug. 25. Text in Department of
State, Bulletin I, 172.

[1] Bulletin I, 396.

[2] Although the power to bar both submarines and armed merchantmen
is included in the same clause of the act.   [3] *Supra*, p. 102 *et seq.*

sive armament against warships and submarines " was unobjectionable.[4]

It was known that large orders for airplanes had been placed here by Great Britain and France early in 1939. Unless the Neutrality Act were changed, these could not be delivered after the outbreak of war. For this and other reasons, the President was determined to have the act amended to accord with his wishes. He succeeded.

On the opening day of an extraordinary session of Congress called for the purpose, the President delivered a stirring address again manifesting his dislike for the " aggressor " — clearly indicated, but not named — and for the arms embargo; what he sought was " greater consistency through the repeal of the embargo provisions and a return to international law." To bolster his argument he derided the " artificial legal distinction " between munitions and other articles, although this distinction was made not merely by the Act of 1935, which he now deprecated, but by the international law he purported to extol. He pointed out the " material . . . advantage " of giving employment here rather than sending raw materials abroad for processing; [5] he intimated that legislative restrictions would impair his exercise of discretion under " international law." Contrary to his former devotion to the " Peace Act " of 1937, he now pictured that legislation as impairing " the peaceful relations of the United States with foreign nations." [6] He repeated his statement of the previous January that the attempt to "legislate neutrality . . . may operate unevenly and unfairly — may actually give aid to an aggressor and deny it to the victim " — a Geneva misconception of the function of neutrality, and indeed an implicit attack upon the whole philosophy of neutrality.

[4] *New York Times,* Aug. 30, 1939, p. 4. See comment, *A. J. I. L.,* XXIV (Jan., 1940), 107–112.

[5] Cf. *supra,* p. 354.

[6] Address, Sept. 21, 1939, *Cong. Rec.* (daily), LXXXV, 8–10.

The President considered that the War of 1812 and the burning of the Capitol in 1814 were due to the embargo policy of 1807–12, a conclusion with which historians might well differ. He argued that the repeal of the arms embargo would *aid* peace, because " this Government . . . will insist that American citizens and American ships keep away from the immediate perils of the actual zones of conflict." Why such precautions could not be taken *without* embargo repeal he did not explain.

With minor modifications, the bill forthwith introduced by Senator Pittman [7] followed closely his bill of the previous spring. Again, the only serious debate turned on the lifting of the arms embargo. It was hard to conceal the fact, though a valiant effort was made, that the motive for the change was a desire to help Great Britain and France. This accorded with the emotional views of most American citizens, but little mention was made of the fact that such a change for such a motive would violate international law and cause America to incur grave risks of involvement. The law does not deny a neutral the privilege of changing his law in time of war, but it may not be changed with the motive of helping one belligerent at the expense of the other; nor may the neutral *weaken* his neutrality, without exposing himself to charges of unneutrality from the handicapped belligerent.[8]

The Research in International Law, conducted under the auspices of the Harvard Law School, with Professor Jessup as reporter, has concluded:

The task confronting the neutral State [in changing its rules during war] is to make certain to itself and clear to other States that the motive inducing the adoption of a new rule or regulation during

[7] As an amendment to the Bloom bill of June 30, thus avoiding the introduction of a fresh bill in the House.

[8] *Supra*, p. 402. See also letters of Charles Cheney Hyde and Philip C. Jessup, *New York Times*, Sept. 21, Oct. 5, 1939. Speech of Edwin Borchard printed in *Cong. Rec.*, LXXXV, App., 415–418. See also letters from J. B. Moore, W. C. Dennis, W. P. Lage, F. S. Dunn, Henry S. Fraser, and others in *Cong. Rec.*, LXXXV, App., 762–763.

the course of a war is the product of its concern to act strictly in accordance with the law of neutrality, and not the result of a desire to aid one or the other belligerent.[9]

We find in the majority report of the Senate Committee on Foreign Relations the following sentences:

The committee is of the opinion that the United States cannot maintain its neutrality so long as such embargo provisions remain on our statute books. It is contrary to the accepted precepts of international law which prescribe that any belligerent may purchase any articles or materials in any neutral country. Belligerents, as well as neutrals, have relied from time immemorial upon this law. . . . It was a voluntary departure from international law by the United States Government . . .

It would be hard to frame four short sentences containing more misconceptions than these. Apart from the fact that never before has an arms embargo been deemed a danger to neutrality, a few legal facts may be stated.

International law does not compel neutrals to supply arms to belligerents. No belligerent has by international law a right to demand arms from a neutral country. But international law imposes no restrictions on neutral traders in selling arms. So far as international law is concerned, a government may permit or forbid its citizens to sell arms. But that was not the issue.

The peculiar defect in the proposed change was that it undertook to lift the embargo during a foreign war with the knowledge, if not, indeed, the intention that it would help one set of belligerents only. This seems a clear violation of international law. Just as the United States Government as a neutral government may not legally furnish arms to either belligerent, so it may not by deliberate change in its law help its citizens to furnish such arms, particularly when the effect is discriminatory.

[9] Comment on Article 13, Supplement to *A. J. I. L.*, XXXIII (July, 1939), 316.

Arguments were advanced, however, to show that the proposed change was purely a matter of American policy which no one could question and that the cash-and-carry provisions as to all commodities afforded a compensating restriction upon the existing law. But the tightening of certain provisions in order to promote abstention does not justify a loosening of other provisions calculated to assist one side only. We can only hope that the handicapped belligerents will not be in a position to exert reprisals. At the moment, the greater danger arises from the United States itself, for if the aid given Great Britain and France does not prove sufficient, the urge to increase it may become irresistible and active intervention may well result. On January 4, 1940, presumably the best the President could say for nonintervention was that " the overwhelming majority of our fellow citizens do not abandon in the slightest their hope and their expectation that the United States will not become involved in military participation in these wars." Perhaps this was an admission that the United States is already being involved in economic and other participation " short of war."

Special exemptions in the new act, passed on November 4, permit trade in American vessels, without prior transfer of title except for munitions, with belligerent states outside Europe. Most trade to Canada is unrestricted, except that title to munitions must be transferred and American vessels are forbidden to enter ports eastward of the Bay of Fundy. Bonds of belligerent governments may not be sold in the American market, as the 1937 act had already provided, and credit may not be extended to belligerent governments or their agents; but credit may be freely extended to private purchasers (except for buying arms and munitions).[10] In view

---

[10] A distinction between munitions and other commodities, once decried (cf. *supra*, p. 406), was here admitted. It was again admitted in the loan to Finland. And by ignoring the fact that there is a war there, the " Fighting Funds for Finland, Inc.," and part of the Hoover Finland Relief Fund, Inc., extended gifts or loans for munitions, thus evading the Neutrality Act.

of a doubt whether the Export-Import Bank is a " person " which may not advance credit to defaulting nations under the Johnson Act, that institution was especially included in such credit prohibitions in an act adopted March 2, 1940, to extend the lending facilities of the Export-Import Bank for non-military purposes from one hundred to two hundred millions.

The provisions as to transfer of title are proving hard to administer, especially in the case of foreign subsidiaries of American corporations; pressure is growing for their repeal. American vessels are still exposed to possible attack, or may be taken into British control ports while proceeding to Lisbon or Genoa, outside the barred zone, with cargoes for neutrals. While the " cash-and-carry " provisions will probably prevent a war boom, the Allies are, quite naturally, buying raw materials and supplies, such as food and tobacco, in Turkey and in British dominions, wherever their political and economic interest dictates. This is producing pressure from American suppliers to lift the credit restrictions of the act. A shortage of shipping creates a motive to use American ships in the combat areas and has led to various transfers to foreign flags, including British, French, and Belgian; transfers to Latin-American flags, however, were for a time viewed with disfavor by the State Department.[1] The ban on loans to belligerents may be seriously affected by Government credits voted to belligerent Finland and China for allegedly non-military purchases, including commercial airplanes, through the Export-Import Bank, which is now apparently used for

[1] A recent transfer of eight United States Lines vessels to a Belgian corporation, to be owned 60 per cent by Belgians and 40 per cent by American citizens, has been approved. *New York Times*, Feb. 18, 1940. Cf. Maritime Commission Release, Press Releases (Feb. 19, 1940), No. 505. Of American ships transferred between September 18 and March 1, the following countries' flags predominate: Panama, 25 ships; Great Britain, 17; Brazil, 13; France, 13; Canada, 12; Belgium, 8. If financial interest is not materially changed, the transfer might be considered an evasion, although not illegal, and may cause further popular loss of confidence in and disrespect for law. American protection must of necessity be withdrawn from such vessels. Cf. Foreign Policy Reports, " The War and American Shipping," April 1, 1940.

political purposes.[2] Soon, there may be an effort to repeal the Johnson Act prohibiting loans to countries in default on their debt to the United States, so that other European loans may be floated.

Unneutral Acts. The United States is permitting finished bombing planes to be supplied to Great Britain and France. To avoid conflict with American statutes, they are being flown from California to the Canadian border by American pilots, title is solemnly transferred, they are pushed or pulled across the border on wheels, and then the flight continues across Canada to the East coast.[3] Just as no warship may be supplied by a neutral to a belligerent, so no finished bombing plane may be supplied. Article 46 of the Draft Convention adopted at The Hague, 1923, though unratified, prohibits such supply and merely codifies, it is believed, pre-existing law. It is now reported that the British Government is supplying funds for the enlargement of American powder and aircraft plants under contract to supply Britain and France with their entire output.[4] This, too, is believed to be

[2] Of the 100-million-dollar increase in the lending facilities of the Bank, effected by the Act of March 2, 1940, 65 millions were promptly allocated to favored countries at war or in danger of war: 20 millions to Finland, 15 millions to Sweden, 10 millions to Norway, and 20 millions to China. Cf. Kendall Hoyt in the *Annalist*, March 7, 1940.

[3] *New York Times*, Nov. 18, 1939. Apparently the latest types are being supplied to the Allies, with the Secretary of the Treasury acting as coördinator between United States and Allied demands. General Hugh Johnson in column, *New Haven Register*, Jan. 24, 1940. Paul Mallon, *idem*, March 15, 1940; *New York Times*, March 23, 1940. It is an unusual experience to find the Secretary of War and the Chief of Staff urging on Congress the importance of speeding planes to one set of belligerents, letting the Allies have 2,100 planes originally ordered for the American Army. The argument advanced was that plant expansion and delivery to the Allies would improve the later product for the United States. The sale was described as " of vital importance to the national defense of the United States." This is certainly true if United States belligerency is contemplated. Kluckhohn in *New York Times*, March 28, 1940; Associated Press Dispatch, *idem*, March 27, 1940, *idem*, March 29, 31, 1940; *New York World Telegram*, March 25, 1940. The sale is defended, however, by the astute Hugh S. Johnson, *idem*, March 25, 1940.

[4] Associated Press dispatch, *New Haven Register*, March 15, 1940.

a violation of American neutrality, in that the funds of a belligerent are used to make the United States a base of military supplies.

On June 23, 1939, Ambassador Kennedy in London signed an agreement with the British Government providing for exchange of British rubber for American cotton, the declared purpose being " to acquire reserves of cotton and rubber, respectively, against the contingency of a major war emergency." [5] Neither the cotton nor the rubber was to be disposed of or released by the receiving government on the general market " except in the event of such an emergency." The agreement was ratified by the President on July 17, 1939, and was to come into force on August 25; it was proclaimed on September 6, 1939.[6]

Meanwhile, however, Britain had declared war on Germany on September 3, and on the fifth this country had proclaimed its neutrality.[7] As a result, it became legally impossible for this country to fulfill its obligations under the agreement without violating its neutrality, for a neutral government, as such, cannot supply either belligerent nation with any commodities, certainly not contraband, without committing an unneutral act.[8] Nevertheless, the cotton has been shipped.

The United States has protested to Great Britain against diversion of American ships from the high seas to the dangerous " combat areas," against the prohibition of the export of goods from Germany, and against the search of American mails.[8a] Great Britain, not unnaturally, is using an unwise ad-

[5] Press Releases, XX, 547–549.
[6] Bulletin I, 240.   [7] *Idem,* p. 203.   [8] *Supra,* p. 7.
[8a] There is no justification for the apparent concession by the Department of State (Bulletin II [Jan. 6, 1940] 3; British answer Jan. 20, 1940, *New York Times,* Jan. 21, 1940; cf. *idem,* March 29, 1940) that letter mail on an American vessel or plane voluntarily entering a belligerent port or letter mail in ordinary transit through belligerent territory may be examined or censored. Cf. *Reports to the Hague Conferences* (Oxford University Press, 1917), pp. 741, 733, 735, 221; Scott, *Hague Peace Conferences* (Baltimore, 1909), p. 616.

mission of Secretary Lansing in May, 1916, to the effect that money orders, checks, and negotiable instruments may be considered merchandise,[9] as a reason for rejecting the American protest on the mails. Thus, American surrenders of the period 1914-17 are coming home to roost, and to impair further the rights of neutrals. As Secretary Hull soundly remarked, but in another connection:

To waive rights and to permit interests to lapse in the face of their actual or threatened violation — and thereby to abandon obligations — in any important area of the world, can serve only to encourage disregard of law and of the basic principles of international order, and thus contribute to the inevitable spread of international anarchy throughout the world. For this country, as for any country, to act in such manner *anywhere* would be to invite disregard and violation of its rights and interests *everywhere*, by every nation so inclined, large or small.[10]

Nor have neutrals been aided by the Pan-American claim of a 300-600 mile immunity zone against belligerent action " from land, sea, or air " around the American continents, excluding Canada.[1] If other neutrals claimed a similar immunity, little of the open sea would be left for belligerent action. But apart from the impracticality of the idea, the fact that the belligerents have not accepted it,[2] that numerous

9 *For. Rel.*, 1916, Suppl. p. 608.

10 Department of State, Publication No. 1146.

1 Called " Declaration of Panama," Bulletin I, No. 15 (Oct. 7, 1939), 321-333. Presumably American belligerents can fight in the zone, especially the United States. The Declaration, which was not submitted to Congress and has not received its approval, contains a reservation that it is to apply only " so long as [the signatories] maintain their neutrality." Evidently it was contemplated that some of the American Republics might become belligerents. The " safety zone " is then abolished for all, presumably. There is no such legal concept as " American waters." In the famous battle between the *Kearsarge* and the *Alabama* off Cherbourg, 1864, in which France sought to have the ships conduct their fight seven or eight miles out, Secretary of State Seward said: " The United States do not admit a right of France to interfere with their ships of war at any distance exceeding three miles." Moore, *Digest of International Law*, I, 724.

2 Bulletin II, No. 35 (Feb. 24, 1940), 199-205.

belligerent naval bases and possessions would be insured against enemy attack, that the attempt to enforce it might lead to conflict with the belligerents, and that failure to attempt enforcement might lead to humiliation, the extraordinary idea encourages the excessive claims of belligerents, and this at a time when neutral rights have already been gravely impaired and must struggle for recognition.

Russo-Finnish War

AFTER his successes in overawing Esthonia, Latvia, and Lithuania into granting the Soviet military and naval bases in their ports on the Baltic,[3] Stalin turned his attention to Finland. Russia desired a rectification of frontiers which were within twenty miles of Leningrad. She offered to give more territory than she asked, but wanted a thirty-year lease of Hangoe, which commands the approach to Leningrad. The terms were not unreasonable as such things go. It must be recalled that Finland had not been really independent since the twelfth century, and that from 1809 to 1918 she was under the control of Russia. Russia did not fear Finland or wish to terminate her post-1918 independence. But, in the modern tradition, Russia wished to prevent Finland from being used as a base of attack by Russia's enemies. Whoever advised the Finns to resist the Russian terms was not astute or acting in Finland's interest. At all events, the negotiations at Moscow ended abruptly in late November, and Russia started bombing the Finnish capital and attacking at various points along the Finnish-Russian border.[4] Finland immediately launched upon a heroic resistance. But in Washington no proclamation was issued under the Neutrality Act. For the administration, Finland and Russia, like Japan and China,

[3] Bulletin I, 543, 542, 705. Cf. Ambassador Bakhmetieff's refusal on June 30, 1921, to recognize, for the Kerensky Government, the independence of those countries, on the ground that they constituted Russia's gateway to the Baltic. *For. Rel.*, 1921, II, 756–759.

[4] *New York Times*, Dec. 1, 1939, p. 1.

were not at " war " and a Senate subcommittee agreed on March 5 that the Neutrality Act need not be invoked.

Irrespective of the sympathies which most Americans have for Finland, this was not an observance of the law.[5] There is no option to treat a foreign war as nonexistent, and thus violate neutral duties. A public loan to Finland, very decidedly at war, was an unneutral act. So was the supply of fighting planes. Sir Edward Grey in 1915 and Neville Chamberlain in 1940 emphasized the fact that a neutral's failure to observe strictly his duties of neutrality afforded the injured belligerent the privilege of retaliation.[6] The irrelevant allegation that war had not been declared only adds to the irregularity.

Upon learning of the bombing of Helsinki by Soviet planes, the President immediately characterized the act as a " wanton disregard for law." [7] Next day, after consultation with the Secretary of State, he issued the following statement:

[5] Even if it be assumed that the Russo-Finnish War did not affect the peace, security, or neutrality of the United States, the ordinary obligations of neutrality under international law applied. After urging as entirely proper a loan to Finland, even for munitions (*New York Times,* editorial, Feb. 8, 15, 1940), the *New York Times* admitted (editorial, March 28, 1940) that the Congress had departed from " strict neutrality in one of Europe's wars, to the extent of giving aid to one nation, Finland, at the direct expense of another, Russia."

[6] Grey in a dispatch to Holland during the European war of 1914, is quoted as having said: " If a neutral Power allows its sovereign rights to be invaded by one belligerent to the prejudice of the other, without effective resistance, it cannot complain if the other belligerent protects himself by similar measures." Quoted by Restor in London dispatch, *New York Times,* Feb. 23, 1940, p. 4. This was applicable to the United States in 1915 and 1916; it ought not to become applicable again. Prime Minister Chamberlain in *New York Times,* Feb. 25, 1940, sec. 1, p. 33. But this can cover only voluntary surrender of rights. It is reported (*New York Times,* March 27, 1940) that France will now maintain that if a neutral is *unable* to enforce respect for its neutrality on the part of one belligerent, the other may intervene " to force observance of that neutral's rights." This is a threat to all small neutrals. Germany apparently took this view in occupying Denmark and Norway after the British had mined Norwegian territorial waters. *New York Times,* April 9, 10, 1940.

[7] Bulletin I, 609.

The American Government and the American people have for some time pursued a policy of wholeheartedly condemning the unprovoked bombing and machine-gunning of civilian populations from the air.

This Government hopes, to the end that such unprovoked bombing shall not be given material encouragement in the light of recent recurrence of such acts, that American manufacturers and exporters of airplanes, aeronautical equipment, and materials essential to airplane manufacture, will bear this fact in mind before negotiating contracts for the exportation of these articles to nations obviously guilty of such unprovoked bombing.[8]

With this new war scarcely two days old, the President thus pledged himself anew to the unneutral policy of " moral embargo."

Following up the President's statement, on December 14 Secretary Hull personally notified every manufacturer of airplanes and airplane parts of this new " moral embargo," enclosing a copy of the President's statement. At the same time, the Secretary also extended the " moral embargo " to include aluminum and molybdenum; i.e., raw materials.[9]

On the heels of these pronouncements, it was announced that the Navy Department had yielded priority to the Government of Finland in the acquisition of some forty-four American naval fighting planes.[10] These planes were of the latest and fastest types then under construction for the United States Navy, types which would ordinarily not have been available to any foreign nation for many months. But since the President had embargoed planes, parts, and even raw materials to Russia, it was perhaps fitting that the Navy should release choice new planes to Finland. It was illegal to threaten private American industry into compliance with the "moral embargo," and the United States Government,

---

[8] Bulletin I, 686.

[9] The sale to Japan and Russia of aluminum, molybdenum and other raw " materials essential to airplane manufacture " was discouraged. Bulletin I, 685.

[10] *New York Times,* Dec. 19, 1939.

by releasing the planes, was supplying one warring nation with military aircraft for use against its enemy. The unneutrality of such action is patent.[1]

Finally, on December 20, the Secretary turned his moral attention to the oil industry; devices for improving ordinary gasoline into high-octane-rating aircraft fuel were placed under another " moral embargo " [2] — again aimed at Russia and Japan.

Meanwhile, the administration was not neglecting its other powerful weapon — money. As in the case of the Sino-Japanese War, where hostile acts against Japan were accompanied by financial assistance to China, so here, after giving effect to its dislike of Russia, the administration began assisting Finland financially through the Export-Import Bank. On December 7 it was announced that the bank was negotiating a large credit to Finland.[3] Finland's last payment on her debt to the United States was segregated for return to her, pending Congressional approval.[4] A remission of former payments was even discussed; as a precedent for remissions to other belligerents this would be a momentous act.

On January 8, 1940, after the expulsion of Russia from the League and the Council's request for aid to Finland, the State Department informed the League of Nations that " the Government of the United States has from the outbreak of hostilities given tangible evidence of its sympathy for the people and Government of Finland in the present situation; " it spoke of the " medical, financial and other aid " extended by

[1] *Supra*, p. 7. More recently American brokers and dealers in rubber have been urged not to make or carry out contracts with the Soviet agency, Amtorg, a New York corporation, for the sale of rubber now in the United States, presumably because some might reach Germany. An agreement among them has been fostered. It will be interesting to observe whether they will be granted immunity from the anti-trust laws, which would otherwise be applicable.

[2] *New York Times,* Dec. 21, 1939, p. 1.

[3] *New York Times,* Dec. 8, 1939.

[4] *New York Times,* Dec. 6, 1939, Dec. 8, 1939, Jan. 13, 1940.

the American Red Cross and private organizations and of consultation with Finnish agencies " with regard to the most effective manner in which such aid may be continued and expanded." [5] The President suggested that voluntary enlistments in Finland would not violate American neutrality,[6] and Great Britain went so far as to suspend the Foreign Enlistment Act to permit recruiting for Finland — with the explanation that England would thus be fulfilling League obligations.[7]

On January 16, 1940, the President consulted with Congressional leaders for the purpose of obtaining a large loan for Finland. Evidently the original intention was to leave it unrestricted. But the leaders were said to object on the ground that Finland was at war, that the loan was intervention, that intervention was an act of war, and that it might be as well to meet the issue honestly by declaring war on Russia.[8] This objection produced merely a limitation in the amount to be lent and it was colored as a move " to promote American agricultural and industrial exports."

The proposal brought wide criticism as an illegal act, a first step toward involvement in the war, a precedent to break down the loan prohibitions of the Johnson Act and the Neutrality Act to debt defaulters and belligerents.[9]

On March 2, 1940, however, an act was passed which, by enlarging the lending facilities of the Export-Import Bank, increased from ten to thirty millions the credits to Finland for the purchase in this country of " agricultural surpluses

---

[5] Associated Press dispatch, Jan. 8, 1940, *New Haven Register*, Jan. 8, 1940. The report to the League of American activity on behalf of Finland did not awaken the criticism usual in such cases.

[6] *New Haven Register*, Jan. 30, 1940.

[7] *New York Times*, Feb. 14, 1940.

[8] Paul Mallon in syndicated column, *New Haven Register*, Jan. 18, 1940.

[9] *Hartford Courant*, Jan. 18, 1940; cf. John de R. Storey's able letter to the *Times* of Jan. 26, 1940, protesting the loan as " a subterfuge available only to powerful and remotely situated nations." *New York Times*, Jan. 30, 1940.

and other civilian supplies." [10] If there was no war, this limitation seems unnecessary. But the Act of March 2 permits such loans — the spending of which would be hard to control — if not contrary to international law " as interpreted by the Department of State." Judging by the excuses made for the Finnish loan, we may have to be prepared for some novel constructions of law, not at all in harmony with the professed desire to " revitalize " international law.

On March 13, 1940, Finland and Russia signed a peace treaty. In London and Paris this was greeted with dismay and there was some recrimination against Sweden and Norway for their refusal to permit Allied troops to cross their territory, assist Finland and, less prominently mentioned, establish a northern front against Germany. This was overlooking the fact that Sweden and Norway hesitated from the knowledge that Germany would at once attack, make Scandinavia a battlefield, and endanger their political life and independence. Washington's chagrin was differently expressed. The President denounced Russia anew and praised Finland. In a public statement he renewed his lament of December 1, 1939, at the spread of force, " the wanton disregard for law," and declared that " all peace-loving peoples still hope for relations throughout the world on the basis of law and order, and unanimously condemn resort to military force." He added that " by virtue of an attack by a neighbor many times stronger they have been compelled to yield territory," and that " the ending of this war does not yet clarify the inherent right of small nations to the maintenance of their integ-

10 *Supra*, p. 410. It is a weak argument to suggest, as did an administration spokesman, that because in 1928 the American republics at Havana — only six have ratified the Convention — agreed not to regard credits to belligerents for the purchase of "food products and raw materials " as unneutral, therefore such loans are now privileged in international law. Hearings on S. 3069 (Jan. 31, 1940), p. 37. Cf. " Panama Resolutions," Bulletin I (Oct. 7, 1939), 329. A few states cannot change international law by unilateral act, as the belligerents have not failed to point out in their refusals to accept the 300-mile zone. Bulletin II (Feb. 24, 1940), 199–205.

rity against attack by superior force." [1] Whether this means that the United States will use measures to clarify that right is left unclear.[2]

The preamble of the Neutrality Act of November 4, 1939, states that it was inspired by the United States' " desiring to preserve its neutrality in wars between foreign states and desiring also to avoid involvement therein." But what has already been done, backed by the presidential declaration of a " limited emergency " in September, 1939, and Navy Secretary Edison's demand of January 4, 1940, for the grant to the President of quasi-dictatorial powers over American industry,[3] has aroused fear and suspicion that the Neutrality Act will gradually be evaded and whittled away to accomplish intervention and involvement. Just as in 1915 and 1916 the American people assumed that neutrality and nonintervention were the national policy which their rulers were carrying out, so now they are comforted by the thought that legislation assures their immunity from war. But as President Roosevelt said at Chautauqua in 1936,[4] that depends upon the wisdom and determination of the man who is President. The observance of the Neutrality Act and the determination to stay out of war cannot be reconciled with " methods short of war " to down " aggressors " or with what has already been done to escape the restrictions imposed by the law of neutrality. Untoward events in Europe might easily tip the scales for active intervention. The danger is especially great because the sentiments of the American people are so emo-

---

[1] *New York Times*, March 14, 1940; Bulletin II, 295.

[2] Cf. the statement of the King of Sweden, Feb. 19, 1940. He expressed his admiration for the Finns and cited the great amount of voluntary aid that had been supplied, but opposed any political intervention " because . . . if Sweden now should intervene in Finland it would cause the direct risk that we should not only be drawn into the war against Russia, but also the war between the great Powers, and I have not been able to take the responsibility to face such a risk."

[3] This was too much even for the *New York Times*, which protested in an editorial, Jan. 5, 1940.

[4] *Supra*, p. 343.

tionally engaged to disapprove the possible victory of Hitler's Germany. Their resolution to resist the temptation to involvement must therefore be exceptionally strong. Whether it will prove strong enough remains to be seen.

The Role of the United States

On February 10 Mr. Sumner Welles, Under-Secretary of State, was commissioned by the President to visit Rome and the belligerent capitals of Western Europe to discover, it was said, the views of the belligerents on war and peace.[5] Some people mistrusted another Colonel House expedition, with the United States committed to supporting Allied peace terms. Others felt that the mission could not be confined to inquiry but would involve presidential mediation, with probable Italian and Papal support. At the moment, the Allies' position is not the best, for they seem to be seeking a widening of the fronts and hesitate to make peace. However that may be, there is the danger that the Allies may make their own assent to peace conditional upon the enforcement or guarantee of its terms by the United States. The American engagement in the European war in 1917 made the United States part of the temporary balance of power of Europe and the drive to take the United States back to Europe will always be strong in certain quarters. The Allies obviously want the protection of the United States military and naval forces. But just as the first intervention proved a disservice to them and to Europe,[5a] so another might well prove equally futile and dangerous to the United States and to them. Under the

[5] Upon his return some six weeks later, little information about his activities abroad was given out. Being an astute diplomat, Mr. Welles was probably careful to avoid another House-Grey memorandum. *Supra,* p. 110. Congress, however, was fearful, and, when Ambassador Cromwell delivered his now-famous speech in Canada, became openly suspicious; investigations were demanded. *New York Times,* April 4, 5, 1940.

[5a] See a British confirmation of this view in Geoffrey T. Garratt, *What Has Happened to Europe* (Indianapolis, Bobbs-Merrill, 1940).

laudable desire to mediate and end a war which must have large consequences in the future, intervention and political entanglements could easily result. In view of the emotional fervor that Finland had aroused, perhaps the peace with Russia closed a tempting door to American intervention.

The President's statement that no troops will be sent abroad, that rumors to that effect were a " fake," [6] does not take account of the fact that his belligerent words and un-neutral acts necessarily arouse fear that they will lead to such consequences. Granting his good faith and good intentions, his assurance that he can safely play with dynamite is *not* reassuring. Even admitting that America's distance from the theater of war permits a recklessness which no European neutral can risk, still, if war comes, there can be no limited liability. Whether troops are sent or not may well prove a matter beyond the President's control. So also a discount must be placed on his promise that we shall not become *military* participants in the current European war. Economic war and military peace cannot long remain bedfellows.

The United States has thus been launched on a policy which purports to be neutral but in reality is far from it. What the effect will be it is still too early to say. In spite of all the efforts of the country to insure American abstention from war and to adopt a policy of genuine national neutrality, the policy of sanctions against aggressors seems to be winning out. Yet the country ought not to be assured that there is no danger in it or that America is following a legal course designed to keep it out of war. The authors still believe that the infinite number of domestic problems which have remained unsolved will require all the energy of the country, and that on their solution the welfare of the nation depends. If that energy is to be dissipated in fresh moral crusades and

[6] Oct. 27, 1939, at *Herald Tribune* Forum, *New Haven Register*, Oct. 27, 1939.

the national welfare is to be risked by participating in foreign wars to help one side defeat the other, the outcome is not likely to be a happy one for the American people [7] or, if the last war and peace are portents, for anyone else.

There is yet another consideration. If post-war reconstruction is envisaged, it must come largely from the United States. That requires economic and mental health which war would gravely impair. Our vast stores of gold afford a means of recharging the processes of industry and exchange, but should be advanced only on conditions not romantic but practical, with a view to satisfying the legitimate needs of Europe as a whole. The United States must recover its role as an impartial healer, and abandon that of unintelligent preacher. Such words as " aggressor " should disappear from the diplomatic dictionary. Instead of supporting mechanized institutions which pursue political aims of domination under hypocritical moral slogans, the United States might encourage regional federations for economic coöperation and customs union, and thus cautiously and gradually expose the short-sightedness of autarchy and high tariffs. All this will require a restoration of confidence which for the past twenty-five years has been shattered. It will take as long to rebuild. But only on such a foundation is there any hope of those voluntary surrenders of national sovereignty which promise coöperation for an intelligible purpose. The reluctance of many Americans to sanction the surrenders demanded of them since 1919 is based upon their conviction that the purpose was not honest, not universal, but for the perpetuation of diseases which cried for healing. If a sensible project of economic planning and exchange can be evolved, deleting every element of coercion, of political domination, of discrimination against certain countries, it will meet with a favorable recep-

---

[7] Cf. John T. Flynn's article, " Can Hitler Beat American Business," *Harpers*, February, 1940, p. 320; C. Hartley Grattan, *The Deadly Parallel* (New York, 1939).

tion from a good many Americans. But that will require an abandonment of the 1919 political machinery which exercised such a fascination for many Americans and which helped, by preventing necessary change, to bring the world to its present pass. If economic coöperation can be made to work, there will be no need to worry about political institutions and armaments. The institutions will grow and the armaments will diminish if conditions justify this development. So also will come more tolerance in social organization generally. Toward such ends, the disillusioned citizens of the United States might be willing to make their contribution. But they will examine carefully the plans submitted for their inspection; they are more astute than they were in 1914. If the old wares are merely exhibited in new dress, they will probably prefer to stay at home, with such minimum coöperation as is indispensable. If Europe can demonstrate that the lessons of the past generation have been learned, there will be no want of American sympathy and tangible sacrifice. It is up to Europe.

APPENDICES

A

AMERICAN MERCHANT SHIPPING LOSSES DURING NEUTRALITY [1]

1. SUBMARINE AND RAIDER

DATE	VESSEL	G.T.		LIVES			REMARKS
		LOST	DAMAGED	U.S.	FRGN.	TOTAL	
1–27–15	*Wm. P. Frye*	3374		—	—	—	Raider
5–1–15	*Gulflight*		5189	3	—	3	Torpedo
5–25–15	*Nebraskan*		4409	—	—	—	Torpedo
7–25–15	*Leelanaw*	1923		—	—	—	Torpedo
8–4–15	*Pass of Balhamas* [2]	[1571]		—	—	—	Surrendered
10–28–16	*Lanao* (Phil. Is. S. S.)	692		—	—	—	Bombs
11–7–16	*Columbian*	8673		—	—	—	Bombs
11–26–16	*Chemung*	3061		—	—	—	Torpedo (Austria)
12–14–16	*Rebecca Palmer*		2556	—	—	—	Shells
1–4–17	*Norlina*		4596	—	—	—	Torpedo
2–3–17	*Housatonic*	3143		—	—	—	Bombs or Torpedo
Total to 2–3–17	Rupture in diplomatic relations	20,866 [1571]	16,750	3	—	3	6 sunk 1 surrendered 4 damaged
2–12–17	*Lyman M. Law*	1300		—	—	—	Captured
3–12–17	*Algonquin*	2832 [3]		—	—	—	Shelled and Bombs
3–16–17	*Vigilancia*	4115		6	9	15	Torpedo
3–17–17	*City of Memphis*	5252		—	—	—	Shelled
3–18–17	*Illinois*	5225		—	—	—	Bombs
3–21–17	*Healdton*	4489		7	14	21	Torpedo
4–1–17	*Aztec* (armed)	3727		12	16	28	Torpedo [4]
4–4–17	*Marguerite*	1553		—	—	—	Bombs
4–4–17	*Missourian*	7924		—	—	—	Shelled
Total to 4–6–17	War declared	57,283 [1571]	16,750	28	39	67	15 sunk 1 surrendered 4 damaged

2. AMERICAN MERCHANTMEN MINED

DATE	VESSEL	G.T.		LIVES			REMARKS
		LOST	DAMAGED	U.S.	FRGN.	TOTAL	
2–19–15	*Evelyn*	1963		—	1	1	
2–22–15	*Carib*	2087		3	—	3	
4–2–15	*Greenbrier*	3322		—	—	—	
9–27–15	*Vincent*	1904		—	—	—	4 injured
11–18–15	*Helen W. Martin*		2265	—	—	—	4 injured
6–18–16	*Seaconnet*	2294		—	—	—	
7–10–16	*Goldshell*		5614	—	—	—	
12–18–16	*Kansan*		7913	—	—	—	6 injured
Total to 4–6–17	War declared	11,570	15,792	3	1	4	5 sunk 3 damaged

[1] Statistics from: Navy Dept., Historical Section, *American Ship Casualties of the World War* (Washington, Government Printing Office, 1923), except for *Rebecca Palmer* which is not included there.

[2] Gibson and Prendergast (*The German Submarine War* [New York, 1931], pp. 47–48) indicate that this capture was effected by the *U–36* between July 22 and July 24, 1915, as that submarine was destroyed by the Q-boat *Prince Charles* on the latter date.

[3] In the Colby Report (S. Doc. No. 419, 66th Cong., 3rd Sess.), p. 29, this tonnage is given as 1805 gross tons.

[4] This may have been a mine loss; see text.

CHRONOLOGY

February 3, 1917 — Rupture in diplomatic relations.
February 26, 1917 — Wilson requests authority to arm vessels.
March 4, 1917 — Congress adjourns; authority not granted.
March 9, 1917 — Wilson summons Congress to meet April 16.
March 12, 1917 — Wilson authorizes arming U. S. vessels.
March 21, 1917 — Wilson summons Congress to meet April 2.
April 2, 1917 — Wilson addresses Congress requesting declaration of war.
April 4, 1917 — Senate passes declaration of war.
April 6, 1917 — House passes declaration of war; it is approved and proclaimed.

COMMENT

(1) The foregoing statistics do not include the airplane attack on the *Cushing* (April 28, 1915); the damage, if any, was slight. (See text.)

(2) The tabulations given in Savage, *op. cit.*, II, Doc. No. 245, p. 596, include attacks on three other vessels: the *Oswego* (8–6–16), the *Sacramento* (1–6–17), and the *Westwego* (1–21–17). No lives were reported lost, and none of the vessels was sunk. The following appears to be the only information available as to these ships:

(a) The *Oswego* is listed as having been attacked by an airplane on August 3, 1916 (Savage, II, p. 596). According to newspaper accounts based on official documents and on the testimony of the master of the ship, the alleged attack was by a German submarine.

On a hazy, windless afternoon, a submarine signaled the *Oswego* to stop. The boats were about three miles apart at the time and the master of the *Oswego* claimed that he saw neither the signals nor the submarine because of the haze. Receiving no response, the submarine fired several shots across the vessel's bow; one of these, striking the water near the *Oswego,* impressed upon the master the fact that he was being summoned to halt. Visit and search having then been carried out, the submarine allowed the *Oswego* to proceed to its destination. The vessel was not damaged in the slightest.

See the accounts in the following issues of the *New York Times:* Aug. 24, 1916, p. 2, col. 8; Sept. 1, 1916, p. 5, col. 1; Sept. 9, 1916, p. 3, col. 6. Ambassador Gerard's cable of August 27, 1916, to Lansing, giving the official German statement of the case, appears at the September 1 citation.

(b) In the case of the *Sacramento,* it was reported in the press in late December, 1916, that the vessel had reached Havre safely with a cargo of Argentine wheat after having been stopped by a submarine. The ship's papers had been examined and the vessel had been released because of its American registry. (*New York Times,* Dec. 27, 1916, p. 3, col. 3.) The foregoing press account, however, is followed by the following significant item of an editorial nature:

" The only steamer of the name of Sacramento listed in available maritime records is reported by the New York Maritime Register to have been transferred recently from American to British ownership."

(c) The *Westwego,* an oil tanker, was reported to have been stopped by a submarine on January 31, 1917. Under threat of sinking, it complied with the submarine's demand for three barrels of oil. In the process of hailing the vessel, several shots had been fired, " none of which took effect." *New York Times,* Feb. 7, 1917, p. 3, col. 2.

B

AMERICAN MERCHANT SHIP CASUALTIES [1]

AUGUST 4, 1914 — FEBRUARY 3, 1917

CAUSE	VESSELS					LIVES		
	ATTACKED	LOST	G.T.	SALVAGED	G.T.	DEAD	INJURED	PRISONERS
Raiders	1	1	3374	—	—	—	—	—
T — S — B *	9	5	17492	4	16750	3	—	—
Mines	8	5	11570	3	15792	4	14	—
Surrendered	1	1	1571	—	—	—	—	—
	19	12	34007	7	32542	7	14	—

FEBRUARY 3, 1917 — APRIL 6, 1917

T — S — B *	9	9	36417	—	—	64	—	—

TOTAL AUGUST 4, 1914 — APRIL 6, 1917

Raiders	1	1	3374	—	—	—	—	—
T — S — B *	18	14	53909	4	16750	67	—	—
Mines	8	5	11570	3	15792	4	14	—
Surrendered	1	1	1571	—	—	—	—	—
	28	21	70424	7	32542	71	14	—

APRIL 6, 1917 — NOVEMBER 11, 1918

Raiders	7	7	5052	—	—	1	—	13
T — S — B *	130	116 [3]	258004 [3]	14 [2]	58543 [2]	366 [4]	49	7
Mines	4	2	5760	2	17225	31	—	—
	141	125	268816	16 [2]	75768 [2]	398	49	20

TOTAL AUGUST 4, 1914 — NOVEMBER 11, 1918

Raiders	8	8	8426	—	—	1	—	13
T — S — B *	148	130	311913	18 [2]	75293	433	49	7
Mines	12	7	17330	5	33017	35	14	—
Surrendered	1	1	1571	—	—	—	—	—
	169	146	339240	23 [2]	108310 [2]	469	63	20

NOVEMBER 11, 1918 — JULY 2, 1921

Mines [5]	7	6	21782	1	5763	11	—	—

TOTAL AUGUST 4, 1914 — JULY 2, 1921

CAUSE	VESSELS					LIVES		
	ATTACKED	LOST	G.T.	SALVAGED	G.T.	DEAD	INJURED	PRISONER
Raiders	8	8	8426	—	—	1	—	13
T — S — B *	148	130	311913	18 [2]	75293	433	49	7
Mines [5]	19	13	39112	6	38780	46	14	—
Surrendered	1	1	1571	—	—	—	—	—
	176	152	361022	24 [2]	114073 [2]	480	63	20

* Torpedoed, shelled, or bombed by submarines.

[1] Statistics from: Navy Dept., Historical Section, *American Ship Casualties of the World War* (Washington, Government Printing Office, 1923).

[2] Includes both times the *Armenia* (5463 G.T.) was torpedoed and salvaged.

[3] Includes the *Kansan* (7913 G.T.) sunk July 10, 1917, with a loss of 4 lives; it is uncertain whether this was a mine or a torpedo casualty.

[4] This includes the 4 lives mentioned in note 3, and also the following lives lost on ships damaged but not sunk:

1917: 9
1918:11

[5] The last reported mine loss occurred on July 1, 1921.

COMMENTS

(1) Because of the evident impossibility, the losses attributed to mines cannot be apportioned between the Entente and the Central Powers. For a discussion of American participation in the mining activities of the Allies, see Navy Dept., Office of Naval Records and Library, Historical Section, Publication No. 2: *The Northern Mine Barrage and Other Mining Activities* (Washington, Government Printing Office, 1920); *idem*, Publication No. 4, *The Northern Barrages — Taking Up the Mines* (Washington, Government Printing Office, 1920).

(2) The Navy Dept. Report does not differentiate between American and foreign lives lost on the American vessels.

CHRONOLOGY

August 4, 1914 — European war.
February 3, 1917 — U. S. breaks off relations with Germany.
April 6, 1917 — U. S. declares war.
November 11, 1918 — Armistice signed.
July 2, 1921 — Joint Resolution terminating war.
November 11, 1921 — Treaty of Berlin.

C

AMERICAN LIVES LOST ON FOREIGN VESSELS

DATE	VESSEL	NATIONALITY	AMERICANS LOST			REMARKS
			PASS.	CREW	TOTAL	
March 28, 1915	*Falaba*	British	1	—	1	Escaping
May 7, 1915	*Lusitania*	British	128	—	128	
c. June 30, 1915	*Armenian*	British	—	21	21	Govt. Service Resisted
July 30, 1915	*Iberian*	British	—	1	1	Escaping
Aug. 19, 1915	*Arabic*	British	2	—	2	
Nov. 7, 1915	*Ancona*	Italian	9	—	9	Estimate
Dec. 30, 1915	*Persia*	British	1	—	1	Armed
March 23, 1916	*Englishman*	British	—	6	6	Escaping (Estimate)
Oct. 28, 1916	*Marina*	British	—	6	6	Armed
Dec. 2, 1916	*Palermo*	Italian	—	1	1	
TOTAL to *Feb. 3, 1917*	10 Belligerent vessels		141	35	176	See Note
Feb. 3, 1917	*Eavestone*	British	—	1	1	Escaping
Feb. 7, 1917	*Vedamore*	British	—	10	10	Armed
Feb. 17, 1917	*Athos*	French	1	—	1	Convoyed troopship
Feb. 25, 1917	*Laconia*	British	2	1	3	Armed
Feb. 27, 1917	*Galgorm Castle*	British	—	2	2	
Feb. 28, 1917	*Sjostad*	Norwegian	—	1	1	French convoy
March 29, 1917	*Crispin*	British	—	1	1	Armed
TOTAL to *April 6, 1917*	16 Belligerent 1 Neutral		144 —	50 1	194 1	
	17 Foreign ships		144	51	195	See Note

NOTE

For the case of the armed British mule transport *Russian* sunk on December 14, 1916, see *M. S. Losses* (1919), p. 28; *A. J. I. L.* XI (1917) Special Suppl., 129. According to press reports at the time it was uncertain whether this vessel had struck a mine or had been torpedoed. Seventeen American muleteers are alleged to have perished in the sinking. See *New York Times*, Dec. 19, 1916, p. 1, col. 4; *idem*, Dec. 21, 1916, p. 6, col. 3. No verification or subsequent confirmation of these alleged American losses having been found, it was not considered advisable to include the vessel in the tabulations. It is not improbable that this ship's occupation was similar to that of the *Armenian* — i.e., engaged in British Government service.

COMMENT

The tabulations shown in Diplomatic Correspondence, etc., *European War*, No. 4, pp. 300–301 (published in 1918 by the Department of State), include, in addition, the following American casualties on foreign vessels:

DATE	VESSEL	NATIONALITY	AMERICANS LOST
Aug. 1, 1915	*Koophandel*	Belgian	1
May 16, 1916	*Batavier V*	Dutch	1
Oct. 20, 1916	*Cabotia*	British	1
Feb. 8, 1917	*Mantola* (armed)	British	1
Feb. 11, 1917	*Roanoke* (armed)	British	1
Feb. 16, 1917	*Mayola*	British	1

	5 belligerent vessels	5
Totals	1 neutral vessel	1
	6 foreign ships	6

These vessels have not been included in the foregoing tabulation or in the text for the following reasons:

(1) The first two vessels could not be located elsewhere. The cause of the sinking of the *Batavier V* is listed as " not known."

(2) In the case of the *Cabotia,* no verification of the American casualty among the thirty-two lives lost in the sinking has been located. See *M. S. Losses* (1919), p. 24; Hurd, *op. cit.,* II, 351–352.

(3) In the case of the *Mantola,* Consul Frost cabled Lansing on February 10, 1917 *(For. Rel.,* 1917, Suppl. I, p. 126):

. . . one American on board, ship's surgeon Earle Rice. . . . All crew and passengers saved except seven Lascars, drowned due to mismanagement. . . . Mantola carried 4.7 gun with two gunners on duty. Have affidavit Surgeon Rice.

The vessel is also listed as armed in *M. S. Losses* (1919), p. 32.

(4) In the case of the *Roanoke,* Vice-Consul Baxter cabled Lansing on February 26, 1917 *(For. Rel.,* 1917, Suppl. I, p. 149):

One seaman killed by explosion; rest of crew, one being American citizen, rescued by patrol steamer.

The vessel was not sunk but was towed in, one life was lost, and the vessel was listed as armed in *M. S. Losses* (1919), p. 137.

(5) In the case of the *Mayola*, Consul Washington cabled Lansing on March 5, 1917 (*For. Rel.*, 1917, Suppl. I, p. 169):

Harold E. Burke, American citizen, affirms member crew British schooner Mayola . . . unarmed. . . . No other Americans on board; affidavit mailed.

The official British records (*M. S. Losses* (1919), p. 33) show no loss of life on this vessel which was captured by a submarine and sunk by bombs.

D

AMERICAN MERCHANT SHIPS SUNK [1] — 1914–1918

DATE	CRUISERS			SUBMARINES			MINES			TOTAL		
	SHIPS	G.T.	LIVES	SHIPS	G.T.	LIVES	SHIPS	G.T.	LIVES	SHIPS	G.T.	LIVES
1914	—	—	—	—	—	—	—	—	—	—	—	—
1915	1	3,374	—	1	1,923	—	4	9,276	4	6	14,573	4
1916	—	—	—	3	12,426	—	1	2,294	—	4	14,720	—
Total 1914–1916	1	3,374	—	4	14,349	—	5	11,570	4	10	29,293	4
1917 — Jan.	—	—	—	—	—	—	—	—	—	—	—	—
Total to date	1	3,374	—	4	14,349	—	5	11,570	4	10	29,293	4
1917 — Feb. & Mar.	—	—	—	7	26,356	36	—	—	—	7	26,356	36
Total to date	1	3,374	—	11	40,795	36	5	11,570	4	17	55,649	40
1917 (Apr.–Dec.)	7	5,052	1	55[2]	140,925[2]	248[2]	1	3,302	1	63	149,279	250
1918	—	—	—	64	130,283	126	1	2,458	30	65	132,742	156
Total 1914–1918	8	8,426	1	130	311,913	410[3]	7	17,330	35	145[4]	337,669[4]	446[3]

[1] This does not include damaged American vessels, nor the one ship surrendered in 1915.

[2] Includes the *Kansan* (7913 G.T.) sunk on July 10, 1917, with a loss of 4 lives; it is uncertain whether this was a mine or a torpedo casualty.

[3] To reconcile these figures with those in Appendix B, the following lives lost on vessels damaged but not sunk should be added: 1915, 3; 1917 (after April 6), 9; 1918, 11; Total — 23.

[4] To reconcile these figures with those in Appendix B, the following should be added: *Pass of Balhamas* (1571 G.T.) surrendered in 1915.

E

DISTRIBUTION OF WORLD TONNAGE LOSSES [1]

NATION	CRUISERS	SUBMARINES	MINES	AIRCRAFT	TOTAL
Great Britain	448,339	6,692,642	681,962	7,912	7,830,855
France	52,905	812,309	34,144	—	899,358
Italy	6,016	803,092	37,280	—	846,388
United States	8,428	364,200	24,431	—	397,059 [2]
Greece	724	334,408	10,384	—	345,516 [3]
Brazil	—	25,464	—	—	25,464 [4]
Norway	15,172	1,043,077	122,067	—	1,180,316
Sweden	8,185	142,493	50,598	—	201,276
Denmark	4,834	201,394	37,478	—	243,707
Netherlands	5,584	131,948	74,310	127	211,969
Spain	—	152,387	16,104	—	168,491
All others	18,350	450,092	31,973	—	500,415
TOTALS	568,537	11,153,506	1,120,732	8,039	12,850,814

[1] Fayle, *Seaborne Trade*, III, 466. The British figures are official; the others are based on British Admiralty estimates. The table has been reproduced here (in somewhat condensed form) merely as showing three groups: the belligerents, the neutrals that became belligerents, and the neutrals. For other American figures, see the preceding Appendices.

[2] Of which the United States lost 55,665 G.T. prior to its entry into the war.

[3] Of which Greece lost 228,497 G.T. prior to its entry into the war.

[4] Of which Brazil lost 13,946 G.T. prior to its entry into the war.

INDEX

Abyssinia. *See* Ethiopia

Adams, John, on American foreign policy, 21, 22, 26

—— John Quincy, on neutrality, 4

Adriatic, 84–85, 96

" Aggressor ": American acceptance of idea through Kellogg Pact, 251–252, 259–260; American urge to suppress, 365, 395; British refusal to accept Geneva Protocol, 263–264; consultative pacts linked with theory of, 299; Davis commitment, 1933, effect of, 301–302; practical nullification of, 302; Davis definition as condemnation of all America's wars, 266; definitions, 261–265; difficulties of definitions, 261, 264, 272; embargoes against, 396, 404; escape clause in Locarno Pact, 262; freedom in selection of, 254; identified, 396; nonrecognition, a weapon against, 302–303; peace organization's approval of selection of, 245; poisonous effects of use of theory of, 246–248; punishment of, 351, 389–390, 422, 423; purpose of attempts to define, 264; Roosevelt proposes quarantine, 367–369, 372; selection of, inducement to war, 265; terminology of, in Kellogg Pact, 290–291; theory based on prompt surrender, 247; " violator of a treaty," substitute for, 295, 400

Alabama, 9, 29, 84, 405

Albania, Italian conquest of, 394

Alien property custodian, 278

Allen, Representative R. G., 398

Allies. *See* individual nations

American citizens: claim of right to travel on belligerent vessels, 42, 113–116, 136–140, 151, 220, 225–227, 318, 346; Congressional action on travel by, on belligerent vessels,

40, 113–114, 139–140, 315, 327, 340–341; travel on belligerent ships by, *see also* Bryan, Gerard, Lansing, and Wilson

—— lives: American failure to distinguish between neutral and belligerent ships, 221–222; basis of American complaint, 225–227; difficulty in checking reported losses, 215, 231; failure of all governments to report losses, 231–232; indemnity offered by Austria-Hungary, 215; indemnity offered by Germany, 142, 150, 166, 224, 225; loss between severance of relations and declaration of war, 227–229; loss compared with Scandinavian loss, 231–233; loss of, cause for entry into war, 138–139, 235; on American ships, 220–233; on armed American ships, 228; on armed merchantmen, 215, 216, 218; on belligerent ships, 183, 212–220, 430–432; on belligerent ship resisting visit, 214, 216; on neutral ships, 219–220; on ship engaged in government service, 214; summary of loss prior to American entry, 220, 230–231

—— Red Cross, aid to Finland, 418

—— ships, airplane attack on, 134; taken to control ports, 410; transfers to foreign registry, 410 n.

—— Society of International Law, Kellogg speech before, 291

Ancona, Americans lost on, 215, 231; sinking of, 166, 215

Anglo-American trade treaty, 367

Anti-Comintern Pact, 371

Arabic, Americans lost on, 215; German offer of indemnity, 166; sinking of, 42, 165

Argentina, specific reservation of food-stuffs and raw materials at Buenos Aires Conference, 333

navigation of, 159–160; real issues not examined, 40, 141; sinking of, 35, 134, 141, 163, 164, 175, 204, 205, 214, 221–222, 233, 237; status of, 40, 141 ff., 149, 150; terms of construction agreement, 91–92, 141, 156; use of American flag by, 129; Wilson, author of first note on, 144

Lytton Report, 266, 271–272

McAdoo, William G., 41

McNair, Arnold D., 260

Madison, James: coercion of states, 247–248; no mention of impressment to Congress, 31; Nonintercourse Act, 30–31, 313

Madrid Government, 356, 357, 359

Mails, seizure of American mails, 42, 412 n.

Malone Report on *Lusitania,* 158

Manchukuo. *See* Manchuria

Manchuria: dispute with Russia, 1929, 297, 360; invasion of, 265, 270–272, 361, 364, 366; League, 244; Lytton Report on, 266

Marina, 216–217

Marshall, Chief Justice John, opinion in *Nereide,* 86, 87, 117, 118–119, 120–122, 181

Mauretania: British classification of, 156; construction of, 91, 156 n.

Maverick, Representative M., 385

May Bill, 385

Mediation: reason for failure of American efforts for, 41–42, 79–80, 109; Wilson's efforts for, postponed for election, 170–171

Memel, history of, 394 n., returned to Germany, 394

Merchant vessels: alleged British warning to British ships on travel, 137–138; American citizens' right to travel on belligerent merchant ships, *see* American citizens; attacks on American, 134; British orders to attack submarines, 39, 85–86, 90, 94–95, 141, 149, 151, 212; conversion of, into cruisers, 83–84, 105; diversion of, 42; pas-

sengers, forcible removal of, 42, 181–182; risks taken by passengers on belligerent, 10, 116, 136, 170; 178, 183, 225, 229, 233; Scandinavian losses, 183, 234–235. *See also* Armed merchantmen

Merion, 85, 96

Mersey investigation of *Lusitania,* 155, 160

" Methods short of war," 382–383

Mexico: not blockaded during Civil War, 69–70; stand on armed merchantmen, 100; United States arms embargo, 281, 336; War of 1846 with United States, 266, 374

Miller, David Hunter, 250

Millis, Walter, 163

Minnesota Mortgage Moratorium case, 389 n.

Monroe Doctrine: compared with British reservations on Kellogg Pact, 293; copied by Japan, 272; natural corollary to American rule of nonintervention, 24; new neutrality legislation in light of, 329, 340

Moore, John Bassett: armed merchantmen and travel on belligerent vessels, 42, 121; consultative pact, 300; law governing vessels on high seas, 178; League of Nations, 52; necessity for restatement of law, 288–289; Pittman Bill memorandum, 327, 331 n.

—— R. Walton, 327

" Moral Embargoes ": alleged purpose, 387; against Japan, 363, 374, 386–391, 404; against Russia, 396, 416; illegality of, 387, 416; on aircraft, 386–387, 416; on gasoline plans, 387, 417; on raw materials, 416; noncompliance with, denounced, 387; unneutrality of, 391, 416–417; violate treaties, 374, 387. *See also* Embargoes

Moravia, 394

Munich, 392

Mussolini, Benito: answers Roosevelt peace plea, 394, 400; bombing of Corfu, 264; conquers Al-